AMERICAN GLASS

Other books from
the pages of *Antiques*

Marvin D. Schwartz, Ed., *American
Glass, I, Blown and Molded*

Constance Greiff, Ed., *Great Houses*

Eric de Jonge, Ed., *Country Things*

Howard Herschel Cotterell, Adolphe Riff and Robert M. Vetter,
National Types of Old Pewter

AMERICAN GLASS

From the Pages of *Antiques*

II. *Pressed and Cut*

EDITED, WITH AN INTRODUCTION, BY
ROBERT E. DiBARTOLOMEO

THE PYNE PRESS
Princeton

Cover photograph, courtesy The Corning Museum of Glass,
Corning, N.Y.: Group of five lacy pressed glasses: sugar-
bowl with cover, shallow bowl, plate, cup plate and salt.
United States, New England, ca. 1830-45.

Library of Congress Catalog Card Number 73-91978

SBN 87861-070-7, paperback
SBN 87861-071-5, hardcover

Printed in the United States of America

Contents

CUT AND ENGRAVED GLASS

Introduction

Of all the varieties of glass produced from ancient times to the present, the type which is peculiarly American is pressed glass. That it may have been made earlier elsewhere on a limited basis does nothing to diminish that statement. No other nineteenth-century glassmakers turned out the quantity of ware or approached the quality achieved by pressed glass manufacturers in the United States.

A view of the glass industry in this country from 1830 to 1900 seems to present a panoply of better methods of pressing glass, improved molds and presses and more economical techniques of production resulting in more items being made more cheaply. These advances, more than any other improvements in glass technology, enabled American makers to control a major proportion of the domestic market and even export large amounts of ware. Lowell Innes, in an article reprinted in this collection entitled "Pittsburgh Pressed Glass, Part I," points out that "the whole country imported about $38,000.00 worth of pressed glass, while Pittsburgh alone in 1878 was exporting over $860,000.00 worth." This to him is ample evidence that American pressed glass production was "tremendous."*

In the late 1820s and early 1830s when pressing first began in the United States, all of this was in the future. It was the economic climate that made it essential to develop a new form of mass production in glass. The Wars of Independence and 1812 were behind us. Tariffs were low or non-existent, and many American industrialists must have been discouraged as their candidate, Henry Clay, was defeated again and again. Economic stability was decades away and the home market had to be shared with foreign producers when the first drawer knobs, lamp bases, and lacy cup plates were pressed. It was essential that an inexpensive product be developed so that our glassmakers could compete. Eastern factories near the centers of population had been established, and the resources of the eastern part of the Middle West, especially the area's huge coal fields in places like Pittsburgh and Wheeling, were beginning to be tapped. Cheap fuel, improving transportation facilities, an influx of skilled workers and growing population would soon enable Midwestern glassmakers to compete not only with their Eastern counterparts but also with European manufacturers.

During this period glasshouse owners had to struggle simply to survive. Each minor downturn in the American economy was apt to be a crisis. Many companies were undercapitalized and totally dependent on this week's profits to pay last week's bills. Before 1865, with a few notable exceptions, glass companies came and went rapidly, leaving little behind as proof of their existence. Large companies like the Central Glass Company of Wheeling, W. Va., pressing a multitude of pieces a year, did not begin to operate on this scale until well after 1870. Gigantic combines like the United States Glass Company were not even thought of.

*All of the articles quoted in this introduction have been reprinted in this collection.

Writers of introductions are expected to bring forth revelations which pull the material they are discussing together. Such revelations usually take on the form of generalities which are intoned with such strength that they appear to be rules. Unfortunately glass does not lend itself to such treatment, because for every "rule" stated there are a host of exceptions. The reader would be wise, then, not to consider the next few paragraphs as dogma, but rather as "a general putting together of material."

Most glass students agree that the first pressed glass items produced were small: drawer knobs, lamp bases, cup plates and salt cellars to name a few. Many of the early patterns, lacy or otherwise, were geometric in nature and/or imitated cut flint glass. During the height of the lacy period much of the surface of the pieces was covered with designs in order to conceal manufacturing flaws, but the stippling utilized to accomplish this added new qualities to the material. For the interplay of light amidst the tiny facets or points of the stippling imparted a brilliance to the glass unknown before in any ware.

After 1850, when the lacy product had run its course, the patterns remained geometric and were in some cases still imitations of cut ware, but a slight element of naturalism began to creep in. The dolphins on those candlesticks could not be mistaken for anything else. The "Bellflower" and "Ribbed Palm" patterns of McKee and Brothers were made up of stylized geometric elements, but in combination there was a hint of realism.

Natural patterns grew in popularity and no buyer could doubt what Hobbs Brockunier and Company's "Blackberry" or "Grape Frieze," or the Central Glass Company's "Cabbage Rose," all issued in 1870, were meant to portray. As the manufacturers continued to stress realistic patterns it must have seemed as if the country's tables were being submerged in an endless stream of fruits, birds, and animals, human or otherwise, on goblets, compotes, covered dishes, celeries, spoonholders and nappies. Some of these patterns covered most of the surface of a vessel, but other motifs were sparse, so that even in this era of increasing mass production, glass could be personalized, by the copper-wheel engraver or the acid etcher, with initials or monograms.

Geometric patterns never really disappeared and by the mid 1880s they became popular again. This was the era of "Daisy and Button" and its many variants. But, as time passed, competition among pressed glass manufacturers grew more intense. Price cutting occurred, and one producer attempted to outdo the other, offering more colors and more eccentric designs. In many cases the quality of both the glass and the patterns on it declined. Styles became more decadent, as, in their search for novelty, the glassmakers imitated one another. Pressed glass was even made to seem like material it wasn't. The early twentieth century was the period of carnival glass, and a piling of one motif upon the other, or of imitating the cut glass of the Brilliant Period. It was only a matter of time until a reaction set in, and patterns in pressed glass reverted to simpler themes.

During the lacy period relatively few pieces of colored glass were made, and of course they are much sought after. In the 1870s opal (milk) glass was popular, and eventually a rainbow of colors was introduced for the Victorian housewife. When single shades were not enough, bi-colored wares like amberina or the arsenic, bone ash opalescents were issued. Whatever other trends in pressed glass may be identified, one of which we can be certain is the ever-increasing use of a variety of hues.

Neither the colors nor the patterns existed in a vacuum. Styles in architecture and furniture were mirrored in pressed glass. Many lacy cup plates are rococo in design. From style classique furniture came the dolphin and the caryatid. Those "Cathedral" sugar bowls from New England contain gothic elements, and "Daisy and Button's" intricacy is symbolic of the Victorian's attachment to detail and ostentation.

If progress from the simple to the complex were the only criterion of judgment, it would be easy to conclude that cut and pressed glass followed parallel lines of development. However, cut wares often set the standards for pressed glass, and in almost every instance the designs on cut pieces were executed with much more restraint.

Largely this is due to the state of the material when it receives its motifs. Cutting is an extrinsic form of decoration. Only so many things can be done to a cold piece of glass with a stone wheel and sand. Its general shape has already been formed. In contrast, glass in its molten state about to be pressed is an empty pliable surface, capable of accepting almost any design. The only limitations are the imagination of the mold maker and some technological consideration. For example, is the design such that it can be pressed into the glass and the piece removed from the mold intact?

Cut glass manufactured in the first half of the nineteenth century owed much to Anglo-Irish cut ware. The motifs used were simple geometric ones like panels, flutes, fans and mitre-cut diamonds. One factory's production resembled another's because design elements were limited. Between 1860 and 1880 the same decorative devices were being used, but in greater combination upon a single piece. Strawberry diamonds might be combined with fans, panels, flutes and ovals. This complexity of design continued, culminating in the cut glass of the Brilliant Period with its pinwheels, hobstars and intricate sunbursts. Still the individual elements making up these complex designs were those of the earlier decade merely presented in new sets of combinations. If the period from 1830 to 1860 was cut glass's sedate youth, then the era from 1890 to the First World War was its matronly middle age. The entire surface of vessels was covered and every set contained large, thick-walled pieces. The glass cut was still the more expensive lead flint with its astounding clarity, rather than the lime glass used in pressed ware after 1864. Cut glass's place was primarily at the table of the affluent. If pressed glass belonged to every man, then cut flint was the ware of the well-to-do.

The articles reprinted in this book are not only a history of a number of aspects of the glass industry, but they also are a record of the phenomenal growth of a hobby—pressed glass collecting. The articles fall into several categories: histories of glass companies and their owners, stylistic influences, methods of manufacture, and how to attribute and identify individual patterns. Before this book's publication this information was available only to those who had access to a full file of *Antiques* and its indices. Now it has been collected in one volume and access to it simplified.

As a chronicle of glass collecting these articles underline how authors may popularize a hobby and even set its standards of taste. A debt is owed to those who came first. Writers like Lura Woodside Watkins, Rhea Mansfield Knittle, Ruth Webb Lee and Harry Hall White provided the foundations on which other research was done. On their heels came a second wave of researchers who almost immediately refined and enlarged existing information. Helen McKearin made collectors aware of the New England Glass Company and its products, and James Rose and Lowell Innes enlarged the horizon of those interested in glass to include the products of Pittsburgh and other Midwestern factories. In the decades that followed others have written, refining the subject matter even more, but their task was made easier by those who came before.

It is not difficult to isolate the trends in collecting which these authors consciously or unconsciously promulgated. For instance, it is obvious that initially many writers were interested in the products of the Boston and Sandwich Glass Company and in all lacy pressed produced anywhere. Authors ardently championed the cause of their favorite factory, describing its ware in glowing terms while denigrating the production of other houses in other regions. Some of the authors became enmeshed in the virtually insoluble problem of who pressed what, where, first.

If Sandwich and other eastern glass was discovered first, it was not long before the supporters of Midwestern factories made their presence felt. The editors of *Antiques* may well have started this trend with an article printed in 1927 entitled "By No Means Sandwich" in which the products of McKee and Brothers were discussed. Ruth Webb Lee wrote pieces which she entitled "Pittsburgh vs. Sandwich." In one of them she declared, " 'When in doubt, say Sandwich!' has been the one collecting commandment heeded. 'When in doubt, don't call it Sandwich!' is far wiser counsel."

The articles on earlier pressed glass in this collection far outnumber the ones on late nineteenth-century pattern glass and cut and engraved wares from any period. One has to suspect that in the case of the late pattern glass it was simply too close to the writers in time to be fully accepted. However, the lack of articles on cut and engraved items needs to be discussed in more detail.

As was noted earlier it is difficult to differentiate between the products of early nineteenth-century cut glass manufacturers. To attribute such ware and write incisively, a handle is needed—glass owned by the descendants of workers, family histories or other documentary material. Those descendants are difficult to find, and once discovered they often know little about their ancestors, or they own no glass. Documentary evidence on pre-1865 cut ware is rarely found, so the articles simply weren't written. During the Brilliant Period some pieces were marked but there were many which were not, so the situation was not improved that much. What appears in this collection is virtually all of the articles on nineteenth-century cut and engraved ware which appeared in *Antiques* from the late 1920s until 1972. It is apparent, then, why articles like Katherine Hait Dorflinger Manchee's three-part series on Dorflinger glass are so valuable to collectors and scholars alike.

The nineteenth-century copper-wheel engraver was not so handicapped by a limited number of motifs as the glass cutter. With his tools he could do many of the things which an artist does with his brush. It is still difficult, however, to tell one man's work from another and little has been done to classify it. Cutters and engravers may have held a privileged position among glassworkers in a factory, but outside of that circle they worked anonymously, and this does not facilitate research. As in the case of the Dorflinger series, articles like Carl Fauster's on Louis Vaupel are welcome.

The desire to make attributions motivates many collectors, museum curators and authors. Whenever anything appears which makes that task easier, it is greeted warmly. Therefore, when immense amounts of glass fragments were unearthed on the site of the Boston and Sandwich Glass Company, the discovery was heralded as extremely important. Over and over, writers claimed these shards as definite proof of point of manufacture. For a time, any fragment said to come from those cullet piles was automatically attributed to the Sandwich Company. Confusion resulted with the addition of evidence showing that some of the items unearthed were not of Sandwich origin. The lack of precise archaeological techniques in their exhumation has been cited as compounding the problem.

Still the shards were there and the non-Sandwich fragments had to be explained. Some companies in New England probably purchased cullet elsewhere. Glassmakers often acquired competitors' ware in order to copy it. In the later periods much Midwestern glass was sold in New England. For a time there was a brisk trade in Sandwich Glass cullet, so it may be that Grandmother's Midwestern compote had more value as bogus Sandwich glass shards than it did intact. Obviously much of the material found in the Sandwich cullet piles is valid, but we are still left with fragments which aren't. How they got there will probably never be known, and as the years pass researchers will continue to praise or damn collections of Sandwich shards as they have done in the past.

Since attribution is taken seriously, it may be helpful to cite some of the advice given to collectors by the authors who have been included in this book. Harry Hall White suggests, in the second part of his series "New Views of Old Glass," that collectors base their "judgments of old glass—or anything else for that matter—not on a single indication or a sign but upon a careful study of many indices, and an appraisal of their relative importance." Ruth Webb Lee, in one of her "Pittsburgh vs. Sandwich" articles, warns us that attribution can become a "mania . . . responsible for much misinformation" because collectors "avail themselves of any peg on which to hang theories that automatically become facts through the magic of speech plus wish." One can't help adding also, "through the power of the printed page."

Attributions are constantly being revised as new information becomes available. Take the case of *The Maid of the Mist* cup plate, a humble little thing made well after lacy styles had passed their peak. Initially it was attributed to a New England factory and it was said to be a view of *The Maid of the Mist*, a boat which traveled back and forth below Niagara Falls. Alice Van Leer Carrick, in "Historical Glass Cup-Plates," clings to the Niagara Falls interpretation, but attributes the piece to an unnamed New York factory. A number of years later James Rose published new material which laid the earlier versions to rest. He stated that the cup plate, indeed, had nothing to do with Niagara Falls, but was made by a Wheeling glasshouse to commemorate the completion of the Wheeling Suspension Bridge, then the longest in the country. The view was not of Niagara Falls, but of a scene on the Ohio River at Wheeling, Virginia, now West Virginia. The maker, however, is still unknown.

Ruth Webb Lee, in "Rarities in Pattern Glass," outlines an intriguing thesis that pressed glass kept interest in antiques alive during the Depression. What she and the other writers who published then leave unsaid is the effect of their work on what collectors bought. Their articles on the "ten best" or the "hundred best" instantly affected prices. If the authorities said it was desirable then it surely was worthwhile to acquire.

At its peak, pressed glass collecting seemed to deal more in quantity than in quality. It became fashionable not to collect one of something but to own dozens of pieces in a pattern—the ultimate being to possess several of every piece in every color in a large set of pressed tableware. Articles praised collectors for owning 400 pieces of "Moon and Star," or any other pattern for that matter. Those who were mentioned must have felt that they had arrived in the world of collecting.

If the hobby has declined in recent years it may be because of this tendency to build large collections. During the Depression, when dealers were interested in low-priced volume items, it was necessary to cultivate the buyer who wanted to complete that set of a dozen pressed goblets. But as affluence returned, stocking higher-priced items became the order of the day. After all, a piece of art glass occupied the same space and brought more money. A fine piece of eighteenth-century furniture occupied more space but the potential for profit was even larger. Queries to several dealers about pressed glass in stock brought me this reply, "I have a little but it's too much bother to specialize in it."

Pressed glass collecting has always been a relatively controversial subject. It has had its ardent group of supporters as well as its detractors. Lura Woodside Watkins considered some Sandwich glass to be the "handsomest pressed glass ever made." Miss Flora Jarves, Deming Jarves' granddaughter, declared that "It is useless to describe this silly fad for Sandwich glass which is trash." In her opinion, pressed Sandwich was inferior to the factory's other wares, which proved too expensive to make, so "they began this pressed stuff much to the disgust of my father (James Jackson Jarves)."

Yet, despite its detractors, pressed glass collecting continues today. The ware is more difficult to find, and much more expensive than when many of these articles were written. Perhaps the interest in it remains high because, as Mary E. Bakewell wrote in her article on "The Bakewell Glass Factory":

> There will always remain an element of the marvelous about glass, a substance resulting from the fusion of a combination of silica with various bases. . . . This beautiful translucent thing which we call glass awakens in us more than response to beauty. For here we are near such transformation as urges our thoughts beyond the confines of a factory.

April, 1974

Robert E. DiBartolomeo
Director, Mansion Museum
Oglebay Institute
Oglebay Park
Wheeling, W. Va.

AMERICAN GLASS

New Views of Old Glass

Intended Primarily for the Neophyte Collector

I. Pressed-Glass Compotes

By Harry Hall White

BY WAY of starting things, let me ask a favor. Will every owner of a pressed-glass compote who can tell, without looking, whether his specimen was pressed in one piece, or in two pieces, please raise the right hand? Not many hands. There might be still fewer if I were to ask what conclusion should be drawn from the evidence that a piece had been assembled instead of formed as a complete unit. Here is a simple point that apparently has escaped some collectors. I know that it has escaped not a few dealers. It is made clear in the accompanying illustrations.

The four compotes pictured in Figure 1 illustrate the highly popular pattern variously known as *thumbprint* or *thumb mold:* one of the earlier pressed designs, which came on the market about 1850 and went out of style about the time of the Centennial Exhibition. These dates are, of course, only approximate, but are based on trustworthy evidence and are generally accepted.

From a note in Antiques for April 1927 we learn that the *thumbprint* pattern is pictured in the 1868 catalogue of M'Kee & Brothers of Pittsburgh, where it bears the name *Argus,* in deference to the hundred-eyed Greek demigod whose visual apparatus was eventually used by Juno for embroidering the tail of her favorite bird, the peacock. Ruth Webb Lee, in her *Early American Pressed Glass,* illustrates the same pattern, under the same name, from an undated catalogue of Bakewell, Pears & Company, also of Pittsburgh. No doubt *Argus* glass was produced by other manufacturers, though apparently not at Cambridge or Sandwich.

Mrs. Lura Woodside Watkins illustrates in *Cambridge Glass* (p. 105) some pressed bowls with a decoration resembling the *Argus* pattern, but differing from it in that the "eyes" are circular instead of oval in outline. The Cambridge factory name for this pattern was *punty.* Again, in the list of Sandwich molds quoted by Mr. Chipman in his *Romance of Old Sandwich Glass,* I find *punty* mentioned on page 69. We may, I think, accept this circular *punty* motive, now generally known as *mirror,* as the Yankee analogue of the Pittsburgh oval *Argus,* or *thumbprint.* Sometimes confused with the latter are the shallow faceted patterns originally christened *New York* and *Vernon,* but now

classified under the head of *honeycomb.* Thus on page 75 of *The Romance of Old Sandwich Glass,* several pieces of *honeycomb* (*New York* and *Vernon*) are pictured as *thumbprint* — a matter of no serious importance except that, since Ruth Webb Lee has so competently done for glass what Adam and Eve did for the animal kingdom, there seems no adequate reason for upsetting her nomenclature. On page 74, however, of Mr. Chipman's volume both terminology and description are quite confusing.

But to return to the structural consideration. The earliest, and perhaps most desirable, of compotes will, on close examination, be found to consist of two distinct parts — the bowl and the foot, which were separately pressed and then fused together with soft adhesive wafers of molten glass. This method was necessitated by the limited capacity and power of the early pressing machines. In Figure 2 this wafer has been blackened so as to show clearly. Later compotes, on the contrary, including the majority of those in so-called pattern glass, will be found to have been pressed in a single piece.

Besides the evident line where bowl and base meet, assembled pieces may also exhibit traces of the pontil used to support the parts at the time of their joining. These traces are additional evidence of early workmanship. All such indices of age must, of course, be employed with discretion. At most they can only point to a method of manufacture; they are by no means a guarantee of date. Many an early process was, and for that matter, still is, continued in certain localities long after its general abandonment by progressive manufacturers.

Except for the device just described, I know of few, if any, technical signs by which the relative age of pressed glass items may be judged. Design, however, affords us a few hints, though they are singularly vague. We are, for example, fairly justified in placing fine lacy patterns between 1830 and 1850. It is, indeed, possible that very little lacy glass was made in this country after 1845. From 1850 to 1870 occur geometric patterns. After 1870 the more or less naturalistic compositions which are designated by the term "pattern glass" attain precedence. Thus the age of a piece may be roughly estimated.

Fig. 1 — Compotes: Thumbprint Pattern (*c. 1850*)

In the terminology of the glass catalogues of the 1860's the taller objects here would be known as bowls; the footed dish as a "nappy" with foot; and the covered dish as a sweetmeat. Apparently, however, a footed nappy was usually classed among the sweetmeats. If it attained a considerable diameter and corresponding depth it became a bowl

Fig. 2 — Detail of Compotes

These pieces were pressed in two separate parts, which were assembled and joined by means of a wafer of molten glass. The wafer here has been painted black to increase its visibility. Note what Mrs. Watkins has to say about this method of making candlesticks (p. 106 of *Cambridge Glass*)

New Views of Old Glass

II. Surface Lines and Rounded Edges on Pressed Glass

By Harry Hall White

PLATES of various sizes, from cup plates to bread platters, have long been collected, and much has been written about them; but to Rose Lohr Ayer, I find, belongs the credit for the first article devoted to glass tea plates (see Antiques for July 1931, p. 34).

The specimen here pictured is larger than any in the six-inch group shown in Mrs. Ayer's article: to be exact, it measures seven inches. Recently brought to me for examination by a collector, it seemed so evidently of early period that it was placed in comparison with the cup-plate collection, where, as expected, a smaller edition was found measuring three and seven sixteenths inches. While, to my knowledge, this cup plate is as yet unnamed and hitherto unpublished, it may be identified as *Marble*, Number 176. Since the ornaments interspaced between the hearts of the border are presumably stylized honeysuckles (anthemia), we may properly christen the pattern *heart and honeysuckle*. Large plate and small show many similarities besides those of design. Among the features common to both, there is one in particular whose explanation my enquiring collector was anxious to learn: namely, the peculiar network of lines, or shallow grooves, observable on the upper surface of each piece — a somewhat fascinating blemish.

These lines have been variously accounted for, though seldom in terms corresponding to the actualities of glassmaking. Their revelation is of certain difficulties in the operation of pressing glass, which the pioneer glassmakers were not able quite to overcome. In short, these hairlike cracks are surface ruptures, shallow fissures that were opened as the face of the glass cooled and shrank more rapidly than the still viscous interior, until, like a too tight garment, it had to yield somewhere to the strain. Such strains might have been avoided if mold and plunger could have been kept at a uniform temperature so as to prevent the occurrence of prematurely cooling areas. But that was something more easily talked about than accomplished.

The reason why the cracks appear most frequently on the plunger side of the glass is that the plunger was generally devoid of pattern, thus allowing a slight slipping under pressure, while the side bearing the design would be quite securely anchored in the mold. Of course, when the mold temperatures were

Fig. 1 — Seven-Inch Tea Plate and Matching Cup Plate
Here christened *heart and honeysuckle*. What appear to be scratches on the larger piece are ruptures in the surface of the glass due to uneven cooling

Fig. 2 — Detail of Plate in Figure I
Taken at an angle so that reflected light will reveal the surface ruptures. Such ruptures are among the evidences of age in pressed glass

pervasively unequal, ruptures would appear on both plain and corrugated faces. The bottoms of the fissures on the pattern side of the glass are usually rough, while those on the face are more smooth and rounded.

Pressed articles were withdrawn from the mold while they were still in what may be called a rather limp condition, and were placed in forms calculated to support them during their stay in the annealing oven.

These curious surface fissures are almost unfailing attributes of the earliest pressed glass, and were largely eliminated as technical methods improved. Yet their presence in a piece of glass is not in itself an infallible sign of age. In truth, glassmakers today encounter troubles of the same kind. Now, as of old, when production is hurried, or the water-cooling of a plunger is excessive, uneven shrinkage becomes manifest in an outbreak of lines. Look for them within the mechanically formed white-glass ointment or cold-cream jars of the "beauty table."

It is the old story: we must base our judgments of glass — or of anything else, for that matter — not on a single indication or sign, but upon the careful study of many indices, and an appraisal of their relative importance.

A chipped or crumbled rim on an early pressed-glass plate constitutes a blemish; an incompleted rim, if smooth or rounded, may be regarded as an asset. The two are easily differentiated. Chipping will show the characteristic shell-like fracture with sharp edge. An incomplete rounded edge, on the other hand, indicates that the mold was not entirely filled with metal, an overcautious or excessively thrifty gatherer preferring to mold a piece scant than to have it too thick. As more precise methods of measuring quantities were devised, and molds were no longer either underfed or overfed, pressed pieces became more perfect from the mechanical standpoint. Yet to me those which fail of complete exactitude are the more attractive. Both of the plates here illustrated exhibit what may be called partially atrophied edges; but the fact makes them no less desirable.

Broadly speaking, if the pattern corroborates other evidences, the presence of the defects described is fair guarantee that a specimen of pressed glass is of collectible age. Since imitations of old patterns are common, this is worth remembering.

Fig. 3 — Detail of Rim *(greatly enlarged)*
Contrasting incomplete, or atrophied, portions and full-pressed portions. This unevenness, due to unequal and insufficient distribution of glass in the mold, is a desirable evidence of somewhat primitive technique

Early Glass Pressing at Cambridge and Sandwich

Part I

By Lura Woodside Watkins

THE longer one studies early pressed glass and the first methods of pressing, the more is one amazed at what seems to be a sudden transition from breath and hand shaping to a complete mechanical technique. In the early 'twenties of the last century the greater part of American glass was blown or molded. By 1827 pressing had become a regular practice in half a dozen factories that we know of, and, probably, in a number of others about which we are uninformed. At the beginning of the next decade virtually every glasshouse was acquainted with the process, and Deming Jarves was already turning out the handsomest pressed glass ever made.

Undoubtedly the shift to machine methods took place less abruptly than it seems to have done. English goblets, bowls, candlesticks, and castor bottles with square, pressed feet were on the market in the late eighteenth century (it is said that feet of this type did not appear before 1775), and advertisements show that the New England Glass Company was making tableware in the same manner before 1820. Jarves imported pressed salts from Holland and other glass of the kind while he was a member of the Henshaw & Jarves firm (*1815–1818*). The squared feet required cutting or polishing to smooth rough edges, as the first pressing apparatus could not finish the work at one operation.

For a long time persons interested in glass research have speculated as to which factory made the first pressed glass as we know it today. The answer should probably be: they all did. Deming Jarves has usually been given the credit for the invention. If his own story can be depended upon, he was certainly the first glass man to press an article like a tumbler. He doubtless showed the way to the use of hinged molds — perhaps by adapting a plunger to a mold intended for blowing. This I have discussed in a previous article (ANTIQUES, October 1931).

The activities of other factories in the direction of mechanical molding have remained in a haze of doubt which a survey of patents could not dispel. Unfortunately, important information was lost when the early Patent Office records were destroyed in a disastrous fire. Nevertheless, there are still enough data to show that Jarves was not the sole originator of the pressing process. Door and furniture knobs were the products of the first attempts at pressing; and several of the earliest patents were for such knobs. One, taken out by J. P. Bakewell of Pittsburgh, September 9, 1825, covered an "improvement in making glass furniture knobs." Another, patenting "glass knobs for doors," was secured by Henry Whitney and Enoch Robinson of Cambridge, November 4, 1826. A third, for "glass knobs pressed in one operation," was granted to John Robinson of Pittsburgh, November 14, 1827.

With no information beyond the names of these patents, it has been impossible to determine whether all were for methods of pressing knobs or merely for knob hardware. A paragraph in a volume entitled *The World of Science, Art, and Industry, illustrated from Examples in the New-York Exhibition, 1853-54,* edited by Professor B. Silliman,

Fig. 1 — SANDWICH KNOB WITH GLASS SCREW
Stamped *Patent*

Jr., and C. R. Goodrich, throws some light on the matter. The value of this evidence may be judged from the authoritative background of the work, and from the fact that Joseph N. Howe, Jr., was an employee at Cambridge as early as 1822 and could give first-hand information.

We have taken some pains to ascertain the history of this branch of glass making in the United States, and have been obligingly furnished with some facts relating to it by Mr. Jos. N. Howe, the Agent of the New England Company. It appears that moulded glass has been made in a certain rude form, but that in 1826 Mr. Enoch Robinson, then in the employ of the New England Company, took out letters patent for the invention of a process by which furniture knobs, door handles, &c., were made of pressed glass. The validity and originality of this patent was fully tested by a closely contested lawsuit in Philadelphia, carried on against powerful parties in Pittsburgh. In 1827 Mr. Robinson, against the ridicule of the craft, succeeded in moulding a salt stand, and various other articles for table use, and from that time the invention, as one of general applicability, may be considered as established. In 1832 about £100 sterling in value of the Boston pressed ware was taken to London by Mr. Ryan, an Englishman, where the articles in question excited much curiosity and sold profitably. But it was only so late as 1837 that a thin vessel like a drinking glass was fashioned by the pressing process, which branch of the manufacture has since steadily increased.

The Jersey City Glass Company was also early in the field. A patent for a glass-pressing mold secured by P. C. Dummer of Jersey City, October 16, 1827, is evidence of that company's progress in the use of mechanical methods. All of the above-mentioned patents antedate Jarves' first claims by more than a year, although we know that Sandwich was making cup plates in 1827.

In his patent papers of December 1, 1828, Jarves claimed a method of "pressing melted glass into moulds." His next device was a furniture knob, which he describes as a "glass knob with a glass screw or shank." One of these knobs, with the word *Patent* stamped on the bottom of the screw, may be seen in Figure 1. Its identity as a Sandwich knob is established by comparison with a sapphire-blue specimen that now reposes in the Harrison Gray Otis House, Boston, in the collection of Sandwich fragments assembled by Doctor Irving P. Lyon. It exemplifies Jarves' ingenuity in turning out an object by mechanical means without waste of time in finishing; for the knob, after being pressed in a two-part mold, was complete and required no metal attachment whatever. Its practicability seems doubtful. The necessity for boring a hole in the wood large enough to accommodate a glass

Fig. 2 — SANDWICH LACY PITCHER
Handle pressed in one with body

screw and the wear occasioned by this sharp-threaded member must have wrought havoc with drawer fronts.

It has been assumed, since so much pressed glass of an early type is known to have emanated from the works at Sandwich, that Jarves was the first glass man to capitalize the sales possibilities of the new process. A comparison of Sandwich glass made in the 'thirties with that pressed at other glasshouses leads to the conclusion that the assumption is sound. Jarves' 1830 patent, perfecting his earlier experiments, secured to him the sole right to press glass by

Fig. 3 — AUTHENTICATED NEW ENGLAND GLASS COMPANY EARLY PRESSED PLATES
a, Clear light green, full of grit and bubbles; *b,* light green opalescent, good quality

the same fundamental method that has been in use ever since. His claim reads as follows:

The improvement claimed is the forming of a handle or handles or other similar projections on glass cups, by pressure at one operation, instead of attaching them to the cup after it has been blown, in the way heretofore practised.

The mould is to be made in the usual manner of brass or other suitable metal, excavations being provided for the formation of the handles. The plug or piston which is to form the inside of the cup is made to fit exactly into a rim which forms the top of the mould, so that when it is pressed down none of the fluid glass which has been put into the mould can escape at the top, but will by the pressure be forced into the cavities described. The claim is to the forming of the mould in the manner above indicated.

This patent was in force for fourteen years. Thus until 1844 no factory other than the works at Sandwich had the right to press pitchers or mugs with handles integral with the body. That attempts were made to infringe on Jarves' patent seems unlikely. It is noteworthy that lace-glass pitchers of known Sandwich origin are pressed in this manner, while one of the few pressed jugs of the period from Pittsburgh was made without the benefit of this invention. A glance at the photographs of a stippled pitcher bearing the mark *R. B. Curling & Sons Fort Pitt* (ANTIQUES, December 1933, p. 207)

Fig. 4 — The Pressing Machine
With shears in his right hand, the presser detaches a portion of glass (*B*) from the assistant's punty. His left holds aloft the arm (*D*) which operates the plunger (*C*).
From "Curiosities of Glass-making," Apsley Pellatt, 1849. By courtesy of the Massachusetts Historical Society

will show that its handle was pressed separately and was then applied.

There is so little general knowledge of the appearance and operation of a pressing mold that it may be well to pause here and examine the diagram of such an apparatus (*Fig. 5*). It may easily be seen that the removable rim or cap plate prevented excess glass from running over at the top. It did not regulate the thickness of the glass. The matter of thickness was controlled by the workman who dropped the glass into the mold. Several writers have stated that molten glass was poured into the mold from a ladle. Any practical glass man will contradict this assertion; and pictures of workmen operating a press show quite a different method of procedure. Two men worked together at a press. One brought a sufficient gathering from the furnace on the end of a punty, from which the second workman cut off the correct portion with his shears. The glass thus released dropped into the mold, which was then pushed into place on the table of the press beneath the plunger. A strong pull on the lever arm finished the operation. The mold was then tipped upside down, and the ejected article carried to the annealing oven on a wooden tray or shovel, or on a pronged stick.

For many years, glass collectors have been puzzled by the so-called "scratch" or "straw" mark that appears almost invariably on early Sandwich glass. The explanation of this defect is simple. In cutting or shearing the gathering of glass from the punty, the presser inevitably pulled a portion of it out to a thin wisp. One can picture this easily by recalling the effect of cutting soft molasses candy. The slight ridge thus occasioned in the lump was bound to show as a line or apparent

scratch after the glass had hardened. Skilled workmen were usually able to give the ball of molten glass a twist as it fell into the mold, thus allowing the cut wisp to melt into the inner portion of the gathering. Accordingly, the "shear" mark, as glassmakers call it, is found sometimes inside, sometimes outside the finished piece. Sometimes it is entirely eliminated.

The process just described was essentially that followed by Jarves as early as 1830. It is obvious that other concerns must have stumbled on the idea of the confining ring without infringing on his patent.

Bearing in mind the method of its production, we may more easily appraise early pressed glass. Just how good was it? The answer is that the virtue of Sandwich lacy glass lies wholly in its clearly defined technique and in the nature of its patterns. It is absurd to say that the glass was of excellent quality. It wasn't. It was full of bubbles, grit, and lumps of quartz. Much of it was off-color. That these irregularities endear it to the collector does not alter the facts. Furthermore, early Sandwich is not to be admired for any subtlety of finish. The glass was slapped into the mold, pressed as quickly as possible, and hurried off to the annealing oven without any sort of hand finishing. The result would have been unbearable had not Jarves or his clever moldmakers retrieved the appearance of their mechanically contrived wares by pressing them in patterns more nearly suitable for the process than any since devised. Where or how the designers in a little country town obtained the idea of lacy glass we may never know. To them, at any rate, goes the credit for a new and beautiful product, and to Jarves the credit for perfecting a means of pressing that made possible the use of such molds.

Early glass in lacy pattern and in designs of similar character from other factories seems to be less brilliant than the ware from Sandwich. This inferiority is due partly to the quality of the glass itself, and partly to lack of skill in pressing. Well-cut molds, however, rather than any inherent quality of the Sandwich metal, produced the sparkle and silvery glitter that is so much admired and often attributed to the addition of barytes. I have seen pressed glass from the New England Glass Company, where barytes was not used, that would be quite as brilliant as anything from Sandwich had it been pressed in a mold of lacy pattern. By such means Jarves developed pressing to a point whence it could progress no further in the direction he had given it. For by mechanical methods alone he had achieved a product whose unique beauty was derived from the special fitness of its designs.

Editorial Note. The second part of Mrs. Watkins' discussion of glass pressing at the New England Glass Company and at the Sandwich Glass Works will be published in an early issue. Part II will be a consideration of fire polishing as it was practised in the two glasshouses in the mid-nineteenth century. The glass pictured in the present article is from the author's collection.

Fig. 5 — Cross-Section of Hinged Mold for Pressing a Footed Bowl
a, body of mold; *b*, core-plate of base; *c*, removable rim, ring, or cap plate; *d*, plunger; *e*, hinge-pin; *f*, bolt-pin; *g*, matrix (which gives the shape of article to be formed). Worth noting is the large volume of metal constituting the mold in relation to the free space into which the molten glass was to be forced by the plunger.
From an 1869 patent specification

Early Glass Pressing at Cambridge and Sandwich

Part II

By Lura Woodside Watkins

JARVES in his lacy glass had brought the pressing process to a point where it could go no farther in the direction he had given it; he had attained unique designs by purely mechanical means. But other glassmakers were dissatisfied with the rough surfaces and raw edges of the lacy ware, for it must be understood that fire polishing played no part in the making of lacy glass. The heat incidental to that process would have melted the delicate stippling beyond recognition. In England little attention was paid to early mechanical methods because of these seemingly inevitable crudities. It was not until 1837 that Richardson of Stourbridge began to press glass. With the English adoption of pressing, careful fire polishing became a general practice. Thus, almost as soon as the Sandwich project was launched, we find other glassmakers working toward an entirely different goal.

The object of fire polishing was to give pressed glass a surface and texture like that of blown glass. It was accomplished by attaching a punty rod to the pressed object and reheating the latter slightly before the open flame of the furnace. The smooth scar of a ground-off pontil mark is to be seen on pieces thus treated, and by this scar they may be dated before the invention of the snap holder in the late 'sixties. By 1840 Jarves himself was finding his lacy glass impracticable and unprofitable. An inventory of that year shows that he too was fire polishing his shank ware.

A review of pressing in the 'forties as carried on at the New England Glass Company will show that the preservation of the lustrous appearance of blown glass was the prime desideratum. As early as 1840 pressed patterns were being changed from dainty feathery and lacy designs to motives imitating early cutting. Four patterns of the 'forties made at both Cambridge and Sandwich were the *Washington, Huber, diamond point* or *sharp diamond*, and the *New York* or *honeycomb*. All of these had previously been known in cut ware. The *Ashburton*, or large thumbprint, seems to have been turned out at Cambridge over a period of thirty years. It was made at Sandwich, too, but not to so great an extent; patents at Cambridge may have discouraged competition.

Some time in the early 'forties, Joseph Magoun became foreman of the pressing department at East Cambridge. Born in 1811, he had gone to work at the New England Glass Company when still a very young man. As a figure in glass history he is notable for a series of patented inventions perfected in the course of many years, by which he succeeded in eliminating mold marks. He seems to have been obsessed by the idea,

eventually developing it so that pressed glass might exhibit no visible mold marks whatsoever.

As a first step in this direction, he secured, September 25, 1847, two patents for molds — one a mold for a fluted goblet and the other for a lamp body. The full text of these patents is worth reading as throwing light on the methods of pressing at this date. Magoun explains in his papers that, previously, it had been customary to make goblets in a two-part mold, contriving that the seams of the mold, which left their telltale ridges, should come at the angles of the flutes or other form of ornamental treatment. He says, "Whenever these mold marks appear in any plane or curved or cylindrical surface, they materially injure the beauty of the article and thereby affect its marketable value." It was, for example, almost impossible to present the upper surface of a goblet foot to the action of the furnace flame in such a manner as to remove these blemishes by fire polishing. Accordingly Magoun invented a mold in which the foot was pressed as a hollow cylinder. In this shape, it could be held to the fire, the joint marks thus eliminated, and the foot worked up to a flat disc with the aid of the glassmaker's tools. Furthermore, the body of the goblet was so formed that the upper part of the mold could be made without seams. Thus, when the lower hinged section had been opened, it was possible to remove the whole goblet by pushing it upward by means of a contrivance devised for the purpose.

The other patent aimed at eliminating the marks on the plain upper surface of a lamp reservoir (*Fig. 1*). The body section of the mold was made in two or more parts, but the plain part was in one section. After the lamp bowl was pressed, the upper part of the mold could be lifted to allow the removal of the article. The plain cylindrical portion, quite free from marks, was then drawn together into its domical shape by hand manipulation.

This second patent is particularly significant. Its term of fourteen years covers precisely the period when whale-oil and fluid lamps enjoyed their greatest popularity. This circumstance indicates that a pressed lamp reservoir whose curved shoulder shows absolutely no sign of mold marks is an East Cambridge product. It does not follow that goblets without visible marks were made exclusively at the New England Glass Company, unless one happens to be certain that they were pressed during the period 1847–1861. The same principle was applied in the pressing of toilet bottles, which were pressed, so to speak, wrong side up, that is, from the base end, and the plain cylindrical portion subsequently

Fig. 1 — Mold Diagram of 1847. Magoun's Patent

Fig: 3 pictures a section of the mold for pressing a lamp bowl without visible mold marks. *A* represents the seamless ring, which may be lifted after the article is pressed; *B* is the hinged body section of mold; *C*, the plunger. *Fig: 4* shows the lamp bowl after removal from the mold. *b* is the seamless cylindrical section to be drawn together by hand manipulation into the neck of the lamp flattened and drawn together to a small nub in the centre of the bottom (*Fig. 2*).

In 1848 Magoun concentrated his inventive powers upon accomplishing the same result with the *Ashburton* pattern. He produced a mold with a series of retracting pistons or cams that shaped the thumbprints. After the plunger had done its work, a handle was turned, withdrawing the little cams from their contact with the glass. The tumbler could then be removed without any opening of the mold.

Many years later — in 1867 — Joseph Magoun carried his ideas to their logical conclusion in a very complicated device that made it possible to press goblets and glasses of many kinds in molds without joints. It is said that the New England Glass Company reaped a goodly profit from the invention, which legally belonged to them, although the patent had been taken out in Magoun's name. Feeling that he deserved a bonus for his invention, he sued the company for part of the profits. His action was fruitless, and he left the company soon afterwards, a broken-hearted man.

Magoun is also to be remembered for having made, in 1845, a pressing machine to which any mold could be adjusted. To quote his description: "Heretofore it has been necessary to have a press or a series of springs and rods applied to each mold used; but now I am enabled to make use of but one press and one series of springs and rods for numerous molds, thus saving much expense."

Aside from the labor of polishing away mold marks, there was so much hand work required in making the heavy early glass that the ware might almost as well have been shaped entirely by blowing. This is exemplified by the pitcher in Figure 3. This piece was first pressed in a straight-sided mold. The pitcher form was then developed by hand. After attaching a punty to the base of the piece, the glassmaker pinched the body in, cut the lip with his shears, and manipulated it into shape. He then fire polished the vessel and applied a handmade handle. When, after all this treatment, the piece had cooled, the pontil mark was ground away. The result is a pitcher whose slight element of pressing

Fig. 2 (left) — Base of New England Glass Company Toilet Bottle
Pressed from bottom end, and drawn in by hand, with resulting nub in the centre

Fig. 3 (right) — New England Glass Company Fire-Polished Pitcher, "Ashburton" Pattern

Fig. 4 — Fire-Polished Mugs
Left: Honeycomb pattern from New England Glass Company; handmade handle. *Right: Huber* pattern from Boston and Sandwich Glass Company; handle pressed with body in one operation. Both have ground pontil marks

does not prevent its having the character of a blown piece. The glass itself is beautifully clear and white, and its texture has a velvety smoothness not usually associated with pressed glass.

During the past year I have examined many pieces of fire-polished pressed ware easily identified as of East Cambridge origin because of their likeness to the series of excellent line drawings in a catalogue printed in 1869. Some of these patterns were in vogue throughout a period of many years and recur in glass ranging in date from the 'forties to the 'seventies. The mugs illustrated in Figure 4 were finished by hand manipulation, as the ground-off pontil marks on their bases testify. The high standard of their metal and finish we shall probably never see equaled. Glass today is fire polished by gas flame while still in the mold, thus entirely eliminating the personal equation. Moreover, flint metal is rarely used at the present time for ordinary tableware.

It must not be assumed that the New England Glass Company was the only concern that so carefully made pressed glass. In the early period similar methods were in use at Wheeling, and doubtless in other glasshouses. But the fact that Cambridge processes were patented made it impossible for competitors to attain quite the same perfection of finish. In the pursuit of pattern glass it would be well for the collector to ask himself whether he is acquiring, at no little expense, glass manufactured without benefit of human handling and of a quality below that of the modern five-and-ten, or whether he is saving for posterity the product of an era before speed and cheapness in production were the all-essential considerations.

Note. Magoun's invention of a pressing machine adjustable to a diversity of molds not only reduced the quantity of apparatus required for making different patterns, but cut time and labor costs by enabling three or four men working at one press quickly to substitute a reheated and refilled mold for one that had just served its purpose and had to be prepared to receive its next molten morsel. By this new though simple process, the output must have been greatly increased and the even quality of the product assured.

Pressed Glass
a Debtor to
Staffordshire?

AN EDITORIAL NOTE

THE collector of early pressed glass will have observed two divergent tendencies in the decorative motives employed during the 1830's. On the one hand, he will encounter pieces whose elaboration reveals a careful adherence to the cut designs of their day. On the other, he will find ornamental devices that would have defied the capabilities of the cutter's wheel. Among the latter is the stippled background which serves so helpfully in giving cohesion to a poorly articulated design in whatsoever medium executed. Stippling imparted brilliance to the early pressed glass; but we may reasonably doubt that the achievement of such an effect was anticipated by the mold maker who first punched tiny dots to fill the voids in a cup-plate border.

Fig. 1 — DETAIL OF STAFFORDSHIRE STIPPLED BOR-DER BY WOOD: GLASS CUP PLATE, SCROLLED BORDER

The procedure was but an imitation of a method become familiar to the artisan through long communion with the printed Staffordshire tableware on which his daily bread was served. From a like experience, also, he may have derived the idea of giving a pictorial flavor to cup plates, and of wreathing the border of larger plates and dishes with acanthus scrolls and, at times, with floral garlands. The theory that many patterns of American early pressed glass owed at least something to printed Staffordshire tableware may easily be pushed too far. Nevertheless, the accompanying illustrations will suffice to suggest its fundamental validity. It is, of course, unlikely that the mold cutter's imitation of an earthenware technique was often conscious. Visual impressions may be most casually received. They are likely to repose latent and forgotten in the mind until evoked by creative necessity. Then they emerge in the guise of original ideas.

Fig. 2 (left) — STAFFORDSHIRE OAK-LEAF BORDER BY R. STEVENSON AND WILLIAMS: PRESSED-GLASS FLORAL BORDER

Fig. 4 (right) — WEDGWOOD PRINTED DISH EARLY PRESSED-GLASS PLATE
Note the background figure of the Wedgwood plate, also the resemblance between major motives in the two items

Fig. 3 — GREEN-GLAZED ENGLISH EARTHENWARE PLATE, GOTHIC BORDER: "HAIRPIN" BORDER IN PRESSED GLASS
From the collection of Julia D. S. Snow

An ANTIQUES survey:

Stylistic influences on
nineteenth-century American glass

BY MILLARD F. ROGERS JR., *Assistant to the director, Toledo Museum of Art*

AMERICAN GLASS FROM 1800 TO 1900, like its European counterpart, illustrates the whole trend of nineteenth-century taste, as clearly as does furniture, architecture, painting, or any other of the fine and decorative arts of the time. We can see in glass forms and decorations the classic, Gothic, rococo, and Renaissance revivals, and even the combination of two or more styles in the eclectic spirit of the late 1800's. This wide range of styles also reflects the American glassmaker's ability to digest European influences and adapt them to native products. His talent for improvisation resulted in a good deal of individuality in designs and patterns. He revived old techniques as well as styles, sometimes adapting them in such a way as to produce pieces quite different from their prototypes.

This photographic survey of style relationships in nineteenth-century glass is based on examples from the collections of the Toledo Museum of Art. That this museum should be associated with the art and history of glass is not surprising, since its founder was Edward Drummond Libbey (1854-1925), an outstanding figure in American glass manufacturing who directed the operations of one of the nation's largest glasshouses. No American or European glass was owned or exhibited in the museum until twelve years after its founding. Then, in 1916, Mr. Libbey acquired Edwin A. Barber's collection, and donated it to the museum as the beginning of what has become one of the most extensive collections in the world.

Neoclassic. Cut-glass decanter, c. 1827-1830. Height 13 inches. Clear glass.

In the first decades of the nineteenth century, classical formalism in glass decoration and form remained supreme. The influence of contemporary English and Irish models on form and decoration is apparent here, but the design of tulips and fine crosshatching in shallow relief shows the labor-saving simplification of American cut-glass design in this period. The restrained fluting at the shoulder of the decanter is a reaction against florid Continental embellishments.

Neoclassic. Blown and engraved urn with cover, c. 1830-1840. Height 12⅜ inches. Clear glass.

Sir William Hamilton's archeological efforts and Josiah Wedgwood's reliance on classical forms and motifs for pottery influenced England and, in turn, America via immigrant glassworkers and imported English and Irish ware. On this covered urn the wheel-engraved oak leaves and narrow wreath on the neck are simplified classical forms occurring frequently in English ware. The relationship to the classical Greek amphora shape, so admired and copied in the late eighteenth century, is also seen in this decorative footed piece.

Neoclassic. Pressed-glass salt cellar, c. 1840. Height 2 inches, length 3 inches. Clear glass.

A piece produced when the Greek revival style in architecture was gaining popularity. Grecian forms were easily adapted to the decoration of glass. The Ionic columns at the corners of the salt cellar suggest in miniature the main elements of this order; even the fluting is reproduced. A frieze of oak leaves beneath the top edge is classic in its simplicity, but does not copy the Greek motif literally.

Baroque revival. Blown-three-mold decanter and cream pitcher, c. 1825-1830. Height of decanter, 11 inches; of pitcher, 4¾. Clear glass.

The flowing and rhythmical line, the full form give its baroque character to this scarce decanter (McKearin, GV-16) and pitcher (GV-8). Soft, rounded edges of shell and gadrooning on the pitcher produce reliefs not unlike those on European seventeenth-century stucco panels and silver. However, the term baroque serves more to distinguish designs of this kind from geometrical and other patterns than to suggest a derivation from the seventeenth-century style, and this blown-three-mold ware was actually made in imitation of English and Irish cut glass. The same technique was employed to produce designs that might be classed as Gothic revival and classic revival.

Gothic revival. Pressed-glass sugar bowl with cover, c. 1840. Height 5¼ inches. Peacock blue glass. Pressed-glass salt cellar, c. 1840. Height 1⅝ inches; length 2¾ inches. Clear glass.

The American gift for capturing the essential elements of a style was never better demonstrated than in pressed glass in the Gothic revival style. This Gothic arch motif was borrowed from architectural examples appearing first about 1830 and representing the innovations of Alexander Jackson Davis, Ithiel Town, and others. The pointed arch was the most familiar decorative symbol of this revival; it is found in pattern books and engravings, and in the design and decoration of furniture, silver, ceramics, textiles, cast iron, as well as in architecture.

Rococo revival. Pressed glass salt cellar, c. 1840. Height 2 inches, length 3. Clear glass.

The rococo was a popular style because it characterized elegance, and in glass the elaborate ornamentation made possible by improvements in the technique of pressing became synonymous with the term. The style of American salt cellars went rapidly from simplicity to the profuse decoration of the 1850's. This fairly common example, its surface crowded with rosettes, baskets of flowers, and scrolls, illustrates the mid-century's choice of motifs and the stippled background characteristic of lacy glass enhances the rococo effect. A kinship with furniture is apparent in the shape, suggesting Victorian black walnut sofas.

Neo-Venetian. Blown vase, c. 1825. Height 8¼ inches. Light blue glass.

Rigaree trailing on handles and body of this simply shaped vase suggest the *façon de Venise* of the sixteenth to eighteenth centuries, though the decoration of this piece is crude in comparison with most European examples.

Neo-Venetian. Bellows bottle, c. 1885. Height 19⅞ inches. Body of rose with opaque white loops; clear glass base and applied trailing and rigaree.

John Liddell of the Mount Washington Glass Company created this bellows bottle as an exhibition piece or keepsake, using the form of similar bottles produced in the first half of the nineteenth century. The looped bands of rose and white in the body of the piece are reminiscent of South Jersey swirling reintroduced by 1830, but applied rigaree and quilling were patterned after Venetian handling of decorative pinched-glass trailing seen on many seventeenth-century examples.

Medieval revival. Tumbler or beaker, c. 1850-1860. Height 6 inches. Dark ruby overlay on clear glass, with gilding.

This drinking glass harks back to medieval prototypes in shape. The early mid-European glasses its resembles, however, were not cut and decorated in this manner. The type is often called Bohemian glass, a term loosely used to describe all ruby glass with cut or engraved decoration.

Naturalistic. Cameo-glass vase, c. 1885. Height 9 inches. Light ruby glass with pattern carved in overlay of opaque white.

The style of this vase foreshadows the *art nouveau* of the end of the century, but it was executed in a medium developed by the ancient Romans and revived by English glassmakers in the last third of the nineteenth century. Joseph Locke (1846-1936), who came to the New England Glass Company in 1883 from Stourbridge, brought the technique to America but it flourished here only briefly. In ANTIQUES, June 1954 (p. 474), Geoffrey Beard said that he knew of the whereabouts of only one example of Locke's work. This vase can now be added to the record.

Fig. 1 — "View of Sandwich Glass Works" (*from a wood cut*)
The above entitlement appears on a wood cut owned by Mrs. P. W. Whittemore. It bears the further entitlement *Glass Manufacture in the United States*. The source of this work of art is, however, not divulged.

The Boston and Sandwich Glass Company

By Priscilla C. Crane

Note — The following article is based on information gleaned, for the most part, on a trip to Sandwich in May, 1924. In spite of diligent search, I have been unable to locate any manuscript records concerning the Company beyond the old account book now for the first time discussed. The material here compiled is derived chiefly from personal interviews. A list of the persons seen, together with a bibliography, is appended— P. C. C.

Beginnings

IN 1825 Deming Jarves, born 1791,* a resident of Boston, living near the corner of Boylston and Tremont Streets† and interested in the New England Glass Company at Cambridge, Massachusetts, started a glass factory at Sandwich, Massachusetts, called The Sandwich Manufacturing Company.

Ground was broken in April, dwellings for the workmen built, and manufactory completed, and on the 4th day of July, 1825, they

Fig. 2 — The Glory That Was Glass
Ruins of the Cape Cod Glass Factory, from the north. The Cape Cod Glass Company was founded in 1858 by Jarves after his withdrawal from the Boston and Sandwich concern.

commenced blowing glass, three months from first breaking ground. In the following year it was purchased of the proprietor, a company formed, and incorporated under the title of the Boston and Sandwich Glass Company.*

The Act of Incorporation may be found in Chapter 99, Acts of 1825, *Private and Special Statutes of the Commonwealth of Massachusetts*, and reads as follows:—

Sect. 1

Be it enacted, etc. That Deming Jarves, Henry Rice, Andrew T. Hall, and Edmund Monroe and such persons as may become associated with them and their successors and assigns be and hereby are made a corporation by the name of the Boston and Sandwich Glass Company for the purpose of manu-

*Deming Jarves is said to have been born in Boston, but he is not listed on the city records.

†Charles F. Dalton, old glassworker, born 1845.

Reminiscences of Glass Making, Deming Jarves, Boston, 1865.

Fig. 3 — SANDWICH GLASS
Three characteristic examples of glass are shown on this page. It would probably be impossible to fix accurate dates for these pieces. *Owned by Mrs. P. W. Whittemore.*

facturing glass in the city of Boston and town of Sandwich in the county of Barnstable and for that purpose shall have all the powers and privileges and shall be subject to all the duties, requirements and disabilities prescribed and contained in an act defining the general powers and duties of manufacturing corporations and the several acts in addition thereto.

Sect. 2

Be it further enacted that the said corporation in their corporate capacity shall and may lawfully hold and possess such real estate not exceeding $100,000 and personal estate not exceeding $200,000, as may be necessary and convenient for carrying on the manufacture of glass in the places aforesaid. As of February 22, 1826.

In so far as I can learn, most of the invested capital came from Boston and not from Sandwich.* The factory was located in Sandwich for two reasons: *first*, the abundance of local fuel; and *second*, easy transportation. At this time the New England glass factories burned wood, and easy access to timber was a chief reason for settling on Cape Cod. At Sandwich, too, there is a tidal creek which reaches back from the ocean for about a mile, and which is navigable for small boats. From Sandwich to Boston by water is approximately fifty miles:—easy transportation was thus assured. The factory was built on the edge of the creek, which was later widened to permit boats to come directly to the plant.†

There is no foundation for the statement that Jarves picked his site at Sandwich on account of the sand to be found in that neighborhood. In fact, the sand at Sandwich contains too much iron, and is too coarse for making fine glass. All of this product used at the factory was imported from Morris River, New Jersey, and from the Berkshires

*William E. Kern, old glassworker, born 1830, started to work in factory as boy of thirteen. See contrary statement by Walter A. Dyer in ANTIQUES for February, 1922 (Vol. I, p. 58).
†John Jones, old glassworker, born 1850.

in western Massachusetts. It came at first by boat, and later by train.

Fact and Tradition

It has been said that, from 1825 to 1858, the factory output was "transported by boat to Boston in the sloop *Polly*, which was able at high tide to come up the creek almost to the doors of the factory."* There seems to be no local record of this boat, and the evidence concerning the creek and the transportation of the glass is quite varied. I was told by one man† that the creek was dredged and water gates were built, and that, when the boat had been loaded, these gates were opened so that the force of the water rushing out carried the boat through the creek. Entrance was only possible at high tide.

Still another man‡ told me that all the glass was loaded on flat-bottomed scows, and poled down the creek on high tide to the boats waiting outside. Supplies of coal, sand, etc., were brought up in the same way. He also said that there was a small railroad, or "bogey," built about 1827,§ to carry the glass across the marsh—approximately a mile—to the shore. This is said to have been one of the earliest railroads of its kind in America.

The merchants of the town had a sloop, the *Osceola*, which was used to carry freight and passengers to and from Boston, and no doubt it carried glass also. The creek now shows no signs of having once been dredged; at low tide it is merely a mud flat.

Early Organization

The Boston and Sandwich Glass Company owned over 20,000 acres of forest land, from which the wood for firing the furnaces was procured. This fuel was cut chiefly by farmers living in the hills back of Sandwich, and was brought by ox team down into the village,—a matter of six

*Walter A. Dyer in ANTIQUES as before.
†Thomas Montagu, old glassworker, born 1848.
‡William E. Kern.
§See contrary statement by Dyer as before.

Fig. 4 — SANDWICH GLASS

Fig. 5 — SANDWICH GLASS

or seven miles. Fifty cents a cord was the pay for cutting and hauling the wood. It is said that most of the town taxes of these early farmers were paid with the money thus received. The old roads through the woods near Forestdale (part of Sandwich township) are still deeply rutted, and show signs of the wear and tear of the heavy hauls which formerly passed over them.*

The men who tended the furnaces were called "shearers"; and the operation was known as "shearing the furnace." In the old account, or sloar†, book of the factory‡ there are listed, "2 shearers $12"; but no information occurs as to whether this is a weekly or a fortnightly rate. I am inclined to believe it to be the former, as the wages in all glass factories were remarkably high for the period.

In this same account book, the first date in which is July 9, 1825, the following glass-workers and their wages are listed:

John Snowdon	17
Jos. Crosby	14
Samuel Kern	8
2 boys	6
	45
Benj. Haynes	17
Benj. Tewkes	14
Alford Green	6
2 boys	6
	43

---

*John Jones and others.

†Sloar is a familiar word in glass phraseology. May it not be a corruption of *slore: to grasp?*

‡Now in the possession of William E. Kern and very kindly loaned to me for reference purposes.

Fig. 6 — Sandwich Candlestick
A piece whose massive outline and heavy base seems to suggest a fairly early date in Sandwich history. Unusually handsome for its type. *Owned by Mrs. P. W. Whittemore.*

John Doyle	16	
John Scott	14	
Isaac Fesenden	7	
2 boys	6	
		43
M. Doyle (Michael)	16	
Arratt	10	
Wm. Lapham	5	
2 boys	6	
		37
Thomas Lloyd	16	
Samuel do	14	
C. Lapham	5	
2 boys	6	
		41
2 shearers $12, 2 shear men $12, 2 W.		
Dryers 12	36	
1 pot-maker 9, 2 assistants 6–12	21	
2 packers 12, 2 stoppers 12, 1 boy 2	26	
Doudy (?) Drake 0.50, 2 laborers 12	24 50	
Blacksmith	8	
		324.50

Deming Jarves was manager of the factory until 1858. Captain William Stetson was his assistant until 1830, when he was succeeded by Theodore Kern, who subsequently served as superintendent for some thirty-six years. George Lafayette Fessenden, or "Lafe" as he was almost universally called, became manager on Jarves' retirement (1858). The former's brother, Sewall H. Fessenden, was agent in Boston for many years. George Lafayette Fessenden was succeeded by Henry V. Spurr in 1882.

First Products

The factory, in 1825, consisted of an eight-pot furnace, each pot holding eight

Fig. 7 — Sandwich Plates
The peacock feather and the bull's scroll of the second example suggest certain French glass patterns of the 1830's. It is worth noting, further, that this same design occurs in the Pittsburgh eagle cup-plates attributed to the decade of the '30's. Compare Figures 3 and 5. The first example appears to be considerably later in date. *Owned by Mrs. P. W. Whittemore.*

Fig. 8 — SANDWICH GLASS IN MINIATURE

Sparkling to the eye and imparting a pleasant sound when struck, such specimens of children's glass possess certain cheerful qualities which, though hardly appealing to the higher aesthetic sensibilities, are admittedly attractive. *Owned by Mrs. P. W. Whittemore.*

hundred pounds. The weekly melts did not exceed seven thousand pounds. The yearly product was valued at $75,000. From sixty to seventy hands were employed.*

The pots in which the glass was annealed were all made directly on the grounds in a special building. In order that the clay of which they were made should be very fine, it was trodden by a man and a boy. As one old worker† said, "I got in a trough and danced all day."

There was one glass house at first with five "shops," as the individual crews were called. In 1849 a second house was built, the two being known as the *upper* and the *lower* house. Each had a ten pot furnace.‡

First Products

The first products of the factory were tumblers, cruet stoppers, moulded hats, toy decanters, twisted cruets, common salts, pint pocket bottles, ½-pint mold jugs, 5-inch mould patty pans, star and ball stoppers.§

The first piece produced at the factory was blown July 4, 1825, by Charles W. Lapham.¶ Chamber and "high blown stem lamps," "lamps on foot," and "peg lamps" were first made on July 30, 1825. "Six-inch round dishes, heavy plain ink, 5-inch molded patty pans, button stem short lamps, common pungeons,‖ flint champaigns, molded salts for cutting, molded mustards, Liverpool lamp glasses, small and large rose foot lamps, oval moulded, 9-inch dishes, fount inks, tulip lamp glasses, cylinder lamp glasses, flint

---

Reminiscences of Glass Making, as before.
†Hugh Brady, born 1830.
‡William E. Kern.
§Account book.
¶William E. Kern.
‖This word is found spelt in many different ways: pungeonts, pungeens, pungrants, etc. May it not be a corruption of the word *puncheon*—slang for a bowl? Bowls would undoubtedly have been among the first products of the factory, but there are few entries of them, while *pungeons* are numerous.

licqueurs, cologne bottles, centers dishes, 38-pound bowls, 21½-pound bowls and bird boxes" are among the entries of the first three months in the account book.

Invention of Pressed Glass

It has been said that the modern method of pressing glass was invented at the Sandwich works. Joseph D. Weeks, writing in 1880* says:

The invention of the American press (for glass) is ascribed to a Massachusetts carpenter in the town of Sandwich about 1827 who, wanting an article of glassware made for some purpose, went to Mr. Deming Jarves and asked him if he could make the article desired. Mr. Jarves told him it would be impossible to make such an article. The carpenter asked if a machine could not be made to press glass into any shape. The idea was scouted at first, but, on second thought, Mr. Jarves and the carpenter fashioned a rude press and made the experiment. This machine was intended to make tumblers, and when the hot molten glass was poured into the mold which was to determine whether glass could be pressed, the experiment was witnessed by many glassmakers of that time. They were nearly all of the opinion that the experiment would come to naught and were greatly amazed when the result demonstrated that it was possible to press glass. The first tumbler that was manufactured in the rough, improvised press remained in Mr. Jarves' possession for many years and then passed into the hands of John A. Dobson, a well-known glass dealer of Baltimore and was exhibited at the Centennial Exhibition by Hobbs, Brockumier & Co., where it was accidentally broken by Mr. John H. Hobbs.†

Mrs. Williams, in *Sandwich Glass*‡ states that the pressing mould for glass was invented in 1827 at the New England Glass Company. In all of this the evidence is purely of the hearsay variety. But the oldest surviving worker§

Report on the Manufacture of Glass, by Joseph D. Weeks, in Department of Interior, *Report on Manufactures in United States in tenth census.*
†In the Philadelphia U. S. International Exhibition, 1876, *Official Catalogue*, J. H. Hobbs, Brockumier & Co. are listed from Wheeling, West Virginia, as exhibiting "soda lime glassware."
‡*Sandwich Glass*, by Leonore Wheeler Williams, N. Y., 1922.
§William E. Kern.

Fig. 9 — SANDWICH LAMPS (*late period*)
The extensive use of petroleum for illuminating purposes is a phenomenon of the last quarter of the nineteenth century. The illustrations here are from the leaf advertisements issued by the Boston and Sandwich Glass Company. They probably belong to the decade 1875–1885. *Reproduced from sheets owned by H. S. Dowden.*

of the Sandwich plant gives credit for the pressing mould to the New England Glass Company. The date appears to have been earlier than 1827, however, since the process seems to have been known to Jarves previous to his establishing of the Sandwich factory.

Hiram Dillaway, an Englishman, was long the head mould maker at the Sandwich factory, and designed most of its patterns.* Without doubt, he and Jarves improved the process of pressing glass, which Jarves had perhaps known at the New England Glass Company.† If such is the case, the story told by Weeks may be the correct one, with merely the change of location to Cambridge, and the date to before 1825. That Jarves was constantly interested in improving the process of pressing glass is without question. On May 28, 1830, for example, he took out a patent for an improvement in glassmakers moulds:‡—

The improvement claimed is the forming of a handle or handles or other similar projections on glass cups, by pressure at one operation, instead of attaching them to the cup after it has been blown, in the way heretofore practised.

The mould is to be made in the unusual manner of brass or other suitable metal, excavations being provided for the formation of the handles. The plug or piston which is to form the inside of the cup is made to fit exactly into a rim which forms the top of the mould, so that when it is pressed down none of the fluid glass which has been put into the mould can escape at top, but will by the pressure be forced into the cavities described. The claim is to the forming of the mould in the manner above indicated.§

---

*Frank Ellis.

†On December 1, 1828, from Boston, Jarves obtained a patent for a method of "pressing melted glass into moulds." Moore, *Old Glass, European and American*, New York, 1924, p. 339.

‡*Repertory of Patent Inventories*, London, 1831, Vol. XI, p. 239, American Patents.

§Deming Jarves had taken out patents for a machine for opening glass blowers' moulds, February, 1821. In June, 1829, and October, 1830, he took out patents for "glass knobs." Moore, *Old Glass European and American*, p. 339.

The moulds employed for pressing glass were for the most part made of brass. For large articles the presses worked with a screw instead of a lever. The designs were cut on the plunger and pressed upside down and the article, while very hot, turned into a receiver of the same shape as the mould.*

Early Cut Glass

That glass was made for cutting in 1825 is indicated by several entries in the account book, but no statement occurs as to whether the cutting was done at Sandwich or elsewhere.

Octagon dishes, sugar bowls, decanters, cruets, 10-inch oval dishes, 7, 8 and 9-inch octagon dishes, ship tumblers, etc., were common articles of manufacture, besides the ones already mentioned. Some of these were doubtless cut.

First Record of Familiar Items

On September 23, 1826, occurs the record† of "310 Dolphin tall pungeants $18.10." On November 4, 1826, are first listed "34 Lafayette Chamber Cylinder Lamps $5.66" and "56 Lafayette lamps $14." Petticoat lamps are noted as first having been made on December 23, 1826: "211 petticoat lamps $25.22." The first entry of cup-plates is on April 20, 1827, and is as follows:

132 No. 1 cup plates	$7.92
305 No. 2 cup plates	15.25
77 No. 3 cup plates	2.98

There is no explanation as to what the difference in the numbering of the cup-plates means. It will be observed that they are listed at six, five and four cents each, but whether these figures represent cost of manufacture or

---

*William E. Kern.

†Account Book.

selling price is not clear. It would seem to be the selling price.

On March 9, 1827, are listed "7 Lafayette Salts $1.16", I should imagine that these are the same as the salt reproduced some time since in ANTIQUES.* It is interesting to note that one salt was worth 16½ cents.

Various Forms and Colors

What is known as *lace* glass must have been turned out quite early in the history of the factory, for it was presumably not made after 1840.† *Colored* glass was first made in the thirties, but its great improvement and extension of manufacture did not occur until after the Civil War.‡ *Snakeskin* glass is supposed to have been made about 1860;§ *hobnail* somewhere in the ten years following the Civil War; *cable* glass at the time of laying the French cable (*1867*); *opaque* after the Civil War.

Fig. 10 — WOOD PATTERNS FROM SANDWICH
Metal moulds used for glass pressing were cast from wooden patterns. The pattern at the left is evidently that of a lamp base. The one at the right is unidentified. *Owned by Frank Lloyd.*

The *diamond* pattern was first cut by "Gaffer"* Cook, who is said to have designed the pattern.† What is known as the *Grant* pattern, i.e., a pattern in which the diamonds are quite fine, was made at the time of Grant's candidacy for president (*1868*). *Alabaster* glass is the bluish white glass, similar in aspect to china ware, which is so often found used in lamp bases.‡

Opal glass, it is said, was first introduced in America by the Boston and Sandwich Glass Company, which sent to England for a man, Rice Harris, who came to this country for six months and taught the process of making it. He received for his services $5000 and expenses.§

Factory Methods

Beginning in 1843 and continuing until 1867, the workmen in the factory were divided into four shifts, or "turns." The first turn was from one A. M. until six. The second turn was from seven until noon; the third from noon until

*ANTIQUES for April, 1922 (Vol. I, p. 152).

†John Chipman, who was told by an old glassworker, now dead. Rather long-range evidence, to be sure.

‡John Jones, and receipt book, dated 1868, in possession of Frank Lloyd.

§This and the other dates were given to Mr. Chipman by the old glassworker, who identified the pieces for him.

*"Gaffer" means the head man of a shop.

†Ella Silsby, corroborated by others.

‡Hugh Brady.

§William E. Kern

Fig. 11 — SANDWICH LAMPS
The influence of mid-century Bohemian types of glass is apparent in these lamps. They probably date from 1870–1885. *Reproduced from sheets owned by H. S. Dowden.*

six P. M. The same men who had served on the first turn came in for the third. The last turn was from six until mid night, with the second turn men on.

This meant that the factory worked night and day and thus required only four working days a week, leaving a holiday for the men from Friday morning at six until the following Monday.

The boys worked tending the glory holes and getting in wood. Every Fourth of July these boys were presented with fifty cents each to spend on fireworks. They were like-wise allowed to gather and work the glass in their spare time, and were encouraged to learn the glassmakers' trade.*

Treatment of Employees

The Company, as was perhaps natural in a small town, looked after its workers in every way. The employees began to work while mere lads, and continued in service until they were old men. If they were unable to make good in one job, another would be found for them. At Christmas time the Company made presents of flour, coal, etc., to the widows of men who had been in their employ.

The Company likewise built workmen's houses and established near the factory a small village, which is still standing.† The houses could be bought on the instalment plan.

Many are the stories told of the kindness of the Com-pany to its employees, and of "Lafe's" personal kindness to individuals. As one old man said, "It was the best place any man ever worked. 'Want for nothing' was Lafe's common saying."‡ Sewall H. Fessenden, the Boston agent, whose offices were at 26 Federal Street for many years, was the hero of all the small boys of Sandwich. He used to visit the works once a month, and the tale goes that on each occasion he wore a new suit of clothes!§

When the Railroad Came

After the railroad came to Sandwich, in 1848, much of the factory's supplies and products was transported by rail. Several years after it had reached Sandwich, however, the Old Colony Railroad raised its rates, to the disgust of the Boston and Sandwich Glass Company. Accordingly, in 1853, the steamer *Acorn* was built. It was at this time that the channel was probably dredged to admit of her entrance.

For several years this vessel carried all supplies, and was also used as an excursion boat, the trip to Boston and back costing one dollar.¶ The railroad soon came to terms with the Company, which then built a wharf at Cohasset Narrows, now Buzzards Bay, where coal, brought up the bay, was landed and was transported nine miles by rail to Sandwich, thus saving the long and hazardous trip around Cape Cod.‖

Shifts and Changes

Much glass was exported to South America, Rio de Janeiro being a port often appearing on the books of the Company.* February 18, 1853, the capital stock of the Company was increased $200,000, making a total of $500,000.† February 26, 1859, this was reduced to $400,-000, par value of shares $80.‡

The Cape Cod Glass Company

In 1858 Deming Jarves resigned from the Boston and Sandwich Glass Company, and, together with James D. Lloyd,§ built the Cape Cod Glass Company works at Sandwich, about half a mile from the old factory. Mr. Jarves built this plant for his son, John, who, however, died a few years later. The works were opened with much ceremony, every person in the town of Sandwich receiving an engraved invitation to a clambake and an inspection of the new factory.

The Cape Cod Glass Company commanded all the modern improvements then known to glass manufactur-ing,¶ and paid ninepence more a day to its workers than did its rival. William E. Kern became superintendent, earning $35 a week as superintendent, and $12 a day as workman.‖

Jarves imported men from England to teach special methods. Among others were Nehemiah Packwood and John Jones from the Stourbridge district in Worcestershire, where there were many glass factories. Packwood worked for the Cape Cod Glass Company for about six months, and then went over to the Boston and Sandwich concern. He was a designer of cut glass, and under his direction the first chandeliers made at the Boston and Sandwich works were cut.**

Troubled Days at Sandwich

During the Civil War John Jarves died, and many of the Sandwich men went to fight. Deming Jarves, too, was growing old. The Cape Cod Glass Company never suc-ceeded in becoming a successful competitor of the Boston and Sandwich Company.

Deming Jarves died in Boston April 15, 1869, aged 78, after a long illness.†† The Cape Cod Glass Company was disposed of by the Jarves family and remained unused for a period of years, until taken over by one Dr. Flower, who experimented with a glass which he called "vassa mur-rhina." It was, however, never commercially successful.

In 1882 the factory was bought by Charles W. Spurr and was used for a veneering plant. This venture was short lived. The factory has since slowly fallen to pieces. Only the stack and part of the building now remain standing. The workmen scattered, some to New Bedford, some to Philadelphia, and some to Brooklyn. Not a few went west, where glass factories were everywhere springing up.

---

*Charles F. Dalton, who remembers, as a child, looking at the names in the record books, and hunting them up on the map in his geography book.
†Acts of 1853, Chapter 12, Commonwealth of Massachusetts.
‡Acts of 1859, Chapter 65.
§Frank Lloyd, son of James D. Lloyd.
¶See account of Delano patent feeder, a new invention, used in the Cape Cod Glass Company, in Jarves' *Reminiscences of Glass Making* appendix.
‖William E. Kern and Thomas Montagu.
**John Jones.
††Mr. Kern says that, on the night of April 15, he had, after seeing that the fires were all right, just left the Cape Cod works when some boys called after him, "Up he goes" referring to the smoke from the fire. It was not until the next day that he learned that Jarves had died. The fires that Mr. Kern stoked that night were never relighted.

---

*William E. Kern.
†This village was contemptuously referred to by the old inhabitants of Sand-wich as "below the tracks," and one's social standing was gauged by whether one lived "above or below the tracks."
‡Hugh Brady.
§Charles F. Dalton.
¶Charles F. Dalton.
‖The Cape Cod Canal has since been cut through—its northern entrance is about a mile from the old factory.

Last Years of the Boston and Sandwich

The later years of the Boston and Sandwich Glass Company may be quickly summarized. In 1870 the Company had offices at 26 Federal Street, Boston, 20 Murray Street, New York, 419 Commerce Street, Philadelphia, 246 West Baltimore Street, Baltimore. They did little advertising and had few travelling salesmen. The factory was run continuously—good times or bad—and the stock, as made, was stored in the old railroad round-house until wanted.

The factory was one of the best known glass houses in the country and its better products were much in demand. Most of its later work was in cut and etched glass, although it still continued to make cheaper pressed glass, together with lamps with metal bases, which last were imported from England.

In the Philadelphia 1876 Exhibition the Company exhibited "Cut crystal chandeliers, rich cut glassware of every description, including the 'Daniel Webster Punch Bowl.'"*

In 1882, George Lafayette Fessenden was succeeded by Henry V. Spurr, who had long been head salesman in the Boston warehouse, and who had originally entered the Company's employ in 1849. The agent still continued to be Sewall H. Fessenden.

Competition from the West

Competition in the glass industry became much keener after the Civil War, the western factories having the advantage over those in the east owing to their use of natural gas for fuel, and to their proximity to coal, sand, etc. The profits of the Boston and Sandwich Glass Company began to dwindle. For several years the works were run with no profit whatever. In 1887, however, a crisis occurred. The men had formed a union, at the instigation of a western "agitator." They presented demands for many new rules. The Company explained that it could not continue its business if these were put into force, and called attention to the good it had done and was doing for the inhabitants of Sandwich. Eventually it issued an ultimatum to the effect that, "If the fires are allowed to go out they will never be re-lighted."

The Finish

The men, unable to believe that the Company meant what it said, struck. The furnaces were allowed to die. On January 2, 1888, the works were closed, never to reopen. The Company's charter was dissolved March 6, 1894, after the books had been destroyed. Cases of glass were dumped in heaps outside the factory, and many of the cheaper kinds of glass were sold to a chain of five-and-ten-cent stores. Then the population of Sandwich began to shrink. In 1857 it numbered 4800; today there are scarcely 1500.

It is said that, during the height of its prosperity, the Company cleared as much as fifty per cent a year for several years; and that, during the sixty-three years of its existence, it produced about $30,000,000 worth of glass.

After the closing in 1888, many attempts were made to start the old works again, but none were successful. Among

others came Cardenio King, who bought the factory and remelted the *cullet*, or imperfect glass, producing a brown and unattractive output. This, too, proved a failure. Since then the factory buildings have fallen to pieces. What remained was torn down in 1920, except for one building used as a fish freezing plant, and a new building erected for a bark factory.

The ruins have been pretty well searched over for pieces of glass, some of which have been mounted into jewelry by a Sandwich woman.* The town has no industry now, and the younger people are gone, leaving a sleepy Cape Cod village with but memories of the industrial city that might have been.

_____

LIST OF PERSONS INTERVIEWED

In *Sandwich*, Massachusetts.
  John Jones, old glassworker.
  Thomas Montagu, old glassworker.
  Hugh Brady, old glassworker.
  Frank Lloyd, son of James D. Lloyd, glassworker in Boston and Sandwich and Cape Cod Companies.
  Frank Ellis.
  William Nye, president Sandwich Historical Society.
  John Chipman.
  Frank Howland, town clerk of Sandwich.
  Fletcher Clark, old inhabitant of Sandwich.
  Mrs. Bertrand C. French, maker of jewelry from glass.
  Miss Eliza Wing, daughter of Paul Wing, Sandwich school teacher.
  Miss Caroline Nye, whose father worked in factory.
  Mrs. Ambrose Pratt, family inhabitants of Sandwich since founding.
  Mrs. Benjamin Webber, East Sandwich.
In *Sagamore*, Massachusetts.
  Miss Ella Silsby, much interested in Sandwich glass history.
In *New Bedford*, Massachusetts.
  William E. Kern, former superintendent of Cape Cod Glass Company.
In *Boston*, Massachusetts.
  Russell Spurr, son of Henry V. Spurr, manager for Boston and Sandwich Company.
  Charles F. Dalton, old glassworker.
  Mrs. Robert T. Swan, whose father, Joshua Crane (my great-grandfather) was, according to tradition, president or one of the main directors of the Boston and Sandwich Company between the years 1839–1846.

BIBLIOGRAPHY OF BOOKS ON SANDWICH, OR RELATING TO GLASS, CONSULTED

Encyclopedia Americana, New York, 1910, under "Glass Manufactures in America."
Reminiscences of Glass Making, Deming Jarves, Boston, 1865.
Account Book of Boston and Sandwich Glass Company, owned by William E. Kern.
Report on the Manufacturer of Glass, Joseph D. Weeks, in Department of Interior, Report on Manufactures in United States in tenth census.
Official Catalogue, Philadelphia U. S. International Exhibition, 1876.
Sandwich Glass, Leonore Wheeler Williams, New York, 1922.
Repertory of Patent Inventories, London, 1831, Vol. XI., p. 239, American Patents.
American Glassware, Edwin A. Barber, Philadelphia, 1900.
Curiosities of Glass Making, Apsley Pellatt, London, 1849.
Private and Special Statutes of the Commonwealth of Massachusetts, Acts of 1825, 1853, 1859, 1894, 1895, 1904, 1907, and *Files* at office of Commissioner of Corporations, State House, Boston.
Reminiscences of the Boston and Sandwich Glass Company, William E. Kern, paper read before American Association of Flint and Lime Glass Manufacturers, July 20, 1906.
Yarmouth Register, August 18, 1906.
Boston Herald, March 23, 1907.
Boston Evening Transcript, September 4, 1920.
ANTIQUES, Vol. I, p. 58; Vol. I, p. 61; Vol. I, p. 152.
Old Glass, European and American, N. Hudson Moore, New York, 1924.

*Mrs. Bertrand C. French.

*In *Official Catalogue* 1876 Exhibition as before. The punch bowl seems to have disappeared, several of the older workers remember that three or four big bowls were sent to the Exhibition, but no one had heard of the Daniel Webster bowl.

Deming Jarves and His Glass-Factory Village

By Mabel M. Swan

NO ONE had ever heard of a glass-factory village when as a boy Deming Jarves went to Sandwich, Massachusetts. Nor, imaginative though he was, did the lad dream of the many brick buildings and the rows of little gray houses which he was later to build on the meadows bordering the creek. The *Dictionary of American Biography* today characterizes Jarves as "chemist, inventor, organizer." True enough; but to me the word "gentleman," as he was called in his father's will of 1823, is his most appropriate designation. He stemmed from the Gervaise family, French Huguenots, who, finding refuge in England, accepted the name of Jarves and became prominent not only because of their wealth but for their staunch Whig principles.

Urged by his republican views, John Jackson Jarves, Deming's father, came to America in 1787, established himself in business as a cabinetmaker in Boston, and advertised:

Jarves
Cabinet, Chair, & Clock Case Maker from London
No 76 Newbury Street, Boston
Respectfully informs Gentlemen and Ladies that he makes the following Mahogany Furniture on reasonable Terms, viz: Library Book Cases, Desks & Book Cases, Chests & Book Cases, Double Chest of Drawers with Desk Drawers, single Chest of Drawers, Desks, Gentlemen's Portable Writing Desks, Counting House Desks, Ladies Commode Dressing Tables with furniture Drawers, Library Tables, Dining Tables in sets, round & square Card Tables, Pembrook, Claw, China, Chamber, Toilet & Night Tables, convenient Stools, China Shelves & Brackets, Balance, Pole, Face, and Hand Fire Screens, Side Boards, Cellerets, Butler's Treys, Knife Treys, Oval Tea Treys, Tea Chests & Cadys, Sconce & Swing Glass Frames, Ladies Urn Stands, Gentlemen's Wardrobes, Sophas, Easy Chairs, carved & plain, Chairs, Four post, Field Bureau & Common Bedsteds, Weight & Spring Clock Cases, Watch Cases, & all kinds of Picture Frames (*Massachusetts Historical Society clipping.*)

This extensive cabinetmaking business, occupying several buildings on Newbury Street and later at 6 Beach Street, was very successful if one may judge from the will of "John Jarves, gentleman decea'd," administered in September 1823. The late cabinetmaker left $25,000, in addition to six buildings, to his widow and two children, Deming and Sally Jarves Hastings, the bulk of the estate going to Deming. The family's comfortable circumstances are further indicated by the inventory item, "Pleasure Boat & Sails $50."

Deming Jarves' mother was Mrs. Hannah Deming, widowed daughter of the celebrated Samuel Seabury (*1729-1796*), who, when the politically prejudiced Church of England refused to consecrate bishops for America in 1783, moved to Scotland, there received the coveted recognition, and became the first American Episcopal bishop.

Jarves was born abroad, where his parents were traveling, and was baptized in the New South Church, Boston, December 9, 1790. He is first listed in the Boston directory of 1813 as in "dry goods 11 Cornhill." In 1815 and 1816 he is listed as a member of the firm of Henshaw & Jarves, dealers in crockery ware; and, in 1818, as a glass factor on Belknap Street. In 1815 he was married to Anna Smith Stutson (often spelled Stetson), a daughter of Captain Levi Stutson, Revolutionary soldier. Nine children were born to the couple: John W., George, Deming, Jr., James Jackson, Anna Maria, Isabella, Mary, and two sons who died in infancy.

Fig. 1 — "Alabaster" Vase, Credited to James D. Lloyd

In November 1817, the Boston Porcelain & Glass Company in East Cambridge, of which Jarves was the clerk, disposed of its property at public auction. This event projected Jarves into the first of his five glass organizations. With several associates, soon to be incorporated as the New England Glass Company, he purchased the Boston Company's works.

From the first it appears to have been his policy to keep his business ventures largely in the family's hands. His father's will records a note to the New England Glass Company for $1,900. Daniel Hastings, Boston merchant and importer and one of the directors, was the nephew of Deming Jarves' sister. Edmund Munroe, also a director, was a wealthy relative of Jarves' wife. The first superintendent of the Boston & Sandwich Glass Company was Deming's brother-in-law, William Stutson. The Southacks also were relatives on his wife's side. A strong family loyalty governed the Jarves family, all of whose members seem to have been at one in their admiration for the young glass organizer.

Well they might be proud of his ability: for his initial attempt to discover a formula for making red lead, the secret of which had long been held by English glass manufacturers, was successful. Thereafter his new company was able to supply native glasshouses with this essential ingredient. Such creative genius as his could not long be content with merely turning out apothecary and chemical wares, electrical apparatus, entry lamps, globes, decanters, and similar merchandise such as the company advertised. In 1821 he obtained his first patent, covering a machine for opening glassblowers' molds. The following year he took out a patent for an improvement in the tubes for glass lamps.

Encouraged by his success, and rendered financially independent by the death of his father in 1823, Deming Jarves the next year made an extended visit to Pittsburgh. Here he saw many superior methods of glassmaking in operation, for the Bakewell & Page flint glassworks of Pittsburgh was one of the most advanced in the country. Many years later Jarves in his *Reminiscences of Glassmaking* wrote of Mr. Bakewell: "He truly merits the *artium magister* so often bestowed on those less worthy of its dignity and honor."

On his return to Boston, he severed his connection with the New England Glass Company and undertook the organization of a new concern. The move was in no wise due to any misunderstandings with his directors, but, almost certainly, to Jarves' desire to experiment independently and without the restrictions imposed by the normal schedules of a large factory.

Though living in Boston, Deming knew Sandwich. There game abounded, and he knew well the extent of the pine forests. He also realized that so remote a spot would offer no urban lure to his workmen, that transportation by water was at hand, and that in the quiet little town he might in many ways reduce sundry manufacturing costs. So he called a meeting of the Sandwich citizens and told them, among other things, that workers in the Pittsburgh factories were making from $2 to $2.50 a day in an employment neither arduous nor dangerous, and that if sufficient interest was manifest he would build a glassworks in the town. (His wage estimate seems to have been optimistic.)

Ground was broken in April 1825, and the

first building erected with a small furnace of eight pots. On July 4 the first piece of glass was blown. The new enterprise was called the Sandwich Manufacturing Company until April 3, 1826, when the capital stock was increased and the concern incorporated as the Boston & Sandwich Glass Company by Deming Jarves, Henry Rice, Andrew T. Hall, and Edmund Munroe.

One week before this reorganization, Deming Jarves and Edmund Munroe established the New England Glass Bottle Company "for the purpose of manufacturing black and green glass wares in the city of Boston and the town of Cambridge." This, the second of Jarves' five glass companies, continued in operation until 1842.

For his first superintendent at Sandwich, Jarves chose his brother-in-law, William Stutson, a young man as forceful and vigorous as Jarves himself. At the age of nineteen Stutson had been in full command of a ship, and during the War of 1812 commanded a privateer, which was captured by the British, who landed the young captain in Dartmoor to remain until the end of the war.

Charles C. P. Waterman, the first clerk and paymaster, was born in Wareham, Massachusetts, and remained in the Boston & Sandwich Company until 1858, when Jarves left to organize the Cape Cod Factory. Waterman went with his employer and remained with him until his chief's death in 1869.

Some of the glassmakers of the New England Glass Company followed Jarves to Sandwich. Others were obtained from South Boston; many others were imported from England. Later Ireland, Belgium, and France contributed to the working force. Wherever he could find the most skilled workmen, Jarves gathered them in, exhibiting a distinct flair for picking good material.

Among the first expert glassblowers whom he obtained from England were Benjamin and Edward Haines, who came from Dudley, England, in 1825. Other English workers of the same period were James McDonald, William Teasdale, Alfred Greene, and George W. Scobie. Subsequently Jarves laid out lots and built houses for his employees in what became known, far and wide, as Glass Factory Village. Some interesting documents in the Sandwich Town Hall record mortgages granted by Jarves, and even by some of the glassblowers, who appear to have had plenty of ready money. The borrowers were mechanics and other laborers, who, giving their furniture as security, paid one dollar a week in liquidation of their debts. During the hard times of 1840 the Company charged no rent to its tenant workmen and at all times recognized the value of good wages and consideration for all classes of help.

One of Jarves' most valuable aids was Hiram Dillaway (1813–1887), a master mechanic to whose skill much of the success attending the manufacture of pressed glass was due. Dillaway drew designs, made patterns, and was the chief moldmaker even after Jarves left the Boston & Sandwich Company in 1858. Dillaway came to Sandwich early in 1828 after serving a year's apprenticeship with E. M. Bartholomew, moldmaker in South Boston. His notebook, now in the possession of his grandson Charles Lloyd of Sandwich, records the receipt of $50 in payment for the first year under Bartholomew. He abandoned the glowing prospect of a second year at $55 to join forces with Deming Jarves. Dillaways seem to have been plentiful in South Boston. Enoch Dillaway, and later, Enoch Junior, were both moldmakers in South Boston. In 1853 Enoch is listed as a moldmaker at 51 Federal Street, sales headquarters for the Sandwich Company.

Deming Jarves organized the Boston & Sandwich Glass Company at a time when experimentation by glass manufacturers throughout the country was in progress. The Bakewells of Pittsburgh, Henry Whitney and Enoch Robinson of Cambridge, John Robinson of Pittsburgh, the Dummers of Jersey City, all crowded forward with patents for improvements in glassmaking. In 1828 Jarves himself was granted his third patent: for an improvement in the mode of pressing melted glass into molds. This was presently followed by two others, and, in later years, by many more. As his son James Jackson said, Deming both made and lost fortunes in his many experiments. Hiram Dillaway's inventions brought this maker ten patents and a sufficient sum in royalties to permit the accumulation of $200,000. He was with the Boston & Sandwich firm until his death in 1887.

Fig. 2 — Cut-Glass Crystal Flashed with Ruby, Credited to James D. Lloyd

Another standby of Deming Jarves was James D. Lloyd (1836–1920), son-in-law of Hiram Dillaway. His father, Thomas, and his uncle, Samuel Lloyd, came to Sandwich from Birmingham, England, where they had been expert glassmakers. James began work in the Sandwich factory as a busboy at the age of eight. He later became the color expert for the Company as well as of the Cape Cod, Mount Washington, and New Bedford Companies. His notebook, now in possession of his son Charles Lloyd, contains such receipts as *Best flint Wm. Kern's recipe; Common flint James D. Lloyd; Flint G. L. F [George L. Fessenden]; Badger's recipe for wine metal; French recipes March 15, 1874; French green for cutting; Best white enamel Hummaberg's; Pluk Glyn recipe for Chinese Glass.*

These and other recorded formulas give not only quantities of the ingredients but explicit directions for making ruby, flint for etching, flint for cutting, flint for coating with ruby, green for hocks, "very good alabaster," best blue, Victoria blue, blue for casing, best white enamel, bottle glass, crown glass, alabaster as used by the old Company, opal in all its various colors — pearl gray, lilac, rose, turquoise, alabaster blue, iris, pale green, lemon, dove, "Imporatria," purple, and many others.

Lloyd developed alabaster, and during his experiments Jarves sent him to England to obtain information and recipes. While there he went on to Ireland and brought home some very lovely pieces of Belleek from the Belleek china factory, which he thought appropriate for model . Lloyd's notebook records certain sources of materials, thus:

Fluorspar you can buy in New York as well as in England. If you get it from England the best house is Hall & Co., Marble Works, Derby. Their price is .75 for 112 pounds but what is bought in France is as good. In Europe the best man for felspar is Monsieur Jouket, Beauvoir, par Lalizolle, Allier, France.

Uranium you can get the best from Poulenc Wittman, rue Neuve, St Mary, Paris. Price $5. It is better than the English. Sulphate of copper get anywhere in Boston. Pick out pieces which have no yellow stains in them.

Jarves evidently insisted upon obtaining the best of everything, whether glassmakers, ingredients, color recipes, or patterns. Never quite satisfied, he experimented with sand from New Jersey, Plymouth beach, Sandwich, Berkshire, Massachusetts, and even obtained supplies from France and South America.

When in 1858 he left the Boston & Sandwich Company and organized the Cape Cod Factory, less than half a mile from the old works, he hoped to interest his son John W. Jarves in the glass industry. Lloyd went with him. John, however, died in 1863, and thereafter his father showed little interest in a business which, for forty-five years, had completely absorbed his time and thought. Jarves was doomed to disappointment in his efforts to launch his sons as glassmakers. Much earlier he had organized the Mount Washington Glass Works in South Boston in behalf of his son George, then in his twenties. But George was not interested in glass, and the new company was conducted for two years by Captain Luther Russell. It then reverted to George, who for a short time had a Mr. Labree as partner. The 1846 Boston directory lists the concern as Labree & Jarves, brass lamps and chandeliers, 71 Summer Street — which was the home address of Deming Jarves. In 1850 Labree was succeeded by Henry Cormerais of Dedham. Operating under the name of Jarves & Cormerais, the new partnership enlarged its business by adding furnaces. Later purchased by W. L. Libbey, in 1869 the enterprise was transferred to New Bedford.

Deming Jarves, Jr., though inheriting his father's versatility and business ability, showed no inclination to pursue glassmaking. At the age of eighteen his chief ambition, that of becoming a professional sailor, was diverted by the wisdom of his father, who gave him a trip around the world, starting him out as the only passenger in one of McKay's clipper ships. After rounding the Cape of Good Hope in the dead of winter, encountering a typhoon in the China Sea, arriving in Calcutta at the height of the Indian Mutiny, he returned to Boston on the *Niagara*, a Cunard paddle-wheel steamer. His ambition for a life at sea had quite evaporated.

For a short time he served as clerk in his father's glass headquarters at 51 Federal Street, Boston, but at the beginning of the Civil War he enlisted, and served throughout the war. From 1866 he sold Sandwich glass and the products of other glass factories in New York, until he was ready to start in business for himself. Organizing a boneblack factory in Michigan, he made a fortune manufacturing commercial fertilizer as a by-product. In 1880 he bought an old farm on the River Rouge, increased the capital of his company, and built three different factories, one for producing boneblack, one for fertilizer, and the third — strange to relate — for making glass. Following his retirement from active affairs, he spent his remaining years in France, where his estate, *Val Fleuri*, at Dinard was filled with choice antiques. In October 1919 he was decorated by the French government with the order of Chevalier of the Legion of Honor for war work.

James Jackson Jarves, another son well known for his interest in art, was permitted to travel abroad when illness and impaired eyesight compelled him to abandon his intention of entering Harvard. From California, Mexico, Central and South America, James went to

Fig. 3 — DEMING JARVES
From a photograph taken about 1863

Paris and later to Florence, where he lived for thirty years, numbering among his friends the Brownings, George Eliot, Trollope, Ruskin, Rossetti, and Hawthorne. In 1866, King Humbert of Italy created him a Chevalier of the Order of the Crown of Italy. In 1880 he was appointed vice consul at Florence, resigning in 1882. (*The Forgotten Man*, by Theodore Sizer, in the *New England Quarterly*, 1933.) His daughter, Miss Flora Jarves of Kingston, Rhode Island, wrote of her father:

It is hardly necessary, I suppose, to correct the statement that my father ruined himself with his collection [now in the Yale Gallery of Fine Arts]. Most certainly he did, but back of him was my grandfather [Deming Jarves] and some credit is due him and something more than has lately been given him of Sandwich glass fame. It is useless to describe this silly fad for Sandwich glass which is trash. The real Sandwich glass is seldom seen and very rare. I have the real pieces and the bad ones. My father tried to bring the art of Venice into the works because of the fine sand there, but there was not enough of it nor could they make it fine enough — so when they gave up the Sandwich glass proper they began this pressed stuff, much to the disgust of my father, but when it sold for twice as much as the real, "cui bono?"

Although Sandwich is over sixty miles from Boston and there was no railroad in the early days of the glass manufacture, Deming Jarves kept his residence in Boston, living first at 47 Hancock Street, then at 71 Summer, and finally at 64 Boylston Street. He spent his summers at the old Stutson place in Swampscott. The Jarves house, still standing in Sandwich and often thought to have been the home of Deming, was built for the son John when the Cape Cod factory was started and Deming was still hopeful of interesting the young man in glassmaking. An interesting note of the family's visit to Sandwich is recorded in the log book of the sloop *Henry Clay* in the Sandwich Historical Society:

"Capt. Gibbs — From Boston to Sandwich July 17, 1830: Deming Jarves & family — state room — Fare $8.75;

[and on July 23, 1830]

Capt. Stetson & wife — 2 passages — $2.50"

The expansion of Glass Factory Village or Jarves Village, as the section of the town adjoining the factory buildings was called, was in no sense a mushroom growth, but reflected the careful planning of Deming Jarves. The tall elms which he planted in the little park in front of the factory are still standing. The typical Cape Cod houses which he built for his workmen are still in good condition although gray and weatherbeaten. The company store, a large brick building, now provides quarters for several families. The bakehouse, bakery, and shoe shop formerly provided for the glassworkers are gone. On a recent visit to the old factory I found children on a platform of one of the factory buildings. They were selling fragments of Sandwich glass which they had dug

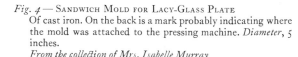

Fig. 4 — SANDWICH MOLD FOR LACY-GLASS PLATE
Of cast iron. On the back is a mark probably indicating where the mold was attached to the pressing machine. *Diameter*, 5 inches.
From the collection of Mrs. Isabelle Murray

Fig. 5 — CAMEO-GLASS CIGAR HOLDER (c. 1880)
Broken white pattern on blue ground. Produced during the régime of James D. Lloyd.
From the collection of Mrs. Charles Lloyd

up from old cullet heaps — broken curtain pulls, bits of broken lamps, inkwells, and salt cellars.

Deming Jarves' tax bill for 1829 from the town of Sandwich recorded "½ homestead (Davis estate) ½ house valued at $1500, lot of land and shop $200, 2 tenements & lot $800, block & tenements $600, carpenter & wheelwright's shop $300, 177 acres of land $1200." By 1858 some of the additional items were: "Store, bake house, bake shop, shoe shop, hammer & pattern shop, planing, saw, and grist mills, Spring Hill stave mill, building and water privileges at Upper Mill, North Sandwich, ice house" — all assessed at

$26,405. In the following year he had built the new Cape Cod glass factory, pot house, machine and blacksmith shop, which were appraised at $15,000.

In 1860 he had added still more: "the Herring River Iron Works upper and lower, $6500, lumber yard and planing mill $3000, stone mill at Spring Hill $1500, pine grove at Cohasset, cutting shop for the new Cape Cod Factory, a cooper shop and new storehouse" — all valued at $40,000.

He made it possible for a glassworker to furnish his home by paying one dollar a week, giving the furniture as security. On moving to another locality the man was little burdened with worldly goods.

It will be remembered that, following labor troubles in 1887, which really started with the advent of the Glass Union in Sandwich in 1879, the old Boston & Sandwich Company closed its plant. At the time Jarves' former lieutenant, Lloyd, was approached by Nathaniel J. Bradlee, president of the Company. In the event of the reopening of the Sandwich works would Lloyd assume the position of manager? Lloyd's answer, here in part quoted, is interesting. Under the date of September 1888 he wrote to Bradlee:

It is very desirable to have a smart energetic man there with much ability for designing and that will insist upon good work from the men. Mr. E. J. Donovan has applied for the position. But this matter can be deferred until we know if the factory is to start.

As I view the situation the factory must be brought to a paying basis and I should not advise starting it until all these things are agreed to by the men. Every point where it is probable there might be disagreement should be understood and settled now, and I think it would be proper for you to frame from these suggestions what you expect from the men and wish your manager to carry out. Then I would suggest calling the men together and having it read and agreed to by them. It seems to me Mr. Seaver is just the man to do it.

Now concerning what I want by means of salary I don't think the situation warrants such pay as you have been giving and I am willing to work for $1500 a year if I should accept the position of manager. But as I have said before if you can find another man to occupy this place I will willingly by suggestion wherever needed help all in my power freely. . . .

Nathaniel Bradlee died shortly after this and, as we know, the old factory was never restored to its former status.

Deming Jarves' will, administered April 8, 1869, recognized what he had done for his children by the clause, "Having in mind all I have done for my children." He left a modest fortune, $200,000, to his wife. His lifelong ambition seems to have been to perfect a glass which would be equal to that of Venice. But his efforts in importing the best workmen, seeking the best ingredients wherever they were to be found, sending his men far and near to learn new methods or receipts, seeking suggestions as to forms from his son in Florence — all availed little. Today his reputation rests on the product that he viewed as potboiler stuff — pressed glass. His granddaughter wrote, "The real Sandwich glass is seldom seen and very rare." We may wonder to just what she refers.

Fig. 6 — SANDWICH RUBY TUMBLER (c. 1840)
Given by Deming Jarves to his granddaughter, Flora Jarves, who was extremely fond of horses.
From the Sandwich Library

Fig. 7 (right) — SANDWICH GLASS ORNAMENT
Not improbably a souvenir of the early days of the factory. Evidently an off-hand piece, and of exceptional interest.
From the collection of Mrs. Charles Lloyd

Acknowledgment. In preparing the foregoing article I have been greatly assisted by Mrs. Charles Lloyd, Miss Flora Jarves, Miss Elizabeth Driscoll, and George S. Burbank, of whose kindly aid I am glad to express my very keen sense of appreciation. — M. M. S.

Notes. To the finding of fresh fragments of information on any subject there is apparently no end, however thorough may have been the previous siftings of material. In an early paragraph of this article, I stated that Deming Jarves was born abroad. I may now add, more specifically, that the "blessed event" occurred in London.

To students of glass who enjoy delving, I suggest search for evidence regarding the scope of E. Dillaway's activities. Dillaway was moldmaker for Jarves, with

In compliance with your request . . . I give you in my opinion the best methods of running your factory. . . . The following would be my way of conducting the business if the gains or loss were to be my own. . . . First — In running the Blowers Department I desire a capable man to assist me. . . . I would prefer to have Mr. Kern. Then I wish it distinctly understood by the men that we want work made in the best possible way and that no poor work will be paid for; no orders to be made in the factory not ordered except by permission; and should the factory be run nights those who work on the night run are expected to be in place promptly as day men — to see that the boys also are on hand promptly to do good work.

Then I should like to say I don't think any factory can be made to pay unless run nights — neither can men stand around outside the factory or elsewhere in working hours as they have in the past. . . .

In regard to the Cutting Shop, in other places it is run by the day. Men going in at 7 o'clock in the morning and working till 6 at night with exception of one hour at dinner, and it seems a fair way to me. Here in the past they have worked by the piece. There are advantages both ways, should wish to consult with you and the directors before deciding about that.

headquarters at the Boston office. I suspect that he served several other manufacturers in a similar capacity. If my surmise should prove correct, it would solve not a few problems. In 1879 many factories were producing virtually identical articles, whose output volume was, however, in each instance regulated by the Glass Union. The purpose of the restriction seems to have been that of preventing any one factory from monopolizing the advantages accruing from its own creative ingenuity. An illuminating story might be written concerning the development of this early union and the resultant effect on the glassmaking industry in New England. — M. M. S.

Fig. 1 — TOUCHSTONES FOR DATING
Eagle, *1831*; Queen Victoria, *1837*; Victoria and Albert, *1840*; President Harrison, *1841*

Sandwich Lacy Glass

By HOMER EATON KEYES

THE more one sees of American glass of the nineteenth century, the more his respect increases for the ware generally known among collectors as "lacy Sandwich." Nor is such meed of admiration due solely to the facts that the metal itself is of high excellence, and that its transformation into useful and ornamental forms was accomplished by mechanisms that owed their origin to Yankee ingenuity and commercial alertness. Rather may it be ascribed chiefly to the realization that lacy glass is not, as generally assumed, a slavish imitation of cut glass, but is, on the contrary, a virtually independent substitute for the more expensive ware. Hence, in its way, this product deserves consideration in a class by itself, just as do the early patterned papers that took the place of tapestries and other expensive fabrics as a covering for walls.

The makers of lacy glass were, to be sure, desirous of equaling, or surpassing, the enticing brilliance of cut glass; but they accomplished their end by technical devices virtually impossible to the cutting wheel. In place of the geometrical, finely crosshatched faceting of cut glass, they employed stippling. With this they combined ornamental motives that are, in aspect, somewhere between cut

Fig. 2 — "PENNSYLVANIA STEAMBOAT," *6 ½ in.*
The palmette or anthemion ornaments of the border thoroughly neo-classic in type, and so strongly reminiscent of the late 1820's as to argue for placing this plate in the very early 1830's

designs and those more skilfully wrought decorations usually associated with the art of the glass engraver. And because the press permitted them to produce intricate patterns in a metal too hard to submit readily to the older methods of hand decoration, they achieved effects of non-prismatic gleam and sparkle beyond anything previously known to ornamental glass.

The labor involved in making the molds for such glass must have been prodigious, and in time, as wages increased, so costly as to forbid its profitable employment by the manufacturer. Hence it is safe to say that the shift from lacy patterns to bolder and simpler designs was compelled less by a change in popular taste than by the relentless force of economic necessity.

Precisely when that shift occurred we have no certain means of knowing, although documents upon which to base some fairly reliable guesswork are at hand in the form of several cup plates that either carry an imprinted date or, because of the nature of their decoration, may be assigned to a specific year. These cup plates are the so-called *1831 Eagle*; the *Queen Victoria*, without doubt issued as a souvenir of the young monarch's coronation in 1837; the *Victoria and Albert*, celebrating the royal marriage in 1840;

Fig. 3 — "ROSE," *6 ½ in.*
The struggle between Victorian naturalism and the neo-classic tradition is here apparent. No doubt contemporary with Fig. 2

Fig. 4 — "CONSTITUTION," *6 ½ in.*
Allied with Figures 2 and 3. The frigate *Constitution*, though condemned to destruction in 1830, was rehabilitated in 1833. This plate may date between those two years, perhaps slightly later than Figures 2 and 3

Fig. 5 (left) — "Flower Basket and Grapes," 7 ⅝ *in.*
In this exceptionally fine plate we encounter motives dear to McIntire in the early 1800's. One of the most refined and logical of Sandwich designs, 1830–1833

Fig. 6 (centre) — Medallions, 6 ½ *in.*
Here the more classic motives have yielded to adaptations of French Regency

details. A lush design, extremely well executed and but little later than the preceding

Fig. 7 (right) — "Eagle," 6 *in.*
Difficult to place, but maintaining a delicacy of pattern and justness of scale that, aside from the classic anthemions of the border, point to the early 1830's (*Fig. 2*)

and the *President Harrison*, bearing the date *1841*. With this final item must be associated the *Bunker Hill* plate, inscribed *Finished by the Ladies 1841*.

We have but to compare the two last-named plates with the preceding three to perceive how quickly simplicity of decoration has supervened upon ornateness. Some slight stippling is discoverable in the border swags surrounding the Harrison profile, but it is reduced to a minimum. The *Ringgold* plate (*1846*) displays no stippling whatsoever, while the various members of the log-cabin series, likewise of the 1840's, are either quite unadorned as to their rims, or carry merely a straggling vine or detached flower sprays.

Similarly, the host of conventional cup plates may be quite sharply divided into two classes: the first usually signalized by an astonishingly detailed richness of quite exquisitely handled motives set off against a stippled background; the second characterized by the virtual absence of stippling and by the employment of bold, large-scale, and often rather coarsely commonplace motives in place of the refined elements for which the first class is notable. If we are justified in believing that the year 1840 establishes the line of demarcation between the gener-

ously enriched historicals on the one hand, and the relatively plain ones on the other, we are equally justified in placing the first class of conventionals prior to that year, and the second, subsequent thereto. What is true of cup plates should be true of the larger plates and dishes. We may not say that all pieces of the kind which prominently display stippling were made before 1840. In fact, the 1860's and 1870's witnessed a considerable revival of that device. Nevertheless, we may confidently insist that all notably brilliant items that liberally employ fine stippling as a background for traceries of exceptional refinement in both form and scale are, without much question, a product of the 1830 decade.

Whether or not it is possible to determine to which half of that decade a particular example should be assigned is another question. No two mold cutters were equally gifted in judgment and skill. The constant demand for new patterns must, at times, have taxed the most lively invention. Not a few experiments, too, were made in the direct imitation of English cut patterns. Considerations such as these must give pause to dogmatic assurance. Yet, in spite of them, it is impossible to resist the temptation to arrange a few of the old patterns on the basis of certain significant attributes of design, and thus to infer a probable chronology.

The accompanying illustrations present such an arrangement. Their captions indicate certain reasons for the position of each item in the sequence. The examples

Fig. 8 (left) — Palmette and Scrolls, 7 ¼ *in.*
Far less delicate than any of the preceding and less well considered as a composition, but placed early because of the predominance of classic or semiclassic motives

Fig. 9 (centre) — Star and Lozenge, 6 ½ *in.*
Very difficult to place on the basis of its pattern, which, on examination,

resolves itself into a thing of shreds and patches, most of which would seem rather nondescript except for the brilliance of the glass

Fig. 10 (right) — Cornucopias, 5 ¼ x 8 ¼ *in.*
A favorite early motive associated with others of a somewhat neutral variety. Unless the work of an inferior designer and mold maker, this and Figure 9 might qualify for a rating in the late 1830's

Fig. 11 (left) — SHELL AND BULL'S-EYE, 7 ½ in.
Obviously indebted to Figure 6 for its inspiration, but not so logically designed or so fine either in scale or in mold cutting. Either somewhat later than Figure 6 or by an inferior artisan

Fig. 12 (centre) — "STAR, FLOWERS, AND LOZENGES," 8 in.
This name, like all the others, is purely arbitrary, and is intended merely to emphasize some feature or features of the pattern. Cup plates, plates, and dishes in lacy glass, particularly if conventional in pattern, are better known

by number than by any descriptive name. This is one of the patterns that, in many respects, follows the geometrical design of cut types. There is no sign of neo-classic influence. Though the workmanship is excellent and the scale beyond criticism, the whorl of flower forms in the centre points forward toward the 1840's rather than back toward the 1820's. Perhaps, therefore, about 1835

Fig. 13 (right) — "STAR, OAK, AND LANCE HEAD," 5 ½ in.
The geometrical character of the rim and the whorl of naturalistic leaves about a starlike centre associate this in type and probably in date with 12

selected are from a carefully picked collection, and, with one or two exceptions, have not hitherto been published. All are rare and well worthy of study regardless of the relative correctness or incorrectness of their date ascriptions.

Conclusions

The reader will no doubt already have remarked that this brief study has stressed peculiarities of pattern and has not even mentioned indications afforded by the character of the glass itself. In general, it may be noted that the metal of all the pieces here considered is of the same high quality. Its handling, however, is not uniformly competent. Some of the examples illustrated are of almost double thickness, usually considered a sign of early period. Some clearly betray the curious surface lines explained by Harry Hall White in AN-TIQUES for April

1933, page 146. Since these lines, or fissures, are due primarily to unequal heating of the mold, they, too, are widely accepted as significant of crude methods and hence of relative antiquity. Bubbles in the body of the glass are similarly viewed.

These various signs and symbols should not be overlooked, or their great importance denied. Yet it may be possible to emphasize unduly their value in determining whether a given piece in which some of them may be discovered is of earlier date than another, in the same general class, which chances to be free from alluring flaws. Between the years 1830 and 1840 the technique of glass pressing as a mechanical process was far from achieving perfection, albeit the artistry of pressed-glass design reached its zenith during that period. Hence we may not rely solely on the inperfections in a single piece of one pattern to reveal the date of the pattern itself. The lone specimen

Fig. 14 (left) — "VICTORIA CORONATION," 6 ½ in.
The year 1837, that in which Victoria was crowned queen, may be accepted as dating this plate. Rose, thistle, and shamrock, signifying England, Scotland, and Ireland, are entwined in the wreath of the rim. The design would be better were the likeness larger and in profile, but, as a whole, the plate is a fine piece of work

Fig. 15 (centre) — PANELED DISH, 6 ⅛ x 8 ¼ in.
This is the first piece in the group whose rim is clearly divided into separate panels. The fanciful centre and the motives of the long sides of the rim are obviously derived from Louis XVI designs; the thistle corners recall the Victoria and Albert cup plate of 1840, the first of the paneled cup plates. The

leaf and anthemion are evidently the selection of desperation. The workmanship is better than the somewhat mixed design. Date of this dish, probably 1839–1840

Fig. 16 (right) — PANELED DISH, 9 ⅜ in.
The paneling here is unmistakably similar to the Victoria and Albert wedding cup plate of 1840. The handling of the motives is quite distinctive; first, for the large size of each element, and the considerable but well-disposed areas of clear glass; second, for a new quality of modeling specially observable in the petals of the dahlia-like centre flower. There is here a curious quality in the detail, as of stamped metal, such as we have not hitherto encountered. Date, about 1840

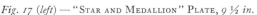

Fig. 17 (left) — "STAR AND MEDALLION" PLATE, *9 ½ in.*

Here again we find large clear surfaces rather subtly modeled instead of being outlined with a ridgy border such as bounds a considerable proportion of the previous examples. The technique is so similar to that of Figure 16 (compare the central motives, and the use of clear glass in the design) that we must ascribe both to virtually the same year, 1840

Fig. 18 (centre) — BONBON OR CARD DISH, *8 x 9 ½ in.*

More or less in a class by itself, though the so-called hairpin motive occurs in cup plates, plates, and dishes. Judged by the weight of glass and the fineness

of workmanship, fairly early in the 1830's — perhaps 1835; but affording few if any stylistic clues. Perhaps based on a silver design. An excellent piece of workmanship

Fig. 19 (right) — "BUTTERFLY, FLEUR-DE-LIS, AND FAN" DISH, *7 ¼ x 10 in.*

Another very puzzling item. So brilliant in quality that when seen in the original it is likely to blind the observer to its imperfections in design, which consists of a rather heterogeneous accumulation of unrelated motives. Again the product of a quite unimaginative shop designer despite its neat workmanship. Date perhaps about 1840

may be heavy in body, bubbly, covered with surface fissures, badly atrophied about the edge. But, unless we can find several more from the same mold, all exhibiting like peculiarities, we shall lack the evidence essential to any really valid conclusion. The possibility that the piece before us is a "second," representing a minor accident rather than pervasive inexpertness on the maker's part, must be recognized and taken fully into account.

At the same time, it must be admitted that attempts to determine dates, in the jumbled eclecticism of the nineteenth century, exclusively on the basis of pattern are fraught with no little peril. They are worth while primarily because they compel con-

mental design and workmanship in the mold. Their results will be indicative rather than definitive, and must, therefore, be checked and counterchecked against the testimony borne by the fabric of the glass itself.

Of one thing, however, our study may leave us reasonably certain. Most of the brilliant, finely stippled American pressed glass, the so-called lacy glass, is a product of the 1830–1840 decade. For reasons that need not be rehearsed it may be credited to the factory at Sandwich. While in quality of metal it varies but slightly, in quality of design it betrays wide divergencies. But, whatever its occasional deficiencies, it is to be recognized as a distinctive and distinguished contribution to our industrial art.

Fig. 20 — THREE LARGE DISHES, *11 and 12 in.*

Arranged in probable order of date from about 1830 to 1840. All three are palpable imitations of English or Irish cut glass. The second, which borrows motives common in early nineteenth-century cut decanters and tumblers, is handsomest

sideration of individual decorative motives and their probable bearing, and, even more important, because they involve the temporary ignoring of merely superficial glitter, and necessitate concentration upon quality of funda-

MUSEUM EXAMPLES OF SANDWICH GLASS

An Editorial Note

IN NOT a few museums of the United States today one may encounter somewhat heterogeneous, often nondescript, and frequently mislabeled accumulations of pressed glass. In so far as we are aware, however, the Metropolitan Museum of Art in New York is the first to place on display a cabinet of selected examples of the pressed glass made under the supervision of Deming Jarves at his factory in Sandwich, Massachusetts, apparently between the years 1828 and 1842. Though these examples are a loan from the collection of Mrs. Charles W. Green of New York City, they were, we understand, chosen by Curator Joseph Downs, to whom, further, must be credited their excellent arrangement in a large alcove cabinet adjacent to the entrance to the American Wing.

In view of the care exercised by all concerned in preparing and placing this display, we see no reason to question the ascription to Sandwich of all the items shown. Nevertheless, the more critically one examines this group of glass, the more astonishing will he find its variety of forms, ornamental patterns, and colors. And the more readily will he admit that the early pressed glass of Sandwich deserves recognition as an important and worth-while contribution to American art-industrial history.

If the mechanically produced glass manufactured by Jarves and his coworkers had been no more than a cheap and imitative substitute for the cut and engraved wares of its period, it would merit little if any attention. Occasionally it descends to such a relatively low level. In the main, however, it owes little or nothing to wheel technique and, unlike the variously produced output of a later generation, nothing to the influence of cast iron. On the contrary, it stands as a really quite new and independent type of glass, often quite original in form, and in general exhibiting a style of decoration exceptionally well adapted to enhance the brilliance of the material in ways feasible for the pressing machine but quite beyond the capabilities of the cutter or the engraver. Such glass could have been turned out only under the favorable conditions created by relatively low labor costs and exceptionally resourceful and progressive management — such conditions as, in its heyday, the Sandwich factory enjoyed and utilized to the full.

While various considerations preclude picturing all the specimens of this glass exhibited at the Metropolitan, we believe that our readers will be glad to examine portrayals of representative specimens from a group considered worthy of a place in an outstandingly great American museum of art. Thanks to the courtesy of the authorities, who went to no little trouble in taking special photographs, we are able to illustrate a number of pieces from the Green collection, accompanied by brief descriptive notes. Most of the pieces illustrated in ANTIQUES for August 1933 are included in the loan to the Metropolitan Museum. One or two of them are republished in the present group of illustrations.

According to Doctor Charles W. Green, specimens of lacy Sandwich glass are most frequently found in New England, the

FIG. 3 — COVERED DISH (*10 ½ by 8 ½ inches; overall height, 5 inches*)
Clear glass, with fluting, stippling, and mingled floral and abstract forms. It was no small undertaking to press these large pieces of irregular shape and to ensure satisfactory fitting of cover to dish. This may account for the scarcity of covered examples in comparison with those made and marketed without covers

FIGURE 4

FIG. 4 — CREAMERS (*all approximately 4 ¼ inches high*)
These patterns, usually occurring in clear glass, are here respectively pressed in sapphire, fiery opalescent, and brilliant but rich blue. Gothic patterns of surbase of *a* and *b* virtually identical. In this couple reversion to a form akin to the much earlier helmet shape is interesting. From the standpoint of design these creamers might properly be rated in the order of their photographic presentation

FIGURE 5

FIG. 5 — BOWLS: ALL BUT ONE COVERED
(*Overall height of covered items, from 5 ¼ to 6 inches*)
Covered bowls, whether blown or pressed, with cover fitting into a galleried rim, are specifically of the nineteenth century. If, as we believe, fine delicacy of detail is indicative of relative age in pressed glass, *b* would be the latest in this interesting quartet. Colors: *a*, sapphire; *b*, exists in *claire de lune*, deep blue-black, and green; *c*, deep blue, oval form; pattern an ingenious combination of bull's-eyes surmounted by scalloped scalelike motives interspersed with thistles; ends show pineapple. As usual, brilliance is enhanced and unification achieved by stippling the ground. *d*, clear butter bowl, circular

FIGURE 6

FIG. 6 — PLATE AND DISHES
a, Sapphire-blue oblong dish with chamfered corners; gothic design with leaves in corners; not uncommon pattern in clear glass, but rare in color. *b*, Six-inch clear plate with serrate edge, acanthus or palmette with *fleur-de-lis* border and eagle centre; a highly refined and consistent design, probably of the 1830's. *c*, Octagonal 6 ½-inch dish with border of rococo implications and six-pointed star centre surrounded by a ring of shells

Hudson River Valley, and eastern Pennsylvania. The last-named locality appears to have been partial to the colored glass. Miniature specimens of lacy glass are now believed to have been made, not as samples, but as a tribute to juvenile interest. The variety of patterns in lacy Sandwich glass defies enumeration. Hitherto unknown examples are constantly turning up. Goblets, tumblers, compotes, a large diversity of plates and dishes, egg cups, small cups and saucers, sugar bowls, creamers, sand shakers were turned out in lacy patterns. So, too, were candlesticks and lamp standards. It seems fair to surmise that Jarves' intention was to compete not only with more expensive glass tableware, but also with Staffordshire earthenware, which, during

FIG. 7 — DISHES (*approximate diameters, 7 in.*)

a, Clear glass, twelve sided; border motives capable of sundry interpretations. *b*, Clear glass with irregular-shaped edge, pressed from an unusually well-designed and cut mold. *c*, Circular dish with pearl or bull's-eye and finely designed oak wreath in centre; for octagonal variant, see ANTIQUES for August 1933 (*p. 60*). *d*, Octagonal; clear glass with well-conceived and executed grape border and flower-basket centre

the 1820's and 1830's, was being imported in vast quantities into the United States. In some instances, at least, it would seem that Sandwich patterns owe their inspiration more to Staffordshire designs than to contemporary ornamental glass. But the point should not be overstressed. As already observed, the early lacy Sandwich is virtually peculiar to itself, and though it was produced in an era when excessive decorative elaboration was the rule, it almost invariably represents a just sense of the inherent quality of glass as a material, and a remarkably sound taste in adjusting patterns at once to the capabilities of the machine and to the nature of the substance employed. Later, and in other localities, this rule was less carefully observed.

FIG. 8 — DISHES OR DEEP PLATES, ALL IN CLEAR GLASS

The meticulous elaboration of fine detail in *a*, *b*, and *c* contrasts decisively with the larger handling of the motives in *d*, and hence may point to a somewhat earlier date for the first three items. It should be unnecessary to call attention to the almost constant employment of stippled grounds in the various examples illustrated. See ANTIQUES for August 1933 (*p. 58*), where is published an article on Sandwich lacy glass which attempts to establish some basis for dating certain patterns

FIG. 9 — PLATES AND DISHES

a, Shallow dish, clear glass, 9 ¼ inches, scroll and sunburst border, double-fan centre. Rare. *b*, Brilliant clear-glass *beehive* dish, 9 ¾ in. Examples vary greatly in degree of brilliance. *c*, Soup plate in clear glass with amber border; while the pattern itself is of not infrequent occurrence, this combination of clear glass with amber is exceptionally handsome and, in so far as known, unique. *d*, Flat plate similar in pattern to *c* but in clear glass

22

NEW ENGLAND GLASS COMPANY INVOICES

Part I

By HELEN McKEARIN

Discovery of the invoices here discussed is an exciting event for students of early American glass, and ANTIQUES *is proud to be able to reproduce them here with Helen McKearin's scholarly analysis. She interprets the often cryptic notations and elucidates their significance for glass collectors. The documents, except for one which is privately owned, were formerly in the Archives of the Maryland Collection at the Enoch Pratt Library, and are now owned by the Maryland Historical Society. They were discovered by Richard Wood of Baltimore, who was able to track down in the Baltimore city directories all but one of the dealers mentioned on the invoices; his identifications are given in the captions. This study will be continued in* ANTIQUES *next month.*

— THE EDITOR

A PROMISING LODE of information as to the early products and business procedures of the New England Glass Company has been discovered by Richard Wood of Baltimore. He has located a bill of lading and four invoices of consignments, sent by water, between September 13, 1828, and 19, 1829, to William E. Mayhew & Company, commission merchants of Baltimore. Heretofore as Lura Woodside Watkins states in her authoritative *Cambridge Glass*, contemporary newspaper advertisements have been the source of nearly all our knowledge of the wares made before 1830. Information so obtained has been general — largely as to genus and species. These newly discovered documents are a little more specific, confirm some old conjectures, and contain evidence for new, tentative if not positive, attributions.

The study of these papers, the ferreting out of factual and implicit information from prices (f.o.b. factory) and somewhat cryptic wording, has been more engrossing than a double acrostic. But the conclusions are not so capable of proof. Since nearly every line has been re-phrased and interpreted in the light of personal experience and research it is not unlikely that, as in the case of many translations, the exact meaning of the original text and idiom may have been missed. So, as a check and balance, the text of the privately owned 1828 invoice is given here as Figure 1 and of the four 1829 invoices now owned by the Maryland Historical Society the three dated January 3, April 18, and May 2 are illustrated as Figures 2, 3, and 4. Each line and column has been numbered so that the entries, as they are discussed, can be identified by L. (line) and C. (column) with the corresponding numbers. Also, an arbitrary division of the material into three parts has been made. Part I is devoted to drinking vessels and tableware.

FIG. 1 — COPY OF ITEMS on the earliest of the New England Glass Company invoices of glass shipped to Wm. E. Mayhew & Co., commission merchants at 22 South Charles, Baltimore. As the document itself is privately owned and not available for reproduction, Richard Wood has supplied the transcript.

		Sept. 13th 1828	
1.	6 pr 3 sq foot cyl-lamps plated caps	13/6	13.50
2.	½ Doz 9 in Straw ◇ fruit dishes on feet		7.50
3.	4 " Tale champaigns	10/6	7.00
4.	3 pr. Qt flute & flute Dects	12/	6.00
5.	12 pr. 3 Pt Dble flute carofts cut rings	3.50	42.00
6.	12 Doz Flint flute & wing Tum	2.75	33.00
7.	3 " " " " " Wines	2.25	6.75
8.	9 " " " " " "	2.25	20.25
9.	6 " " " " " Clarets	2.75	10.50
10.	6 " " Fluted champaigns	3.50	21.00

Decanters and drinking vessels almost invariably led the glassware lists in the innumerable contemporary advertisements of merchants and auction houses. So, as one would expect, a large proportion of these comparatively small shipments consisted of these objects. In all there were 231½ dozen glasses — wines, clarets, champagnes, and tumblers. Of these 16 dozen were plain stem wines at 3/ (equivalent to 50¢) a dozen: 8 dozen entered on Line 2, Column 1 (*Fig. 3*) and 8 on Line 9, Column 1 (*Fig. 4*). It is a fair assumption that they were free-blown with an applied, unadorned stem and the flat circular foot of the period. As to the bowl, who knows?

It is probable that another and one of the most common of the free-blown forms is indicated by the "taper" wines — 3 dozen tale at 3/ (*L.5, C.2, Fig. 3*) and 3 dozen common at 3/ (*L.24, C.1, Fig. 4*). These were wines similar to Figure 5 with drawn bowl and stem.

Tale, which characterized other items also, indicated a quality of glass. Whenever it was impossible to secure pure ingredients for glass a scumlike substance, sandgall, was formed on top of the batch by the impurities carried upward by the bubbling of the cooking metal. While this was removed as completely as possible, the metal at the top was usually inferior to that below. Wares made from the best metal were the fine glass, for instance that used for extrinsic decoration. Those made from the top were considered inferior as a rule and were called tale. I suspect the term is of English origin because weight of glass and excise taxes went hand in hand for so very long in England. And "tale," which according to Funk & Wagnalls may be a "numbering as distinguished from a weighing," "a valuing by tale and not by weight," might have seemed a logical term for the cheaper glass.

In the 1828 shipment (*L. 7 and L. 8, Fig. 1*) there were 12 dozen "Flint flute & wing" wines. That descriptive phrase, no reference to molding, the high price — 2.25 a dozen as compared with 50¢ a dozen for taper wines — point to free-blown wines fashioned from fine lead glass (called flint from the days of the Englishman, Ravenscroft) and with wheel-cut decoration. This was a field of manufacture which the New England Glass Company cultivated almost from its inception in the spring of 1818. Its patterns, like its heritage of technical and decorative practices, undoubtedly were as British as the shillings and pence which peppered its invoices. Flute was, and is, a common British cut-glass term, apparently first used in the eighteenth century to designate a vertical decorative element resembling half a flute or reed divided lengthwise. Eventually, it embraced all similar motifs — convex or concave, long or short, shallow or deep, broad or narrow, tapering or even horizontal. Often a differentiating adjective such as flat or fan was

FIG. 2 — JANUARY 3, 1829, INVOICE of apothecaries' wares and blanks for cut glass, the latter for a Mr. Tingh, probably one of the many independent glasscutters who were located in our cities, especially along the seaboard, some even prior to '76. Mr. Wood was unable to locate Tingh in the directories, but he did find a Baltimore Steam Glass Cutting establishment. *This and Figures 3 and 4, courtesy of the Maryland Historical Society.*

FIG. 3 — APRIL 25 COPY of the April 18, 1829, invoice of glass consigned to Wm. E. Mayhew & Co. for the accounts of Albert Koster, china, glass, and queensware merchant at South Calvert, and Thomas Sutliff, owner of a furniture store at 60 West Lexington, both of Baltimore. Across the face of the invoice is a notation enough of which can be read to learn that "this invoice by the Marshall Ney did not come to hand . . . having been lost on her passage . . ." *Fig. 2 above, Fig. 3 below, facing page.*

added. Sometimes very fine flutes were called finger flutes; fine and slanting, blazes. And the broad, convex vertical flutes — ribs to us — introduced by Irish designers after 1790 were known as pillar flutes, or just pillars. These flute and wing wines might be described as having fine flutes in winglike formation above a band of vertical flutes around the lower part of the bowl.

The same suppositions may be held, regarding the 6 dozen "Flint flute & wing" clarets (L.9, Fig. 1), billed at 2.75 a dozen and totaled at 10.50! The arithmetical error is especially irritating since the price might provide a clue as to whether the clarets were larger or smaller than the wines. Obviously they were unlike in some respect. In fact, for centuries the claret glass appears to have had an identity of its own: it occurs in English lists far back in the seventeenth century. But so far I have been unable to identify one. Since, however, this *claré* French wine was light-bodied and usually taken with meals it seems likely that it was served in glasses having more capacious bowls than those used for a heavier and headier wine. Jerome Strauss, an outstanding student and collector of drinking vessels, concurs in this opinion. It is not impossible, of course, that the shape was similar to that of the *Ashburton* so-called claret, the much later pressed form resembling a stubby and chubby parfait glass. Whatever its shape, one thing seems certain, if the claret was larger than the wine a dozen would have been 2.75; if smaller, 1.75.

During the prosperous 1820's and '30's another French wine, champagne, long a favorite of the wealthy, appeared with increasing frequency in the daily newspaper notices of wines and spirits for sale. An immediate corollary was the more regular inclusion of champagne glasses in the listings of cut glass for sale. So it is not surprising to find them on the 1828 invoice of the Cambridge firm — 4 dozen tale at 10/6 a dozen (L.3), and 6 dozen flint fluted at 3.50 a dozen (L.10, Fig. 1). It can be inferred that both types were free-blown; the first, probably plain; the second with simple cut flutes probably rather flat and extending only part way up the bowl. Their shape is a matter of conjecture. One probability is the French "flute" like that in Figure 6 which from the seventeenth century had been used for this sparkling wine. Another is the Victorian champagne or "coupe" which supposedly came in vogue about 1830 and had a shallow "saucer" bowl with foot or very tall stem. A third is a glass with a large tulip-shaped bowl which André L. Simon maintains in his *Champaign* was the proper form.

The tumblers, 181¼ dozen in all, outnumber all other drinking vessels. Two descriptions, I believe, admit of easy translation — 12 dozen flint flute and wing at 2.75 a dozen (L.6, Fig. 1), and 67¼ dozen ⅓-pint flute and tree at 67¢ a dozen (L. 21, C.3, Fig. 4). The first presumably were free-blown lead glass and matched the cut wines and clarets in pattern. The second, I believe, were blown-three-mold in the *arch* pattern G.IV-2 (as classified by McKearin, *American Glass*), or possibly G. IV-3 (*Fig. 7*). Two tumbler molds have been determined in G.IV-2. One, because of tumbler fragments unearthed at Sandwich, has been attributed to that factory. The other mold and the rare pieces from it have never been associated with any glasshouse. Nor has the one determined mold in G.IV-3, a tumbler mold.

The knob tumblers at 67¢ a dozen (12 dozen, L.1, C.1, Fig. 3 and 12 dozen, L.7,

C.1, Fig. 4) are as yet an unsolved puzzle. Diligent search through many books on drinking vessels has been unrewarding. Newspaper research has revealed only their popularity in the 1820's and '30's. Cask upon cask of English knob tumblers were imported, many in 1825 by George Dummer & Company of New York City, founders in 1824 of the Jersey Glass Company. The Brooklyn Flint Glass Works of John L. Gilliland & Company as well as Cambridge made them, and in quart, pint, and ½-pint sizes.

The remaining type of tumbler which, if I have translated the abbreviations correctly, was named "fingered," presents one of the most intriguing problems in these documents. A careful scrutiny of the letter before *Tum* (L.10, Fig. 2) and the beginning of the word after *Mold* (L.16, C.2, Fig. 3) leaves no doubt in my mind that in the former invoice the tumblers for cutting (blanks) at 12/ a dozen, were also "fingered." Nowhere in the many illustrations I have surveyed have I found a tumbler or other article so labeled. Nor have I found any certainty as to its meaning among the students I have consulted. One suggestion, which would fit the molded glasses but not the blanks which were free-blown, was a band of finger flutes. Another suggestion, quite likely the correct one, I feel, comes from Frederick Carder, noted glassman and founder of the Steuben Glass Works. He writes, "These must be what were called thummers and had deep depressions, pushed in while hot, in the lower part so that when one had too much to drink he could at least hold onto the glass." Mr. Strauss is of the same opinion. Such a shape could be formed in a mold as well as by hand. Whatever they were, the molded variety was in popular demand and was cheap, 50¢ and 62½¢ a dozen. The total number destined for the Baltimore dealers was 61¼ dozen (L.16, C.2, Fig. 3; L.6 and L.19, C.2, and L.10, C.3, Fig. 4).

Three other articles might be mentioned briefly: flasks, jars, and stopper rounds. In the April shipments there were 295 11/12 dozen oval black flasks at 3/ a dozen (L.9–15, C.1, Fig. 3); in the May, 233 1/12 dozen of the black at 3/ or 50¢, and 39 2/12 dozen oval green flasks at 62½¢ a dozen (L.3–6, C.1 and L.11, 12, C.3, Fig. 4). These undoubtedly were plain blown or molded flasks from the affiliated New England Bottle Glass Company. The 72 gallon jars and 105 half-pint stopper rounds (L.1, 2, 7, Fig. 2) were probably on their way to apothecaries. I have found stopper rounds — wide mouth containers with meticulously fitted stoppers — advertised under the heading *Apothecary Wares*. The New England Glass Company like most of its competitors produced quantities of such goods. It may be that the method of glass stoppering described by Apsley Pellatt in his *Curiosities of Glass Making* was used at Cambridge.

Other articles of tableware included vessels for serving wine, spirits, and water; castors and peppers; plates and hats. Only the carafes and three pairs of decanters were in the September 1828 shipment; the others were all sent in 1829. The consignments of decanters, carafes, and pitchers were even larger than those of their boon companions, the drinking vessels already discussed. In all there were 120 11/12 dozen pitchers, 12 pairs of carafes, and 70½ dozen decanters. The last, as I interpret the entries, were of three species — blanks, cut glass, and blown-three-mold.

Of the two tierces of blanks sent on January 3 for a Mr. Tingh, one contained 25

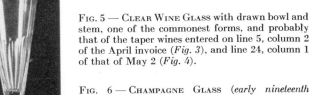

FIG. 5 — CLEAR WINE GLASS with drawn bowl and stem, one of the commonest forms, and probably that of the taper wines entered on line 5, column 2 of the April invoice (*Fig. 3*), and line 24, column 1 of that of May 2 (*Fig. 4*).

FIG. 6 — CHAMPAGNE GLASS (*early nineteenth century*). So-called French flute (shape) with simple flute cutting around the lower half of the bowl. Possibly the form, and decoration of the New England Glass Company's "Fluted champaigns," line 10, Figure 1.

FIG. 7 — BLOWN-THREE-MOLD TUMBLERS in the arch patterns (McK. G.IV-2 and G.IV-3) which might be described as flute and tree. That having the single motif springing from the spandrels of the Roman arches of G.IV-2 is perhaps the more tree-like so more likely to exemplify the "flute and tree" of the tumblers entered on line 21, column 3, Figure 4 than the one having two sprig-like motifs from the spandrels of the Gothic arches of G.IV-3. *Collection of George S. McKearin.*

quart and 20 pint decanters "for cutting" (*L.8, 9, Fig. 2*). Blanks, heavy free-blown forms usually of the finest quality of lead glass, were to the glasscutter as sheets of silver to the silversmith, a raw material and the medium for displaying his art and skill. As a rule they sold by the pound, not by the dozen as did the tumblers. And, as a comparison of prices shows, they were far more costly than finished molded glass. Even at the average weight of nearly 2¾ pounds one of these American-made decanter blanks cost nearly twice as much as a pair of molded quart decanters. Undoubtedly foreign rather than domestic imports were the most favored blanks with Mr. Tingh as with the majority of our independent glasscutters and firms prior to 1824. That year marked the passage of a truly protective tariff which included the imposition of a duty of 2¢ a pound plus 30 per cent ad valorem upon the glass including blanks. The American System began to function and the New England Glass Company as well as other producers of fine glass got a nice slice of the melon.

The Company's own cut-glass wares would have shown the influence of currently fashionable European styles — if it wished to sell them. Among them were designs of simple flute cutting. In one of the May consignments there were three pairs of pint *fluted* decanters at 84¢ a pair (*L.13, C.1, Fig. 4*); in that of April 18, three of pint *flute and flute* at 1.50 a pair, (*L.8, C.1, Fig. 3*); and in the September 13, three of quart *flute and flute* at 12/ ($2.00) a pair, (*L.4, Fig. 1*). The exact form of the flutes is a matter of surmise. But judging from known examples of the period, one might assume that the *fluted* had merely a band around the lower part of the body. A simple and not expensive cutting seems indicated by the price which was much lower than that of the pint *flute and flute* decanters. The latter doubtless had two bands, probably one around the lower part of the body and one running from the shoulder to the base of or into the neck. There may have been only one type of flute motif, as on the decanter in Figure 2; or two types, for example, a narrow shallow flute at the bottom and a broad tapering one at the top.

Whereas, even at wholesale, the presumably cut decanters were sold by pairs, the much cheaper — about 30¢ a pair — molded decanters sold by the dozen, and, as would be expected, in much larger quantities. The invoices included 65 ⅔ dozen molded quart decanters at 1.75 a dozen which, I believe, belonged in what we call today the blown-three-mold category. In the first place the full-size piece mold was used almost universally for both shape

and pattern at this period. In the second, the Company's descriptive *Arch flute, Arch, Gothic Arch,* and *Cornucopia* immediately call to mind recorded blown-three-mold patterns, not one of which has been associated heretofore with any specific glasshouse.

The first three would fall in the *arch* group. As pattern G.IV-5 (*Fig. 9*), has an arch over a broad pillar flute or rib, need we look further for the design of the 2 dozen quart molded *Arch flute* decanters of the April shipment (*L.22, C.1, Fig. 3*). At present I have a record of only two molds in this pattern, each of three pieces, one for a quart and one for a pint decanter. Though it is quite possible that the 2 dozen quart *Arch* decanters (*L.15, C.1, Fig. 4*) were in an unfamiliar pattern I suspect they were molded in G. IV-5 and "flute" was omitted because of cramped space. The 20 dozen quart molded *Gothic Arch* decanters, (*L.18, 19, 28, C.3, Fig. 4*), I believe, were in the pattern G. IV-6 like the pitcher in Figure 10. A three-piece mold in each of three decanter sizes — quart, pint, and half-pint — has been determined in this blown-three-mold pattern. Incidentally, neither Mrs. Watkins nor I found any pieces in either of these *arch* patterns among the Sandwich fragments we examined. Nor does Mrs. Lee mention having identified any.

This is true also of the decanters in the so-called *horn o' plenty* pattern (*Fig. 11*). It seems far more than a possibility that this *baroque* pattern G. V-17, of which only one mold has as yet been determined, was the *Cornucopia* of the New England Glass Company. That it was popular, perhaps a new design, is attested by the 41¼ dozen sent to Baltimore — 2 dozen (*L.25, C.1, Fig. 3*) in the lost April shipment and the others in May (*L.16, C.1; L.23, 24, C.2; L.3, 20, 27, C.3; Fig. 4*).

In the September 13 lot of glassware were "3 Pt Dble flute carofts" with "cut rings" (neck rings or collars) at 3.50 a pair (*L.5, Fig. 1*). Caroft, without doubt, was a corruption of carafe, still in 1829 a very young English word for water bottle. Its liquid capacity and, surely, a wider neck were probably the features distinguishing this member of the bottle family from normal decanters. Apparently these items went in pairs even though not intended for wine or spirits. It is possible that *double flute*, because of the short entry line, was a contraction of *flute and flute*. Quite likely it meant two bands as on the decanter in Figure 8. At any rate it may be assumed that the carofts were free-blown and wheel cut, because of their price, the phrase "Dble flute," and because of their cut rings.

"Jug" rarely calls up any image other than that of a bottle-like vessel with a very short narrow neck with or without a flange and pouring lip, and a small handle. Merely by widening the neck, flaring a rim, forming a lip, and perhaps enlarging the handle a bit, a jug could be transformed into a "pitcher." Perhaps some such evolution, plus the fact that most molded pitchers prior to mechanical pressing were patterned in bottle or decanter molds, explains in part the persistence of the old name though, except in Britain where jug is still in common usage, it was used here from the 1830's on about as seldom as pitcher was in the eighteenth. During that period, when tea with cream was a dictate of fashion, the small vessels for serving cream were called cream jugs no matter from what substance they were made. Even Steigel listed cream jugs and cream pots among his products. In these invoices the old-fashioned "jug" was used for large pitchers, the nineteenth-century "creams" for the half-pint size.

Surprisingly, jugs and creams far outnumber the decanters. In the total of about 120 dozen, three methods of fabrication were represented: free-blown, molded, and mechanically pressed. Of the free-blown there were 6 "Qt. Jugs for Cutting" averaging 1.10 each (*L.4, Fig. 2*) and, presumably, the 4¾ dozen quart plain heavy jugs at 37½¢ each (*L.25, 26, C.3, Fig. 4*). Except for the pressed creams the remainder was the cheaper molded glass. The half-pint molded creams at 1.00 a dozen — 15 dozen on the April invoice (*L.16, C.1, Fig. 3*) and on the May, 56 2/12 dozen (*L.2, C.1; L.10, C.2; L.13, C.3, Fig. 4*) — might have been pattern-molded. But it is more likely they were blown in a full-size piece mold since that method required less hand work.

Evidently pitchers as well as decanters were popular in the *arch* patterns already discussed in connection with the decanters. And doubtless, as was customary, they were patterned in the same molds. Although I have never seen a pitcher of any size in G.IV-5 (*Fig. 9*), I have expected to do so. For in my experience, decanters and pitchers in the same blown-three-mold patterns are as inevitable as death and taxes. There were 10 dozen quart and 10 dozen three-pint *Gothic Arch* pitchers (*Fig. 10*) on the May invoice (*L.4, 5, 22, 23, 24, C.3, Fig. 4*); 8½ dozen *Arch flute* on that of April 18 (*L.22, 23, 26, C.1, Fig. 3*); 10½ dozen *Arch* on that of May 2 (*L.7, 8, C.2, Fig. 4*). That these pitchers should cost 25¢ each and their decanter companions in pattern about 15¢ is quite understandable, a matter of time and labor. To finish a decanter blown in a full-size mold required only forming a flange and, after annealing, fitting a stopper which, no matter how it was formed, cost little. That of a pitcher necessitated widening the neck, forming rim and lip, attaching and forming a handle, operations not only involving more manipulation but three or more re-heatings at the furnace to maintain the metal's plastic state.

Molded hats at 42¢ a dozen, 3½¢ apiece, were more numerous than any other article except the pint flasks. In the April shipments there were 49½ dozen molded hats (*L.17, C.1, Fig. 3*); in the May 99½ dozen of unidentified color, 50 dozen blue, and 50 dozen white (*L.1, C.1; L.9, C.2; L.14, 9, 15, C.3, Fig. 4*). It is safe to assume that those without color designation were clear glass. But while white in a glassman's language often meant colorless, Mrs. Watkins states in *Cambridge Glass* that when used by the New England Glass Company it invariably meant milk-white glass. The period was one, of course, when fine quality milk-white glass was being produced almost everywhere. As to the design, one cannot go beyond the assumption that, like the known blown-three-mold hats of the period, they resembled the popular beaver hat. It is probable too that they were blown in full-size three-piece molds.

Other molded articles on the April and May invoices which probably would fall in the blown-three-mold category were peppers and castor bottles — 12 dozen peppers at 5/3 a dozen (*L.3, C.1, Fig. 3; L.10, C.1, Fig. 4*); and 3 dozen old molded castor bottles at 75¢ a dozen (*L. 25, C.1, Fig. 4*). While "old molded" may be open to more than one interpretation, my own guess is that it referred to discontinued patterns, especially as at least 46 patterns in 75 different molds are known today. It is of interest that the glass manufacturers supplied the castors for the bottles. In the May

consignments there were a few 4- and 5-hole japanned castors and 4-hole plated (probably silver) castors (*L.14–16, C.2, Fig. 4*).

The indisputable evidence that early pressed 5″ and 6″ plates and 3″ and 3½″ cup plates were produced by the New England Glass Company is most gratifying to those of us who for years have maintained stoutly that they just *must* have been. In the April shipment were 3 dozen 3″ cup plates at 3/ a dozen (*L.9, C.2, Fig. 3*), and 3 dozen 3½″ at 3/9 a dozen (*L.10, C.2, Fig. 3*). They were duplicated in one of the May consignments (*L.2, 3, C.2, Fig. 4*). The May shipment carried also the 5″ and 6″, second quality, pressed plates, 20 dozen of each (*L.8, 16, C.3, Fig. 4*) at 1.50 a dozen — or 12½¢ apiece. The factory prices were surprising to me — a second quality 6″ pressed plate only about 3¢ less than a quart molded decanter, a 3½″ cup plate more than a molded hat! But then, pressed glass was still "new" in 1829 and molds for it were intricate and expensive as compared with piece and dip molds.

(*To be continued*)

Illustrations below, left to right:

Fig. 8 — CLEAR GLASS DECANTER, typical of the early nineteenth century, with simple decoration of cut flutes, possibly the type used on the New England Glass Company's flute and flute decanters or double flute carafes, line 8, column 1, Figure 3, and lines 4 and 5, Figure 1. *Collection of the Connecticut Valley Historical Society.*

Fig. 9 — RARE QUART BLOWN-THREE-MOLD DECANTER in *arch* pattern (McK. G.IV-5), which, having a broad vertical rib or pillar flute under an arch, easily fits the New England Glass Company's descriptive "Arch flute" of the decanters and pitchers of the April invoice (*Fig. 3*), and probably also those of the May consignments described as "Arch" (*Fig. 4*). Heretofore there has never been any kind of evidence for even a tentative attribution to any glasshouse. *Collection of George S. McKearin.*

Fig. 10 — BLOWN-THREE-MOLD PITCHER in *arch* pattern (McK. G.IV-6), probably the pattern in which the "Gothic Arch" pitchers and decanters of the May shipment (*Fig. 4*) were molded. The only articles recorded in this pattern to date are the scarce pitchers and decanters which were molded in the same three molds of quart, pint, and half-pint sizes. The three-pint pitchers undoubtedly were patterned in the quart decanter mold. Until now there has been no inkling as to their possible source. *Collection of George S. McKearin.*

Fig. 11 — BLOWN-THREE-MOLD QUART DECANTER in the *baroque*, so-called *horn o' plenty* pattern (McK. G.V-17), with original stopper. Probably the *Cornucopia* of the New England Glass Company's decanters (*Fig. 4*). As in the case of the *arch* patterns G.V-17 has never been associated with any glasshouse. *Collection of G. S. McKearin.*

NEW ENGLAND GLASS COMPANY INVOICES

Part II

By

HELEN McKEARIN

THE DISCOVERY *by Richard Wood of Baltimore of several invoices of the New England Glass Company dated in 1828 and 1829 has furnished new and important documentary material regarding the products of this firm. The documents themselves were illustrated through the courtesy of the Maryland Historical Society in Part I of this article, which appeared in September 1947. There the author discussed the drinking vessels, jugs, pitchers, decanters, hats, peppers, castor bottles, and cup plates listed in the bills. Her analysis is continued here, and will be completed in our December issue. References to the bills are given here by date, and, as in Part I, L. means Line, C. means Column. The view on this page is a detail taken from a view reproduced on the invoices discussed here.* — THE EDITOR

A SIGNIFICANT CONTRIBUTION made to the history of American glass by these New England Glass Company invoices is that they bear witness to the fact that the Company was well launched in the field of mechanical pressing before 1830. I know of no earlier documentary, specific evidence of the long-accepted conclusion that many articles besides knobs and salts were pressed at Cambridge before that date. Plates of cup-plate size and of five-inch and six-inch diameter have been mentioned in Part I. We now turn to other articles in this category, even more exciting, particularly sugar bowls and creamers. Unfortunately there is no clue as to the shape and decorative patterns of the pressed creams at 4.50 a dozen and sugars at 6.00 a dozen, both second quality (*L. 7, 6, C. 3, May 2*). However, Mrs. Watkins believes, and many of us will agree with her, that there is a strong possibility they were similar to, if not exactly like, the very early pressed examples in Figures 1 and 2. One would expect 1829 designs to be simple, and the forms to be reminiscent of other bowls of the period and also to lend themselves readily to mechanical pressing.

The April 18 shipment contained one dozen "new molded" sugars (*L. 11, C. 2*). "New molded" is a somewhat puzzling phrase open to many interpretations, such as new pattern, new method, or both. Since the presumably blown-three-mold quart pitchers were 3.00 a dozen and as, I figure, the time and labor needed for fashioning a cover would not double the expense of production,

FIG. 1 — (*two views of each*) Two EXTREMELY RARE and early creamers pressed in simple designs and forms reminiscent of many Staffordshire creamers of the 1820's. Unusual applied handles formed by free-blown techniques. While there is no way of knowing what the creams entered on line 7, column 3 of the May invoice (*Fig. 4, Part I*) may have been like, it is far from impossible that they were similar to these. In fact it is probable. The heart on the creamer at the left is a pressed-glass motif long associated with the New England Glass Company and one of the designs mentioned in the 1826 patent for pressing knobs. *Collection of Lura Woodside Watkins.*

FIG. 2 — (*two views*) EXTREMELY RARE and early pressed sugar bowl. The bold, simple, but effective design is similar to those of the creams in Figure 1, probably typical of such pieces made by mechanical pressing prior to 1830. The shape carries on a popular rectangular Staffordshire form and is similar to that of the heavy bowl blown-molded in the earlier 1820's, presumably by the New England Glass Company (*see* ANTIQUES, *August 1939, page 69*). Probably the pressed creams of the May invoice and "new molded" sugars of the April and May were similar in shape and pattern, perhaps even the same. *Collection of Grace Lyman Stammers.*

it seems unlikely that these sugars were blown in full-size piece molds or, for that matter, in pattern molds. There were two outstanding "new" methods of molding at the time, mechanical pressing and pillar molding, either of which would have been more expensive than the others. Still, since these particular sugars, like those entered as pressed, were *second quality* and *6.00 a dozen* I am inclined to believe they too were pressed, not pillar molded.

Incidentally, two facts about these pressed, and presumably pressed, sugars and creams are arresting. One is the smallness of the lots; the other that they were all second quality. The implication might be that the type of ware was still in its infancy and practice had not yet made it perfect, for either or both of which reasons the public had not taken it wholeheartedly to its tables.

Another fascinating description is the "½ Doz 9 in Strawberry diamond [symbol used for diamond] fruit dishes on feet" at 15.00 a dozen (*L. 2*), on the September 1828 invoice. Obviously they were distinguished by strawberry diamonds, either in a diaper or as the pattern's dominating feature. This diamond, one of the most ubiquitous cut-glass diamond motifs of the period, was exceedingly popular with the composers of our early pressed patterns, many of which boldly aped cut glass. However, inasmuch as a quart pitcher blank was 1.10 and a B. S. bowl nearly 2.00, the price of 1.25 each for these footed dishes seems much too low for cut glass. And their price seems equally high for molded glass since a quart molded *gothic arch* pitcher could be sold for only 25¢. I think the logical conclusion is that they were pressed glass.

Equally thrilling entries were those for "Pine Apple" dishes which were made in three sizes. The 7-inch size sold at the factory price of 6.00 a dozen or 50¢ each, (*L. 2, C. 2, April* and *L. 21, C. 1, May*); the 8-inch, at 7.50 a dozen or 62½¢ apiece,) *L. 5, C. 1; L. 3, C. 2, April* and *L. 8, 22, C. 1, May*); the 9-inch, at 9.00 or 75¢ each (*L. 6, C. 1; L. 4, C. 2, April* and *L. 14, 23, C. 1, May*). The descriptive phrase "Pine Apple" may have had reference to design or function or both. The pineapple, a favorite motif of that period with artisans in many crafts, was incorporated into more than one pressed glass design. If, in this case, the words signified a design, or the characterizing motif of one, the dishes may have been the same as or

similar to that in Figure 3. And, of course, there were precedents galore for christening a dish or any vessel for something to drink or eat. The times were ripe for one to be used in serving pineapples. They were a West Indian delicacy sufficiently newsworthy to be listed among imports even when brought into the country in very small quantities. As to whether or not the method of production was pressing, even if there were no other considerations, price again seems to indicate an affirmative answer.

The "B. S." of the 12 bowls for cutting (*L. 5*) of the January 3 invoice is an intriguing abbreviation. If the article were a wine any glass student, without a second's hesitation, would say "baluster stem." Perhaps it was just that. Such compotes were made. Perhaps Mr. Tingh ordered compotes intending to embellish them with cut strawberry diamonds. Another possibility is that it stood for "Big Salad." Salad bowls were advertised by the New England Glass Company before 1829 and, in contemporary newspapers, they appear often in the cut-glass invoices given in auction announcements. (At this time by far the majority of advertisements of glass for sale were those of auction houses, not of manufacturers or independent merchants.) But whatever its form, the B.S. bowl was a comparatively large object; the average weight was 5¾ pounds, 2 pounds more than that of the quart jug blanks and quite a bit more than the average of the "58 Dishes for Cutting" entered on line 3 of the invoice. That there is no clue to the shape and sizes of these dishes and bowls is regrettable. Perhaps they were assorted.

Like the pitchers, the salts in these consignments presumably were free-blown, pressed, and blown-molded. The free-blown were the 24 blanks (*L. 6, Jan. 3*), remarkable for an average weight of nearly ¾ pound each and costing 35¢ apiece. The "Rose" and the price of the 6 dozen salts (*L. 4, C. 1*) of the lost April shipment, an order duplicated in that of May (*L. 11, C. 1*), leads to the inference that they probably were pressed in one of the New England Glass Company

FIG. 3 — HEAVY EARLY PRESSED GLASS dish having a pineapple motif in each corner of the base and, on the sides, a Gothic arch, another popular motif of the day of these invoices. Possibly similar in design and shape to the New England Glass Company's "Pine Apple" dishes in the April and May 1829 shipments. *Privately owned.*

FIG. 4 — EARLY PRESSED GLASS salt marked on the bottom in four lines *N E Glass Company Boston;* on sides, a well-modeled version of the popular basket-of-flowers motif, and on the ends, a rose from which perhaps the Rose salts in the May shipments took their name. While there are at least three other similar Basket of Flowers-Rose salts, one also marked *N E Glass Company Boston,* this rose differs widely from its fellows. *Privately owned.*

salt patterns having a rose on each end, one of which is shown in Figure 4. The inference is bolstered by the fact that, according to Joseph Howe, Jr., who became the Company's agent in 1822, pressed salts were produced in 1827. If only he had mentioned their design! In connection with these Rose salts it should be noted that they were 1.25 a dozen whereas the pillar molded salts (*L. 13, C. 2, April*) were 1.50. This is the only instance in the scale of costs in which, according to my interpretation, pressed glass was less than blown-molded.

The pillar molded salts sent in April and the molded pillared salts, in May (*L. 5, C. 2*) also at 1.50 a dozen, give rise to considerable speculation. The paramount question is whether the May lot was a replacement of the April and the words reversed in making the entry or whether two distinct types were meant. Only one thing seems absolutely certain: regardless of the method of molding, the design contained vertical ribs, or, in English-Irish terminology, pillars or pillar flutes. If molded pillared or pillar molded meant only design without reference to method there is a possibility, to my way of thinking a very, very slight one, that the salts were the same as or similar to that illustrated in ANTIQUES for August 1939 (Fig. 1, lower A, p. 68). As the method of molding this type of salt (described in the article referred to) required little, if any, more time and labor than a blown-three-mold salt, I doubt very much if it would have sold for as much as 12½¢ apiece. If a molded hat, probably blown-three-mold, was 3½¢, a salt would hardly have been more than 5¢.

If on the other hand, pillar molded was the proper phrase and can be taken literally — as I believe it can — the question as to how the salts were made is easily answered and the high price reasonable. About this time pillar molding, a method known and practiced by the Romans, was "re-discovered" by an English glassman and hailed as a great modern improvement. Two gathers of glass were used. After allowing the first to cool to a greater degree of hardness than was customary, a second was made over the first, and, while it was as hot as possible, the whole was rammed into a small fluted dip (pattern) mold. Because of this procedure pronounced ribs or pillars projected on the outside while the inside remained smooth. After the gather had been impressed a piece was fashioned by free-blown techniques.

In this case the fact that neither I nor anyone whom I have consulted has seen an identifiable pillar-molded salt fails to shake my belief that they were made at

Cambridge and some of them sent to Baltimore in April and May 1829. There are other reasons for such a conclusion besides the use of the words in the invoices and the existence of such a method. For one thing, Apsley Pellatt, who gives a lucid and detailed account of the method in his *Curiosities of Glass Making,* mentions salt cellars among the articles for which it was "used advantageously." Moreover, there is evidence that at this time there was a demand here for such wares. For instance, "half pint pillar molded tumblers," "pillar stem champaigns," and "pillar molded sets" were imported in quantities from England. Bowls, pitchers, and vases, many attributed to the Pittsburgh district, are known which have the earmarks of having been molded in this fashion. So why should not the progressive New England Glass Company have used it? Even the price might be positive evidence if the Rose salts at 1.25 a dozen were indeed pressed. Pellatt, speaking of "American pressed glass," states that while its effect was not so good as pillar molding it was less expensive. If that was true in England, it probably would also have been true at Cambridge.

Inasmuch as since November 1826 the Company had had control of the second United States patent for pressing glass knobs it would be a disappointment not to find these articles on the invoices. They are there. The knobs in Figure 5 could have been made at Cambridge; they bear the physical signs of having been pressed in the type of mold called for by the patent specifications. Apparently, if one can judge from the prices, each size of knob had its number by which it could be identified. In the April shipment there were 15 dozen #1 pressed furniture knobs at 2.25 a dozen (*L. 18, 19, C. 1*); 15 of #2 at 1.75 (*L. 20, C. 1*), and 4 of #3 at 1.25 (*L. 21, C. 1*). In May there were the same quantities of the 2.25 and 1.25 knobs but entered respectively as 2⅜ inches (*L. 11, C. 2*) and 1⅜ inches (*L. 13, C. 2*). At 1.75 there were 17 dozen 2⅛ inch knobs (*L. 12, 22, C. 2*). In addition there were a dozen 2⅜ inch and 2 dozen 2⅛ inch knobs with round spindles at 12/9 (2.13) and 9/9 (1.62½) a dozen. It might be startling to know what designs the faces of these knobs wore, if they were listed in the patent specification: ". . . circles, rings, hearts, roses, fruit, animals or any other fancy or ornamental shape that has been or may be used in brass or other ornaments . . ."

To be Concluded

FIG. 5 — Two GLASS furniture knobs which were pressed in a mold the same as or similar to that described in the patent of 1826 obtained by the New England Glass Company. Simple geometrical pattern. *George S. McKearin.*

NEW ENGLAND GLASS COMPANY INVOICES

Part III

By

HELEN McKEARIN

The discovery by Richard Wood of Baltimore of several invoices of the New England Glass Company dated in 1828 and 1829 has furnished new and important documentary material regarding the products of this firm. The documents themselves were illustrated through the courtesy of the Maryland Historical Society in Part I of this article, which appeared in September 1947. There the author discussed the drinking vessels, jugs, pitchers, decanters, hats, peppers, castor bottles, and cup plates listed in the bills. Her analysis was continued in October 1947 and is completed here. References to the bills are given here by date, and, as in Part I, L. means Line, C. means Column. — THE EDITOR

ONLY TWO ARTICLES remain to be considered in this final part of the discussion of the New England Glass Company documents. But these last, the lamps and enameled deep plates, are far from the least important and interesting. They are further evidence of the fact that when our tariff-sired production of fine glassware was beginning to ride the 1820's wave of industrial expansion, the company was quick to counter competition at home and from abroad and alert to the possibilities in developing new and old types.

Glass lamps which, before many decades, were to form one of the vertebrae in the backbone of the glass industry were among the "lines" steadily increasing in popularity. In the many 1827-1829 newspaper advertisements of imported or domestic lamps which I have found, glass ones — cut and plain, sometimes even painted and enameled — appeared frequently, whereas a few years earlier they seldom were included. And advertising is a fair yardstick by which to measure a growing demand. The presence

FIG. 1 — ONE OF THE earliest types of glass lamp with pressed base made by the New England Glass Company. Free-blown font, probably one styled "cylindrical" by the Company, attached by heavily ringed knop to square three-step base or foot. Quite likely the design of "3 sq foot cyl lamps plated caps," Line 1 of the September 13, 1828, invoice. *Photograph courtesy of Lura Woodside Watkins.*

in the Baltimore shipments of six, or eight, apparently distinct designs representing two methods of production, added to the evidence of its own and its agent's advertisements, testifies to the New England Glass Company's enlargement of its line of lamps.

Among the articles "lost" in April 1829 when the *Marshall Ney* of the Union Dispatch Line went aground on Handkerchief Shoal and "sunk in 6 fathom water" were six dozen "½ arch ribed" peg lamps, one half dozen "cyl" lamps with square foot and round shoulder, and two pairs of "bulb" lamps with three-square foot and brass caps (Part I, *Fig. 3, C.1, L.7; C.2, L.7 & 8, 14 & 15*). Since Parts I and II of this discussion have been written I have found that the possibility of raising the brig noted on the May invoice by the agent, Mr. Whitney, became a certainty, and also that about $1000 worth of merchandise had been washed ashore. On May 1 the brig was drawn by two schooners into Chatham harbor where she remained in five fathom of water until suitable tackle could be procured by Captain Howes whose services had been retained to raise her. Six months later she was once more plying between Boston and Baltimore. So it is not impossible that the company recovered its wares — fit for cullet if not for customers. In any event it is unlikely that the firm suffered any financial loss since there was $7000 insurance. As for Wm. E. Mayhew & Co., the consignment of lamps appears to have been replaced in the May shipment (Part I, *Fig. 4, C.1, L.12, 17, 19*).

The "½ arch ribed" immediately calls to mind a well-known dip-molded decoration of an arch, more commonly called a panel, usually formed by an almost hair-like rib. On small articles, such as peg lamps, the arch extended about halfway up the body or, in this case, the font. Many articles besides peg lamps were so ornamented. It is probable the "arch rib ⅓ pint tumblers" which were listed in an 1820 advertisement of the New England Glass Company were made by the same method and bore the same type of arch or paneled decoration as the peg lamps.

Around the other lamps itemized in the invoices of September 1828, April and May 1829, an elaborate fabric of conjecture can be woven. The entries, grouped according to foot or base, are listed and numbered for reference as follows:

No. 1 — 6 pr. 3 sqr foot cyl lamps, plated caps (Part I, Fig. 1, L.1.)		13/6	13.50
No. 2 — 2 pr. 3 sqr foot bulb lamps, brass caps (Part I, Fig. 3, C.2, L.14 & 15; Fig. 4, C.1, L.19 & 20)		10/6	3.50
No. 3 — ½ doz. sml sqr foot cyl lamps round shoulder (Part I, Fig. 3, C.2, L.7 & 8)		4.50	2.25
No. 4 — ½ doz. sml sqr foot high cyl round shold. lamps (Part I, Fig. 4, C.1, L.17 & 18)		4.50	2.25
No. 5 — 2 pr. sml sqr foot bulb lamps and glasses (Part I, Fig. 4, C.2, L.17)		1.50	3.00
No. 6 — ½ doz. cup plate foot bulb lamps (Part I, Fig. 4, C.2, L.18)		2.25	1.12
No. 7 — 20 doz. cup plate foot cyl lamps (Part 1, Fig. 2, C.3, L.17)		1.75	35.00

In the fabrication of all these lamps it may be inferred, I believe, that the company was combining the ancient and the modern in lamps having free-blown fonts and pressed bases. Undoubtedly "cyl" and "bulb" referred to the fonts, the part of

Fig. 2 — Clear Glass Lamp with large free-blown pear-shaped font and cup-plate foot pressed in one of the sheaf-of wheat patterns. Possibly the "cup plate foot bulb lamps" in the May shipment were of this type — or of that shown in Figure 4. *From the collection of George S. McKearin.*

the lamp which held the lighting fluid. From a rather wide survey of glass lamps and illustrations of them the opinion seems tenable that the cylindrical fonts were those with straight sides, whether vertical or tapering from a flat or slightly rounded shoulder to a· narrow base as in the lamps of Figures 1 and 3; and that the bulb fonts were the various types with rounded sides such as the round or spherical font of the lamp in Figure 4, the pear-shaped in that in Figure 2, or one resembling the modern electric light bulb. All of the vertically straight-sided cylindrical fonts I have seen have been quite small. In size and oil capacity they would compare to the font in Figure 1 as the round in Figure 4 would to the pear-shaped in Figure 2. If a tall lamp was desired the height was achieved by joining the font to the base or foot by a shaft fashioned by free-blown techniques. The forming of a straight-sided font with either vertical or tapering sides would require a little more of those cost-increasing factors, time and labor, than a bulb. A bulb, after all, would be the more natural result of just inflating a gather of metal. This may account in part at least for the fact that, with the exception of the cup-plate foot bulb lamps (No. 6), the lamps with cylindrical fonts were more expensive than those with bulb fonts — 2.25 a pair for No. 1 and 75¢ for Nos. 3 and 4 as against 1.75 a pair for No. 2 and 1.50 for No. 5 which included the cost of a pair of glasses or globes. Probably a third or more of the cost of the last can be attributed to their being fitted with globes. I find no clue as to which type, or types, of "bulb" were used.

It is a fair assumption that the three types of base — three square foot, Nos. 1 and 2; (small) square foot, Nos. 3, 4, and 5; and cup plate foot, Nos. 6 and 7, — were pressed. The time and the price were right for them. As it seems likely that the mold for many of the known pressed square bases would have been neither more costly nor more complicated than that for a knob, probably lamps with such bases were made by, if not before, 1826. That was the year in which the Whitney-Robinson patent for pressing knobs was obtained. The "three square foot" doubtless was like or identical with that shown in Figure 1, a square base with three steps. In fact, lamps Nos. 1 and 2 might well have been counterparts of that shown in Figure 1, of which Lura Woodside Watkins writes, "This lamp was one of the earliest types made at Cambridge."

There are so many known different square pressed bases that it would be silly to speculate as to which one supported the fonts of Nos. 3, 4, and 5. Because the cylindrical lamps with round shoulders and square base, Nos. 3 and 4, were being sold by the dozen and at a comparatively low figure, I feel there is a strong probability that "small" modified the whole lamp as well as the base or foot. On the other hand, I have never seen or heard of one of these early lamps shorter than that shown in Figure 1 which was equipped with glasses. Therefore, though recognizing the possibility of short lamps being so fitted, I should conclude that "small" as applied to No. 5 probably referred to the foot only.

Of the dozen or more cup plates which show outward and visible signs of having been used as feet or bases, the best known is one of the common so-called sheaf-of-wheat (version of the classical palmette) patterns like that of the lamps in Figures 2, 3, 4. Tradition long ago attributed this design to the New England Glass Company; though it never, to my knowledge, has been confirmed. It is quite likely that the "cyl" lamps I have listed as No. 7, which were only 25¢ more a dozen than the peg lamps, were like that in Figure 3.

As far as description goes, the bulb cup plate foot lamps, No. 6, could have been like either Figure 2 or Figure 4. Probably either would have been about 50¢ more a dozen than the cylindrical: one has a much larger font; the other a knop stem the making of which required more metal, minutes, and movements. In the past, cup plate foot lamps have been attributed to Sandwich and to Cambridge, as was quite reasonable and logical. In my mind there is no doubt that other makers of fine wares produced them likewise. Still, insofar as I know, the only *documentary proof* of an origin is contained in the May 2, 1829, invoice of the Cambridge firm.

Two kinds of caps are mentioned, plated and brass. The plating was probably silver; the brass is news. Mrs. Watkins tells me that

Fig. 3 (*below, left*) — Clear Glass Lamp with "cylindrical" free-blown font and cup-plate foot pressed in a sheaf-of-wheat pattern. Possibly the "cup plate foot cyl lamps" of the May shipment were of this type, and also fitted with the cork and tin disc burner. *This and Fig. 4, courtesy of Lura Woodside Watkins.*

Fig. 4 — Clear Glass Lamp with round spherical bulb font, applied knop stem, and pressed cup-plate foot in a sheaf-of-wheat pattern.

the general belief has been that the cork disc burner was used until about 1830, to be followed by pewter fittings. The cup plate foot lamps undoubtedly had cork disc burners like those shown in Figures 3 and 4.

The last article to titillate the glass student's imagination is the enameled deep plate. The bill of lading, dated September 19, 1829, for the tantalizingly described package of 25 dozen is shown in Figure 5. No one whom I have consulted has seen a deep plate of any kind or color with enameled decoration. Nor have I. Yet, putting together bits of information gleaned from many sources, I believe they were just that.

The period was one when many facets of fashion reflected French styles. In tablewares richly colorful and gaily bedecked china, made chiefly in France itself, was enjoying a tremendous vogue here as well as in Europe. The newspapers abounded in announcements of its arrival. Such phrases as "elegant sets of French gold band Festoon," "light blue and gold embossed," "painted and gold," and "every description of French china gold burnished and lustered" called attention to this ware which was a luxury in reach of the few. One dealer quoted dinner sets from $75 to $500. So glassmen in England, Ireland, France, and Germany, scenting profit in simulating fine china in their less costly medium, had created a line generally called enameled or porcelain ware. In England, perhaps elsewhere, it had been done before, in the mid-eighteenth century, when Chinese porcelains had captured Occidental fancy.

A large proportion of the nineteenth-century wares, as of the eighteenth, were of opaque white glass often but not always bearing enameled decoration plus gold embellishment. Included in the same category was enameled and gold-decorated clear and transparent colored glass. Mr. Frederick Carder tells me the decoration was done "in impasto or paste applied by brush or spatula and fired in the muffle." He says also that in this period "the French did some very fine work in this manner as well as two English firms." In Germany the term enameled glass seems to have been as inclusive as elsewhere, except Ireland where it was reserved for the opaque white glass with and without decoration.

If enameled glassware was made in Europe, why not in the United States? Is it improbable that an enterprising firm like the New England Glass Company should have entered the lists? While the price of $2.75 for a dozen deep plates may seem very low for a fancy glass, it must be remembered that the decoration would not have been costly since at that time women could be hired at about $1.00 a week to paint and gild glass. Moreover, two very important items of information tip the scales definitely toward an affirmative answer, in my opinion. Mrs. Watkins found an early recipe for white enamel in Thomas Leighton's recipe book of compositions used at Cambridge. And the following from the New England Palladium for June 23, 1829, four months before the shipment, speaks eloquently: "New Articles: The New-England Glass Company has, within a few weeks, commenced the manufacture of ENAMELLED GLASS WARE, which resembles the finest Porcelean and Pearl and, surpassing what has been done in Europe, has extended it to the making of dishes, plates, nappies, cups, saucers, jelly, custard and egg cups, salts, knobs, etc. They are most beautiful articles — attract general attention — and so strike and interest the public taste, that already large

orders have been given for them./A rich assortment may be seen at the Company's extensive Warehouse, South Row,/ Washington-street, Boston."

Perhaps a wide bias in favor of home industries led the editor of the *Palladium* to place this bit of news at the head of column one on page one of his paper but it hardly seems likely that a plain piece of transparent or opaque glass would have aroused so enthusiastic a report. (Incidentally I found not one New England Glass Company advertisement in that paper during the entire year.) Also the same item, omitting only the final sentence, was published in *The Hartford Times* for June 29. In July it appeared without the reference to the Boston warehouse, in the Baltimore *Weekly Register* of Hezekiah Niles, intensely loyal and vocal advocate of the American System. The news was obviously considered important by those interested in domestic manufactures.

Questions immediately arise as to what happened to the nappies, the salts, deep plates and the "etc." of the announcement. Perhaps the whole line was not so eagerly received by the buying public as other types which have survived in quantity, or else was so popular that constant usage has left no specimens for posterity. On the other hand, it is possible that known enameled pieces have not been recognized as belonging in this period, for instance the *Remember Me* mugs. My own experience with glass which would fall in this category is too limited for me to do more than speculate on the question. Maybe someday one of us will find and recognize a deep enameled plate. In the meantime if anyone has light to shed upon these plates or any other article listed in the invoices, let him not hide it under a bushel.

(Conclusion)

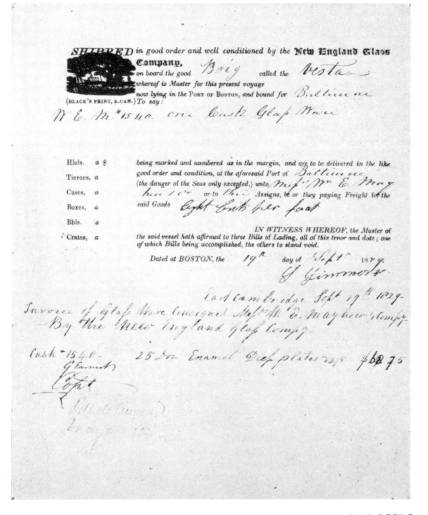

FIG. 5 — REPRODUCTION of Bill of Lading of shipment sent by the New England Glass Company to Messrs. Wm. E Mayhew & Co. of Baltimore, September 19, 1829.

448

New England Glass in Toledo

BY DOROTHY DANIEL

To speak of the "development" of American glass as though it were a gradual climb from primitive to aesthetic values is scarcely accurate. Glass progresses or declines in design and fabric in direct relation to the tastes, habits, and purses of the people with whom it enjoys a common environment.

This is clearly seen in the products of the New England Glass Company of Cambridge, Massachusetts, for this glass works kept close pace with the trends and tastes of American society in the nineteenth century. Some of these trends are well illustrated in a collection of Cambridge glass at the Toledo Museum of Art.

The museum was founded by Edward Drummond Libbey, who in 1888 moved the New England Glass Company from Cambridge to Toledo, Ohio, where it eventually became the Libbey Glass Division of the present-day Owens-Illinois Glass Company. On its fiftieth birthday in 1951, the Toledo Museum received as a present from the Libbey company its own collection of New England glass, along with a number of technically interesting Libbey pieces, as an addition to its permanent American glass exhibit. For the birthday celebration, Miss Nell Jaffe of the museum staff was able to augment the permanent gift with loans from the families of former New England Glass Company workmen and officials who migrated to Toledo with Edward Libbey in 1888.

From the earliest lead glass produced in Cambridge to the twentieth-century Libbey glass, each example was identified by family or company records. The pieces selected for illustration here show the scope of the New England Glass Company's output, and also reflect the times in which they were made.

Editor's Note—The New England Glass Company was founded in 1818, with Deming Jarves serving as manager until 1825. Our knowledge of the early products is scanty, based for the most part on advertisements. We do know, however, that "the company was well launched in the field of mechanical pressing before 1830" (Helen McKearin in an article on New England Glass Company Invoices, Antiques, October 1947).

The cut and engraved glass was of the greatest richness and delicacy. According to Lura Woodside Watkins, author of the pioneer work on this firm, *Cambridge Glass,* the cut-glass department at one time employed as many as a hundred men. The early cutting was simple, frequently combined with engraving; later designs, in the taste of the times, covered practically the whole object. "In the closing years of the factory," Mrs. Watkins writes, "the fashion changed from heavy substantial glass to ware of almost paper-like delicacy." Colored glass was produced in a wide range of shades, with various types of art novelty wares.

The New England Glass Company maintained a consistently high standard of fine quality lead glass, even in the face of the almost overwhelming competition provided by the introduction of lime glass in 1864. The financial problems which began in the 1860's grew acute in the 1870's. In 1878 the works were leased to William L. Libbey, with his son, Edward D., as partner, the latter becoming head of the firm at his father's death in 1883. Five years later, beset by strikes and other difficulties, Libbey moved the company to Toledo, and continued the business there under the name of the Libbey Glass Company.

Summing up the company's achievements, George S. and Helen McKearin have this to say in their comprehensive volume, *American Glass:* "From the very beginning, and throughout its long career, the New England Glass Company produced glass which in quality and purity was not excelled by any other manufacturer in America, or for that matter in any country."

Pressed glass *(c. 1870). Left to right:* waffle and bull's eye compote; New England pineapple cream pitcher; Huber compote; Ashburton sugar bowl; Ashburton compote. *All except the Huber compote, from the collection of Mrs. E. M. Belknap.*

Covered urn. Gold ruby flashing over clear glass *(c. 1845)*. Fine example of partitioned cutting. Overall height, 29¾ inches.

Milk glass (c. 1870). *Left*, covered dish, sawtooth pattern with acorn finial. *Right*, bowl, thumbprint pattern. *From the Belknap collection.*

Mid-nineteenth-century engraving. *Left*, cased glass, ruby over clear. *Right*, clear glass with stained panels.

Early decanter with panel cutting. Fine lead metal of good color. Note unusual flat rings. *From the collection of Mr. and Mrs. P. R. Hughes.*

Photographs, courtesy of the Toledo Museum of Art. Except as noted, all examples are in the Museum's permanent collection.

Tumbler engraved by Henry Fillerbrown at the New England Glass Company *(1875-1880).*

Pressed glass salt cellars. *Right*, opalescent glass, basket of fruit on sides, rose at each end. Marked on base *N. E. Glass Company Boston. Below*, base of an example in same design in clear glass.

Clear glass decanter engraved with inscription *New England Glass Co. Boston Mass. Genl. Head Qrs.* Made for the Centennial Exhibition in Philadelphia in 1876. Probably not original stopper. Height, 10⅝ inches.

Crystal and gold ruby goblet (*probably c. 1850*). Pressed and cut.

Fig. 1. Latticinio glass. Goblets; white and clear with band of red at rim, c. 1840; height 6 inches. *Henry Ford Museum.* Decanter, white and clear, height 10 15/16 inches; and vase, white and clear with applied ruby prunt, height 8 1/4 inches. Both c. 1860-1870. *Collection of Marion H. Pike.*

The New England Glass Company:
some discoveries

BY MILLARD F. ROGERS JR., *Assistant curator, Toledo Museum of Art*

CONSIDERABLE INTEREST in American glass has been generated lately by archeological excavations of such glasshouse sites as those at Jamestown; New Bremen (Frederick), Maryland; and Glastonbury, Connecticut. However, museum exhibitions and their resultant catalogues remain invaluable tools for any study of American glass. The New England Glass Company, perhaps America's most important nineteenth-century glass factory, has been the subject of an important book by Lura W. Watkins (*Cambridge Glass 1818 to 1888*) and of many articles in ANTIQUES and other magazines, but the first major exhibition devoted to this company's glass was that held at the Toledo Museum of Art from November 8 to December 15, 1963. Two hundred and seventy-three objects chosen from over one thousand illustrating this important phase of American glass history were studied during the exhibition, and its monograph-catalogue incorporates past scholarship, recent studies, and newly discovered material.

The most impressive glass made by the company was the free-blown ware of 1818 to 1850, which was generally of clear lead metal. Until 1850, Anglo-Irish design influences were strong. Colored glass was produced in quantity as the century progressed. Cut and engraved glass was a company mainstay between 1818 and 1888, reaching its zenith from 1855 to 1860 under Louis Vaupel and Henry Fillebrown, when the Bohemian style became fashionable and wheel-engraved decoration was superlative.

Mechanically pressed glass, introduced by the ingenious Deming Jarves, had a revolutionary effect on the market and on glassblowing operations. The company's pressed glass, which ranged from early lacy products to Victorian pattern glass, shows an especially conservative choice of design motifs. It is thought that mold-blown ware, intended as an imitation of cut glass, was never produced here in great quantity although several articles in this technique have been attributed.

New England Glass Company lamps, pattern glass, and paperweights had not been surveyed thoroughly until this recent study accumulated new evidence on the company's activity in these fields. Two other areas of importance received special study as well: glass formulas used by the company, and examples of marked glass indicating company provenance. The *Journal* of Thomas Gaffield, an important Boston diarist of the New England glass industry, also yielded many interesting items about the company (the four volumes of this *Journal*, covering the years from 1858 to 1894, are now in the library of the Massachusetts Institute of Technology).

Such an exhibition and study could not fail to provide discoveries and interesting reappraisals. Those that are perhaps most meaningful are included in the following discussion.

Latticinio glass (Fig. 1). The quality of the New England Glass Company's rare latticinio glass is excellent, and it has a sophistication not often seen in nineteenth-century American glass. It is not known whether the company workers acquired this technique by contact with Venetian glassmen or whether it came to Massachusetts from England, where it had been known for some time. Apparently this "filigree" glass was not produced in any quantity, nor was it ever marketed.

Ruby and Bohemian-style glass (Figs. 2, 3). What John Leighton called a "simple solution of gold" gave the company's ruby glass its color. The earliest formula for it in the Leighton recipe books is dated about 1848, but it is known that the company made it practically throughout its entire existence. Gaffield saw "ruby ware" made at the factory in 1875, and a year earlier he had watched company workmen making ruby plated glass for cutting purposes.

Bohemian-style glass, which began arriving here from abroad at least by 1820, was a popular product of the company by mid-century. A writer in *Gleason's Pictorial* stated in 1852 that: "We were repeatedly struck by the fact, new to us, that most of the exquisite, highly colored and decorated glassware, which is so much admired under the name of Bohemian glass, is manufactured at these works." The writer noted, too, that the company's Bohemian glass had an orange tint in comparison with true Bohemian pieces. It often involved gold enamel decoration combined with cut designs, and this technique occasionally was used with green glass instead of ruby. The company must also have explored the less expensive staining technique, since in 1827 the Franklin Institute of Philadelphia awarded it an honorary mention for stained glass.

Flasks (Fig. 4). Several flasks, because of the letters impressed in their sides, are identified with the New England Glass Company. The McKearins, in their book *American Glass,* tentatively attributed the flasks illustrated here and one more, Masonic flask GIV-15, which is marked N. G. Co., to the Marlboro Street glasshouse in Keene, New Hampshire, but added that GIV-27 might have been made there for the New England Glass Company. It is here suggested that the marks on all four of these refer to the New England Glass Company and that they were all made by the company or by the New England Bottle Glass Company, also of East Cambridge, which was organized in 1826 by Deming Jarves and Edmund Monroe for the sole purpose of making bottles. This latter company ceased operations in 1845; a price list dated November 1, 1829, listed "flask bottles" in half-pint, pint, and quart sizes in "black and green ware." The New England Glass Company listed "oval black flasks" and "oval green flasks" on an invoice. It should be noted that in neither instance is there any proof that the seller was also the manufacturer of these flasks.

Astral lamps (Figs. 5-7). Astral lamps of classical design made by the New England Glass Company are among the few objects marked with the company's initials and business location: N. E. GLASS Co./BOSTON. Lamp shades for this type of lighting device were advertised on January 15, 1825, in the *Boston Evening Gazette.* When the company began blowing astral lamp stems is not known. Those in black glass are simply tooled in baluster shape, and some stems in clear glass were cut in broad fluted and faceted patterns. An interesting variation of the black-stem astral lamp is a composite of an astral lamp stem (about 1825-1850) with a kerosene font which must have been made about 1865, after kerosene became popular as a lighting fuel. The metal fittings for the astral lamps probably were made in the company's trimming shop, where, in 1855, fifty men were employed.

Fig. 2. Ruby glass. Vase in so-called Chinese form, c. 1865; height 11 15/16 inches. *Brooklyn Museum.* Vase on clear foot, c. 1865; height 13 1/4 inches. *Collection of Dorothy-Lee Jones.*

Fig. 3. Bohemian-style ruby glass cased with clear; gold decoration. Three-piece toilet set; height of bottles, 9 3/4 inches. C. 1860-1870. *Pike collection.*

Fig. 4. Flasks. McKearin GIV-26: Masonic flask, half-pint size; marked NEG. *Collection of Charles B. Gardner*. McKearin GIV-27: Masonic flask, pint size; marked NEG/Co. *Gardner collection*. McKearin GII-77: concentric ring eagle flask, quart size; marked NG/Co. *Collection of George Austin*.

Fig. 5. Astral lamp, height 16⅝ inches; c. 1825-1850. Marked on metal plate near burner N.E. GLASS Co./BOSTON. *Collection of William J. Elsholz*.

Fig. 6. Pair of blown, pressed, and cut lamps, c. 1825-1850; height 16⅝ inches. *Jones collection*.

Fig. 7. Lamp with blown, clear and frosted shade engraved in grape design; height 18⅝ inches; c. 1865. *Collection of Dorothy Donovan Farrell*.

Fig. 8. Three-piece toilet set made for Eliza Leighton, wife of Thomas Leighton Jr. Opaque white glass with transfer printing and gold enamel decoration; c. 1860-1870. Height of bottles, 9¾ inches; of jar, 4 inches. Each piece inscribed *Eliza* in gold. *Collection of Mr. and Mrs. Stephen H. Sampson.*

Decoration (Fig. 8). Enameling, painting, and transfer-printing with decalcomanias on glass were company decorating techniques at various times during its seventy-year existence. As early as June 23, 1829, according to an advertisement in the *New England Palladium* noted by Helen McKearin (ANTIQUES, December 1947, p. 448) enameled glassware resembling porcelain was offered for sale by the company. Hand-painted decoration is common on company glass, usually on opaque white examples.

The most interesting new discovery regarding decorated glass was found in the Gaffield *Journal,* where it is recorded by the diarist that when he visited the company on March 17, 1873, to see William L. Libbey, the agent, he saw "nice painting on lamp shades . . . transferred." Bound into this *Journal* are two examples of paper transfers of birds, probably samples given to Gaffield by Libbey during this meeting. Gaffield also saw artists painting directly on glass.

1876 Centennial glass (Figs. 9, 10). The New England Glass Company first sponsored an exhibition of its products at a world's fair at New York City in 1853, a fair patterned after the Great Exhibition of 1851 at the Crystal Palace in London. At the 1876 Centennial Exposition in Philadelphia the company was one of forty-five entrants representing the manufacture of glass; it was awarded an honorary mention for its fluted tableware and decorative pieces. Photographs record sections of the company's lavish array of goblets, decanters, epergnes, and chandeliers elaborately cut and decorated. Thomas Gaffield learned from William L. Libbey (*Journal,* June 19, 1875) that the large and impressive display was suggested by the glass cutters themselves: "It seems that the idea of a display arose in the minds of some English workmen in the cutting shop, a committee of whom waited upon Mr. Libbey only a few days before the 17th and told him that in trade processions in London, they had seen the finest show made by the glassworkers, and they guaranteed a similar success here." The men worked night and day building a furnace on wheels to be drawn by horses in a parade opening the exposition; glass was actually blown during the parade's progress.

Volume III of Gaffield's *Scrapbook* gives a detailed description of the company's glass displayed in the Centennial Exposition, a valuable record of company design and decoration at this date.

Art glass (Fig. 11). The popular glass associated with the company in its last years was art glass of exotic and ornamental nature (see ANTIQUES, June 1964, p. 671). Amberina, Agata, Pomona, Wild Rose, and Maize art glass were all made in the five-year period between 1883 and 1888, and several patents testify to the company's need for legal control of these products. The observant Thomas Gaffield wrote in his *Journal,* July 20, 1883, that the "new" art glass, Amberina, already enjoyed a large sale; it was not patented, however, until July 24, 1883, when its inventor, Joseph Locke, assigned it to William L. and Edward Drummond Libbey.

After William L. Libbey died, his son operated the business. Art glass production continued. Edward Drummond Libbey showed Gaffield, according to the *Journal* entry of January 7, 1884, new types of colored and etched glass to be marketed soon. In spite of Gaffield's concluding note, "The Amberina has had quite a successful run," the company lost between five and six thousand dollars in 1883 because the works were closed in deference to a ruling of the Glass Manufacturers Association after the market became glutted.

Because of the amount of Amberina in private and public collections, and because it was produced at least a year before other types of company art glass, it is better known than the other art glass objects attributed to the New England Glass Company.

In an undated entry in Gaffield's second *Journal,* about 1864-1874, he records a visit to the company where he saw mechanical etching and cutting operations. This etched glass was the immediate forebear of Pomona, first produced in 1885. Gaffield records a day at the company, February 23, 1885, as follows: "We saw in the decorating rooms a new kind of glass, called Cremona [*sic*] glass. It is etched by acid and the upper portions stained so as to give a gilt and an iridescent effect also. The glass has not yet been introduced into the market and will not until Mr. Libbey has manufactured a considerable amount of stock to meet the first demand." In a later entry Gaffield noted that this glass was properly called Pomona.

Fig. 9. Goblet cut in hobnail-diamond pattern, c. 1876; height 6¼ inches. *Brooklyn Museum.*

Fig. 10. Wineglass, c. 1876; height 4 7/16 inches. Engraved on bowl *New Engld. / Glass Co. / Boston,* and *Mass. Centl. / Head Qrs. Corning Museum of Glass.* Decanter, c. 1876; height 10 5/8 inches. Engraved *New Engld./Glass Co./ Boston,* with *Mass. Centl. / Head Qrs.* on reverse. *Toledo Museum of Art.*

Fig. 11. Amberina, c. 1883-1888. Mug cut in Russian pattern, height 5 11/16 inches. *Toledo Museum of Art.* Twenty-six rib pattern-molded decanter, height 9 7/8 inches. *Corning Museum of Glass.* Pattern-molded jar with cover, diamond pattern; height 8 1/8 inches. *Metropolitan Museum of Art.*

New England Glass Company marks

BY MILLARD F. ROGERS JR., *Assistant curator, Toledo Museum of Art*

THE NEW ENGLAND GLASS COMPANY of East Cambridge, Massachusetts, founded in 1818 and a prominent American factory for the next seventy years, marked its glass in several ways: by cutting, engraving, metal stamping, etching, and molding, and by affixing printed labels to bases. At least eighteen different company marks came to light in an exhibition of products made by the New England Glass Company held at the Toledo Museum of Art in 1963. In addition, there are a number of presentation pieces directly associated with the firm by engraved inscriptions that do not, however, include the company's title or an abbreviation of it. A large presentation goblet made for Thomas Leighton on the occasion of his retirement from the company was the superlative in this class. Its inscription did not identify the firm by name or initials; instead, the silhouette of the factory complex on the Charles River in East Cambridge was depicted on one side, and on the other was an engraved tribute: *Thomas Leighton/east Cambridge/August 1843/—a token of great remembrance.* Unfortunately, this rare object has disappeared; it was last shown in 1935 at the Fourth Exhibition of the National Early American Glass Club, when it was owned by Mary Leighton.

While eighteen New England Glass Company marks on glass are now known, some have never before been recorded, and few were listed in Lura Woodside Watkins' definitive history of the company (*Cambridge Glass*, Boston, 1930). Practically the entire seventy-year span of production at East Cambridge is represented by these marks. The earliest was applied about 1825; the latest identified certain art-glass creations of about 1887. There appears to have been no particular reason for marking some pieces and not others. Items produced in quantity, such as pressed saltcellars, were marked, as well as astral lamps, which are quite rare today. Some positive dating of marks may be made by means of actual dates incorporated in the mark itself, and other dates are based on stylistic analysis of the marked object.

The New England Glass Company's cutting and engraving reached its zenith in its display at the Philadelphia Centennial Exposition of 1876; a spectator there, Thomas Gaffield, recorded that most of the glass it showed belonged in one or both of these categories. This decanter and goblet were part of a set made specifically for the exposition. *New Engl^d/Glass C^o./Boston* is engraved in script on one side of each piece, and on the reverse is inscribed *Mass. Cent^l./Head Q^{rs}*. See Millard F. Rogers Jr., *The New England Glass Company 1818-1888*, catalogue of the Toledo Museum of Art 1963 exhibition: Nos. 62, 63.

The following marks were used by
the New England Glass Company
between 1818 and 1888:

1. NEG/Cº in serif letters in relief within beaded oval.
Illus. A, detail of mold-blown flask, c. 1826-1850. Height
of letters, ⅜ inch (9 mm.); George and Helen Mc-
Kearin, *American Glass* (New York, 1948), pp. 556-557,
GIV-27, and Rogers, No. 79. Any bottles marketed by the
New England Glass Company probably were manufactured by the New England Glass Bottle Company in East
Cambridge, a firm incorporated on February 15, 1826, by
Deming Jarves and Edmund Monroe, and operated until
1845. Only this one flask exactly abbreviates the parent
company's title, avoiding the contraction of the name
appearing on other flasks (on most specimens the o is
almost indiscernible). According to McKearin, fragments
were found by Harry Hall White at the site of the Marlboro Street Glass Works in Keene, New Hampshire. As
the New England Glass Bottle Company was closed after
1845, perhaps the Keene factory made such marked containers to fill flask requirements for the New England
Glass Company between 1845 and 1850, when it too
went out of business.

2. NEG in serif letters in relief. Illus. B, from a mold-
blown flask, c. 1826-1850. Height of letters, ⅜ inch
(9 mm.); McKearin, pp. 556-557, GIV-26, and Rogers,
No. 78. Masonic and American eagle motifs appear on
three of the flasks marked with company letters. Flasks
with this mark may have been made by either the New
England Glass Bottle Company or the Marlboro Street
Glass Works.

3. N.G. Cº. in serif letters in relief. Illus. C, detail of
mold-blown flask, c. 1826-1850. Height of letters, ½ inch
(13 mm.); McKearin, pp. 554-555, GIV-15. "Flask bottles" in "black and green ware" were made by the New
England Glass Bottle Company in half-pint, pint, and
quart sizes. The firm for which these bottles presumably were made, the New England Glass Company, listed
"oval black flasks" and "oval green flasks" on an invoice,
and these entries may refer to such marked bottles. An
invoice, however, records only the shipper—not the manufacturer.

4. NG/Cº. in serif letters in relief. Illus. D, detail of
mold-blown flask, c. 1826-1850. Height of letters, ⅝
inch (16 mm.); McKearin, pp. 548-549, GII-77, and
Rogers, No. 80. A rare quart flask with concentric-ring
ribbing, bearing the abbreviation here associated with the
company, which may have been made at the Marlboro
Street Glass Works.

E

F

G

5. N.E./GLASS/COMPANY/BOSTON in serif letters raised in relief, within inverted-keyhole cartouche. Illus. E, pressed glass saltcellar, c. 1825-1850. Height of cartouche, 1 3/16 inches (3 cm.). Rogers, No. 118; and L. W. and D. B. Neal, *Pressed Glass Salt Dishes of the Lacy Period, 1825-1850* (Philadelphia, 1962), NE 3; see NE 1, NE 2, and NE 4 for variations. The most common company mark, this is frequently encountered on clear glass salts though opalescent and opaque-white examples are also marked in this way. Generally the keyhole cartouche is surrounded by a garland of flowers, but on this scarce salt (NE 3) the garland is missing. The word *Boston* appears on other objects as well as the salts but these are of slightly later date.

6. NE/GLASS/COMPANY/BOSTON in serif letters raised in relief, within inverted-keyhole cartouche surrounded by garlands. On pressed saltcellar, c. 1825-1850. Height of cartouche, 1 3/16 inches (3 cm.); *cf.* Neal, NE 1a. (Not illustrated.) This pressed mark, perhaps the earliest one employed by the company, is rare. It duplicates the mark on other saltcellars, except for the periods after the N and E. It may be a poor or late pressing from the same mold. There were examples in the George McKearin and Louis Lyons collections, according to L. W. Neal. Mr. McKearin felt that his salt was a good pressing and had never had periods on the die.

7. N. E. GLASS CO/BOSTON. in serif letters stamped in relief on metal plate. Illus. F, detail of lamp fixture, c. 1825-1850. Height of plate, 3/8 inch (9 mm.), length 7/8 inch (2.2 cm.); Rogers, No. 196. Small metal plates carrying this mark were attached to tubular fixtures just below the fuel reservoir of Argand lamps. Such a large factory as the New England Glass Company had several non-glassmaking operations subsidiary to the manufacturing and marketing of glass; its own metal and trimming shop probably made these plates.

8. N.E.G.C.o/E.R:S.R. in serif letters in relief. Illus. G, on pressed opaque white glass lamp base, c. 1825-1845. Diameter 7/8 inch (2.3 cm.); Rogers, No. 104. Certain whale-oil lamps with pressed square plinths decorated with lions' heads and flower baskets are attributed to the company's great competitor, the Boston and Sandwich Glass Company, when they do not carry this mark. The mark is pressed within a circular depression located inside the hollow plinth. Clear glass, light blue, and opalescent white lamps are known in this pattern. Half of the enigmatic second line of the mark may represent the initials of Enoch Robinson, the company employee who secured a patent for pressed-glass knobs in 1826.

9. NEG C°. in serif letters. Illus. H, from glass plug in base of "mercury glass" vase; c. 1850-1860. Diameter 15/16 inch (2.4 cm.); Rogers, No. 28. Small glass vessels lined with silver nitrate had clear, circular plugs in the base marked on the reverse in the glass, or on a piece of metal or foil which was then applied to the plug. The company first exhibited silver, or mercury, glass in 1850 at the Twentieth Exhibition of the Franklin Institute, Philadelphia. Glass plugs for silvered objects were carefully ground to fit the opening in the base. Base and plug were numbered with a diamond point to avoid confusion during assembly operations.

10. PATENT APPLIED FOR N. E. GLASS CO. in serif letters. Illus. I, stamped in crescent on base of railroad lantern, c. 1854. Height of letters, 1/8 inch (3 mm.); Rogers, No. 201. Railroad lanterns were produced by the company in 1854 and later. The locking bases for these were first produced about 1854, the date of their patent, but this rare mark on the underside of the base indicates a production date prior to the granting of the patent. Lantern assemblies may have been made in East Cambridge, in the company's own metal shop.

11. N.E. GLASS CO. PATENTED OCT. 24. 1854 stamped in serif letters. Illus. J, from base of railroad lantern; 1854. Height of letters, 1/8 inch (3 mm.); Rogers, No. 202. The date refers to the official recorded date of the patent for the snap base of these lanterns. Occasionally a lantern bears the railroad's initials cut into its glass globe.

12. N.E. GLASS CO. in serif letters. Stamped in crescent on base of railroad lantern; c. 1854. Height of letters, 1/8 inch (3 mm.). (Not illustrated.) This mark occurs on the base of a railroad lantern at the Henry Ford Museum. It bears no patent date but is otherwise similar to the more complete marks on other lanterns. Cornucopia, circle, and five-pointed star motifs pierced in the metal of this lantern and in others without marks suggest that the company's metal shop produced lanterns for other firms. All marked New England Glass Company lanterns I have seen have cornucopias only on the top assembly.

13. N.E. GLASS CO. PATENT OCT. 24, 1854 EXTENDED OCT. 24, 1868. in serif letters. Stamped in crescent on base of railroad lantern; c. 1868. Height of letters, 1/8 inch (3 mm.). (Not illustrated.) This mark occurs on a lantern in the Walter Simmons collection. The success of the patented snap base on railroad lanterns produced by the company no doubt warranted the extended patent protection.

14. N.E. GLASS C°. PATENTED JAN. 16, 1855 in serif letters. Stamped or engraved on pewter shank of mercury glass curtain knob; 1855. Length of inscription, 2 inches (5.1 cm.); Rogers, No. 95. (Not illustrated.) Mold-blown curtain knobs of mercury, or silver, glass were marked on the pewter shank. The patent may have been for an improvement in the molding and related to Enoch Robinson's earlier patent of 1826.

H

I

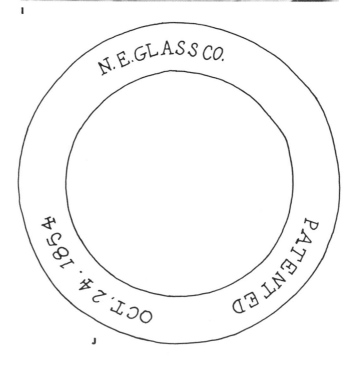

J

15. NEGW/AMBERINA/PATᵈ/JULY 24, 1883. Illus. K, oval paper label, red ink on buff, on a covered jar; 1883-1888. Height of letters, ¼ inch (6 mm.), length ½ inch (1.3 cm.); Rogers, No. 255. During the company's last five years in East Cambridge, printed labels pasted to the bases and pontils of art-glass objects gave the trade name of the glass as well as that of the manufacturer. Simple and economical, this new type of mark was unfortunately subject to loss by washing. The Amberina mark used for the first time the company's changed name (New England Glass *Works*), adopted in 1880; subsequent paper labels all carried the initials NEGW. There were other patents for Amberina glass (November 13, 1883; July 29, 1884; June 15, 1886), and these may have had separate paper labels, although no examples are known.

16. NEGW/POMONA/PATᵈ/APRIL 28, 1885. NEGW/POMONA/PATᵈ/JUNE 15, 1886 (?). 1885-1886 (?). (Not illustrated.) The second paper label to be used on company glass was applied to the base of Pomona pieces. Although this glass did not enjoy great success during the company's history, it was produced in some quantity before formal introduction into the market. Thomas Gaffield witnessed extensive production on February 23, 1885, when he visited the factory and noted it in his diary as "Cremona." Two patents were awarded Pomona, the second referring to an easier method of decoration than the original for the amber, blue, and rose-color stained ware. The first of the two patent dates has been seen on Pomona objects (McKearin, p. 420, and R. W. Lee, *Nineteenth Century Art Glass*, p. 53), but I have not seen an example. If the second date was used on a label, it has not been recorded.

17. NEGW/WILD ROSE/PATᵈ/MARCH 2, 1886, on a diamond-shape paper label, red ink on buff, 1886-1888. Height of label, ½ inch (1.2 cm.), length 1 1/16 inches (2.7 cm.); Rogers, No. 269. (Not illustrated.) This example is from a vase in the ware known today as New England Peachblow, which was patented under the name Wild Rose and produced for only two years, from 1886 to 1888. An early mention of this label occurs in a note by R. W. Lee (ANTIQUES, August 1934, p. 59) who mistakenly called it "a triangular mark." J. Stanley Brothers (ANTIQUES, April 1935, p. 129) recalled seeing "a label on the bottom of a vase, which read, *N.E.G.W./ Peach Bloom/W.L. Libbey & Son*—a mark which may well have been related to this one.

K

18. NEGW/AGATA/PATᵈ/MARCH 2, 1886 (?), or JAN. 18, 1887 (?), on round label, printed in red ink on buff. Illus. L, label on Agata vase in the Bennington Museum; diameter of label, 7/16 inch (1.1 cm.). The latest of the four paper labels used by the company, employed only one year before it moved from East Cambridge to Toledo, captures the character of the *art nouveau* movement in the exotic type face used for the name of the ware. The date on the lower edge of the illustrated label, the only known example, is illegible except for the last two digits and the first letter of the date line. The month of March or May is indicated by the first letter of the date line, and the last two digits appear to be 86. The official patent date granted to Agata was January 18, 1887; March 2, 1886, is the patent date for the company's Wild Rose art glass. Is the date on this Agata label a printer's error?

L

In addition to the well-authenticated marks
catalogued above at least three have appeared which
for one reason or another seem to be questionable.
All have been found on pieces acquired in the
vicinity of Newburyport, Massachusetts.
They are described and illustrated below.

M

N.E.G.CO. in serif letters engraved or stamped on brass
fixture. Illus. M, detail of lamp, c. 1865 (?). Height of
letters, 1/8 inch (3 mm.); Rogers, No. 200; No. 196 is
similar. This mark appears on the brass fixture joining
the glass stem of a lamp to its font. The tooled stem is
similar to those dating forty years earlier, yet the font
is a kerosene type, c. 1865; it may be assumed that the
lamp is a composed piece. Lamps marked with the
metal plate shown in Illus. F do not bear an additional
marking of this type, as far as is known. The mark illustrated here may be a later addition to the lamp.

N. E. GLASS CO. in sans-serif letters etched or engraved
in a rectangle. Illus. N, detail of base of cologne bottle,
c. 1865-1870 (?). Height of rectangle, 3/16 inch (5 mm.),
length 5/8 inch (1.6 cm.); Rogers, No. 210. The
cologne bottle on which this mark appears was illustrated
in an 1869 catalogue of New England Glass Company
pressed glass. This mark may be a later addition.

N

O

New England Glass Co in script, etched or engraved
within a circle. Illus. O, detail of base of overlay bowl,
possibly Czechoslovakian in origin; c. 1865-1870 (?).
Diameter of mark, 9/16 inch (1.4 cm.). This mark occurs
on the polished pontil of a few pieces attributed to the
company; there is no mention of it or of that shown in
Illus. N in the company's books or papers. The vase bearing this mark which was exhibited in the Toledo Museum
of Art show in 1963 (Rogers, No. 37) may be a modern
piece by the H. C. Fry Glass Company of Rochester, New
York.

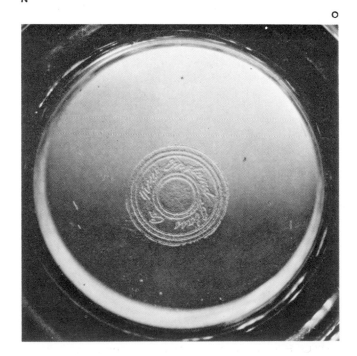

For assistance in obtaining photographs of the objects, and
for helpful suggestions, I am grateful to George Bird and
C. W. Brown of the Henry Ford Museum, Dorothy-Lee Jones,
Richard C. Barret of the Bennington Museum, Paul Perrot
and Kenneth M. Wilson of the Corning Museum of Glass,
A. Christian Revi, L. W. and D. B. Neal, and Paul V. Gardner
of the Smithsonian Institution.

GLASSMAKING IN SOUTH BOSTON

The first part of this article appeared in *Antiques* for September 1945, pages 140-142.
It covers blown wares made at South Boston.

By LURA WOODSIDE WATKINS

THE PHOENIX GLASS WORKS. Patrick F. Slane, who took over the old South Boston glasshouse in 1848, was the first lessee to establish a thriving business there. Something of his work is told in Part I of this article. Slane, William A. Hayes, and Reuben H. Ober were incorporated as the American Glass Company, April 28, 1854. After 1848 the city directories list this company's agency at 13 Doane Street, Boston; from 1854 to 1857 they were at 15 Kilby Street, and a year later back at 17 Doane. Thereafter the firm name disappears, presumably shortly after Slane went out of business. In 1880 a corner of the old Boston Glass Manufactory was still standing, but part of the land had been sold to the railroad.

The fortunes of Thomas Cains ran a smoother course than did those of other South Boston glassmakers. In 1817 he had purchased from Edmund Munroe two lots of land on B Street running down to low-water mark. He had built a house on Second Street and there he continued to live even after he had put up his brick factory in front of it (*Fig. 11*). Later he acquired virtually all the land between B and C Streets from the waterfront to Broadway. Cains's glasshouse was comparatively small, employing only fifteen men, but as business grew he enlarged his building and superseded his first furnace with a ten-pot structure.

According to his son William, Thomas Cains was invited to positions in Sandwich, in Richmond, Virginia, and in New York before he embarked upon his independent career. His decision to run a glasshouse of his own was a wise one. The Phoenix Glass Works, as he called it, naming it perhaps after the Phoenix works in Bristol, where he may have received his training, was able to operate continuously and successfully until 1870. Cains became one of the wealthiest citizens of South Boston. In the mansion house that he later built near the crossing of B and Bolton Streets, he entertained lavishly and enjoyed the fruits of his labor.

William Cains, who was born in South Boston June 24, 1814, went to work in the glasshouse in 1832 and became his father's right-hand man in the enterprise (*Fig. 10*). Also associated with the business and with the family was William Johnston, who married Cains' daughter Susan. He and young Cains ran the factory for about three years after the father retired in 1852. But when Johnston died in 1855, Thomas Cains returned to his furnace and managed the works again until he, too, passed away ten years later. William Cains kept the fires going for five more years. At the time of his retirement his affairs were somewhat involved, and it is evident that the father was the more capable businessman. William Cains lived on for some thirty-five years. He was known as the "grand old man" of South Boston, and, indeed, by virtue of having seen the district grow from a village to a city, he

FIG. 10—WILLIAM CAINS, son of Thomas Cains.

was thoroughly identified with its development.

Recently I acquired a batch of papers — letters, memoranda, circulars, and inventories — relating to the closing of the works. From these I have been able to glean some interesting material as to how the glasshouse was run, and, better still, a fair knowledge of its products at that time.

The Phoenix works ran one ten-pot furnace, each pot of 2,000 pounds capacity, and employed about thirty men and boys (*Fig. 12*). The organization of workers was the usual one — three men and two boys to a shop: the gaffer or blower, one servitor, one footmaker, a "sticker-up" boy, and a "taker-in." There were five of these crews, which, however, required the services of only two footmakers. The other employees were firemen, "slower" men, packers, laborers, a potmaker.

The principal materials were New Jersey sand at $7.00 a ton, lead, and soda ash. St. Louis clay was used for the pots, which cost about forty dollars each to manufacture. Ten tons of this clay lasted for one year to a year and a half. An estimate of the materials consumed in one week includes coal — 18 to 20 tons; sand — about one ton; soda ash — 450 pounds; lead — 600 pounds; cullet — one and one half to two tons; packing hay — one quarter ton. The expense for labor in the same period was between $350 and $400.

To the glass students the most important item in this list is cullet, for it offers definite proof that glasshouses of this period *bought* cullet. The Phoenix Glass Works spent about $300 a month for it. With this fact in mind, we should view with some reserve the evidence of fragments excavated at Sandwich or elsewhere as proof of manufacture there.

Several grades of glass were mixed. Men-

FIG. 11—HOME of Thomas Cains on Second Street, South Boston.

tion is made of "best batch" for the wine shop, soda batch, lime batch. Flint glass was used for lamp chimneys, an important part of the output. A circular published in February, 1870, reads:

> A general complaint from housekeepers of the trouble and expense caused by the brittleness of the glass, has induced us to recommence the manufacture of chimneys.
>
> Our chimneys are made of a superior quality of flint glass.
>
> Each chimney will have Mr. Cains' name pasted on it, and a paper in it, showing that the responsibility for the higher prices asked, rests with the manufacturer and not with the dealer.
>
> We claim that they are less liable to crack than those now in common use.

Sun and *lip* chimneys were produced in large quantities, while *bulb, star, Argand, Ashley,* and *petticoat* were other designations. One type was called the *15th Amendment* chimney. Globes for gas and kerosene lamps, some of them roughed or cut, also appear in the inventory. *Egg blown* and patent *Jenny Lind* lantern globes, the latter with two rings, and saucer, tulip-shaped, or conical shades were other lighting equipment. Three kinds of glass lamps are mentioned: the *Boston Beauty* hand lamp, the *Tom Thumb,* and ring handle.

The blown ware for cutting and decorating seems to have been limited in these closing days of the factory to stem ware, tumblers, lemonade mugs, and nappies. Among these glasses were goblets, wines, champagnes, clarets, and cordials. They were made in shapes such as *Astor, Mitchell, bell, band,* and *straw stem* — terms employed by all glassmakers of the period. Usually they were cut, although engraved leaf goblets are mentioned. Nappies and mugs had star-cut bases.

More easily identified by the average collector is the pressed glass, itemized in a number of familiar patterns. There were complete sets — creamer, covered sugar bowl, spoonholder, and covered butter dish — in the *diamond, grape, leaf,* and *reed and lily* patterns. These sets sold at wholesale for $4.50 to $5.00 per dozen — about ten cents for each piece. The *diamond* pattern also included goblets, salts, and three-inch cup plates. The manufacture of cup plates at this late date may seem strange, but early styles were frequently carried over a long period of years. In the *leaf* pattern, goblets, egg cups, and four-inch nappies (sauce dishes) appear.

A mold known as *split diamond* was utilized for six-inch plates, four- and six-inch nappies, and seven-inch nappies on foot (compotes), with and without covers, for individual salts, and for three-inch cup plates. Four-inch nappies were also made in the *cable* pattern or were sometimes plain with frosted finish.

Various patterns are listed in one form only. The greatest variety is in goblets, which were made in *plaid, huber, crescent, punty and flute,* and *mirror* design, as well as in other simple patterns for bar-room use. Ice cream tumblers are also mentioned. Table salts, salts on foot, and individual salts appear in this list: the first in *punty* pattern; the salts on foot in *diamond, diamond and star,* and *diamond and bead* designs; and the individual containers in *diamond, split diamond; cog wheel, punty,* and *diamond and bead.*

Of the earlier products of Cains's glasshouse we have little information. An advertisement in the *New York Journal of Commerce* in the early spring of 1829 gives a list of glass for sale by "Johnson & Neilson, 46 South Street, Agents of the South Boston Glass Works." Since the old South Boston flint works was unoccupied in 1829, this notice was probably inserted by Cains, and "Johnson" may have been William Johnston, whose name is frequently misprinted with that spelling. The advertisement reads: "Glassware — A complete assortment, consisting of Decanters, Wines, Tumblers, Lamps of various patterns, Salts, Cruets, Castor Bottles, Moulded plates and platters, Specie Jars, Stopper Rounds, Salt Mouths,

Fig. 12—Phoenix Glass Works.

Jewelers Globes, Retorts, Funnels, Breast Pipes, Nipple Shells, Frosting, etc., etc."

THE BOSTON GLASS BOTTLE MANUFACTORY. From the files of the *Boston Commercial Gazette* we learn that there was also a bottle works in South Boston in the early period. The concern was incorporated June 20, 1826 by Charles Wade, Thomas Haskins, and William Underwood "for the purpose of manufacturing bottles and other glass ware." Wade was the owner of a "porter cellar" at 12 Merchant's Row; Haskins was a distiller of cordials on Front Street; and Underwood had a mustard factory on Broadway, South Boston. Bottles evidently played a large part in their vocations. The company advertised its wares as follows September 21, 1826:

Wine and Porter Bottles, Demijohns, Carboys, &c.
For sale, 100 gross Wine Bottles — 100 do. Porter and Cider do. The public are respectfully informed that the South Boston Glass Bottle Manufactory is now in full operation, where they may be supplied with Wine, Porter and Cider Bottles — Demijohns — Carboys, from one to ten gallons. Also, all kinds of Ware, made of black or green glass. Samples of the Bottles and other Glass ware may be seen at Store No. 2, Union-street, where orders will be received.
Cash paid for empty Hampers, Crates, and Broken Bottles.

An advertisement in the *Boston Commercial Gazette,* March 15, 1827, gives a more itemized list of bottles. The flasks mentioned may well have been of the historical variety whose attribution is so often a puzzle to collectors.

BOTTLES
The Boston Glass Bottle Manufacturing Company offer for sale at their Ware House, No. 5 Battery-March-street

350	groce Porter
450	do Wine
150	do Pint Porter
50	do Pint Wine
50	do Quart
50	do Ink
15	do Gallon
10	do 2 Gallon
10	do 3 Gallon
10	do half gallon salt mouth do
8	do quart salt mouth do
50	do pint Flasks
25	do half do
5	do ½ gallon salt mouth, ground stoppers
12	do ½ pound Snuff Bottles
1	do Case Bottles
260	do 5, 7, and 9 gallon Carboys

FIG. 13—SUFFOLK GLASS WORKS.

At their works, South Boston, they now manufacture all kinds of black Glass Bottles, with any stamp or device required, of a quality equal to Bristol Bottles.

Cash paid for hampers and black glass. Orders addressed to John Stimpson, Agt., will receive due attention.

THE MOUNT WASHINGTON GLASS COMPANY. It is well known that the Mount Washington Glass Company had its beginnings in South Boston, that it was built by Deming Jarves and managed by Luther Russell. "Capt." Russell, whose transition from a wharfinger to a glassman seems to have occurred overnight, was first engaged in running a small glassworks near the old South Boston company. The management of this venture appears to have been in the hands of one William Eayrs, whose history defies research, except that he was probably the same William Eayrs who was placed in charge of the short-lived Providence glasshouse. When Jarves in 1837 put up this new factory on the waterfront next door to the Boston company, Eayrs was out of the picture and Russell became Jarves' superintendent.

The Mount Washington Glass Company was organized for the benefit of young George D. Jarves, who was not actively concerned in its operation except perhaps in the salesroom. In 1846 he had joined with John D. Labree under the style *Labree & Jarves*. Labree died very soon after the association was formed. Thereafter, until 1860, Henry D. Cormerais was the other member of the firm.

The history of the Mount Washington company merits more space than can here be given it. It has continued under different firms until the present day. Known until recently as the *Pairpoint Manufacturing Company*, the concern still makes fine glass in New Bedford, Massachusetts.

SUFFOLK GLASS WORKS. The Suffolk Glass Works was in existence for thirty-three years (*Fig. 13*). The Boston Directory first mentions it in 1852 in the list of glass manufactories, with the address "Second Street." Whether the factory building at that time was actually on Second Street or whether the office is indicated is uncertain. The business is usually mentioned in connection with its proprietor, Joshua Jenkins. Throughout the 1850's, however, he is listed as a painter. Not until 1859 does he appear for the first time as the proprietor of the Suffolk Works with offices at 13 Liberty Square, Boston. It is possible that someone else owned or managed the establishment during its initial period; it may even have started in the small glasshouse on Second Street once operated by Luther Russell and William Eayrs. Later on, the factory stood near the foot of Mercer Street, at some distance from the other glasshouses. A description of the glasshouse in 1885 says that it was a large brick structure with "2 cones of 7 pots each."

Joshua Jenkins ran the Suffolk Works without interruption until 1880, when he retired and moved to Scituate. For five years thereafter it was carried on by S. B. Lowland, who had been agent for a time under Jenkins. The buildings, after remaining idle for many years, were burned in 1900.

Jenkins made a general line of ware. In the *Boston Directory* of 1862 he advertised as a manufacturer of "all kinds of Flint-Glass Ware, Blown, Pressed, and Cut. Kerosene and Gas Shades. Rich Cut Table Ware. N. B. Particular attention paid to Kerosene Lamps and Chimneys; also, Druggists' and Chemists' Ware." This advertisement shows a cut of Jenkins's "Tubulated" lamp fount (*Fig. 14*). By his patent, dated September 18, 1860, he secured the rights for blowing a lamp reservoir in such a way that two openings could be made in it, one for the wicks and the other for receiving oil. This was done in one operation.

FRANKLIN GLASS COMPANY. A bill in the possession of Warren C. Lane, dated November 17, 1859, reveals that the Franklin Glass Company manufactured "Plain, Molded, Colored, & Cut Flint Glass-Ware in all its Varieties." As this concern appears only in the 1859 and 1860 directories, it is probable that it represents a brief attempt at revival of the former American Flint Glass Works after Slane's departure.

TREMONT GLASS WORKS. All that we know about the Tremont Glass Works is contained in an advertisement in the Boston Directory of 1860. From this we learn that the factory was at 70 Second Street, South Boston, and that J. M. Cook was the proprietor. He made "Plain, Cut, Pressed and Colored Flint Glass, Gas, Kerosene and Solar Shades, Plain and Rough Chimneys, Homoepathic and Chemical Glass Ware of every description." These articles were for sale by Horace Farrington, Commission merchant, at 87 Kilby Street.

In conclusion it may be of interest to note a few facts gleaned from the *Statistics relating to certain branches of Industry in Massachusetts,* which were published at ten-year intervals. In 1845 there were but two glasshouses in operation in South Boston. Ten years later, when Slane's American Flint Glass Works was in full swing, we see what happened during a business boom. Five hundred and eighty-six men were employed in the three glasshouses, making in one year glass worth $1,190,000. The South Boston glasshouses were actually producing nearly twice as much glass as was being turned out either by the combined New England and Bay State Works in Cambridge or by the two companies at Sandwich. Nine Boston Glass manufactories were in operation in 1865 (all those of which account has been given and four others), but only 332 hands were at work in all of them, with a glass production worth $611,600 annually. After that period the production dwindled. At Cambridge it had increased, giving employment to 653 men and women. The situation at Sandwich, also, had improved, with 590 employees in the two glasshouses.

FIG. 14—ADVERTISEMENT from the *Boston Directory*, 1862, showing Jenkins' patented lamp. Illustrations from *History of South Boston* by John J. Toomey and Edward P. B. Rankin.

The Portland Glass Works

By Martha York Jones

MAINE now qualifies as a member of the family of states known to have possessed old glass works. The Portland Glass Company's pressed tableware may today be collected in authenticated patterns. This will be pleasant news, particularly to the many persons of Maine birth or ancestry who visit New England during the summer and like, when possible, to carry back to their adopted homes worthwhile souvenirs of the Pine Tree State.

Not so early in its inception as the New England works at Cambridge, or the famous Boston and Sandwich Glass factory on Cape Cod, the Portland Glass Works ceased operations in 1873, about fifteen years before the closing of either of the Massachusetts plants. Hence Portland's final products are antecedent to the New England, or Sandwich, or Pittsburgh-district wares of the last half of the 'seventies or the early 'eighties. For instance, they are a little earlier than the patterns brought out for the centennial, of which the *liberty bell*, the *three face*, and the popular *Westward ho* are examples. They are quite a bit older than the New England *amberina*, *pomona*, *agata*, and *peachblow*, and precede the blown, colored, threaded glass made at Sandwich in the early 'eighties.

According to the Portland directory for the year 1869, the Portland Glass Company received its charter in 1863, and, with a capital of $150,000, began making glass in 1864. For nine years it ran at full factory capacity, turning out lamp chimneys as well as pressed-glass tableware in sets, both clear and colored. In 1865, its output is said to have totaled 105,300 pieces. The Company was no less valiant than its rivals in claiming high excellence for its products, thus: "Portland Glass is not inferior to any made in the country and is, indeed, superior to most." Portland patterns, all of which were locally designed, won favor in the principal markets. The sole reason for closing the factory in 1873 was the impossibility of meeting the price competition of glassworks more favorably situated for obtaining fuel supplies and for shipping their output to inland localities.

John B. Brown was the Company's first president, J. S. Palmer its treasurer, and W. C. Davis its superintendent. Its directors were J. B. Brown, Rensellea Cram, Charles E. Jose, George Brock, and Joseph Walker. The works occupied a fine brick building on what is now Commercial Street, very near the old Boston and Maine station at the foot of State Street. It was equipped with the best facilities, and its staff workers originated the designs for the molds, which they made themselves. When the Company discovered that its special designs were being copied, it took measures to secure patents. That a patent was secured, in at least one instance, we know from *tree of life* goblets, spoonholders, and compotes, the bottoms of whose feet are marked *P. G. Co.* with the word *Patented* below. I possess a goblet thus marked. Two unmarked colored pieces of the same pattern I have recently found. One is a six and a half inch plate in light amber; the other, a deep blue finger bowl. I have also seen a green egg cup in *tree of life*, and a light blue dish. There is a yellow color, too; but I have encountered no one who has seen

a piece of Portland glass of any type in any shade of red. Let me say in passing that the patent mark on Portland glass is not readily seen against the elaborate interlacings of the *tree of life* pattern. It is more quickly revealed to touch than to sight.

Both the *tree of life* goblet and the finger bowl have a band of plain, clear, undecorated glass, about three-eighths of an inch wide, around the top. Except for this, the glass is covered with a raised pattern consisting of small, irregular facetings resembling uncut crystals, though perhaps intended to suggest foliage, tucked into the spaces between the endlessly twining branches of the *tree of life*. These branches bear a delicate tracery simulating the bark of a tree. By the casual observer the crystalline elements of the decoration might be mistaken for snakeskin glass. But true snakeskin is really quite different, and is achieved by an entirely distinct process. An undecorated piece of glass, while still hot, is rolled in finely ground particles of glass, which adhere to the soft metal and give a curiously variegated surface. *Tree of life*, on the contrary, received its entire ornament from a mold in which the pattern had been cut.

It may be remarked that the *tree of life* pattern was slightly rearranged after the design had been patented. In order to make room for the patent mark, such of the decoration as had formerly been impressed on the bottom of the base of footed pieces was transferred to the upper side, thus leaving a free surface for an imprint beneath the foot. I recently examined a green egg cup whose decoration appeared on the outside of the bowl and on the under side of the foot, a circumstance that permits classification of the item among the pre-patented pieces. A small, clear-glass berry or honey saucer carries the design on the outside. The patent mark, almost indistinguishable, is in the interior centre.

Other seemingly well-authenticated patterns claimed for the Portland factory are those belonging to the *loop and dart* group. Ruth Webb Lee, in Chapter XVII of her book *Early American Pressed Glass*, remarks: "It would seem that one factory must have had a monopoly of this design; but just why so many similar variants were made is a question." She further remarks that these designs are suggestive of the late 'sixties. This observation accords rather well with the dates of our Portland factory, and with other links in the chain of evidence binding the *loop and dart* to the Maine establishment. Other Portland patterns are the *Roman rosette*, sometimes called *pinwheel*; the *grape, leaves, and buckle*; the *horseshoe*; the *melon*; the *shell and tassel*; and the *shell and jewel*. The *shell and jewel* pattern comes in a fine, very brilliant deep blue, as well as in clear glass. I have seen water sets consisting of a large pitcher and tumblers of this pattern — both in clear glass and in blue. The *shell and jewel* is a very well-authenticated Portland product.

Collectors who wish to see Portland glass will have opportunity to do so at the glass show in Sandwich — if they were not at Plymouth. They will also welcome the information that a good collection of this glass, the gift of Miss M. H. Jewell, is on permanent display at the Harrison Grey Otis House, Cambridge Street, Boston.

Fig. 1 (right) — TREE OF LIFE:
PORTLAND GLASS OF THE 1860's
Sometimes marked *P. G. Co./
Patented.* Probably the earliest
and, in many respects, the best
of Portland designs

Fig. 2 (below) — LOOP AND DART
BOWL, AND ROMAN ROSETTE
PITCHER: HERE ASCRIBED TO
PORTLAND
The *loop and dart* pattern has
many variants. The handle of
the rosette pitcher is of later
type than the off-hand shaped,
crimped handle of the *tree of
life* pitcher

Fig. 3 (below, at left) — SHELL AND JEWEL
PITCHER: HERE ASCRIBED TO PORT-
LAND

Fig. 4 (below, at right) — SHELL AND TAS-
SEL COMPOTE: HERE ASCRIBED TO
PORTLAND
Quadrilateral, with rounded corners.
Another version of this pattern occurs,
in which the items are circular in
horizontal section. The treatment of
the shells recalls the *tree of life* design

*The items illustrated are from the col-
lection of the author*

Fig. 1 — PITTSBURGH GLASS (*1868*)
    Sprig Pattern.
    This and other illustrations are from the Catalogue of M'Kee and Brothers of Pittsburgh, and are facsimiles of the original cuts, errors included.

By No Means Sandwich

Some Examples of Late Pittsburgh Glass

By THE EDITOR

VALUABLE information as to the source and approximate date of manufacture of certain types of pressed glass which, under the general entitlement of *Sandwich*, have been popular with a number of collectors, is discernible in a little brochure which Harold Rugg of Hanover, New Hampshire, has very thoughtfully loaned to ANTIQUES for examination. This brochure is a price list of glassware issued by M'Kee and Brothers, "flint glass manufacturers," of 17 Wood Street, "corner of Wood and First," Pittsburgh, under date of April first, 1868. The work consists of thirty-two pages of woodcut illustrations, and sixteen pages of itemized prices. It was printed by W. S. Haven, whose press was conveniently located at Wood and Third Streets. One "Seymour," whoever he may have been, is credited with the adequate but totally uninspired "engravings."

Besides the usual run of household and hotel glassware, M'Kee and Brothers produced "carbon oil lamps," candlesticks, lanterns for burning either oil or candles, sundries such as toys, shoemakers' globes, butter prints, soap slabs, hyacinth glasses, and apothecaries' shop furniture, including jars, funnels, mortars and pestles, and show globes of various sizes. These last are advertised and pictured as *cone or globe shape*, *pear shape*, and *French style*. They run from two to four stories, or sections, in height, and the large specimens in the French style, when engraved, are priced at $18.00 each.

The price list closes with a note as to terms of sale, which are "net cash, less (blank to be written in) per cent discount, to be paid within ten days from date of invoice." The customer is "at the same time assured" that "there is nothing elegant or extra in Flint Glass Ware, made or furnished in this vicinity, but we make and supply." This is followed by a disclaimer of responsibility for breakage (comforting word) of glass in transit except when special insurance has previously been arranged.

Round Ind. Salt.

Fillmore Salt.

Mason Salt.

Rope Salt.

Tomato Salt.

Imperial Salt.

Fig. 2 — PITTSBURGH GLASS (*1868*)

Vine C. O. Lamp, 5 in. Base.   Stedman C. O. Lamp 5 in. Base.   Prism Lamp, C. O 5 in. Base.   Vine Footed C. O. Lamp.   Shell Footed C. O. Lam

Fig. 3 — PITTSBURGH LAMPS (*1868*)
C.O. stands for *coal oil*.

The most interesting aspect of this catalogue, however, is its pages of pictures with entitlements of the different patterns illustrated. There is, for example, the *sprig* pattern, in dishes, goblets, bowls, "sweetmeats,"* pitchers, "nappies," and so forth. The sprig consists of a somewhat ungainly anthemion, or palmette, displayed against vertical ribbing. One design, in imitation of faceted cut-glass, is given the name *New York*; another, quite similar, is entitled *Cincinnati*. Certain goblets decorated with a kind of bull's-eye pattern are called *mirror* goblets, others, quite appropriately, *argus* goblets. That widely popular pattern which many persons have hitherto inclined to believe might have been derived from a peacock's feather is listed as *comet*; though a typographical error in the catalogue confuses it with the *leaf* pattern.

Collectors who have assiduously gathered items of glass in the well-known *bellflower* design, for table use, will be more or less pleased to learn that this pattern, too, is listed among the multifarious products of M'Kee and Brothers,

in 1868. But in the catalogue it is not identified by the pretty and now popular name of *bellflower*, but by the mysterious initials *R. L.*, the meaning of which has thus far eluded discovery. The letters may, of course, stand for *ribbed leaf*.

In 1868, M'Kee and Brothers were likewise advertising two types of candlesticks which enthusiastic amateurs of glass now look upon as highly valuable members of the Sandwich tribe. These are the *Boston* candlestick, whose name suggests frank borrowing from a Massachusetts source, and the dolphin candlestick, which, though we must all agree that it had no right to be manufactured some hundreds of miles from the seaboard, is here so pictured and labeled as to establish its Pittsburgh affiliations beyond peradventure.

There were, most certainly, other dolphins in other crystal seas than those owned and operated by the enterprising brothers from Pittsburgh. The M'Kee cetacean, it may be remarked, displays one peculiarity which differentiates it from others of the general school. In its extraordinary act of balancing, wherein it emulates Old Father William's feat of posing an eel on the end of his nose, it plants its chin firmly upon a *circular* base instead of upon a *square* one.

Sweetmeats appear to be *covered* bowls of six-inch diameter on a high foot. Items of the same form and size, or smaller, with or without covers, and without foot, are *nappies*. When a sweetmeat adds one or two inches to its diameter, it is listed in the M'Kee catalogue as a *bowl*.

6 in. Comet Sweetmeat and Cover.   6 in. Comet Nappy and Cover.   in. Leaf Nappy and Cover.   7 in. Leaf Sweetmeat and Cover.

Fig. 4 — PITTSBURGH GLASS (*1868*)
Obviously the labels of the first item and the last have been mistakenly transposed. This *comet* pattern is sometimes known as *peacock tail*.

½ gall. R. L. Pitcher.   Qt. R. L. Pitcher.   Qt. Ribbed Pitcher.   ½ pt. Plain Cream.

Fig. 5 — Pittsburgh Glass (*1868*)
The first two pitchers exhibit the so-called bellflower pattern, here designated by the letters *R. L.*

Dolphin and Boston holders, as they are pictured in the Catalogue, are both here reproduced. The prices quoted for them, in 1868, were: for Boston candlesticks, $7.50 per dozen; for dolphins, $6.75 per dozen.

On the same page with the Boston candlestick and the dolphin, appear, among other things, a glass butter print, a three-inch plate — *not indicated as a cup plate* — and a bird bath. On another page — here in part reproduced — appear a number of glass salts of a type which many persons have esteemed as possessing a greater antiquity than inclusion in this catalogue would appear to indicate.

Over the M'Kee line of tumblers, goblets, ale glasses, and beer mugs, it is perhaps well to draw a veil. All the items of glass specifically dedicated to the dispensing of enlivening beverages are, virtually without exception, of a form and pattern which — though extremely simple — yet seem artfully calculated to turn mortal mind to thoughts of thirst. Their comfortable contours invite the clasping hand; the wide circle of their rims suggests potations generously broad as well as comfortingly deep.

The purpose of these notes, however, is not to review in detail the glass of M'Kee and Brothers, of Pittsburgh, but to point to one or two fairly obvious deductions to be drawn from a study of the catalogue issued by these gentlemen. In the first place, we may rest satisfied that many so-called *Sandwich* patterns, if produced in the Cape Cod establishments at all, were certainly not an exclusive spe-

cialty of Jarves and his associates. On the whole, it seems probable that, at various times, the same, or similar, patterns were turned out by a number of unrelated and widely scattered concerns, which either copied each other's successful designs, or else purchased their molds from mold-makers who impartially supplied all their clients with the same thing.

Again, the actual age of the various patterns pictured may not fairly be judged by the fact of their publication in an 1868 catalogue. Some of these patterns were, no doubt, novelties which made their début among the iron-clad engravings of Seymour. Others may have been in use for a generation or more — indeed from the beginning of the pressed glass period in the 1830's; for, whatever of antiquity the firm of M'Kee may have boasted, there were probably luckless predecessors from whom the concern inherited many varieties of both patterns and molds.

The vagaries of design in glass hollow-ware have always been such as to render hazardous any attempt to determine dates of individual pieces on the sole basis of stylistic peculiarity. What in earlier times was confusion develops into sheer chaos during the mid-nineteenth century. Hence we are safe in assuming only that the designs pictured in the M'Kee catalogue under consideration were more or less popular as late as the year 1868. As to their previous status and subsequent fate, no present means of knowing is available.

Boston Candlestick.   Butter Print.   3 in. Diamond Plate.   Bird Bath.   Dolphin Candlestick.

Fig. 6 — Pittsburgh Glass (*1868*)
Here are two familiar candlesticks to prove the wide prevalence of Sandwich types.

PITTSBURGH PRESSED GLASS, I

By LOWELL INNES

In Antiques *for December and January Mr. Innes, honorary curator of glass at Carnegie Museum in Pittsburgh, published articles based on the first large exhibition of Pittsburgh glass ever held, which he had organized for the Historical Society of Western Pennsylvania in 1947. This year he has staged a far more comprehensive exhibition of the locally made glass at Carnegie Museum. Opened in April, it is being kept on view, by popular demand, until November. For the excellent catalogue of this exhibition* Antiques *released some material by Mr. Innes which was already in manuscript in our files. This manuscript, with new additions, is now presented here, and illustrated by courtesy of Carnegie Museum with pieces shown in the exhibition. We shall publish shortly a further article by Mr. Innes, on the pattern glass of the Pittsburgh district.*

—THE EDITOR

WHEN THE COMPLETE STORY of American pressed glass is written, we shall undoubtedly read that the factories of Pittsburgh produced contemporaneously the cycles of pressed glass hitherto attributed only to the eastern seaboard. For instance, John P. Bakewell, Jr., actually held the first American patent for pressing of glass knobs, 1825. Several indentures of the early 1830's support the evidence. One in particular shows the interweaving of glass families in the trade. An indenture of Robert Bryce, aged fifteen years, eight months, and twelve days, to Benjamin, Thomas, and J. P. Bakewell, Jr., and John Palmer Pears states that young Bryce will be taught in the best manner they can "the art and mystery of a Glass Blower and Presser." That document, dated December 26, 1836, indicates that pressing glass in Pittsburgh had been well under way in the early thirties. Wheeling also, at the southern boundary of the Pittsburgh district, in the same decade had several firms advertising pressed glass: Ritchie and Wilson, Plunkett and Miller, and the Sweeneys. So the tri-state district formed an attractive center for experienced glassmen.

Although marked Pittsburgh pieces like the J. & T. Robinson plates and boat-shaped salts and the Curling creamer and Fort Pitt eagle cup plates advertise the district, most convincing evidence of its supremacy lay in the presence of many flourishing moldmakers' establishments. In 1860 the capital value of five metal mold works was $285,000, the value of raw material alone was $105,211, and these works employed 334 male workers. Not all of these were skilled mold designers and cutters. The Joseph D. Weeks' 1880 *Report on Glass Manufacture* numbers moldmakers at 120 with daily pay running from $1.50 to $6.00. Factories like Bakewell's or Lorenz and Wightman contained their own moldmaking establishments within their plants. Besides, there were always itinerant journeymen moldmakers.

Washington (Wash) Beck, to whom Mrs. Knittle paid tribute in *Early American Glass,* was the most famous and enterprising of all the moldmakers, known at home and abroad. For twenty years his factory, possibly the largest establishment of its kind in the United States, flourished and prospered. Other men also deserve notice. Andrew Thompson, born in Ireland in 1818, took over the A. J. Miller & Co. machine shop in 1849, two years after it had been founded. By 1880 his building at 90 Eighth Street, South Side, compared favorably in size and equipment with Beck's. It was said to be "the first establishment in Pittsburgh devoted to the manufacture of flint and green glass molds, presses, and light machinery and mechanical appliances for the production of glassware." Certainly one 12-horse-power engine was not to be sneered at even in 1880. Robert M. Jones, who worked a number of years as pattern-maker at the Fort Pitt Works, went into patterns for castings and models of every description. The Birmingham Foundry and Machine Shop of George Fisher and Peter Wentzel advertised in *Industries of Pennsylvania* (Richard Edwards, Ed. & Pub., 1879): "They take

FIG. 1—EARLY PRESSED COMPOTES with blown bases, and cobalt dish. Stars, ribs, and diamonds were favorite early geometric patterns.

FIG. 2—MIDWESTERN LACY, showing characteristic patterns of the Pittsburgh district.

special pride in their ability for turning out machinery and castings adapted for glass works." Their annual $30,000 business even in depression years when low prices were prevalent employed eighteen skilled workers. *And the product was bought almost entirely in Pittsburgh!*

Molds and statistics seem much less exciting and alive than a well-designed, sparkling piece of early pressed glass. We should remember, however, that pressing by mechanical means in metal molds is largely an American invention, and that the improvements between 1870 and 1880 enabled manufacturers to turn out a finished product which would belie the faults of the early mold. New pieces could be fire-polished, could be designed with sharp angles like cut glass, could be removed from the mold with spring snaps, could have the mold marks almost obliterated. When one recalls that the whole country imported about $38,000 worth of pressed glass, while Pittsburgh alone in 1878 was exporting over $860,000 worth, he will realize that production was tremendous. Weeks' *Report* of 1880 tabulates Pennsylvania as leading all the other states in production of pressed ware (called in his catalogue "glassware") at 51% of the total. New York is second with 12.10% and Massachusetts a weak seventh with 7.3%. Of producing localities Allegheny County (Pittsburgh) was out in front with 26.79%. Certainly in quantity Pittsburgh led the field.

As to quality the debate is still raging. It is pleasant now, however, to have a friend return from California with two handsome goblets purchased at twice our local price. "Why did you pay so much?" we asked. She said that she had demurred but that when she had actually complained the dealer announced triumphantly, "Oh, but these are Pittsburgh!"

Midwestern Lacy

Any showing or discussion of lacy glass is provocative because the origins are still in doubt. Today most students can recognize the sophistication, the classic designs, the clarity and brilliance, and the redundance of Baccarat decoration. American collectors still argue bitterly as to whether most of our lacy is Sandwich or midwestern. It is too bad everyone interested cannot see two authentic Sandwich pieces set amidst thirty-odd midwestern lacy pieces, all showing well against a background of dark green velvet. The general differences between the two types of American lacy are these: the Sandwich product is more brilliant, the stippling finer, the metal clearer, the designs more sophisticated. Yet those generalizations often break down.

In addition to the four pieces illustrated in Figure 2 there were three bowls (two *princess feather* with lifeless stippling) and one of soda-lime metal such as appears in McKearin's Plate 144, Figure 2. The small open compote in our Figure 2, with arrowhead design and the circled rim, one of a pair, was originally presented to a minister of the German Lutheran church on the South Side of Pittsburgh in the early fifties. Possibly these pieces were made at the Bakewell factory after it moved from the early location in the city proper following the fire of 1845. The plate beside it in Figure 2 was duplicated except that the outer rim on the second plate carried no circles, only the ordinary scalloped edge. The plate at far right in Figure 2, also one of a pair, exemplifies well the early combination of simple geometric patterns with an unadorned arch. The rim is a popular one on larger plates and compotes of our locality.

Easily the finest workmanship and most brilliant stippling were revealed by a rare *eagle* toddy plate resting on extended acanthus leaves, illustrated in Figure 3 on the following page (lower left), and also by McKearin (Plate 142, Figure 3). It seems so much more vital than the other pieces in sparkle and so much more elaborately designed that one immediately thinks of lacy Sandwich. With little chance of documentary authentication the student asks two questions: If the *eagle* plate is midwestern, as Mr. McKearin thinks, can it be that Pittsburgh paralleled Sandwich in the production of lacy? If it is midwestern, can it be that only a limited amount of first-quality lacy was made here? Mr. McKearin has owned this *eagle* plate in all three sizes, he tells me, but considers the 7-inch octagonal one the most important and characteristically midwestern.

About two weeks before the exhibition opened, the plate shown at upper right of this same illustration was discovered. Though the pattern has not yet been identified, the center design and rays are reminiscent of Pittsburgh-district cup plates. The border scroll, the circular edge, and the eight circles at the corners, each impressed on the under side with a star, mark the new find as typical of the midwest. The

Fig. 3.—MIDWESTERN LACY GLASS. (*Upper right*), brilliant octagonal plate in an unknown pattern, recently discovered; (*lower left*), *eagle* plate, illustrated by McKearin; other examples of unknown origin, showing coarse stippling and bold design.

metal is unusually heavy and clear and though the stippling may seem coarse, the piece has a great deal of brilliance. The specimen in the same figure, upper left, furnishes an admirable contrast—a much later piece with obviously bold circles and arches and decadent design. Like many midwestern plates it rests on a series of dots (eight in this case). But the metal, undoubtedly with the lead content decreased, is dull compared to that of the one on the right. The illustration makes a nice comparison between two pieces typical of one area yet of different times.

Certainly the sound generalizations made by James H. Rose and George S. McKearin are borne out by the examples illustrated: coarser and smoother stippling, sometimes even to the point of dullness; bold and coarse designs, the frequent use of circles in the body of the piece, in the rim, and even as

supporting feet; rather stiff conventionalized scrolls and figures such as the acanthus; serrations on the rims (Figures 2 and 3 give a good idea of adequately usual types); metal that was often heavy with the lead content steadily decreasing. The very weaknesses of midwestern lacy, however, give it a virility and individuality which bespeak pioneer life and clearly remove us from Baccarat (French) influence, often confusing to collectors of lacy Sandwich.

Cup Plates

Through the scholarly work of James H. Rose and Mrs. Ruth Webb Lee in their *American Glass Cup Plates*, it is apparent that Pittsburgh and the midwest produced generously. Nevertheless, probably neither Mr. Rose nor Mr. Marble, who compiled the first list of cup plates, would unequivocally name more than fifteen plates that could be assigned with certainty to Pittsburgh itself. For the exhibition we were content to display those that characterized the district, and in general mirrored the designs and patterns popular in midwestern glass.

Naturally two variations of the *Fort Pitt eagle* were shown: one with the smooth rim decorated with the twenty-four bull's eyes, the other with the attractive ridges running toward the border and with serrated edges minimizing the

Fig. 4—SUGAR BOWLS. (*Left to right*), cobalt pressed; opaque white Ihmsen (*1851*); blown, deep pink lined with opaque white.

170

prises from 1807 to his death in 1828. Christian took over his father's interests then, had his own factory by 1850, and in 1851 conceived the idea of trying papier-mâché and wooden molds. Not being certain of success, he planned an advertising venture: a sugar bowl that would illustrate in the design of its side panels forms and patterns produced by the Ihmsens. Thus we know that the Ihmsens made *excelsior* as did McKee; made *flute* and *Ashburton* as did Bakewell. The inside of the lid has smaller figures impressed: an *excelsior* footed tumbler with a handle, a champagne and a goblet in *flute,* and odd pieces of *excelsior.* (See ANTIQUES, August 1938.)

importance of the eyes. These well-known plates were manufactured by R. B. Curling & Sons in the 1830's. Other eagles were Rose #670, 675A, and 677. Allied to this group the popular *liberty torch* (Rose #158) and the octagonal *steamboat* (Rose #612A) seems to strike a pioneering note. Though much later, the *anchor* (Rose #693) belongs to the same decorative scheme.

The emotion of recognition is stirred pleasantly in looking at most of the cup plates. The conventionals with wide scallops, point serration, shells, and circles, making use of the stiff scroll designs, employed the same devices incorporated in larger pieces. Most of them have what Mr. Rose calls "a clothlike stippling." His #124A, 136, 150, 165, 183B, 253, and 262 give a true picture of what the west liked and was making. Yet #203 assigned by Mr. Rose to Pittsburgh might be called a Sandwich piece by many dealers and new collectors. A problematical plate (#341), the clear seven-sided one, cannot be attributed on the basis of either distribution or manufacture. An intriguing theory that Bakewell made it is based on its likeness to a famous large plate divided into twelve looped and arched sections very similar to those on the cup plate. It is amazing to anyone studying Mrs. Lee's and Mr. Rose's new book to realize how important and prolific the midwest and Pittsburgh really were in cup-plate production.

Marked Pieces

No American glass district has furnished many marked pieces except the nineteenth-century historical and decorated flasks. From Pittsburgh, two marked plates and a cobalt blue boat-shaped salt dish by J. & T. Robinson are shown. Strictly speaking, the magnificent milk-glass Ihmsen sugar bowl is not a marked piece, but it is as good as marked, since it was devised as a means of factory advertisement and identification. Charles Ihmsen, the father of Christian, had worked in Pittsburgh glass enter-

Another striking bowl is the low open compote of two colors, fiery opal and clear (*Fig. 5*). Under the apron at the base is printed: *B. P. & Co. Pat. Sept. 29, 1874* (Bakewell Pears & Co.). This patent number 155,403 drawn by Bakewell & Kerr, attorneys, was issued to Benjamin Bakewell, Jr., who claimed the following: "As an improvement in the method of forming glass articles of two or more colors, pressing one color upon another successively by means of interchangeable plungers and rings or molds, substantially as and for the purpose specified." In the diagram from the U. S. Patent Office the article pictured is a footed tumbler called *double bouquet.* Apparently, however, the process was not too easy to carry out or else the style did not appeal to the public, for such specimens seem exceedingly rare. An obvious technical difficulty was to have the welding heat for all the subsequent operations constant. A two-part mold was used. George McKearin owns a two-color goblet which he attributes to Ihmsen (McKearin, Plate 58, Figure 2). In the Pittsburgh exhibition two goblets of milk white and clear are shown.

Rather coincidentally, two milk-white marked Atterbury ducks also exemplify the use of double color: one has a blue head and neck; the other has amethyst. These large ducks, often called Sandwich in the east, were patented on March 15, 1887, by Thomas Bakewell Atterbury, president of the Atterbury Glass Company at Carson and Tenth Streets, South Side. It was called *Design for a Dish, Patent No. 17,192* and represents another very popular piece of old Pittsburgh glass.

To be Concluded

FIG. 6—MILK GLASS ITEMS, including rare boar's-head covered dish and two Atterbury ducks with amethyst and blue heads.

PITTSBURGH PRESSED GLASS, II

By LOWELL INNES

In this discussion of the pattern glass of Pittsburgh Mr. Innes concludes his series of articles (December 1948, January, and September 1949). The exhibition at Carnegie Museum, from which many of the illustrations were drawn, has been extended by popular demand to January 1. This exhibition, staged by Mr. Innes as honorary curator of glass, has focussed attention as never before on the glassmaking activities of Pittsburgh.

THE PRESENT large and comprehensive exhibition at Carnegie Museum emphasizes Pittsburgh's contribution to American pattern glass. Though only 450 of the 890 specimens in the exhibition are pressed, it would be a simple matter to fill the Museum. One local collector, for instance, has over four hundred pieces of *Argus* (Bakewell's *thumbprint*); another has several hundred pitchers of different pressed designs. The amount of pressed ware is evidenced not only in statistics from *Weeks' Report on Glass Manufacture in the United States 1880* but also in the concentration of factories in the Pittsburgh area. Between 1830 and 1870 at least fourteen pressed-glass establishments were operating, with a yearly average of three thousand workmen, the capital value of all being better than one million and a half. Annually, from 1848 to 1872, thirty-two thousand tons of pressed tableware at Pittsburgh would be a conservative average. More than 50 per cent of the output was packaged west, the remainder going east to compete directly with the wares of some of the famous-name factories.

Not long after Sandwich and the New England Glass Company had closed their doors, the United States Glass Company formed the greatest combine in glass manufacturing history. In 1891 it joined twelve factories from the Pittsburgh-Wheeling district to six from Ohio. The shifting of the center of influence from east to west had definitely taken place before the merger. The pioneering spirit which encouraged research in a project like Leighton's lime-soda formula of 1864 is shown by the fact that John Adams of Adams, Macklin & Company, Pittsburgh, had been experimenting along the same lines in the 1850's. Though Leighton at Wheeling deserves the final credit

ARGUS, OR THUMBPRINT, by Bakewell, Pears and Company (*1836-1882*), noted in a family catalogue by Thomas Pears as one of the earliest and most popular patterns. On view in the case is a bill of sale: Pittsburgh, 1863, from Henry Higbee, Importer and Dealer in China & Glass and Queensware, 122 Wood St., to Calvin Adams for a 7-inch *Argus* footed saucer at 45 cents. The popularity of *thumbprint* with its adaptations (*diamond, almond, Victoria,* and the New England rival, *punty*) continued through the 1870's. A late edition put out by the United States Glass Company after 1891 has smaller "prints" and decidedly inferior metal.

for having perfected the formula, Pittsburgh men had been trying contemporaneously with a degree of success.

Besides the appeal of experiment and innovation, manufacturers found the proximity of basic materials and cheap fuels desirable. Western labor also was inclined to be more reasonable. Finally, rail and river transportation could effect any market distribution needed on a sound competitive basis. These hidden factors appear in the number of pieces and patterns and in the variety of wares in this show.

The line of demarcation between eastern and western pressed glass can never be clearly drawn. The best example of the interdependence of glassworkers and companies is the case of William O. Davis, an experienced foreman in the employ of J. B. Lyon and Company at the O'Hara factory in Pittsburgh. In 1854 he was credited with a patent for a press for molding glass. Nine years later he patented another improvement in glass presses. In 1868 he was put in complete charge of the newly formed glass company at Portland, Maine. While Davis was directing this enterprise, he designed the popular *tree of life* pattern, working his own name into the tree and branches. Sandwich soon adopted this pattern. In 1873, after the Portland enterprise folded and Davis returned to Pittsburgh, George Duncan and Sons, later the Duncan Miller enterprise of Washington, Pennsylvania, produced *tree of life* and *shell and tassel,* another popular pattern of the Portland Glass Company. Admittedly, the Duncan *tree of life* is heavier than that of either Sandwich or

BELLFLOWER. Established as a Pittsburgh pattern by a Bryce, McKee catalogue of 1868, but the design probably originated at Sandwich in the 1830's. Among variations acquired over the years are fine or coarse ribs, single or double vines, scalloped, beaded, or plain rims, ribbing extended to the edge or stopped by a plain band, plain or knobbed stems of hollow pieces, and differences in base patterns.

SAWTOOTH. Several pieces are pictured in a McKee catalogue of 1868, but the pattern can be assigned to no single factory. That it is an early one was evidenced a few years ago when a pair of wines was found with the pontil ground out. It was made at several eastern factories as well as in Pittsburgh.

over Ripley and Company in 1874 the idea of incorporating a woman's face in the stem of pressed ware resulted in the selection of Elizabeth Blair of Steubenville, Ohio, as a model. Miss Blair (Mrs. Ernest Miller, 1847-1943) stated that she posed when twenty-eight. Rumor has held that *three face* won a prize at the Centennial Exhibition in 1876, but facts cloud the picture. The Free Library of Philadelphia, in studying the *International Exhibition, 1876, Reports and Awards* (J. B. Lippincott & Co., 1878) found no specific mention of *three face* among the Duncan wares, nor was this pattern registered at the patent office until 1878.

This phase of decoration called into play other devices: frosting, engraving, and the wide use of color. *Wildflower* exemplifies well the popular colors used. Often a simple pattern like Bakewell's *prism* would be elaborated by engraving. The final period of western, or should we say American, design was marked by a return to the classical figures—*plume, thousand eye, ribbon candy*—a return made decadent by heaviness and over-ornamentation as in *moon and star (palace)*. A disturbing fact is that there are few large sets of the plain and early patterns in private collections, yet sets in the naturalistic and decadent patterns are numerous. A weakness in American taste may be repeating itself today.

Obviously the Pittsburgh district produced so many patterns that no exhibition could show them all. Each of the patterns illustrated here, and discussed in the accompanying captions, is given a whole case, and so also are *wildflower, three face, deer and pine,* and *shell and tassel*.

No Pittsburgh exhibit would be complete without *wildflower*, largely because the midwest promoted naturalistic designs. The pleasant blue pieces in our display are a credit to the business acumen of John Adams, who had worked for Bakewell, Pears & Company in the forties and formed the first partnership in 1851 with Macklin. By 1861, when this firm became Adams & Company, the plant covered two acres

Portland, yet the pattern is similar enough to confuse the inexperienced. One authority believes that the McKees also made *tree of life*.

A series of comparison pieces in the exhibition included *tree of life* from Portland, Sandwich, and Pittsburgh; *sawtooth* in the fine diamonds of the New England Glass Company, the medium-sized and coarse ones from Sandwich and Pittsburgh; *plume* from Sandwich and from Adams and Company of Pittsburgh; *bellflower* in the coarser ribbing often attributed to McKee as well as the conventional Sandwich; and even such identical patterns as *loop* (Sandwich) and *leaf* (McKee, Pittsburgh). The adaptation of patterns and the close relationship brought on by competition are typical of our American system.

A point of great interest to students of pressed glass, in addition to the relationship of patterns, is the popularity of certain design forms. Glass mirrored taste. The earliest patterns of the thirties and forties (*Argus, colonial, Ashburton*) were spare in ornament and followed the simplest geometric figures. Though Sandwich temporarily loosed the Baccarat lacy influence, most of its ornateness persisted in cup plates and tea plates rather than in pattern glass, *princess feather (Rochelle)* being one of the few lacy patterns which lasted. *Horn of plenty* and *arabesque* represent more practical adaptations of the lacy, for the intricacies and the costliness of molds forbade too frequent change. Therefore, except for commemorative patterns, design went from plain geometric figures to ornamented ones representing a combination like *tulip and sawtooth*.

Then a new lime-soda formula effected a cheapness of production and a lowering of quality in resonance, weight, and brilliance. It allowed more money to be spent on molds and increased the number of patterns. To offset limitations of poor quality, Pittsburgh went in for naturalistic motifs.

About the time George Duncan took

THOUSAND EYE. In the 1870's and 1880's this was made in quantity by Adams and Company of Pittsburgh in two varieties, plain with knobbed finials or stems, and with the fan; and by Richards and Hartley of Tarentum, with scalloped edges. Colors include amber, canary, blue, and apple green.

PRESSED PITCHERS in popular Pittsburgh patterns. (*Top row*), *Rochelle* (*princess feather*), Bakewell, Pears and Company; *tree of life*, George Duncan and Sons; *tulip*, Bryce, Richards; *cherry*, Bakewell, Pears and Company. (*Bottom row*), *Ashburton*, several firms; *ribbed palm*, McKee; *Stedman*, McKee; *almond thumbprint*, Bakewell, Pears and Company.

and had all the necessary machinery and appliances for huge-scale operations. It achieved a weekly payroll of better than $2,000, a yearly volume of better than $200,000, and markets in Cuba and South America, too. Probably because Adams himself had been one of the pioneers in helping to develop the lime-soda formula, the firm's glass retained an attractive clarity even through the late years of the century. In addition to tableware, Adams & Company made lamps, chimneys, and bottles. Finally it was absorbed by the United States Glass Company. *Baltimore pear,* another naturalistic Adams pattern, runs a good second to *wildflower* in popularity.

We planned two small cases of pitchers and one of miscellaneous pieces. Old-favorite pitchers like *Stedman* (McKee), *almond thumbprint* (Bakewell), *Jacob's ladder* (Bryce), *stippled grape and festoon* (Doyle), *maple leaf vaseline* (Gillinder), *Baltimore pear* (Adams), and *wheat and barley*

(Bryce, Walker) covered a range of time and taste. Among the odd pieces a few that stood out were *excelsior* candlesticks, *Rebecca at the well* frosted compotes, *pillar* variant pieces and bowls in *loop* (or *leaf*, to use the Pittsburgh name), a good amethyst paneled salt, a *honeycomb* celery worthy of New York state, *colonial* and *Ashburton* tumblers, and a McKee *colonial* covered sweetmeat in cobalt.

It seems anticlimatic to close a discussion of Pittsburgh glass with miscellaneous pieces and the decadent patterns of the nineties. The only way for any student or collector to gain a rounded picture of the variety of products, the skill of workmanship, and the soundness of design is to visit the exhibition at Carnegie Museum. No other American glass center can equal the continuous time of operation from 1797 to the present and the amount of glass produced, or can show greater versatility in its craftsmanship and wares.

PLUME, by Adams and Company (*1874-1890*). Often used as premiums by merchandising firms. This pattern, like its fellow *moon and star*, was continued by the United States Glass Company. *Moon and star*, more widely known, possessed a dignified heaviness of design, useful as a table set and appealing enough to modern collectors to be reproduced.

Pittsburgh white and clear and the Bakewell patent

BY LOWELL INNES

THE USE OF WHITE AND CLEAR glass together may be traced throughout the history of glassmaking. Loops, dragging, marvering of white in a matrix of another color were techniques popular in earliest times around the Mediterranean. The combination has long appealed to glassmakers as dramatic, and the Venetians particularly employed it widely and successfully.

All the glass made by these early techniques was, of course, free blown and hand manipulated. American examples in the white and clear group include blown clear glass pieces with white loopings, as well as cased articles such as the blown sugar bowl of about 1835 in Figure 1 and the mid-century pillar-molded vase in Figure 2. Figure 3 shows another type, a pressed white vase on a clear blown foot; and Figure 4 still another, a clear goblet blown into a pressed base.

It remained for Benjamin Bakewell Jr., of the famous Pittsburgh glass firm which bore the Bakewell name from 1808 until 1882, to devise and patent a mechanical technique of pressing together glass of two different colors. In this process neither layer envelops the other, as in cased glass; the two colors join only at the contact surfaces. (Apsley Pellat in his *Curiosities of Glassmaking* describes clearly the steps in casing glass. The gaffer blows a bubble of the lining color; at the same time his assistant prepares one of the next color layer, opening the end of his bubble, or parison, and widening it almost like a bowl. To steady and to shape it, the assistant may insert it into a metal shell or he may merely rest it on the shell. Now the gaffer blows his lining bubble into the bowl-like aperture, and the two layers of glass adhere. Perfect fusion is accomplished by reheating in the glory hole, and the cased bubble is then worked into its final form. This process can be repeated for three or more colors.)

To quote from the patent itself (it was applied for on July 18, 1874, and is dated September 29 of the same year):

My invention consists in the manufacture of glass articles by pressing glass of different colors, one upon or above another, in a mold or molds, so as to form an article made up of two or more colors . . . by means of interchangeable plungers and rings or molds . . .

The patent drawing shown here (Fig. 5) does more to clarify the process, perhaps, than the long and involved description contained in the patent application itself.

At the close of this technical description Bakewell adds: "I am aware that bas-relief glass-work has been united to the outer surface of blown glassware by first pressing articles of bas-relief, and then blowing a glass article so as to unite therewith, and do not claim such a

Fig. 1. Free-blown sugar bowl, milk-white with clear casing; Pittsburgh type, c. 1835; over-all height, 7½ inches. *Except as noted, illustrations are from the author's collection.*

Fig. 2. Pittsburgh pillar-molded vase in white with clear casing, on clear blown base; c. 1850; height 10⅜ inches.

process"—a remark which sheds an interesting light on a well-known piece of white and clear glass, the Ihmsen goblet now at the Corning Museum of Glass (Fig. 4, here, and Plate 68, McKearin, *Two Hundred Years of American Blown Glass*). Frederick Carder, the noted glass technologist and founder of the original Steuben Glass Works, says that the Ihmsen goblet was produced in exactly this way; the process described, he says, is one that he himself used over many years.

In spite of the ingenuity of Bakewell's new method, the very scarcity of surviving specimens in double glass, as the pressed white and clear was called, shows that the new product did not "catch on." In the Bakewell and Pears catalogue of 1876 only four pieces are pictured, on page 47: three fruit bowls identical in design but of different sizes (Fig. 8, here, and Revi, *Nineteenth Century*

Glass, p. 154) and the footed tumbler (Fig. 6) which the catalogue calls a Boquet and which is also shown on the patent drawing. Only one other piece, the goblet with swirled stem shown in Figure 7, is known. The white portions of these five pieces of double glass are all formed of a definitely fiery opal except for that of Figure 7, which is of opaque white with only the faintest of opal shadings on the edge of the bottom rim.

Whether the fiery opal texture, which had appeared intermittently in American glassmaking without ever paying its way, made the cost of the new glass prohibitive I would not venture to guess. We do know, however, that until the formula for cheap "milk" glass was developed toward the end of the century, fiery opal never became a major product of one factory or swept the market as a separate fashion.

The few surviving pieces made by the Bakewell patent of 1874 have an undoubted charm of their own, but to anyone with a knowledge of other forms of white and clear glass it is plain that the artistic possibilities of this combination were better realized by craftsmen of the old world and by individual artisans in the new than they could ever have been by Mr. Bakewell's "new and useful Improvement."

Fig. 3. Pittsburgh vase with fiery opal pressed top and clear blown base, c. 1850; height 8⅜ inches.

Fig. 4. Goblet with clear top blown on opaque white pressed base; attributed to Ihmsen Glass Works, Pittsburgh; c. 1850. *Corning Museum of Glass.*

Fig. 5. Diagrams forming part of the Letters Patent of Benjamin Bakewell Jr. dated Sept. 29, 1874: "Figure 1 is a vertical section of the mold and the plunger and ring first used therewith. Fig. 2 is a like view of the mold with the second plunger and ring used therewith, and Fig. 3 is a view of the article formed by the mold and plungers shown."

Fig. 6. Double glass "Boquet" tumble clear on fiery opal pressed glass; Bakewell, c. 1875; height 4½ inches.

Fig. 7. "Double glass" goble clear and opaque white pressed glass Bakewell, c. 1875; height 6 inche

Fig. 8. Double glass open fruit or salad bowl of clear and fiery opal pressed glass; marked B.P. & Co. Pat. Sept. 29th 1874; height 3⅝ inches.

THE BAKEWELL GLASS FACTORY

By MARY E. BAKEWELL

BENJAMIN BAKEWELL by
James R. Lambdin.
*Courtesy of Mrs. T. H.
B. McKnight.*

This article was written by the great-granddaughter of Benjamin Bakewell, the pioneer glassmaker of the Pittsburgh area. It was first published in Carnegie Magazine, *Pittsburgh, for July 1947, and is here reprinted by special permission. Lack of space prevents inclusion of Mrs. Bakewell's recollections of a childhood visit to the glasshouse — "a Crystal Abode of the Fairies."*

A DAMNING adjective was applied to Pittsburgh by the recent writer who spoke of "the disconsolate Monongahela." One must admit that the term might be deserved for certain aspects of the city: begrimed, incomplete, really inchoate — begun, but not yet finished and realized.

Yet some hundred and thirty years ago, to a newcome young Englishman, it doubtless seemed all of Utopia. For here were green hills, full-flowing rivers, a new settlement with opportunity at every hand; here he found the stuff of which life weaves good patterns.

Benjamin Bakewell was born at Derby, England, in 1767, the son of Joseph and Sarah Woodhouse Bakewell. Married in young manhood to Anne White, for support of her and their future family he became an importer of French goods. Through his constant expeditions across the Channel young Bakewell received a wide education, not only in another language but in another history, another culture than his own — in architecture, beautiful objects in church, museum, shops, in men and women different from those he knew and yet much the same. Furthermore, since he was to become a Liberal in outlook, it is interesting to note that he was a spectator of the French Revolution. Thereafter came the grim chapter of war between France and England — and the business of importation was ended.

In 1794 Benjamin Bakewell with his wife and children set sail for that new and promising country of the United States of America, to which many English eyes had turned. He established his family in New York City and started his old business of importing, but with little success, for the French and English war had effect even upon this far land, and when President Thomas Jefferson laid a stern embargo upon all foreign trade, importation died.

Why or how my great-grandfather's attention was drawn to glass manufacture has not been ascertained. England had known glass since the end of the first century A.D. With his intelligence and esthetic sense well developed it is reasonable to think that he may have mulled over certain ideas. Practically considered, Pittsburgh, ideally situated on navigable rivers, was in strategic position for any manufacturing. The art of glassmaking was older than history; a factory was at hand. Mr. Bakewell was an astute business man and grasped the possibilities. More than that, he had appreciation of beautiful things. Why not produce glass, then, in this new country just emerged from the wilderness? Records are few, but we have the information that, in 1808, a small glass plant in Pittsburgh, Pennsylvania, was purchased by Benjamin Bakewell from the firm of Robinson and Ensell, unsuccessful operators. The factory was located at the foot of Grant Street on the bank of the Monongahela River.

Over those almost impassable mountains, then, came his wife and children, the loyal housekeeper, and the "bound boy," the long journey made in what must have been a variety of the Conestoga wagon. After life in London — think of it, so to settle on the frontier. Pittsburgh had been a lonely outpost against a savage wilderness, a collection of rude log cabins surrounded by a stockade. In 1794 the little town had barely one hundred and fifty houses and, though by 1808 these had become frame or brick, even so, civilization was not far advanced.

Difficulties abounded for the mother of the family, not only in household supplies but in the matter of watching the children with the fear of Indians not yet driven from her mind. There were difficulties for the man in charge of family and business. Construction of the factory was poor; each glasshouse must have specially built furnaces to receive the melting pots of fire clay, in which was placed the combined ingredients — the sand, the potash, oxide of lead, sometimes saltpeter, and so on — to be fused in the ovens; materials were poor and costly and had to be transported by long distance on wagons or barges — pearl ash and red lead might come from Philadelphia, pot clay from New Jersey, white sand from Missouri; skilled workmen had to be brought in from considerable distance. The occasion was "piled with difficulty." For Benjamin Bakewell, it was to rise to the occasion.

Pittsburgh, however, grew with amazing speed. Not only were houses multiplied, but many of them became mansions whose architects were rightly proud. Niceties of existence began to be evident. The little town could boast of a post office, a canal, a stagecoach route providing a mere four days' trip to Philadelphia. Trade and commerce began to flourish.

For the Bakewell glasshouse the difficulties were gradually

PAIR OF PRESSED-GLASS COMPOTES with *Rebecca at the well* base. One is owned by Mrs. Douglas Stewart and the other by Henry King Siebeneck. COVERED SUGAR BOWL pressed in *Argus* pattern now known as *thumbprint*.

surmounted, by intelligence and persistence overcome, and the first successful flint-glass factory in this country became a reality. To the West Indies, Mexico, Bermuda, Buenos Aires, Lima, eventually were shipped crates filled with tons of glass — white, clear-metaled, beautiful. A reputation was made.

Though to modern ears it sounds a small affair, consider the time, the very early nineteenth century. A typical year was 1825 — the year, by the way, when the Sandwich glass began its career. In the Bakewell factory were sixty-one hands, exclusive of designers and engravers, sixty-one workmen trained in and brought from England, Belgium, and France. For these workmen was all consideration, the firm taking utmost interest in the men's welfare. With the living quarters nearby, the close association made for friendliness and high morale. Games and contests were staged, swimming, skating, and racing enjoyed. The sick or injured, widows and orphans were all cared for.

In this year $45,000 worth of glass was sold and shipped. Apothecary sundries, bottles, tumblers, épergnes, decanters, perfume holders, bureau knobs, and so on, had already gone down to Rio. Bakewell glass, furthermore, was on the shelves of the White House, President James Monroe in 1817 having ordered, in the words of the Pittsburgh *Mercury*, "a splendid equipage" of wineglasses, decanters, and tumblers of double flint, each bearing the engraved coat of arms of the United States. President Andrew Jackson, too, in 1832 ordered a set of Bakewell glass for his own use.

For nearly fifty years Bakewell's was a showplace in Pittsburgh, given loud acclaim from a never-ending stream of visitors. Elias Pym Fordham in his *Personal Narrative of Travel* in 1817 wrote, "Mr. Bakewell's works are admirable . . . His cut glass equals the best I have seen in England."

The following year Henry Bradshaw Fearon in his *Sketches of America*, published in London, wrote: "Witness such perfection on this side of the Atlantic, and especially in that part of America which a New Yorker supposes to be at the farther end of the world . . . It is well to bear in mind that the demand for these articles of elegant luxury lies in the western states! the inhabitants of Eastern America being still importers from the Old Country."

In 1825 Bakewell glass won the silver medal of the Franklin Institute for the best specimen of cut glass, in a competition that included the whole country.

Mrs. Anne Royall, who visited Pittsburgh in 1828 and published *Mrs. Royall's Pennsylvania, etc.* in Washington the following year, exclaimed, "Bakewell's is the place! . . . This establishment is entirely devoted to the manufacture of white or flint glass, and has succeeded in producing the best specimens of this article ever made in the United States . . . There is scarcely a stranger visits Pittsburgh who is not desirous of taking a peep at Bakewell's Glass House . . . The quality, variety, beauty, and brilliance of the endless piles of glass at Bakewell's is the greatest show I ever saw."

It is significant that Deming Jarves, thoroughly familiar with the flint-glass industry in the eastern states, and also proprietor of the Sandwich glassworks, writes in *Reminiscences of Glass-Making* in 1865: "We may well consider Mr. Bakewell as the father of the flint-glass business in this country; for he commenced the work in 1808, and by untiring efforts and industry brought it to a successful issue."

The pioneer position of Bakewell's in the history of American glassmaking was later substantiated by Joseph D. Weeks' *Report on Glass* in the Census of 1880, an exhaustive study of the whole subject. This concludes, "There can be no doubt that Mr. Bakewell is entitled to the honor of erecting and operating the first successful flint-glass house in the United States."

Magazines and newspapers of the time tell the story of Lafayette's visit to Pittsburgh in 1825. It was a flower-strewn, flag-waving, drum-resounding occasion for the city, and an occasion for Bakewell's as well: workmen pulling the forelock, "making a leg," grinning, and bashful; the owners, pleased, and all of graciousness; the General and his escort proving most admiring guests.

At the glasshouse of Bakewell, Page and Bakewell, as it was then known, were presented to General Lafayette two cut-glass, double-flint vases, beautiful in quality and design. These vases were lent by Lafayette's granddaughter to the World's Fair in Chicago in 1893. The letter of acknowledgment, written by the distinguished visitor, is a treasure in the Bakewell family:

Gentlemen:
The gratification I have felt at the sight of your beautiful manufacture is still enhanced by the friendly reception I have met from you and by the most acceptable present you are pleased to offer me. Accept my affectionate thanks, good wishes, and regards.

Lafayette

Benjamin Bakewell died in 1844. The glass firm continued under management of the two sons, Thomas and John Palmer, also a nephew, John Palmer Pears. Benjamin Bakewell and Benjamin Bakewell Campbell, both grandsons, and Benjamin Page Bakewell, grand-nephew, later joined the firm, and still later, more distant relatives, Thomas, Benjamin, and Harry Pears.

Through success and vicissitudes the factory wrought on. In the great fire of 1845 it was totally destroyed, with what loss one can guess. It was rebuilt immediately on the same location, however, and in 1854 moved to the south side of Pittsburgh. In 1881 the business dissolved.

There will always remain an element of the marvelous about glass, a substance resulting from fusion of a combination of silica with various bases. That such diverse constituents as sand, lime, lead, even bone, iron filings, cobalt, can be fused into this beautiful, transparent, translucent thing we call glass awakens in us more than response to beauty. For here we are near such transformation of matter as urges our thought beyond confines of a factory.

SPOONHOLDER, CREAMER, SUGAR BOWL, and BUTTER DISH, pressed in sawtooth pattern. *Collection of Mr. and Mrs. Donald Campbell Bakewell.*

PRESSED GLASS DECANTER in honeycomb pattern. BLOWN CELERY GLASS and WATER GOBLET. *Collection of Mrs. Charles Wharton, Jr.*

Fig. 1 — GLASS BY BAKEWELL OF PITTSBURGH
The two bell goblets are of blown glass, and appear to be of the early period. The "patent" shell dish and the dolphin-footed dishes are of pressed glass, and belong to the mid-nineteenth century or somewhat later. This dolphin design was popular with many different factories.
Owned by Miss Mary E. Bakewell

The First Successful Flint Glass Factory in America

Bakewell, Pears & Co. (1808-1882)

By THOMAS C. PEARS, JR.

Illustrations furnished by Mrs. T. H. B. McKnight, from collections as noted in the text

WHEN the Marquis de Lafayette visited Pittsburgh on his famous tour in the year 1825, he expressed a wish, according to the account of Levasseur, his secretary, to see

some of the ingenious establishments which constitute the glory and prosperity of that manufacturing city, which, for the variety and excellence of its products deserves to be compared to our own Saint-Etienne or to Manchester in England. He was struck by the excellence and perfection of the processes employed in the various workshops which he examined; but that which interested him above all was the manufacture of glass, some patterns of which were presented to him, that, for their clearness and transparency might have been admired even by the side of the glass of Baccarat.*

These patterns consisted of two beautiful vases of cut-glass, on one of which, engraved in a medallion, is shown a view of the chateau at La Grange, the salon of which the pieces were to adorn, and on the other, the American eagle, likewise in a medallion. These vases were loaned by a granddaughter of Lafayette to the French Commission and exhibited at the World's Fair at Chicago in 1893. Miss Mary E. Bakewell of Sewickley, Pennsylvania, is in possession of the original autographed letter in which Lafayette expresses his thanks for these handsome specimens of early American glass. It reads as follows:

*A. Levasseur, Lafayette in America in 1824 and 1825. Philadelphia, Carey and Lea, 1829, Vol. II., page 183.

Pittsburgh, May 31, 1825.

Gentlemen,

The patriotic gratification I have felt at the sight of your beautiful manufacture is still enhanced by the friendly reception I have met from you and by the most acceptable present you are pleased to offer me. Accept my affectionate thanks, good wishes and regards.

LAFAYETTE.

Messrs. Bakewell, Page and Bakewell.

In the same year the proprietors of this establishment were awarded the silver medal by the Franklin Institute, for the best specimen of cut-glass. Several years previously, 1817, they had made a service of glass to President Monroe's order, which is described in part in a contemporary editorial in the Pittsburgh *Mercury*, as

a splendid equipage of glass . . . consisting of a full set of Decanters, Wine Glasses and Tumblers of various sizes and different models, exhibiting a brilliant specimen of double flint, engraved and cut by Jardelle, in which this able artist has displayed his best manner, and the arms of the United States on each piece have a fine effect. The glass itself must either have been selected with great care, or the spirited proprietors must have made considerable progress in their art, for we have seldom seen any samples so perfectly pellucid and free from tinct. Upon the whole we think the present service equal, if not superior to the elegant Decanters presented to the President when he passed through Pittsburgh last year.*

Again, a few years later, 1832, another President of the United States, the redoubtable Andrew Jackson, ordered from this same firm:

*Pittsburgh Mercury. November 10, 1818.

Fig. 2 — GLASS BY BAKEWELL OF PITTSBURGH
Two *prism* pattern footed dishes, a cake or fruit dish, *Rebecca at the Well*, a blown and engraved decanter showing an interesting development of the earlier *Chestnut* bottles, and a six-inch pressed plate in *Saxon* pattern. Of the group, the decanter is perhaps the earliest. The *Rebecca* probably belongs not far from the Centennial period. The cover of the first dish should be omitted.
Owned by Mrs. T. H. B. McKnight.

a set of glass for his own use, consisting of large and splendid bowls, with and without stands, celery glasses, pitchers, quart and pint decanters, tumblers, wine and champaign glasses, salts, etc., all executed in the very best style of workmanship. The glass is as pellucid as crystal; and the beautiful cuttings give a brilliancy of effect not easily described. We understand the order is valued at about $1500.*

These examples will suffice to indicate that the old Bakewell, Pears & Co. glasshouse enjoyed an unusual reputation in the early days of the last century; hence it is not surprising to find that it is the one establishment in the city that is always mentioned by name and described in detail by all the early travelers who passed through the Gateway of the West.

When Alexander Wilson, the famous ornithologist, visited Pittsburgh in 1810, he wrote a letter wherein he remarked particularly on the various glass works, and stated that,

Mr. Bakewell, the proprietor of the best, shewed . . . yesterday a chandelier of his manufacture highly ornamented . . . for which he received 300 dollars. It would ornament the . . . in Philada. . . . and is perfectly transparent.†

Fordham in his *Personal Narrative*, 1817, says:

Mr. Bakewell's works are admirable. He has excellent artists, both French and English. His cut glass equals the best I have seen in England.‡

Fig. 3 — GLASS BY BAKEWELL OF PITTS-BURGH
Blown and cut flint decanter.
Owned by Mrs. Charles Wharton.

And Fearon in his *Sketches of America*, 1818, remarks his astonishment

to witness such perfection on this side of the Atlantic, and especially in that part of America which a New Yorker supposes to be at the farther end of the world. At Messrs. Page & Bakewell's glass warehouse I saw chandeliers and numerous articles in cut glass of a very splendid description; among the latter was a pair of decanters, cut from a London pattern, the price of which will be 8 guineas. It is well to bear in mind that the demand for these articles of elegant luxury lies in the western states! the inhabitants of Eastern America being still importers from the Old Country.*

This same note of astonishment appears in *A Journal of Travel into the Arkansas Territory (1818)* in which Thomas Nuttall writes:

The day after my arrival (in Pittsburgh) I went through the flint-glass works of Mr. Bakewell, and was surprised to see the beauty of this manufacture, in the interior of the United States, in which the expensive decorations of cutting and engraving (amidst every discouragement incident to a want of taste and wealth) were carried to such perfection. The productions of this manufacture find their way to New Orleans, and even to some of the islands of the West Indies. The President, Monroe, as a liberal encourager of domestic manufactures, had on his visit to those works given orders for a service of glass, which might indeed be exhibited as a superb specimen of this elegant art.†

And so the testimony goes, all of it

*John Newton Boucher, *A Century and a Half of Pittsburgh and Her People*. The Lewis Publishing Company, 1908, Vol. I, page 236.

†Letter to Alexander Lawson. Quoted from Francis Hobart Herrick, *Audubon the Naturalist*. New York, D. Appleton and Company, 1917, Vol. I, pages 205 and 206.

‡Elias Pym Fordham, *Personal Narrative of Travel*,

Cleveland, The Arthur H. Clarke Company, 1906, pages 75 and 76.

*Henry Bradshaw Fearon, *A Narrative of a Journey*, London, printed for Longman, Hurst, Reese, Orme, and Brown, 1818, pages 206 and 207.

†Thomas Nuttall, *Early Western Travels*, Vol. XII, page 45.

bearing out the judgment of the eccentric Mrs. Royall, who visited Pittsburgh in 1828, that "Bakewell's is the place!" And indeed it was for fifty years or more the show place of Pittsburgh. Mrs. Royall's description is too long to quote in full, so we shall content ourselves with one or two brief extracts. She writes:

This establishment is entirely devoted to the manufacture of white or flint glass, and has succeeded in producing the best specimens of this article ever made in the United States. The admiration of this glass is not confined merely to home observers, but the great amount of it which has been exported testifies the reputation it enjoys abroad; and there is scarcely a stranger visits Pittsburgh, who is not desirous of taking a peep at Bakewell's Glass House. . . . The quality, variety, beauty and brilliancy of the endless piles of glass at Bakewell's is the greatest show I ever saw. Everything made of glass is found here, — and I would say, the patterns and clearness of the pieces, is equal, if not superior, to the Boston glass. It cannot be exceeded. . . . In the manufacture of this article Pittsburgh and the surrounding country enjoys an extensive reputation. . . . The glass of Pittsburgh, and the parts adjacent, is known and sold from Maine to New Orleans. Even in Mexico they quaff their beverage from the beautiful white flint of Messrs. Bakewell, Page and Bakewell.*

Fig. 4 — GLASS BY BAKEWELL OF PITTSBURGH
Blown and cut decanter, and a celery holder. Of the two, the decanter seems much the older. The type suggests the earliest period of the factory.
Owned by Mrs. George I. Holdship.

on page 86 of his *Report on Glass*, Census of 1880, says, "There can be no doubt that Mr. Bakewell is entitled to the honor of erecting and operating the first successful flint-glass house in the United States." In a letter dated December 17, 1836, and reproduced in Lyford's *Western Directory* (page 103), Mr. Bakewell himself states that his establishment for the manufacture of flint glass "is the oldest of the kind now extant in the United States." And Deming Jarves, who was thoroughly familiar with the flint glass industry in the Eastern States, and was the proprietor of the Sandwich Glass Works, writes in his *Reminiscences of Glass-Making* (page 71):

We may well consider Mr. Bakewell as the father of the flint-glass business in this country; for he commenced the work in 1808, and by untiring efforts and industry brought it to a successful issue. For the skill, judgment, labor and perseverance devoted by him to the progress of the art, he truly merits the *Artium Magister* so often bestowed on those least worthy of its dignity and honor.

It is not within the scope of this article to write the history of Bakewell, Pears and Co., interesting as that history is, and important in the development of the American glass industry. The concern was always a family affair, and,

These rather extended notices will prepare the reader for the statement that the old glasshouse of Bakewell, Pears & Co., founded in the year 1808, and continuing in uninterrupted operation for nearly three-quarters of a century, or until the year 1882, was the first successful flint glass factory in America, a claim for which there is abundant testimony which it would be entirely outside the purpose of this article to cite. We shall, however, record the deliberate judgment of three competent authorities.

Joseph D. Weeks

*Mrs. Anne Royall, *Mrs. Royall's Pennsylvania, etc.*, Washington, 1829, Vol. II, pages 110, 113, and 125.

under the successive management of Benjamin Bakewell, the founder, Thomas Bakewell, his son, and John Palmer Pears, who, on his death in 1874, is spoken of as "the oldest person in this country engaged in the business," it spanned the entire period of that development from the very beginning which it inaugurated, up to the point where the making of flint glass had become one of the most important branches of manufacturing in

Fig. 5 — GLASS BY BAKEWELL OF PITTSBURGH
Two engraved tumblers in the Bohemian style; and a pressed goblet.
Owned by the author.

the country.* When the fires were finally allowed to go out, in the year 1882, it had indeed an honorable record to show from the day when, in Albert Gallatin's *Report on Manufactures (1810)*, the recently established works at Pittsburgh were cited as the only works of the kind in the United States, and were described as, even then, making "decanters, tumblers, and every other description of flint-glass of a superior quality."

The recent death of my own father, Thomas C. Pears, of Pittsburgh, removed the last surviving member of the firm. It was "a famous institution in its day, but now numbered among the things of a forgotten past." It seems strange to the writer that it is referred to only in a brief note in Mrs. N. Hudson Moore's excellent work, *Old Glass*.

In concluding this article let us glance at some of the patterns made at the old Pittsburgh Flint Glass Works. A number of fine specimens are still in existence, and are cherished by various members of the family and by other fortunate possessors. We have already described the glass made for Presidents Monroe and Jackson and for the Marquis de Lafayette. There is mention also in the family correspondence of a Clinton tumbler, made in the year 1826.

Mrs. Sicard has pointed out that the pattern described by Mrs. Royall, on her visit to Pittsburgh this same year, is identical with that of the hound tumbler shown in Figure 221 of *Old Glass*, and attributed to the Kensington Works. Indeed I strongly suspect that there are other specimens of Bakewell-Pears glass that are described as unknown or are wrongly attributed.

For instance, in a little handbook, *Sandwich Glass*, 1922, by Lenore Wheeler Williams, is to be found a section on *The Dolphin Group*. The Dolphin pattern is described, and several illustrations are given. On page 73, the author says:

Illustration 8, page 68, is a very remarkably clear white Dolphin dish on standard. It measures 9 by 10½ inches. There is a full size Dolphin, early type, with hollow head supporting a balanced shell. The piece is unique.

Not quite so unique as it appears. The writer of the present article possesses one

Fig. 6 — GLASS BY BAKEWELL OF PITTSBURGH
Heavy pressed decanter finished by cutting and engraving.
Owned by the author.

duplicate specimen, and another belongs to Miss Mary E. Bakewell. It is not a Sandwich, but a Bakewell-Pears product. The specimens referred to have been in the family from the day they were brought from the old factory. In fact my father was manager of the factory at the time they were made, and an old catalogue shows several cuts, one in opal glass. There is likewise a very beautiful and graceful *Pony Dolphin* champagne.

The illustrations which accompany this article include, in addition, from the collection of Miss Bakewell, a shell dish which was made in various sizes and styles of glass; two very old bell goblets; and another dolphin supporting a dish of a pattern designed by Thomas C. Pears, and used to good effect in other articles, especially in a set consisting of tray, water pitcher, and goblets (*Fig. 1*).

The specimens from the collection of Mrs. T. H. B. McKnight of Sewickley, consist of a six-inch plate in the *Saxon* pattern; a fine old whisky decanter; a bowl and cover, and a comport, both of the *prism* pattern. The comport should not have a cover on it as in the illustration. This has evidently been supplied from another piece. The gem of Mrs. McKnight's collection, however, is the *Rebecca at the Well* supporting a dish of the pattern above referred to (*Fig. 2*). The *Rebecca at the Well* was also used as a candlestick. Mrs. McKnight has the punch bowl which was exhibited by Bakewell, Pears & Co. at the Centennial at Philadelphia in 1876 and the medal which was awarded for it. The piece was designed by her father, Benjamin Bakewell, Jr.

I would likewise call attention to the decanters and the bell goblet owned by Mrs. Charles Wharton and Mrs. George I. Holdship. They are very old, and the cutting is excellent. From my own collection I have shown illustrations of two engraved tumblers, and a goblet of the *diamond* pattern, called, by the layman, *pineapple*. The two carafes are cut, and are engraved with the family initial. The cake plate is likewise good (*Figs. 5, 6, 7*). It is of very heavy flint, and of great brilliance. It was purchased by my grandmother, Mrs. Sarah

Fig. 7 — GLASS BY BAKEWELL OF PITTSBURGH
Cake plate of heavy flint glass. Purchased in 1853.
Owned by Mrs. Thomas C. Pears.

*J. Leander Bishop, *A History of American Manufacture*, Philadelphia, Edward Young and Company, 1864, Vol. II, p. 156.

Fahnestock, at the old factory, in 1853. I have noted the origin and ownership of these various specimens as evidence of their authenticity.

Two other very interesting specimens remain to be described. One of them appears as an illustration of this article. It is a communion cup presented by Benjamin Bakewell to the Unitarian Church in Meadville, Pennsylvania, where it is still in use. One of the handles has been broken off and has been replaced.

For the information concerning my final specimen, I am indebted to W. J. Holland, Director Emeritus of the Carnegie Museum, Pittsburgh. In the Museum is a glass prism that is truly famous. It was made from a piece of flint glass, part of a large mass found in the ruins of Bakewell, Pears & Co.'s glasshouse after the disastrous fire, which, on April tenth, 1845, nearly destroyed the city of Pittsburgh. The prism was cut by Dr.

Fig. 8 — GLASS BY BAKEWELL OF PITTSBURGH

A fine old communion cup presented by Benjamin Bakewell to the Unitarian Church in Meadville, Pennsylvania, where the piece is still in use. One of the handles is a restoration. On the other side of the cup appear the words *This Do In —*.

David Alter, of Freeport, Pennsylvania, "a physician of inquiring and ingenious mind, who was early in life attracted to the study of electricity and chemistry, having as a boy read the story of Franklin, and who, quite independently, and yet in fact before the discovery of Morse, invented a crude system of telegraphing." It was by the use of this prism of Bakewell-Pears glass that the doctor made the experiments which entitle him to be known as the first discoverer of spectrum analysis.

Among the many patterns used again and again in various articles turned out by the old glass works may be mentioned the following: *argus, thistle, prism, flute, flute and mitre, arabesque, cherry, lace, heart, Rochelle, Etruscan, Saxon,* and so on. How many of them I used to see on the shelves of our pantry when I was a boy, and how comparatively few of them have survived the hazards of subsequent years!

Concerning William Peter Eichbaum and Bakewell's

By RHEA MANSFIELD KNITTLE

"STRIKE the drums!" shouts the Comte d'Oyat. Dr. Guillotine's knife descends; blood spurts; and the head of Louis XVI rolls from the block. Grotesque shadows of Marat, Danton, Paine, seem to draw the curtains, but the act is not done. At the palace, a scintillant chandelier of crystal crashes to the floor, a shattered mass; and the heart of William Peter Eichbaum, glass cutter to the King of France, bleeds as he hears the ill-omened tidings.

Ever to America from the trouble spots of Europe, come the emigrés — staggering now from the cataclysm of the French Revolution. It is 1793, and they are docking at the wharves of the City of Brotherly Love, where the persecuted of many lands have found a haven. A year passes, and William Peter Eichbaum is now superintendent of a small glasshouse on the Schuylkill River, above Philadelphia.*

Two more years elapse, and we find this man, who has fashioned exquisite glass buttons for the little Dauphin's

*Eichbaum was born in Attenbach, Saxony; migrated to Burgundy; was recognized by the Court of France. He came to America to escape the Revolution. He came to be recognized as a leading citizen of Pittsburgh, where he died in 1866.

blue velvet coat, joining his fortunes with those of the irrepressible Irish-American James O'Hara, and plodding over the Alleghenies to the garrison town of Pittsburgh, where O'Hara and Isaac Craig are about to erect a glasshouse. Eichbaum directs the building of the works, where, in 1797, the first bottle is blown. Eichbaum is recognized as the best glass expert of the district.

But for a time he cherishes ambitions in another direction, for we read the following in the Pittsburgh *Gazette* of September 12, 1800:

WILLIAM EICHBAUM

Begs leave to inform the public that he has opened a house of Entertainment at the Sign of the INDIAN QUEEN, on Front Street, near Market street, where he shall use his utmost endeavors to give satisfaction to travellers and others who may please to call upon him.

Pittsburgh May 15, 1800:

N.B. He wishes to acquaint the public that he follows the glazing business and cutting of glass to any pattern.

Again, from *The Tree of Liberty*, a new name for the *Gazette*, under the date of February 12, 1803, this self-explanatory notice appears:

NOTICE

William Eichbaum requests all persons indebted to him to come forward and settle their respective balances on or before the first day of April next. Those who neglect this notice are informed that longer indulgence cannot be given.

Eleven years go by after Eichbaum has come to the fast-growing little town. And then we find him engaged by two young Englishmen, Benjamin Page and Benjamin Bakewell, who have taken over an unsuccessful glasshouse from Robinson and Ensell. Bakewell is an arrival from Derby, England, in 1808. So the famous house of Bakewell's starts on its way. Eichbaum is its leading glass cutter. In 1810 he cuts the first crystal chandelier in America, six lights and shower upon shower of rainbow-casting prisms.

* * *

Early chronicles state that Ensell owned an interest in the works for about a year, or until 1809, and then withdrew, and that Thomas Kinder had a share in the new management. The house was represented in New York by another member of the Kinder family, Robert, who handled the trade along the coast and acted as commission merchant for foreign exportations. Bakewell's was, from the start, a glasshouse of pretensions, with shipments from the Manhattan port, and, by the water-ways of the Ohio and the Mississippi rivers, to the Gulf.

This southern artery, afforded by the navigable river system, gave the early Pittsburgh houses a far-reaching channel of commerce; for, loaded on flat boats — and later, on steamers — at the point where the Allegheny and the Monongahela conjoin, boxes and boxes of glass started on their way to Mexico City, Bermuda, Rio de Janeiro, and around the Cape to Buenos Aires and Lima. And today, a Yankee in almost any Latin port may gaze upon some glittering lighting fixture "ravishingly beautiful" (as Mark Twain described those later lights on the Mississippi River boats), believing them products of English, Irish, French, or Spanish glasshouses; whereas, truth to tell, they are more than likely to be Bakewell products from the magic hand of Eichbaum.

The early output of the firm was surprisingly large. To note a few at random: vases, decanters, pitchers, bottles, flasks, cruets, candelabra, tumblers, wines, sweet-meats. In 1828, the Pittsburgh *Mercury* carried the following advertisement, which speaks for itself:

BAKEWELL, PAGE & BAKEWELL
Flint Glass Manufacturers
Have for Sale, an Assortment of
ASTRAL, OR SINUMBRAL LAMPS
On Pedestals and for Suspension.
Also, Tuscan, Vase, Mantel and
Chamber Lamps
Which, in addition to their usual stock of
Plain and Cut
FLINT GLASS
Patent Moulded, Plain
and Cut
Bureau Mountings (etc. etc.)
Will be disposed of on the lowest terms.
Pittsburgh, November 20

To go back to the year 1811, Bakewell and Page moved from the old Monongahela works to more commodious buildings on Water Street, corner of Grant, with a warehouse on Wood Street, near Second. Theirs was recognized thus early as the largest flint glasshouse in the Western Hemisphere. Distance had no more terrors for a Bakewell than for a Ledyard, a Crowninshield, or a Perkins. All roads led to and from their glasshouse. Their saltpeter, until 1825, was brought from the caves of Kentucky, and then, for a time, from Calcutta, India. Holland clay was used. The world gave; they assembled and produced; the world assimilated.

During the red letter year of 1825, sixty-one hands were employed, exclusive of twelve engravers and ornamenters; $45,000 worth of goods was turned out; and the plant consumed 30,000 bushels of coal in its furnaces. For a period of ten years one employee alone blew six hundred tumblers daily. The firm took great pride and interest in their workmen, who are said to have excelled both in quantity and quality of production. The living quarters of the men, adjacent to the works, developed a friendliness of intercourse and a high morale which might well turn a modern welfare worker green with envy. Games and contests of all kinds were staged; skating, swimming, and boating races were engaged in; and the injured, the sick, the widow and the orphan were never forgotten. It was, in a manner, an ideal condition, similar in many ways to that which made for satisfaction at Sandwich. Pity that neither could endure!

They made opal curtain holdbacks, mirror and bureau knobs which cannot be distinguished from those of Sandwich, and turned out all manner of river-boat equipment, which, at that period, was elaborate to the last degree. The finest grade of bar goods also came from their furnaces, and much glass which now is catalogued as "Baltimore" is also Bakewell. From compotes to cup plates the list continues. The popular bellflower and dewdrop came from Bakewell's firm as they did from every other flint glass factory of the period.

A diversified list, not at all inclusive, taken from one month's production, gives us an idea of the versatility of the concern:

Apothecary sundries.	Perfume and unguent bottles.
Confectionary jars.	Bottles, vials, flasks.
Decanters.	Glass canteens.
Carafes.	Table glass.
Lighting devices.	Bar goods for river boats.
Bureau knobs in amber.	Lantern glasses.
Mirror knobs — ditto.	Colored glasses for ships.
Holdbacks — ditto.	Toothpick holders.

Tons of glass, tons of beautiful, clear-metaled glass: in a line, this sums up the accomplishment of this house. Yet the collector in general knows little about it.

In 1836, John P. Pears entered the firm, and remained with it until his death, in 1874. During this period the house was generally known as *Bakewell's & Co.* — Benjamin, Thomas, and John Bakewell being the other members of the firm at the time of Pears' joining. Harry C. Pears entered the business in 1878, and, I believe, all the later owners of this well-known establishment were descended from the original founders. The plant ceased operation in 1881–2.

THE FORT PITT GLASS WORKS

By JOHN RAMSAY

FIG. 1 — "FORT PITT" EAGLE CUP PLATE. Made at the Fort Pitt Glass Works, Pittsburgh. Occurs likewise with plain edge and with alternating large and small scallops

FIG. 2 — FROM THE PITTSBURGH AND ALLEGHENY DIRECTORY, 1856–1857

THE first glasshouse in Pittsburgh was that built by O'Hara & Craig in 1797. These men were not glassmakers, but promoters, who played a large part in the development of the city. They brought William Peter Eichbaum, a German glasscutter, from the Schuylkill Glass Works in Philadelphia to manage their plant. In December 1798, they leased it to Eichbaum, Wendt & Company, a firm made up of employees, but as this arrangement proved unsuccessful, the owners regained control in 1801. Eichbaum left, to start a tavern and later a glasscutting establishment, and William Price, an Englishman, became manager of the reorganized firm.

The plant had been making green window glass and bottles, but Price evidently understood the making of flint glass, and the owners decided to enter this field. A letter from Craig to O'Hara states that he "offered to show a specimen of his abilities without charge." The flint-glass furnace was built in 1802. In the same year the equipment of the unsuccessful Ohio Glass Company, organized by General James Wilkinson, Hugh Scott, Ebenezer Denny, Anthony Beelen, and others, was bought by O'Hara and Craig. They likewise engaged that company's superintendent, J. B. LaFleur, a Frenchman. He may have managed the factory's green glass production, but no record of him after 1802 has been found. According to

Cramer's *Almanac*, however, the factory was in 1804 turning out cut and blue flint glass, and was still making "flint glass tumblers, decanters, wine glasses" in 1810.

Price was the first of a number of Englishmen who entered the glass industry in Pittsburgh. He was followed by Bakewell & Ensell (the firm later became Bakewell, Page & Bakewell), who built a flint glasshouse in 1807 and were so immediately successful that they drove the earlier establishment from the field. They attracted other English glassmen to the town. One Robert B. Curling is listed as a "pot-maker" at Bakewell's in the Pittsburgh directory of 1815. Price does not appear in this or other directories of the period, but in 1827 William Price, Robert B. Curling, and his sons, William and Alfred B., built the Fort Pitt Glass Works at Washington and Franklin (later Fourth) Streets,

in the downtown section of Pittsburgh proper. This is Price's first reappearance in available records since 1802. A year later, in September 1828, Price left the firm, which became R. B. Curling & Company, made up of the three Curlings and Henry Higbee (also spelled Higby). The latter, a merchant, was in charge of the sales end of the business.

FIG. 3 — LACY PRESSED-GLASS PITCHER. Base marked *R. B. Curling & Sons Fort Pitt*. Probably made between 1828 and 1834

The Fort Pitt Glass Works is listed in the directories of the period as making flint glass, and later describes its wares with the familiar term, "Cut, Moulded and Plain." In accordance with the custom of the times, the firm probably made a variety of tableware, and anything else in flint glass that it found salable. But the Curlings were obviously alive to new developments in glassmaking. A pressed-glass pitcher (*Fig. 3*) shows that they were quick to adopt the new method of pressing glass developed at Cambridge and Sandwich. The piece also shows that they copied with considerable fidelity the delicate "lacy" designs so closely identified with the latter factory. In my opinion the inscription on the base, *R. B. Curling & Sons Fort Pitt*, dates the pitcher between 1828, when Price left the company, and 1834. For on July 13 of the latter year, Higbee retired from the firm and it became Curling, Robertson & Company. It may be noted in passing that Higbee, after a period of dealing in imported and presumably domestic "China, Glass, and Queensware," re-entered the glass manufacturing business in 1847 as a partner of Higby & Gallagher.

Robert B. Curling remained as head of the Company, but apparently retired before 1839. He is listed in the directory of that year as "gent," not "glass mfr.," invoking the old definition of gentleman as a man with no visible means of support. William Curling remained a member of the firm until about 1840, Alfred until 1856. Morgan Robertson and Henry A. Ringwalt represented the new interest. In 1856 another partnership, Curling, Ringwalt & Company maintained what was probably a sales office or warehouse on Penn Avenue opposite the Pennsylvania Railroad Station.

The manufacturers continued to produce the same "line," though there is little evidence regarding it beyond their advertisements. The fairly common Fort Pitt eagle cup plate (*Fig. 1*) was undoubtedly made at this glasshouse, but it cannot be dated accurately, since the name Fort Pitt was used throughout the life of the factory. It is probable, too, that the Curlings, with two or three other Pittsburgh firms, made lacy glass, although in most cases exact identification is impossible and even tentative attribution is dangerous.

But one or two lacy cup plates, in addition to the *Fort Pitt*, can be traced to Pittsburgh factories. And those shallow bowls, from three and a half to eight inches in diameter, bearing a design of shields with three stars — the "Washington arms" — on a stippled ground may be Pittsburgh products; likewise bowls, up to eleven inches in diameter, with a design of acanthus scrolls and fine stippling. For one thing, they seem to be found more commonly in the middle west than in the east. Moreover, they frequently show poor pressing and poor metal, in clear glass as well as in aquamarine, green, and pinkish shades. And it is worth noting that the marked Curling creamer shows crude workmanship, both in the glass itself and in the making of the mold with its "off-center" motives and incomplete band of serrations. The *Fort Pitt* cup plate has been found with the pinkish tinge that is due to the use of too much manganese dioxide as a "decolorizer" — a characteristic of other early Pittsburgh flint glass — and in a rather unsuccessful light amethyst. It is usually, however, sharply pressed in sparkling clear glass, and also occurs in beautiful shades of deep amethyst and sapphire blue. Hence the Fort Pitt glasshouse could, on occasion, turn out first-class ware.

The Pittsburgh directory of 1856–1857 contains a full-page advertisement of the Fort Pitt Glass Works (*Fig. 2*). This shows, in addition to a number of examples of tableware in heavy pressed designs similar to those made by other Pittsburgh houses, a lacy-glass covered sugar bowl. The artist has sketched the pattern crudely, but accurately enough to indicate the octagonal paneled shape and delicate detail. Among the pieces of pattern glass that are portrayed appear two new patterns, exemplified by two covered sugar bowls. Since neither is shown in Ruth Webb Lee's *Early American Pressed Glass*, they may be considered rare.

Of the other pieces shown, the decanter and goblet at the top

of the page are in the pattern classified by Mrs. Lee as *waffle and thumbprint* and credited to the New England Glass Company, with the notation that it was copied by other houses. The Fort Pitt decanter lacks the "patent stopper" of the New England original. *Waffle and thumbprint* occurs again in what appear to be a wineglass and cordial illustrated in the group on the right-hand side of the page. The other pieces at the top are a small bitters bottle in unusual shape with square base, and a wineglass in the pattern called *colonial* by Mrs. Lee. Other pieces in apparently the same pattern, though with hexagonal base and slenderer proportions, are shown on the right: a footed tumbler, a wine, and a cordial. A tall slim *colonial* goblet with plain base, matching the piece at the top, is illustrated in the left-hand group.

The same group includes a hexagonal paneled tumbler. This type was made by many of the midwestern flint glasshouses and is found in a wide variety of colors, as well as in a number of design variations. This example has an applied handle, but that fact should not encourage attribution of all such handled tumblers to the Fort Pitt Glass Works. The tall flared tumbler in the same illustration is also a common type; in fact, the pattern continued to be made until very recent times. But the footed tumbler on the other end of the row is unusual.

Finally, the advertisement adds, in the old tradition, "Also Window Glass of Every Description. Also Druggists' Ware, Demijohns, and Black Bottles." Possibly the factory actually made these; possibly they were bought from green glasshouses and carried in stock at the warehouse which, at 17 Wood Street, was some distance from the plant.

The firm of Curling, Robertson & Company was dissolved in 1857. Edward Dithridge, who is named as a partner in the advertisement, was a glassblower in the factory in 1839, and is so listed again in the directory of 1850. By 1856 he had been admitted to the firm. In 1863 his name appears in directories as owner of the business. The introduction of kerosene and of chimneys for oil lamps had created a great demand for lighting glassware, and Dithridge entered this field, abandoning the manufacture of tableware. He was highly successful and made some fine engraved and etched lamps and globes. The firm continued in business until the turn of the century.

SOUTH GERMAN SAMPLER (*1737*). No motive enjoyed greater favor among makers of samplers — German, English, French, or American — than did flowers. These are unusually realistic. *From the Boston Museum of Fine Arts*

THE IHMSEN FAMILY:
PIONEER PITTSBURGH GLASSMAKERS

By JESSIE and DELPHINE McCREADY

THE more one studies the subject, the more completely one agrees with Rhea Mansfield Knittle's statement, "The various members of the Ihmsen family became associated with so many glass-making endeavors that it is next to impossible accurately to chronicle their undertakings" (*Early American Glass*). However, thanks to acquaintance with a member of the Ihmsen family, we think that we may throw considerable light on a hitherto obscure chapter of personal history. At any rate, we have established the relationships of the various Ihmsens engaged in glassmaking in this country. The following genealogical table, though lacking some dates, presents the case in compact form:

```
                    ┌ William   ┌ Charles II────Christian IIIa
                    │           │ William II────Christian III
Charles    │ Christian │ Christian Jr.
  (died 1828) │ (1804–1862)│
                    │           └ Frederick────Joseph D.────Christian IV
                    │                           (Our informant)
                    └ ?      ───Dominick───Dominick
```

Charles Ihmsen was born in Steinbach, Westphalia, Germany. For over two hundred years his ancestors had been glassmakers, the business always descending to the eldest son in each generation. Charles came to America about 1795 and settled at Frederick, Maryland, where he was doubtless in the employ of Amelung's glass factory at the time of its collapse in 1798. We find him next, in 1807, after the embargo had been imposed against English goods, stopping at Friendship Hill, to confer with Albert Gallatin. Advised by that extraordinary person to undertake glassmaking in Pittsburgh, Ihmsen trekked westward to the smoky city. He was by no means penniless, for we find him almost immediately in partnership with Ensell, Wendt & Company. Theirs was the fourth glasshouse to be established west of the Allegheny Mountains, and the second to produce window glass. The factory, located in the Birmingham district of Pittsburgh, also turned out bottles and vials. We are sure that this pioneer Ihmsen was Charles, and not Christian, as Mrs. Knittle states in *Early American Glass*, because Christian was not born until 1804, at least nine years after Charles had begun his career in this country.

From this time on Charles Ihmsen seems to have been connected with several different concerns. We may suspect that the associations were concurrent rather than consecutive, since the dates available curiously overlap. Ensell, Wendt & Company became Ihmsen, Wendt & Company. In 1812 we find the name Impson, instead of Ihmsen, among the owners of the concern to be known as Beltzhoover, Wendt & Company, whose articles of copartnership have come to our attention. The latter document, inscribed on parchment, is the property of H. J. Cochran of Aliquippa, Pennsylvania, whose maternal great-great-grandfather was Frederick Wendt. Thanks to Mr. Cochran's courtesy we are able to summarize the contents of this valuable piece of historical evidence.

The agreement, dated January 17, 1812, names George Sutton and John K. McNickle and Daniel Beltzhoover, who on the one hand were to supply the necessary capital to start the venture, and Frederick Wendt, Charles Impson, Peter Hane, Daniel Tucker, and Edward Ensel Jr. (glassblower), who were to receive wages and varying shares in the hoped-for profits in return for their services. It would appear that the working partners of the concern were at the time in the employ of James O'Hara, since the agreement states that they are to join forces with the new concern "as

soon as their present contract or engagement" with that individual expires. The paper was never signed. Mr. Cochran believes it to be a duplicate of a fully completed contract. Mention of the firm of Beltzhoover, Wendt & Company will be found in George Thurston's *Allegheny County One Hundred Years Ago*.

During subsequent years the corporate name underwent several changes. In 1822, according to Thurston, we encounter Sutton, Wendt & Company, in which figure Daniel Beltzhoover, George Sutton, John McNickle, Edward Ensell Sr. and his son, Frederick Wendt, Charles Ihmsen, and Peter Hane. About this time we find Charles Ihmsen's son William entering the glass business near Williamsport, now Monongahela City, where in 1826 he established a factory.

In 1828 Charles Ihmsen died and his interests were taken over by his second son, Christian, an enterprising businessman. He was associated at various times with Thomas I. Whitehead, William Phillips, and Frank Plunkett, and apparently prospered. In 1850 he was operating as C. Ihmsen (Knittle); in 1855 as C. Ihmsen & Company. In 1862, the year of his death, Christian took two of his sons, Charles and William, into the firm. But the younger men lacked their father's ability and failed within a few years. In 1865 we find another member of the family, Dominick, entering the glass business in company with Wilson Cunningham, under the name of Cunningham & Ihmsen. According to Mrs. Knittle, Dominick's interests were later disposed of and Dominick himself disappears from the record.

We now come to the third generation of the Ihmsen family in America. In 1885 Christian Jr. opened a glassblowing house on the site of the old Beltzhoover, Wendt & Company factory. Called the Ihmsen Glass Company, this enterprise lasted only ten years. With its demise the Ihmsens went out of the glass business forever.

Concerning the profitable business conducted by Christian, which in the 1830's had an annual glass production worth $100,000 to $120,000, Mrs. Knittle observes, "Almost nothing has appeared in print concerning this very large establishment — a glass-works which was turning out as much flint-goods as any house in the United States. What did it make? We ought to know as much about its 1836 production as we do concerning that of Sandwich, the New England Glass Co., or Bakewell's."

Though we are unable to give a specific answer to Mrs. Knittle's question regarding the products of this factory in 1836, we do possess information concerning a few of the items turned out in 1851. Fifteen years was, of course, a long time as measured by the vicissitudes of the glassmaking industry in that period and by frequent changes not only in personnel but in the character of the goods produced. While we know that patterns in pressed glass which proved popular were continued over a term of years, it seems probable that those produced in 1851 were recently introduced novelties rather than repetitions of those devised when pressed glass was first coming into vogue. The 1850 decade, it may be recalled, was one of newly awakened activity and wide competition in the manufacture of glass.

The sugar bowl of which three views are here pictured is not only an 1851 product of the Ihmsen factory; it also furnishes evidence regarding the character of other products of the establishment. Until recently acquired by us, it had been cherished by an old lady, now eighty-four years of age, residing on 12 Street near Sarah Street, two squares from the site of the old glass factory

SUGAR BOWL: THREE
VIEWS (c. 1851)
Reliably ascribed to the
Pittsburgh-district factory
operated by Christian
Ihmsen. Said to be the
product of experiments
with new methods of
moldmaking, the bowl
was evidently intended to
advertise the sundry articles and diverse patterns
of glass tableware pro-
duced by the Ihmsen con-
cern. The three views
pictured exhibit in the
order given a variety of
items, framed in arched
panels. *Diameter:* 5 inches; *overall height:* 5 ½
inches.
From the authors' collection

A: bowl — *Ashburton* decanter; *flute* goblet;
spillholder in *star* or *sunburst* pattern; cover
— *excelsior* compote; *flute* champagne;
flute goblet

C: bowl — *excelsior* covered sugar bowl; *excelsior* decanter;
excelsior champagne; cover — what appears to be a hexagonal salt above an inkwell; *flute* champagne; *excelsior*
footed tumbler

B: bowl — *excelsior* ale glass; hexagonal
six-banded candlestick; *excelsior* spillholder; cover — *excelsior* footed tumbler
with handle; bitters bottle; *excelsior* tumbler

at 14 and Bingham Streets, Birmingham, Southside, Pittsburgh, then operating under the name of C. Ihmsen
and Company (*1851*).

The late owner's elder brother was
an employee of the Ihmsen factory.
By him she remembers having been
told that, about 1851, a series of experiments was undertaken to improve
upon the wooden molds then in use,
which soon became charred and worn
and hence incapable of producing a
distinct impression. To remedy this
defect an attempt was made, she said,
to utilize pasteboard (probably *papier-
mâché*); but in what manner she was
unable to recall.

Whatever the method attempted, it
proved to be a failure, since the process was not only time-consuming but
expensive because of breakage of the
article upon removal from the mold.
An article that escaped such destruction is the sugar bowl here illustrated.
Though this piece shows several
fractures on the base, near the bottom, they are interior and
do not involve either surface. They may have resulted from temperature changes subsequent to manufacture. A number of tiny
nicks and chips on the approximating rims of base and cover
affords evidence of considerable use.

Aside from the more or less reliable tradition attaching to it,
and to its portrayal of contemporary styles in Ihmsen pressed
glass, the bowl appeals on other grounds. It appears to be a unique
medium for advertising the products of a glass factory. The former
owner stated that, had the experiments proved successful, it was
intended to utilize the sugar bowls for advertising other items.
The bowl itself is fairly heavy, while the lid is thinner and lighter
in weight. The glass is quite clear, and bubbles and heat checks
are comparatively few. Resonance of the base is somewhat im-

paired by cracks, but the lid responds
to the lightest touch with a clear bell
tone. The design, which occurs on the
outer surface of the bowl and the inner
surface of the lid, is well defined.

Ruth Webb Lee does not mention
the Ihmsens as the makers of any of
the patterns described in her *Early
American Pressed Glass*. She attributes
the *excelsior* pattern to McKee Brothers and reproduces a page of items in
that pattern from that firm's 1868
catalogue. She remarks, however,
that this pattern also appeared in an
earlier list of about 1859. *Excelsior*
would seem to have been a favorite
with the Ihmsen factory, to judge by
the relative number of items in that
pattern found on the sugar bowl.

Of *Ashburton*, Mrs. Lee observes:
"It has been definitely established
that this pattern was made in three
factories, though doubtless it was produced at others as well." She names
the New England Glass Company and
Bakewell, Pears and Company as among the firms producing it.

The *flute* pattern was probably made at numerous factories,
among which Mrs. Lee mentions the Sandwich works and Bakewell, Pears and Company. The Ihmsen factory may now be added
to the number of those to which it may safely be attributed.

NOTES

1. The confusion of baptismal names among the Ihmsens is due to the fact
that members of the family were prone to indicate their first name only by an
initial. Our informant, Joseph D. Ihmsen, tells us that his son follows the same
custom, always signing himself C. Ihmsen instead of Christian Ihmsen IV.

2. Frederick Wendt's daughter, Charlotte, married John McKee, a brother
of Samuel McKee of the firm of S. McKee and Company, one of the largest
concerns in its field. The unsigned contract referred to was found in an old
McKee family Bible.

Fig. 1 — COVER OF
GEORGE DUNCAN &
SONS CATALOGUE
(c. 1875)

The Duncan Trio

By RUTH WEBB LEE

IT IS generally conceded, at least by dealers, that, at the moment, collectors of American things are more interested in early pattern glass than in other kinds of antiques. The sales prove it. Naturally, the desire for fresh historical information has been intensified by the increased demand for the material. Knowledge, or at any rate the ability to talk learnedly about their prizes, has always been sought by owners of antiques. According to Edwin Lefevre, no deaf mute can be a collector: no talk, no use collecting. Q. E. D.

From the beginning of the interest in American pressed glass there has been much speculation as to the date, origin, and meaning of the trio of countenances in the pattern known as *three face*. Many legends, all apocryphal, circulated for years. For example, there was the tale of the beautiful member of a well-known Philadelphia family who ordered a portrait from a distinguished artist, but was told that her extraordinary beauty could be captured only by three likenesses — full face, profile, and fifty-fifty. Getting three commissions instead of one was not only high art but high finance.

Classical students called the ware the *three Graces*. However, Aglaia has exactly the same face as Euphrosyne, and Thalia is a dead ringer for her

sisters. None of the three looks like either father or mother. Other stories circulated. Many well-meaning souls contended that *three face* was a Sandwich product, though without any corroborative evidence other than the desire to call everything in pressed glass Sandwich. No collector knew even approximately the date when this pattern was made, or where it was made.

It is, therefore, gratifying to find, in an old trunk, a catalogue issued by George Duncan & Sons of Pittsburgh, Pennsylvania, in which several pages are devoted to *three face*, known simply to the trade in those days as *Pattern No. 400*. It is to be doubted that *three face* was made at any other factory, for no variants of any of its forms have been found. When a factory copied a pattern that had been originated by some

Fig. 2 — PAGE FROM DUNCAN'S CATA-
LOGUE SHOWING "PATTERN NO.
400"
This pattern, now known as *three face*, shows, reading left to right: half-gallon biscuit jar (rare); half-gallon pitcher; 8-inch bowl, round (the same bowl occurs also in 7- and 9-inch diameter, with and without cover, and in 10-inch without cover); 4 ½-inch comport (occurs also in 4-inch size); 7-inch bowl (the same bowl occurs in 8- and 9-inch diameter with and without cover, and in 10-inch without cover)

Fig. 3 — LAMPS PLAIN AND ENGRAVED Each type of lamp was procurable in three sizes

Fig. 4 — ROUND BOWL COVERED This bowl is shown without cover in Figure 2

rival concern and had proved popular enough to be plagiarized profitably, slight differences or variations were introduced, either because they could not be avoided or because they were considered a safeguard against accusations of infringement. In the case of *three face*, no variations have been found to indicate that more than one master model was used for any of its different items as produced by George Duncan & Sons.

Collectors always wish to know when and by whom a particular pattern was made, as well as to have a full list of its various items, in order to know when the "series" is complete. It is also desirable to know the original trade name, though we are all agreed that only confusion would ensue were collectors to substitute long-forgotten pattern names for familiar descriptive titles now in use.

For most pattern glass it is obviously impossible to establish the date of manufacture, the reason being that, as a rule, the old catalogues are not only scarce but undated. Nobody deemed trade lists worthy of preservation for the benefit of collectors yet unborn. Moreover, the memory of glass blowers and salesmen is untrustworthy. It is too much to ask the average man to recall

exactly the first making of an article, which may have been one of dozens that he sold year after year four decades ago. The only way to judge the age of glass is by ascertaining its period, which, in turn, is determined by the character of the pattern and the number and variety of articles made in the particular design.

In the earliest days of pressing, very few pieces were considered necessary to complete a set. A "set," for instance, consisted of sugar bowl, creamer, butter dish, and spoon holder. Goblets were made in the same pattern but were not inevitably sold with the set. The changes in fashion between 1870 and 1885 afford the most reliable guide to the age of certain forms. It was between these years that many of the combined frosted and clear effects were produced, as, for example, *three face*, *lion*, *Westward-Ho*, *polar bear*, and so on. For years Eastern collectors have credited many of these to Sandwich; but we now know that they were made in the Pittsburgh district. Incidentally, *camphor glass*, used to designate a frosted finish, was a term unknown to the old glassmakers, who always referred to it as *satin finish*.

The trade name of *three face* in the Duncan catalogue is *Pattern No. 400;* but among the Duncan workmen it was known as *the*

Fig. 5 — BUTTER DISH, CREAMER, SPOONER, SUGAR BOWL

Fig. 6 (extreme left) — Goblet Likewise obtainable in plain form. Three smaller sizes of same form were known respectively as *wine, claret,* and *champagne*

Fig. 7 (left and right) —Celery Glasses of Two Types

Fig. 8 (extreme right) — Pickle Jar Hardly of the pattern; but none the less a pickle jar

Fig. 10 (bottom of page) — Saucer Champagne Probably very few were made, since the demand would have been limited

three sisters. One old glass blower assured me that he recalled making it at the Duncan factory in 1872. Though he was very aged, his memory was apparently as reliable as human memory ever is. It should be borne in mind that much pressed glass was made in 1874 and 1875 in expectation of an active demand from the souvenir-loving public that was planning to attend the Philadelphia Centennial Exposition in 1876. Many novelties were manufactured then, some at Sandwich, some at the old Pittsburgh glasshouses.

Parts of the pages illustrating the *three face* pattern are here reproduced from the George Duncan & Sons' catalogue. I also present a list of the articles in this design illustrated in the catalogues of the 'seventies. It is a pleasure to settle the dispute about the piece in this pattern which was originally intended for a butter dish (*Fig. 5*). For years, collectors have insisted that the covered dish on high standard, now proved to be a butter dish, was really a sweetmeat dish, similar vessels in earlier patterns being so designated by the makers. They undoubtedly based their argument on the fact that in the 'fifties all butter dishes were without standards. The salt shaker was called *salt bottle.*

Everyone knows that in the *three face* pattern, the bowls of the dishes are found both clear and engraved. The factory sold them "plain or engraved." The design for the engraving was selected by the purchaser from a pictorial list submitted by the salesman, and

Fig. 9 — "Salver" (This form came in 9-, 10-, and 11-inch diameters)

the work was done to order. The cracker jar listed in my book *Early American Pressed Glass* is shown in Figure 2. It is listed in the catalogue as "half gallon biscuit jar." I know of but one of these jars that has been found in recent years. The saucer champagnes are so scarce that we may safely assume that very few of them were made (*Fig. 10*). A slight demand yesterday means collectors' heartaches today.

The *pickle jar* (*Fig. 8*), apparently intended for use with *three face* ware, is so unlike its associates that the reason for including it in the series is not apparent. The little salts, which many dealers and collectors have called *celery dips,* are listed as *individual salts.* It is interesting to note that compotes were made with both rounded and flat-bottomed bowls, and were either open or covered in all but the largest size.

List of articles made by George Duncan & Sons in Pattern No. 400, now known as "three face"

Butter dish; sugar bowl; creamer; spoon holder; goblet; champagne (deep bowl); saucer champagne; claret; wine; comport (footed sauce) 4", 4½"; half-gallon water pitcher; biscuit jar; pickle jar (not really matching); salt and pepper shaker; individual salt; celery (scalloped edge); celery (plain edge); salver (cake plate on standard) 9", 10", 11"; lamp (3 sizes) plain bowl; lamp (3 sizes) fancy bowl; round bowl (compote) covered and uncovered 7", 8", 9", uncovered 10"; bowl (compote with angular profile) covered and uncovered 7", 8", 9", uncovered 10".

Pittsburgh *versus* Sandwich

Adams & Company

By Ruth Webb Lee

THE mania for attributions is as old as collecting. It is responsible for much misinformation, for even conscientious students avail themselves of any peg on which to hang theories that automatically become facts through the magic of speech plus wish. During the past thirty years the line of least resistance has led not only dealers but collectors of American pressed glass in the direction of the Cape. "When in doubt, say Sandwich!" has been the one collecting commandment heeded. "When in doubt, don't call it Sandwich!" is far wiser counsel.

For some time, nevertheless, it has been widely recognized that certain patterns of glass were made by more than one factory in the Pittsburgh district, and elsewhere; but accurate information was not easy to obtain. Moreover, the name "Sandwich" was too good a selling point to be willingly abandoned. Shrewd buyers cheerfully pay for misattributed ware, and proudly help to spread the error. This misuse and abuse of the Sandwich name is particularly true of the later patterns — those, say, which date from the 'seventies.

Almost all the old Pittsburgh houses made what dealers and collectors, east and west, still call "genuine Sandwich." They began before 1850, and some of them have kept at it. Adams & Company was among the leaders after 1850.

In an old account book of Bakewell, Pears & Company for 1846 appears the name of John Adams, a presser, who "made $1 per turn." He earned as little as $16.50 during February of 1846, and as much as $38.33 in July of the same year. For the six months he made $116 in all. And yet, in 1851 this same Adams established the firm of Adams, Macklin & Company, which started its first glass factory at the corner of Ross and Second Streets. It is easy to visualize here an American industrial romance; but imaginative tales are not for these pages. It was this same John Adams who, in that same factory, succeeded in making the first lime glass, which became a substitute for the heavier and costlier lead glass previously produced by American manufacturers of tableware. To this substitution, and to the improvement in the pressers, is due the rise of the manufacture

Fig. 1 — Adams & Company, Pittsburgh. "No. 140 Pattern"; Known to Collectors as "Wildflower" (*c. 1870*)

were made by more than one factory in the Pittsburgh district, and elsewhere; but accurate information was not easy to obtain. Moreover, the name "Sandwich" was too good a selling point to be willingly abandoned. Shrewd buyers cheerfully pay for misattributed ware, and proudly help to spread the error. This misuse and abuse of the Sandwich name is particularly true of the later patterns — those, say, which date from the 'seventies.

when the Civil War broke out and the government needed money, a twenty-five per cent duty did the trick, and an amazingly rapid development of the industry followed. To be sure, in addition to the twenty-five per cent duty, many improvements were made in the molds and appliances used in the production of pressed ware. Handy levers on presses, the mold oven, the interior cooling of plungers with water, the eccentric key in place of the old lock, and the use of a cold blast around molds and plungers, all contributed to a much larger and more economical production. According to an anonymous article in an old trade paper, Pittsburgh, in 1856, boasted thirty-two factories, of which fourteen were window-glass houses, eight made flint-glass tableware, eight turned out vials and drug ware, and two produced black bottles. In that year, the Pittsburgh factories fabricated 6,340 tons of flint glassware, valued at $1,147,540. I am certain that in all that output were many "Sandwich" pieces. Ten years later the tonnage of Pittsburgh pressed tableware was 4,200 tons. I am equally certain that many of these 1866 Pittsburgh patterns are still called "Sandwich."

of pressed glass to a commanding place among the important industries of the United States.

From the very start the concern made pressed, figured tumblers and tableware. In 1860, the firm name was changed to Adams & Company. The works were then on South Tenth and Washington Streets, Pittsburgh, according to accounts in old numbers of the *National Glass Budget*.

During the decade beginning in 1850, the development of the pressed-glass industry did not show the rapid progress that was later manifest. Pennsylvanians, of course, declare that the chief reason for this was the lack of an adequate protective duty on pressed ware. At all events,

This statement implies no slur on Sandwich glass. On the contrary. In an old and, unfortunately, undated catalogue of Adams & Company, I found one of the best-known of the more popular patterns collected today. We now call it *wildflower*. In the Adams & Company lists it is called *No. 140 Pattern*. Scarcely a day passes that my mail does not bring one or more enquiries

Fig. 2 — Adams & Company, Pittsburgh. "Gipsy Pattern," Previously "Fig"; Known to Collectors as "Baltimore Pear" (*1888*)

about "the *wildflower* pattern of Sandwich glass." Apparently there are hundreds and perhaps thousands of pressed-glass buyers who either wish to know whether *wildflower* was made at Sandwich, or else assert that it was. As a matter of fact, it was made and sold by Adams & Company. An old moldmaker who worked at the latter factory told me that it was made and sold by them in the 'seventies. Its popularity lasted during two decades; and, as a matter of fact, it still sells — as an antique! (See *Fig. 1*.)

We find this ware in crystal, amber, blue, canary, and apple green. Certain forms, or pieces, which did not sell freely were discontinued from time to time; but, as a whole, the pattern had strong sales vitality. I hazard the personal opinion, for reasons that I consider adequate, that *wildflower* was never made at Sandwich. Moreover, I believe it to have been exclusively an Adams product. Incidentally, I would ask those critics of what has been accepted as the standard nomenclature, to consider whether this pattern should be known as *wildflower*, the name given to it by modern collectors and dealers, or as *Adams No. 140*, which was its official designation. In the matter of rechristened patterns, what is true of *wildflower* is true of scores of others that originally were known merely by catalogue numbers or trade names, forgotten years ago. Better a recognizable alias than a meaningless birth certificate!

Certain persons, anxious to cater to collectors' demands or prejudices, have assured buyers that the pattern known today as *moon and star* was made at Sandwich. This ascription has found its way even into books on Sandwich glass. In Adams & Company's catalogue the pattern appears under the name of *palace*. An old glassblower, who worked at the factory, assured me that the design was first brought out in the late 'eighties. I found it in a catalogue printed after the Sandwich Company went out of business. It was listed in my book as *moon and star* because it had gone by that name for years. Nobody would have recognized it as *palace*. In any event, it never was Sandwich. Other Pittsburgh houses may possibly have made it, but I am sure of only Adams & Company (*Fig. 4*).

Another question that I am asked almost daily concerns a pattern that I did not include in my book because I confined myself to patterns collectible in sets; and, at the time of going to press, I had not come across examples other than goblets. As usual, my correspondents wish to know whether or not this is Sandwich. In an old Adams & Company catalogue it appears under the name of *plume*. It is probably an earlier pattern than *palace*, though I find both in a trade list of the 'eighties. As the *plume* pattern was not

Fig. 3 — ADAMS & COMPANY, PITTSBURGH. "NO. 130"; KNOWN TO COLLECTORS AS "THOUSAND EYE" (*1870's*)
The tumblers are of a different pattern

illustrated in my book, collectors may now find it in a goblet shown in Figure 5.

Another so-called "Sandwich" pattern that was made by Adams & Company is the *daisy and button with thumbprint*. Adams & Company made a complete line of it, including a claret glass which few collectors have seen. In the catalogue the line is known as *No. 86 Pattern* (*Fig. 8*).

It will interest collectors to learn that Adams & Company were the makers of several other patterns in demand today. To satisfy the constant enquiries as to where these were made, a study of the accompanying pictures will be instructive. Thus, it will be news to thousands that the *hobnail with fan edge* is also an Adams product (*Fig. 7*). Most of its items were sauce dishes and bowls. Among its forms not included in my book are six-inch, seven-inch, and ten-inch berry bowls and a five-inch sauce dish. Individual salts and a flanged butter dish, without the fan edge, are shown with this group in the catalogue. A toy set in *hobnail* with thumbprint base, made by Adams, included an individual sugar, creamer, spoonholder, and butter dish. A puff box to match is an odd item.

Some of the ten goblets shown in Figure 5 are of patterns familiar to collectors. With the exception of the *Nevada*, complete sets were made. Incidentally, the catalogue spelling followed the English fashion, "sett." When did "setts" become "sets" in the glass trade? I surmise, in the early 'nineties.

No end of dealers and collectors have asserted that what we now know as *Baltimore pear* (called in certain localities *twin pear* and *Maryland pear*) was made by a glasshouse in Maryland. As a matter of fact, it was first made in 1888 by Adams & Company. In the beginning it was known as the *fig* line. Later, the name was changed to *gipsy*. Today collectors and dealers call it *Baltimore pear*, even though it is neither Baltimore nor pear. In Figure 6 is pictured the *Hidalgo* pattern, which is not included in my book. This line was made to be sold either plain or engraved and included many interesting forms. Among other patterns made by Adams & Company, which likewise are not illustrated in my book, though they are collectible in sets, are the *crystal wedding*, plain and engraved, *art*, and *Apollo*, samples of which may be seen in Figure 5.

It will interest collectors to learn that the very popular pattern known as *thousand eye* was made by Adams & Company, who called it *No. 130* (*Fig. 3*). It came on the market in the 'seventies, and for many years was a good seller. The firm produced the square plates in three sizes and the unusual oblong covered dish, listed as a "honey and cover." Two distinct

Fig. 4 — ADAMS & COMPANY, PITTSBURGH. "PALACE PATTERN"; KNOWN TO COLLECTORS AS "MOON AND STAR" (*late 1880's*)

Fig. 5 — Adams & Company, Pittsburgh. Various Goblets
From left to right, first row: *No. 329, Apollo, Cottage, Nevada, Gipsy (Baltimore pear)*. Second row: *No. 65, Palace (moon and star), Plume, Crystal Wedding, Art*. With the exception of *Nevada*, all of these patterns were made in sets

Fig. 6 — Adams & Company, Pittsburgh. "Hidalgo Pattern"; Both Plain and Engraved

styles of this glass are found, one having three round knobs forming the handle of the cover for covered dishes, and also adorning the stems of compotes, and so on; and a second style, produced by Richards & Hartley of Tarentum, Pennsylvania (another old factory of the Pittsburgh district) and widely advertised by them during the 'eighties (*Fig. 9*). This latter style is referred to by its makers as *No. 103 Pattern*.

The same firm made a wide variety of shapes in crystal,

Fig. 7 — Adams & Company, Pittsburgh. "No. 150 Pattern"; Known to Collectors as "Hobnail with Fan Edge"

amber, blue, canary, and crystal-opalescent. All the Richards & Hartley pieces are scalloped at the top and base, except those which obviously could not be so made, like the twine holder and salt and pepper shakers. "Crystal-opalescent" was a combination of opal and a decided blue tone. That the Tarentum output of "Pattern No. 103" was inconsiderable may be assumed from its marked scarcity today. Collectors eagerly seek it, doubtless because of its attractive color and its rarity. The Adams pieces can be identified by the three knobs noted in the preceding paragraph.

Fig. 8 — Adams & Company, Pittsburgh. "No. 86 Pattern"; Known to Collectors as "Daisy and Button with Thumbprint"

Fig. 9 — Richards & Hartley, Tarentum, Pennsylvania. "No. 103 Pattern"; Known to Collectors as "Thousand Eye" (*decade of 1880*)

Fig. 1 — From Richards & Hartley's Catalogue (*1888*)
"No. 544 Pattern." The bowl occurs in 7- and 8-inch diameters, and the "comport" in diameters of 4, 7, and 8 inches

Fig. 2 — From Richards & Hartley's Catalogue (*1888*)
"Tremont Pattern." "Comports" occur in 4-, 7-, and 8-inch diameters. Specimens of this pattern are relatively scarce.

Pittsburgh *versus* Sandwich

Richards & Hartley

By Ruth Webb Lee

ONE is brought to a constant realization of the difficulties besetting the glass historian by the exasperating dearth of documentary evidence — and even of trade gossip — concerning well-known firms that were active not in the comparatively remote era of James Buchanan, but as late as the presidency of Grover Cleveland. For example, after a diligent search of directories and price lists, and a careful examination of scrapbooks assembled by glass men with a fondness for trade history and anecdote, nothing more could be definitely ascertained about the Richards & Hartley Company than that, having organized in 1866, it built its glassworks during the same year at

the corner of Pride and Marion Streets in Pittsburgh, Pennsylvania, and that, some years later, in order to secure better railroad facilities, it moved its manufacturing plant to Tarentum, Pennsylvania. The firm remained in business until the end of 1891. From three large trunks full of old trade catalogues, I obtained one Richards & Hartley volume, dated *1888*, and an incomplete copy of an earlier edition. Incidentally, it may be recorded here that, in 1892, the principal American manufacturers of glassware operated in the states of Pennsylvania, Ohio, and New York.

To collectors of pattern glass, Richards & Hartley are

Fig. 3 — From Richards & Hartley's Catalogue (*1888*)
"Clover Pattern." A variant of what is now known as *daisy and button*

Fig. 4 — From Richards & Hartley's Catalogue (*1888*)
"Hanover Pattern"

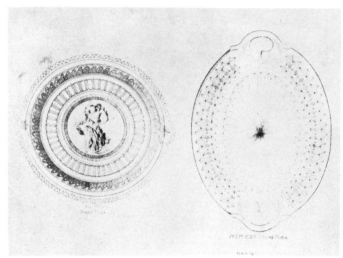

Fig. 5 — From Richards & Hartley's Catalogue (*1888*)
Bread plate in pattern "No. 500," known as *Cupid & Venus; also called
Cupid and Psyche.* Another in "Peerless" pattern

Fig. 6 — From Richards & Hartley's Catalogue (*1888*)
"No. 900 Pattern." Nappies occur in 4-, 6-, and 8-inch sizes; bowls, 7 and
8 inches; goblets in water and wine sizes

important chiefly because they produced so many of the patterns in popular demand today. For example, the *lion, Cupid & Venus, thousand eye, three panel,* and several varieties of the *daisy and button* were all specialties of this concern. In the company's 1888 catalogue the *lion* is called the "No. 525" pattern. *Thousand eye* is "No. 103"; *three panel,* "No. 25." The *daisy and button with crossbar* appears as "No. 99 Pattern" and also as the "Mikado." The Richards & Hartley "Clover" pattern, another *daisy and button* variant, is today found in antique shops in three-petaled sauces and preserve dishes (*Fig. 3*). Another variant, little known to collectors, appears in the catalogue as the "Tremont Sett." It is safe to assume, from the present scarcity of this particular pattern, that it did not prove commercially successful and was discontinued before a large quantity was issued.

In glass, as in politics and every other human interest, truth is not only stranger than fiction, but far more difficult to obtain. Where a demand exists, some kind of supply is sure to be forthcoming. We may not blame collectors for wishing to know everything that bears on their individual specialties, nor be surprised that every meeting of glass enthusiasts inspires sometimes extraordinary accounts of the origin and *raison d'être* of sundry patterns. In default of facts, ingenious fairy stories are eagerly absorbed. The publication of reliable evidence contradicting such tales does not put an end to them. Collectors continue to welcome fictitious accounts of how such patterns as *three face, Westward-ho, peachblow,* and others came into being.

The *lion* pattern has gathered more than its share of legend. It has been attributed to Sandwich, the almost inevitable fate of Pittsburgh designs. There is no valid reason for doubting that *lion* belongs to that group of frosted and clear glass known to have been made just prior to the Centennial Exposition in 1876, perhaps for display during that event. The fact that the *lion* bread plate appears in a catalogue as late as 1888 merely indicates that its particular popularity was maintained

Fig. 7 — From Richards & Hartley's Catalogue (*1888*)
"Etched" bread plate, "No. 525," popularly known
as *lion* pattern

over a long period and survived the decreased demand for other forms. Several variations of the *lion* exist, one made by James Gillinder & Sons. They are differentiated by the lid knobs of the covered pieces. But which of the unidentified variants came from Richards & Hartley works it is impossible to tell, because no covered dishes are shown in their available catalogues.

The picturing of the *Cupid & Venus* plate, without accompanying items, in the 1888 catalogue implies that the demand for plates in this pattern also persisted beyond that for other forms. Incidentally, the firm's prosaic name for this design was "No. 500" pattern — a circumstance that should end controversy as to whether the relief was intended to portray Cupid and Psyche or a guardian angel, as some collectors still believe.

Several patterns made by Richards & Hartley were not included in the first edition of *Early American Pressed Glass.* Among them are the "Richmond," or "Pattern No. 190"; "Peerless," often mistaken for *Hamilton,* particularly in the six-inch plates; "Hanover Pattern"; and patterns "No. 544" and "900," illustrated here for the first time, from the original catalogue. The *leaf and dart* pattern, resembling the *loop and dart* and others of that group, was made by Richards & Hartley. Similarity in design is a dangerous basis for the attribution of patterns to any one factory. The manufacturers cheerfully entered into gentlemen's agreements not to plagiarize from one another, and they kept scant faith by making slight changes. The variants, therefore, may have been turned out by different glasshouses. The exceedingly popular *thousand eye,* made by Richards & Hartley, was fully described on page 67 of ANTIQUES for August 1933.

Of all the patterns produced by the firm, the most important is the *three panel.* In quality of glass and in design it is one of the best of our later commercial colored patterns. I believe it to be one of the earliest designs of colored ware to be made in complete sets. The color range covers only amber, blue, yellow, and crystal. Amethyst was not included because it did not become popular until later. But the reason for

Fig. 8 — From Richards & Hartley's Catalogue (*1888*)
"No. 25 Ware," now called *three panel*. So-called cracker bowls in 7- and 8-inch diameters, and two sizes of mugs, are shown in the catalogue. In design, and in quality of glass, this is the firm's most important pattern

Fig. 9 — From Richards & Hartley's Catalogue (*1888*)
"'Mikado,' No. 99 Pattern," now called *daisy and button with crossbar*. Besides tray, pitcher, finger bowls, and goblets, a tumbler, wine glass, and mugs of two sizes appear in the catalogue. Crystal, amber, blue, and canary

excluding green is difficult to surmise. No plates in this pattern were made, and only one size of footed sauce dish. It should be noted that the low, footed compotes with flaring bowls were listed as "cracker bowls," while bowls with straight sides, like the goblets, were called "comports." Both were made in two sizes, as were also the water pitchers. The *three panel* pattern has much to recommend it to collectors.

The *daisy and button with crossbar*, or "Mikado," pattern was obviously a favorite, for it is extensively illustrated in the catalogue. The color range is the same as for the *three panel*. Incidentally, goblets in *oval panel* were also made at Tarentum.

To the novelties, so popular today, for holding matches and cigarettes, is devoted one catalogue page. Clearly, Richards & Hartley did not go in for these so extensively as many other factories in the "old Pittsburgh glass district." The page in question is dedicated chiefly to odd salts; but it portrays several toothpick holders usually attributed to Sandwich, such as the attractive rabbit with a large container strapped to its back;

the kitten, in amber, blue, or canary, reclining on a cushion and supporting the same container found in the *daisy and button* pattern. Still another curious "tooth-pick" consists of a monkey's head. It looks more like a salt, and is appropriately listed as the "Darwin." A "gem horse radish" is an odd dish, displaying a horse head as cover knob; and a bird salt is clumsier and much less attractive than the one with the cherry in its beak generally ascribed to Sandwich.

Richards & Hartley could not have been in business for much more than twenty-five years; but they contributed their share of items that are sought by present-day collectors. First in importance is the six-inch "Peerless" plate, now universally used as a substitute by *Hamilton* collectors, because, so far, no credible evidence has been adduced that any size of *Hamilton* plate was ever made. The mere sight of a single specimen would bring joy to the hearts of those *Hamilton* hunters who accept "Peerless" *faute de mieux*. We have heard the assertion of its existence. Where is the plate?

Fig. 10 — From Richards & Hartley's Catalogue (*1888*)
"Richmond Pattern," also listed by the manufacturers as "Pattern No. 190"

Fig. 11 — From Richards & Hartley's Catalogue (*1888*)
"No. 103 Pattern," known today as *thousand eye*. Nappies in 5-, 6-, and 8-inch sizes. Colors: crystal, amber, blue, and canary

Glassmaking in Wheeling, West Virginia

By Rhea Mansfield Knittle

ALL is not Sandwich, Cambridge, or Pittsburgh pressed glass that glitters, or, for that matter, that loops the jewel, or that hails the comet. Bellflowers blow in the breeze as gracefully in West Virginia as in Massachusetts. Hearts and flowers, hearts and stars, fade not, falter not along the old Ohio. For in Wheeling-Martin's Ferry pressed glass was extensively made. Not that Wheeling manufactured lacy glass and the later types of pressed tableware to the exclusion of blown, molded, and cut-flint varieties, or cylinder and bottle glass. All of these were made. Almost from the day of its settlement, Wheeling made glass. Between the years 1845 and 1870, the local output of clear glass overshadowed that of any other centre of the industry in America, with the exception of Pittsburgh. The glassworks responsible for this industrial triumph were operated by the finest technicians, trained in the Cambridge, Sandwich, and Pittsburgh flint furnaces. Yet they have never received adequate recognition from the historian.

It is out of the question even briefly to describe the flint-glass factories of Wheeling in this note, or more than to mention some of the green-glass or bottle works. The earliest Wheeling furnace on record was built near a good-sized coal hill at the edge of the little town, one hundred and thirteen years ago. Similar happy solutions of the fuel problem were the chief influence in establishing glasshouses in this district. Coal in hitherto undreamed-of abundance was to be had from the sides of the Monongahela-Ohio hills.

George Carothers built the first furnace, and his little factory was referred to as "an elegant establishment." Its output was advertised as "fine flint." Undoubtedly it was. It was too fine, in fact, for the times and the locality. Forced to abandon his notions of quality, Carothers transformed his furnace into a green-bottle glasshouse. Within a few years these "Virginia Works" (West Virginia had not been created) were taken over by Knox & McKee of Pittsburgh, who retained Carothers as superintendent. The new owners enlarged the plant, and were soon turning out large quantities of window glass and bottles. Later they altered it into a clear-flint hollow-ware factory under the trade name of Wheat, Price & Company. The output was shipped "to Boston and all ports of New England," to New Orleans and New Mexico. During one period it was known as the Fairview Glass Works.

In 1829 the first cut-flint-glass factory in the district was established by John and Craig Ritchie.

Figs. 1, 2, and 3 (top and centre of page) — WHEELING GLASSHOUSE ADVERTISERS OF 1851
From the directory of the City of Wheeling & Ohio County
Fig. 4 (right) — WHEELING NEWSPAPER ADVERTISEMENT OF 1832

The production also included blown tableware, molded ware, apothecaries' supplies, vials, flasks, and "household necessities." Michael and R. H. Sweeney built their first furnace in 1835. Eusell & Wilson, S. G. Robinson, R. C. Knowles, Plunket & Miller, and House & Taylor were manufacturing glass in Wheeling prior to 1850. Ownership of these various plants changed frequently, but nothing is to be gained by listing all of the firm and trade names.

John L. Hobbs, James Barnes, and their sons, John H. Hobbs and James F. Barnes, all expert operators from Massachusetts, came to Wheeling, and, in 1845, erected works patterned after those at Cambridge. In 1854 the furnace capacity was greatly enlarged, and the concern developed into one of the finest flint-glass factories in the land. Many of its forms and designs were similar to or identical with the molded and pressed patterns turned out at Cambridge, Sandwich, and Pittsburgh. It would be folly to award to any one glasshouse between 1845 and 1875 priority in the invention and production of more than a few pressed designs. I have met three men, each of whom asserts that his grandfather positively brought the secret of ruby-colored glass to the United States from Europe.

Hobbs, Barnes & Company built another furnace of good size directly across the Ohio River at Martin's Ferry, Ohio. In 1863 the firm name became Hobbs, Brockunier & Company. For a number of years the mass tonnage of this house exceeded that of Cambridge, of Sandwich, and of several among the Pittsburgh plants. The quality of the metal was excellent. Production included almost everything from large chandeliers with many prisms to small cup plates. This firm also introduced sundry improvements and took out patents for several significant inventions. They did more to better the wage scale than any other house in their district.

Three of the advertisements here reproduced are from the directory of the City of Wheeling & Ohio County, compiled by Oliver I. Taylor and printed at the office of the Wheeling *Daily Gazette*, in 1851. Accompanying statistics show that, next to iron (bar, sheet, and nails), glass was the chief local output. In 1850 the flint glasshouses employed 500 hands, paid in wages $187,200, and produced glass to the amount of $568,456. The green glassworks employed 348 hands, paid in wages $105,866, and produced glass to the amount of $300,000. The hollow-ware houses listed in this directory are: *flint glass*, Sweeneys & Bell, Hobbs, Barnes & Company, D. H. Southwick & Company; *green glass*, Quarrier, Ott & Company. I am quite sure that, at this time, two other bottle houses were operating in the vicinity.

Sweeneys & Bell were capitalized at $75,000, with $12,000 in miscellaneous materials. The

Figs. 1 and 2 (above, and centre, top) — WOODCUT OF THE FIRST PRESSED TUMBLER, MADE BY DEMING JARVES
See ANTIQUES FOR OCTOBER 1931, page 220

Figs. 3 and 4 (above, and centre, bottom) — TWO VIEWS OF TUMBLER IN THE PENNYPACKER COLLECTION Probably one of the original group produced by Jarves

employees numbered 131, and wages totaled $30,796. In commenting upon Sweeneys & Bell, the directory remarks:

The quality of their glass is unsurpassed in all respects, and especially in transparency and beauty. They have succeeded in making the largest vessels, composed entirely of solid cut glass, which have, perhaps, ever been produced. Their three magnificent vases, one of which is in the possession of the Hon. Henry Clay, and another of which has for some time been on exhibition at Washington City, have been objects of universal admiration and wonder. The largest one is 4 feet 10 inches high, holds 21 gallons and weighs 225 pounds.

They have received gold and silver medals from the Franklin Institute, Philadelphia, and the American Institute, New York, for the best cut glass designs and finish to be exhibited at these institutions.

The outstanding achievements of both Sweeneys & Bell, and Hobbs, Barnes & Company, were blown, molded, and pressed tableware; and river-boat, hotel, and barroom flint-glass supplies. Wheeling became the centre of the glass-lamp industry, just as Steubenville did of the tumbler, and as Sandwich had been of the glass candlestick, and Pittsburgh of the cup plate.

It would be much simpler to list the articles of glassware that were not manufactured at Wheeling, than to record those that were.

Exhibitions and Sales

IN ANTIQUES for October 1931, Lura Woodside Watkins presented the history of the first glass tumbler pressed by Deming Jarves at Sandwich, Massachusetts, in 1827, and therewithal a woodcut picture of this important vessel, evidently based on a crude pen and ink drawing. In the course of her article Mrs. Watkins remarked, "It is not outside the bounds of possibility that other examples from the same mold may still be in existence and will some day come to light."

Happily, A. J. Pennypacker is a consistent reader of ANTIQUES. Just at the time when Mrs. Watkins' note appeared in the magazine, he was busily engaged in packing and sorting his stock of old glass for transfer to a newly opened branch shop at Colmar, on Bethlehem Pike, Pennsylvania. With the picture of the old Jarves tumbler in mind, he was peering at the jumbled contents of a dusty top shelf when his astonished eye encountered an actual tumbler, apparently twin brother of the woodcut portrayal in ANTIQUES. Forgotten and neglected during some ten years, this crude bit of glass suddenly assumed an extraordinary importance. Today it is one of Mr. Pennypacker's proudest possessions.

Not long after the epochal discovery, I made a special pilgrimage to Colmar, where Mrs. Emilie W. B. Hennings, who is in charge of the shop in that community, permitted me to examine the historic tumbler. The piece stands 3 ¼ inches high and tapers slightly to a top diameter of approximately 2 ⅞ inches. The bottom shows a pontil scar. The pattern, strongly marked on the outside of the tumbler, presents corresponding ridges and depressions on the interior surface, fair evidence that the tumbler's shaping was not accomplished solely with the aid of a close-fitting plunger. Faint mold marks about the rim indicate the employment of a sectional mold.

In all important particulars this tumbler conforms to the woodcut rescued from oblivion. It has fewer swags below the bull's-eye, and the twelve rays of its sunburst base are of equal rather than unequal size. On the whole, I think it fair to assume that the woodcut was taken from a preliminary sketch from which, in behalf of simplicity, depar-

tures were made in the preparation of the actual mold. Hence I have no hesitation in accepting Mr. Pennypacker's find as, without reasonable doubt, a member of the first group of articles shaped in Deming Jarves' improved press of 1827, to the consternation of the glassblowers whose threats against his life compelled him to go into hiding for six weeks.

Figure 1

A Glance at Glass Knobs

By Letitia Hart Alexander

Illustrations from the author's collection

DESPITE the present furor over early American glass, I have come upon little or nothing in print concerning the glass knobs used on old furniture. It may be that knobs have been exhaustively discussed, and that the fact has yet escaped me, though I have, in a lazy way, long been looking for something authoritative on the subject. In so far as I know, therefore, while many writers make a cursory allusion to glass knobs, few seem to think that these charming bits of glass are of any importance.

Looking back, I think my interest in knobs began with my admiration for a set attached to the toilet table of an ancestress. The table had been bought in Philadelphia, in 1832, and shipped by sea to New Orleans, where the ancestress commenced her married life. Later it came, *via* the Mississippi and Ohio Rivers, to Kentucky. It was a veritable aristocrat among furniture, this much traveled toilet table. The knobs were of clear glass, shaped like melons, and their brass bolts passed through little washers of mother-of-pearl. In the eventual division of the possessions of my ancestress, the toilet table and its alluring knobs passed to a descendant in another branch of the family. Nevertheless, my childish admiration for those gleaming attachments of an early day continued, and I never could resist acquiring a stray specimen, even though *one* was of no use. I have found almost as many patterns as Solomon had wives, so I take it for granted that all factories made them.

N. Hudson Moore, on page 339 of *Old Glass*, says that Deming Jarves, June 13, 1829, and October 19, 1830, took out patents for glass knobs; though what style of knobs these may have been she has been unable to determine. Alice Van Leer Carrick, in an article describing a visit to the Sandwich Factory, observes that an old lady had, among other treasures of glass, "pressed glass knobs on her bureau that were things to dream about." These two statements indicate that at least a fair proportion of knobs must have been produced at Sandwich.

I have always been curious to know what was the nature of Deming Jarves' patents. But, in my prowlings, I have found only one knob that bears a name. If you rest your eye for a moment on Figure 1 *h*, you will notice a specimen bearing cable rim and an old pewter headed screw. On the round base of this knob a square projection, about one eighth of an inch thick, is superimposed. This projection fits into a mortise on the front of the drawer and prevents the knob from twisting, as time and use loosen the grip of the screw.

Around the screw hole of this knob appears the inscription *Bakewell's Patent*, the two words separated by a five pointed star. N. Hudson Moore, in her list of American glass factories, under *Bakewell and Page*, notes that this firm began business in Pittsburgh, in 1808. The firm name was Bakewell and Anderson in 1820; Bakewell and Company in 1824. From 1845 until 1880 the concern operated under the name of Bakewell, Pears and Company. The device described was a happy thought on Bakewell's part, for, as I have said, it held the knob firm and kept the drawer from being abraded by its movement.

After finding this knob, I discovered another exemplifying much the same idea, though there was no name to indicate whose brain had produced the improvement. If you care to look at Figure 2 *f* you will observe this specimen. On either side of the screw hole, at the back, appear two spikes of glass each about one eighth of an inch long. These fitted into holes in the drawer front and thus steadied the knob.

Speaking of knobs that are out of the usual, I would mention the find of a whole set which came to me nearly twenty years ago. I was walking on a mean street, when, through the door of a little shop dealing in secondhand pianos, I saw a twin of the ancestral toilet table! It did not take me long to secure the treasure, though the "song" asked for it approached the price of the warblings of a prima donna. The table had to be done over, but, as it boasted no handles, I let it board with the cabinetmaker, asking his good offices in securing me glass knobs that would not shame my lovely find. Hope was almost dead when my cabinetmaker friend invited me to inspect a set of knobs that had come into his hands. He had just purchased a bed and a sideboard from a broken down wagon, the driver of which told a story of having bought in the pieces at a country auction. After the furniture had been disposed of, the driver pulled out a dirty buckskin bag from which rolled a set of unusual knobs, quite good enough to satisfy my fondest dreams. You will see one of them in Figure 1 *l*.

These examples have about the diameter of a silver half dollar and are beautifully fluted on top and flank. But, instead of being pierced with a *metal screw* through the centre, they carry a heavy *glass screw* molded in one with the knob.

This screw is so heavy that it is in no danger of breaking when turned into the wood. These knobs show three-mold seams. After years of daily use, they remain as firm as a stone wall.

The more knobs one examines, the greater become both knowledge and interest. The first knowledge gained is that hunting glass knobs is like hunting brass candlesticks. Secure a single one, and, however conventional its design, you seem never able to match it *exactly.* You may think

Figure 2

it easy to find a mate; but try it. When you joyfully bring home a stick that you are certain will complete a pair, and set it beside the one you had in mind, it will show so many small differences that you register a vow never to try again—but you do. Matching glass knobs is much the same kind of sport. It matters not how clearly a junk shop find seems to resemble one of your home collection, when you compare it with its presumptive twin, the identity of pattern vanishes.

I think that I have seen all the varieties of knobs which N. Hudson Moore quotes from the advertisement of M. Nisbit, 77 South Front Street, Philadelphia: "plain, fluted, fine twisted, molded, and sunflower." This advertisement also offers "same as the above in deep blue, turquoise, opal, pearl, agate." The only colored knobs I recall are those commonly called "opal." "Deep blue, turquoise, pearl, and agate" knobs I have never met with.

I have shown in Figure 1 *d* a pair of opal knobs. They are not larger than a silver dime and carry circular fluting on the top, much like that of the large knob below. When held to a strong light, they show the colors of a real fire opal. I have always wondered whether these fairy knobs were made for a doll's chest of the eighteen hundreds. I shall use them on a fragile Sheraton dressing stand.

I have found, not only a variety of designs in knobs, but a variety of technical methods in manufacture: knobs showing no seams, molded knobs showing seams, and blown knobs of various patterns. The blown knobs, as I suppose the hollow ones to be, are generally plain, resembling a squat vial, with a

hole for the screw; though some display elaborate patterns. *All* the cut glass knobs that I have seen are hollow, the greater number of them cut in simple diamonds; though now and then an intricate cutting turns up, such as that shown in Figure 2 *c*. Another point is that all the cut knobs are of fine, clear glass, with no bubbles or imperfections.

Molded knobs are liable to be coarser than the cut specimens: sometimes their glass shows a purplish or greenish tinge. Frequently the heavy, common knobs look as if their molds had been used until the outline of the design had become blurred. I have four heavy, large ones, that, except for the screw holes, might be taken for salt cellars. Hoping to complete the half dozen, I succeeded in finding one more of the same queer style, but when I compared it with the four, it agreed in pattern but not in size. Another was found, but alas! though a duplicate in design, it was not of the same dimensions as any of the others.

I once discovered a black walnut chest, of graceful Sheraton lines, bearing a full set of knobs showing well designed whorls that extended around the neck of the knobs. The chest may have been of domestic origin, for, on many large farms in Virginia and Kentucky, it was the custom to apprentice a bright slave to a cabinetmaker for a sufficient time to give him at least an elementary knowledge of the trade. I have seen one or two pieces of furniture made by such slave cabinetmakers. Of course, the hardware and trimmings for such pieces were probably purchased in the near-by town.

Now I come to the last of my knobs. These are the three *a, b,* and *c* in Figure 1. The centre one was picked up in a junk shop many years ago. The other two boast the same origin, but were acquired much later. They are of clear glass, artistically cut, and are sunk in brass cups, to which the screws are attached. The glass seems to be backed with silver foil, as is the case in mock jewels. I have never been able to place this pair. The first knob in the row was already impaling its present oak nut when I found it in a junk shop. I have often pondered what the pieces looked like that bore such expensive fixtures and where such fixtures were manufactured.

I once saw at an auction a clumsy elephant of a walnut bureau, whose knobs were bits of mirror surrounded by tiny frames of wood, about the thickness of a straw. They were unique in my experience. I am yet waiting to see the "deep blue, turquoise, pearl, and agate" mentioned in M. Nisbit's advertisement quoted by Mrs. Moore. M. Nisbit states that his glass is "from the Jersey Glass Company." George and P. C. Dummer? I am hopeful, too, that someone will tell us what Deming Jarves patented in the way of knobs and will, if possible, show the pattern of those articles. Meanwhile, I trust that my pictured bits of glass will interest some collectors who have hitherto neglected such "small deer." I can assure them that knobs, besides exercising something of the fascination of jewels, are not expensive, and that they occupy but little space.

THE CASE OF THE PRESSED GLASS KNOBS

By HELEN McKEARIN

Helen McKearin, a long-time contributor to ANTIQUES *and the co-author of those indispensable books* American Glass *and* Two Hundred Years of American Blown Glass, *has recently catalogued the antique items in the Museum of Glass opened by the Corning Glass Company in May. In this article she presents new documentary evidence that the pressing of glass by machine was first developed in America.*

FIG. 1—PRESSED GLASS KNOB marked *Bakewell's Patent (three views)*. Probably pressed under John P. Bakewell's patent of 1825. *From the McKearin collection.*

THE TERM "PRESSED GLASS," today reserved for glass produced by mechanical pressing, applies to any molded glass forced into a plain or decorated form, not by blowing but by pressure exerted upon the metal. Whether the instrument of pressure be a hand-operated mold or tonglike device or a mechanically controlled pressing machine matters not. But whereas "hand pressing" dates from the early Christian era, mechanical pressing is generally conceded to be an innovation of the 1820's. Where and by whose ingenuity the hand-operated molds evolved into the mechanized are topics of a perennial debate.

Deming Jarves' 1865 remarks on pressing glass have become standard quotes as evidence in this debate. He mentions there English candlesticks and bowls with ". . . square feet, rudely made, somewhat after the present mode of molding glass" and Holland "salts made by being pressed in metallic moulds." These are always cited in evidence against American responsibility for the mechanization of glassmaking. But unless Jarves was using "pressed" in its broad sense rather than in the particular sense of machine-pressing, he had executed a neat about-face sometime during the eleven years between the editions of his *Reminiscences*. In 1854 he had written: "soon after the introduction of the business (flint or lead glass) into this country a very great improvement in the mode of manufacture was introduced . . . Pellat in his admirable work on glass alludes to the American invention in only a few words and passes it by as but of slight importance, but it has brought about a very great change, and is destined to exert a still greater; in fact it has revolutionized the whole system of flint glass manufacture simply by mold machines for the purpose of pressing glass into any form." This seemed nearly clinching evidence that mechanical pressing was a Yankee invention, until the case of the pressed glass knobs cast doubts from another direction.

Apparently mechanical pressing finally hatched from glass knobs, not from "square feet" or "Holland salts." And success in even the most rudimentary stage of the process inevitably led to experimentation by glassmen tumbling to its inherent possibilities. Between September of 1825 and June of 1829 no less than four patents pertaining to making glass knobs were granted—the first to John P. Bakewell of Pittsburgh's Bakewells, for a *method;* the second to Henry Whitney, agent, and Enoch Robinson, mechanician, of Cambridge's New England Glass Company, for a *new and useful improvement;* the third to John Robinson of Pittsburgh's Stourbridge Flint Glass Works, for *pressing in one action;* the fourth to Deming Jarves of the Boston and Sandwich Glass Works, for pressing *glass knobs and screws.*

So far as we know, no glass has been identified with the Robinson patent. The knob marked *Bakewell's Patent (Fig. 1),* probably pressed under John's patent, is a poor thing necessitating disfiguring cutouts wherever it was attached. The Jarves knob proclaims itself as one of doubtful popularity *(Fig. 2).* Glass screws making more than half-inch holes in faces of bureau drawers! The Bakewell and Jarves knobs must have been weak competitors of the type produced by the New England Glass Company. That *type (Fig. 3)* has been determined from the patent specifications, an exact *copy* of which was appended to the Whitney-Robinson Bill of Complaint sworn to on April 25, 1829, and, on May 2, filed by their lawyer, John Cadwalader, with the Philadelphia Circuit Court of Equity.

In that bill Whitney and Robinson of the New England Glass Company swore that their "new and useful improvement" was of much greater use than any mode before known or invented, for "such knobs were manufactured more easily, expeditiously and neatly and by fewer hands than for any former mode." They were "more solid and better adapted to their ordinary purposes . . . more readily made to correspond exactly in size, shape and appearance one with another." Too, they required "less finishing after their form was given them in the first instance" and were "more readily accommodated to the reception of a spindle of the shape best calculated to secure them to the article." During the brief period (about two years) in which the patentees enjoyed exclusive benefit of their improvement, 300,000 knobs or trimmings worth $5000 had been produced and shipped to the principal markets of the United States, including "Boston, Providence, New York, Philadelphia, Baltimore, Washington, Richmond, Charleston, Louisville and New Orleans." To some competitors aware of this new industrial plum mere rumors of such production, sales, and markets could but be an irresistible temptation to bypass the rugged road of experimentation for the shorter one of infringement. All of which happened . . . so a Philadelphia jury decided.

"The validity and originality of this patent was fully tested by a closely contested lawsuit in Philadelphia carried on against powerful parties in Pittsburgh." Thus in 1854 Professor Benjamin Silliman quoted Joseph N. Howe, Jr., of the New England Glass Company *(Industry of All Nations).* Was the Fort Pitt Glass Works, origin of some eagle cup plates and the Curling creamer, involved? Probably not. No glass was made there until May 1828, and even in 1830 only cut and plain flint glass were being advertised. Were J. Robinson and Son guilty? Were the "300 sets of Patent Glass Knobs" on hand and for sale at reduced prices at their Cincinnati Pittsburgh Glass Warehouse in June 1830 made under John Robinson's patent or not? Or were the culprits Bakewell, Page and Bakewells? They were the most famed makers of fine glassware in the Pittsburgh area and, even though "Patent Moulded Knobs" apparently were not advertised until November 1827, John did hold the 1825 patent. Those Pittsburgh "powerful parties" have been puzzled over for some years.

Now light cast by legal documents and records reveals only the Union Glass Company of Kensington, Philadelphia, *provably* caught in the act. Still, there was no doubt in the minds of Whitney *et al.* that the Union Glass Company in the persons of Emmett *et al.* were not alone guilty; they were "combining with divers persons at present unknown," whose names when discovered should be added to the list of defendants. And events following the trial did point a finger toward Pittsburgh. If they gave no real substance to the charge, they certainly strengthened any suspicion that the Union Glass Company was the scapegoat of a conspiracy. They undoubtedly were the cause of Howe's categorical

statement which was made about ten years later.

As nearly as can be determined from the Court records still extant, the alleged infringement began in the fall of 1828. Possibly the deed was uncovered and reported to the home office by William M. Muzzy, then the comparatively new Philadelphia agent of the Cambridge firm. In any event, Whitney and Robinson deposed that, prior to October 1828, they as well as their agents had asked Emmett *et al.* to forswear making or selling knobs, and they were asked to render an account of those made and the money procured by their sale since the patent date. It was also asked that they be ordered to hand over the total receipts and to deliver up or destroy any knobs on hand. If the charges were disputed or the conditions rejected by the accused, then a trial on the law side of the Court was demanded. William Muzzy gave surety for costs. Thereupon the Court of Equity granted an injunction whereby Emmett *et al.* were "informed and commanded under penalty of $400.00 each to desist from making knobs" until they had fully answered the Bill of Complaint.

This they did within five days. On May 7 C. T. Ingersoll, attorney for Emmett *et al.,* filed their confident denial of nearly all allegations and a demand of their own. Let the complainants be required to prove they had sold upwards of 300,000 knobs for $5000, "which from the respondents knowledge of the subject would be difficult for them to do." As for the alleged warning, they had never even heard about the patent until three weeks previous when William Muzzy spoke to Charles B. Austin. If anyone had been informed about it prior to that time, he must have been William Granville. *He* was named in the Bill of Complaint, to be sure, but not only had he been an ex-member of the company for over a year but one with whom no member had had any correspondence whatever about knobs. In fact, all Emmett *et al.* knew of the patent was the copy affixed to the Bill of Complaint and there was nothing startlingly new about that. (It seems odd indeed that not one of them had read the description of it in the March 1828 issue of the Franklin Institute's magazine.) The Union Glass Company in the persons of William Emmett (once with the New England Glass Company), William Bennett, Joseph Capewell, Richard Synar, James Venables, and Charles B. Austin, had made no knobs until about October 20, 1828. Of about 650 dozen produced, 300 dozen were still unsold. On the others, sold at $1.75 to $2.00 a dozen with 5% to 15% discount, the profit was inconsiderable owing to the expenses "attending an experimental undertaking not yet carried far enough to be profitable."

The crux of the reply for us is the disposition concerning

FIG. 2—PRESSED GLASS KNOB marked *Patent.* Pressed under Deming Jarves' patent of 1829 *(two views). Collection of Lura Woodside Watkins.*

FIG. 3—PRESSED GLASS KNOB of the type made under the patent of the New England Glass Company in 1827. *From the McKearin collection.*

FIG. 4—RECONSTRUCTION of a press for making glass knobs, drawn from descriptions of the machine patented by the New England Glass Company in 1826. The description given in the *Journal* of the Franklin Institute is slightly less complete than that attached to the *Bill of Complaint*, which is the only known surviving copy in the original wording, since the records of the Patent Office were destroyed by fire in the 1830's. The exact forms of the parts shown here are theoretical only, and do not necessarily reflect the machine design practices of the early nineteenth century. *Drawing by James L. McCreery.*

the pressing. They asserted that the method and equipment of Whitney and Robinson in no way inspired their own. William Bennett, an Englishman brought up in the glass business in England, had introduced them. Bennett declared Whitney and Robinson were "wrong in supposing themselves to be either the first or the true inventors and discoverers thereof . . . or that anyone ever enjoyed sole right to or use of the improvement" before or since the alleged patent. Before he came to the United States in 1822 he was perfectly familiar with the method. In fact, while he was employed by Wm. Smith & Company in Cork, Ireland, the glass cutters Graham & Brown brought in a mold just like the mold described and "in all respects as to the machine, application, object and results, precisely the same . . ." Bennett himself had used it to make knobs for Graham & Bell. The defendants had no objection to a trial.

From this point on the records are meager. There is little or no evidence of the actions leading to the few maddeningly skeletal entries in the dockets of the law and the equity sides of the Court. Not until May 21 was it recorded that Whitney and Robinson were to institute action on the law side of the Court. At the same time, the injunction was dissolved, but, until further notice, the defendants were ordered to keep account of all glass knobs made and sold by them. About three months later, August 28, Mr. Muzzy gave surety for cost of a trial. Even so it was October 12 before all the defendants were served with subpoenae. And thus ended the first year of the case of the pressed glass knobs.

On April 6, 1830, the case reopened. By the 18th Whitney *et al.* had asked that a commissioner be sent to Cork, Ireland--obviously to investigate Bennett's claim. For some unmentioned reason the chosen Nathaniel Staniford was unacceptable to Emmett *et al.* On an affidavit from Charles B. Austin the Court ruled on May 29 that Whitney *et al.* show cause why another should not be appointed. Seemingly they were unable to defend their man, or did not care who went: they were given three months in which to name another who, as far as the record goes, is nameless. A single entry on August 19 reads, "Exit commissioner to Cork"; on October 6 an-

other, "Exit commissioner to Boston." Thus we know that the rival claims were assessed, presumably by impartial experts, and on physical evidence. Whatever their content, the reports apparently disturbed the assurance of neither party. Far from being intimidated by them Emmett *et al.* pleaded "not guilty" on December 7. The Court ruled for a trial.

On April 6, 1831, just one year after the case had gone over to the law side of the Court, a jury was called. The trial was short and sweet for Whitney *et al.* On May 7 the jury returned a verdict which gave them a moral victory though, in the light of their demands, hardly a financial one. They had charged that "on September 1, 1828 and divers other days to commencement of action October 1, 1828 and afterward . . ." Emmett *et al.* had "unlawfully made 500,000 infringing knobs and sold 100,000," thereby damaging Whitney *et al.* to the extent of $10,000. Therefore $30,000, a sum three times the alleged loss, should be recovered. The jury awarded damages of $500 plus 6/100 for cost; judgment for $1500 plus 6/100 was handed down. Within two days Ingersoll filed for a retrial. About seven months later, on December 12, the judgment was sustained. But not until April 12, 1832, did Henry Baldwin, the judge in the Court of Equity, sign the final judgment whereby the "defendants were perpetually enjoined and prohibited from making or causing to be made or selling" the knobs. On March 18, 1833, the epitaph of the case was entered in the docket: "Costs paid."

In the meantime there had been an aftermath to that judgment; one which undoubtedly called forth louder hallelujahs in the offices of the New England Glass Company than any $30,000. It was probably in Howe's mind when he spoke of "powerful parties in Pittsburgh." Our evidence of it is the following advertisement in the Pittsburgh *Statesman:*

Pressed Glass Knobs

The subscribers, having purchased from the New England Glass Company the exclusive right to make Patent Pressed Knobs west of the Allegheny mountains, hereby caution all persons against making, buying, or selling the same, except such as are manufactured by the patentees, or *Bakewell, Page & Bakewells.* May 9, 1832.

Historical Glass Cup-Plates

By Alice Van Leer Carrick

[Editor's Note — The following discussion is based upon Miss Carrick's own remarkably comprehensive collection of cup-plates. Additional material has, however, been derived through the generous co-operation of Mr. John Overholtzer, of Norristown, Pa., and Mrs. E. C. Hoyt, of Stamford, Conn. Most of the plates mentioned are common to the collections of all three. Notable exceptions are the scalloped Fort Pitt Eagle, belonging to Miss Carrick; the acorn-bordered Log Cabin; the shell-bordered Bee Hive; the crude Sun-burst Eagle and the smooth-edged Fort Pitt Eagle, belonging to Mrs. Hoyt; the pseudo Henry Clay, belonging to Mr. Overholtzer. Illustrations are from all three collections, but, in the main, from a superior series of photographs loaned by Mrs. Hoyt.]

CUP-PLATES

Our Forbears, whom they call polite,
And used to good society quite,
Would without straining any rule
In saucer pour their tea to cool.
Quaffing from which (as they would fain
The tablecloth protect from stain),

They placed their cups which might be wet
In "cup-plates" for the purpose set.
Some of the small glass plates portray
The visage mild of Henry Clay,
On others, through the workman's craft,
Stands Bunker Hill's Memorial shaft.

Advancing taste set up a wail,
That such a fashion should prevail.
The plates were thrown aside forlorn,
Treated with carelessness and scorn,
Thus added value do they gain,
As coveted, but few remain.

      Mary Saltonstall Parker.

PRESSED GLASS was first made in the United States by Deming Jarves, a Boston merchant, in 1825; and Sandwich, Massachusetts, a quaint and still charming little town on Cape Cod, was selected as the place where the works were to be built. To quote from Deming Jarves's *Reminiscences of Glass Making*, a slender volume, which modestly tells you all too little of his own successful venture, "Ground was broke in April, 1825, dwellings for the workmen built and manufactory completed; and on the 4th day of July, three months from first breaking ground, commenced blowing glass." Equally important, and to my knowledge never before quoted, is the first advertisement of the glassworks published in the *Columbian Centinel*, November 9, 1825.

FLINT GLASS

The subscriber informs his friends and the public that his Flint Glass Manufactory in Sandwich is now in full operation, and is ready to receive and execute orders for any article in that line—particularly Apothecaries, Chemical and Table Wares. Also, Chandeliers for Churches and Halls, Vase and Mantel Lamps, Lamp Glasses, and all other articles usually made in similar establishments, and on as favorable terms. Orders directed to Sandwich, Mass., will receive prompt attention.   Deming Jarves.

It is a pity that the old pattern-books of the factory are not to be found; so many disputed points might be proved by them. I have heard them discussed at Sandwich, and have talked with several of the people who remember to have seen them in their childhood, but no search, so far, has revealed them. It is certain, however, that the Sandwich glassworks were started in imitation of and competition with those already established in England, where pressed glass had been made for some years. Deming Jarves imported English workmen experienced in this trade, probably as foremen and expert glass-blowers only, since, in 1832, of the two hundred men and boys employed at the factories, two-thirds were American.

I was so fortunate on a visit to Sandwich as to meet the son of one of these Englishmen, old Mr. Lloyd, who, as a lad, had worked pressing cup-plates after school hours. That was in the early forties, and he told me that the price was then about thirty-five cents a dozen, and that a man and a boy working together could turn out sixteen hundred a day. He also told me that he remembered pressing Bunker Hills, Log Cabins, one or two Eagles, and some of the heads — from his description I judge the smaller heads of Henry Clay. He insisted, too, that the Heart designs were made "out West" (by which I suppose he meant Pittsburgh, where there have been flourishing glass-factories since the last decade of the eighteenth century).

I have seen an English cup-plate made in Birmingham, and dated 1862. Suppose, then, that our first cup-plates were stamped in 1825, the Sandwich glassworks' initial year. That gives them over thirty years of continuous making, though, of course, the English piece was pressed on especial order, since it bore the owner's name, and may, therefore, reflect only an individual whim. But, certainly, we may not date our latest American cup-plate *The Maid of the Mist*, sometimes called the *Niagara*, earlier than 1855, for the Suspension Bridge was not built until that year. Oddly enough, then, a ship begins and a ship ends the list, for, to my thinking, the *Cadmus* design was the first used.

I base this statement upon two things; first, that Lafayette's visit to the United States was one of the great events of its time; next, that I have what I believe to be one of the first pieces of glass to be pressed at the Sandwich works. It seems, even, experimental as well as commemorative, for this round salt-cellar is not only stamped alternately with the eagle and the *Cadmus* (the ship that brought Lafayette to this country in 1824), but it has a crude aspect and is straw-colored rather than white, as if the process of its making had not yet been perfected. But the *Cadmus* is so frequently met with that I can but suppose the design to have been popular enough to continue long after 1825. It is the only other pattern besides the small Henry Clay that I have ever found in half-dozens, a sure proof of its vogue.

But the list of commemoration glass cup-plates includes more than ships. Here is my classification of them:

The Ship Cadmus (*Fig. 1*) — A plate three and a half inches in diameter, with a scalloped edge consisting of alternating scallops and points; the outer border shows scrolls and formalized acanthus leaves spaced with four stars; the inner border very

Fig. 1 — The Cadmus

Figs. 2 and 3 — The Chancellor Livingston

Fig. 4—The Benjamin Franklin

Fig. 5 — The Constitution

Fig. 6 — The Robert Fulton

Fig. 7 — The Maid of the Mist

GLASS CUP-PLATES

much the same except that there are two shields and two stars. The central design measures about an inch, is set in tiny dots, and shows a ship, the *Cadmus*, under full sail. A variant shows a large scallop and two small ones, repeated to form the edge.*

THE CHANCELLOR LIVINGSTON (*Figs. 2 and 3*) — A plate three and a half inches in diameter, even scalloped edge; outer stippled border of scrolls, stars, shields, and hearts. There are three variants of this plate. All are side-paddled steamboats (the rigging is accounted for by the fact that, in those early days of steam, sails still had to be depended upon). In all of the plates the ships face to the right. The slight difference between these examples is that in one plate the ropes are indicated by straight lines, in the other by twisted lines. Both show waves indicated by dots. In the third example, the ship is faintly printed, the flag hardly shows, waves are indicated by lines instead of dots, and the hearts in the border are clear glass, not stippled. In all three plates *Chancellor* is impressed above the ship, *Livingston* below. The ship was one of the first steamboats—certainly as early as 1827—plying between New York and Providence. It was named for Robert Livingston, the patron of Fulton, and one of the five drafters of the Constitution.

THE BENJAMIN FRANKLIN (*Fig. 4*) — A companion plate, the same size. The stippled border has scrolls, anchors, large and small stars, and at the top the American Eagle, shield on breast. *Benjamin Franklin* is printed in a semi-circle over the top of the ship, which faces toward the left. The ropes are twisted, not straight lines, the waves indicated by short, curved lines, and the ship flies three flags: one marked B. F., a pennant, and the Stars and Stripes. F. is marked on the paddle-box also. The name, of course, needs no explanation, and the *Franklin* took the same route as the *Livingston*.

THE FRIGATE CONSTITUTION (*Fig. 5*) — One of the three octagonal plates; the size is a full three and a half inches. The edge shows small scallops, the outer clear glass border has a slight decoration of stars and formalized sprays; the inner rim is stippled and spaced by stars and a conventional motif. Around the center of clear glass is a circle of large raised dots almost like small knobs; the waves are clearer and more natural than in the

other plates, and the ship design is a frigate under full sail. It is commemorative, of course, of *Old Ironsides*, the fighting frigate of 1812, vanquisher of the *Guerriere*, and commanded by Captain Isaac Hull. The plate is rare and valuable.

THE FULTON STEAMBOAT (*Fig. 6*) — A companion piece, octagonal also, with the same scallops and outer edge. The inner border, however, is different; lined, not stippled, and adorned with scrolls and shields. The plate lacks the large glass dots; the central circle is stippled, and the boat is shown as a real steamboat, not with sails, which may indicate that the design was taken from a later drawing. A pennant and the Stars and Stripes are displayed, a star marks the paddle-box, and the waves are flowing and clearly indicated. A very rare and desirable piece.

THE MAID OF THE MIST, OR NIAGARA (*Fig. 7*) — A very crude and ugly piece of glass, made evidently when the worker's art had degenerated, since it could not have been stamped before 1855, the date of the completion of the Suspension Bridge. (The *Maid of the Mist* we know from Prescott's letter to have been already running some years in 1851, and in 1850 Frederika Bremer mentions a Suspension Bridge as well.) This plate, probably, symbolizes the larger, and, perhaps, more imposing structure. The rim is plain, the border has a design of pressed circles, and the central design shows the Suspension Bridge, a part of the Falls, the *Maid of the Mist*, and a most primitive sun. An unbeautiful cup-plate, but valuable on account of its rarity. It is certainly *not* a Sandwich piece — it is a popular fallacy to ascribe any and all pressed glass, it matters not what date or design, to Deming Jarves's factories — but was probably made at some New York State glassworks. Barber does not mention any in his "History of American Glass," but I have seen early nineteenth-century advertisements of factories both at Bristol and at Albany.†

HENRY CLAY (*Figs. 8, 9, 10, 11*) — The three and a half inch cup-plate stamped with the small head of Henry Clay is one of the most frequently found designs. There are six variants of this pattern, the least rare having a scalloped rim precisely like the *Cadmus* variant, a border of cornucopias, and a double-topped shield that resembles nothing so much as an opened umbrella. The elements of this border are common to all Henry Clay cup-plates, but are not equally well handled. Sometimes two, sometimes four, of the shields occur, — an inner circle of sprawling sprays and flowers, and a cameo-like bust of Henry Clay within a

---

*Not illustrated.

†Van Rensselaer: *Early American Bottles and Flasks*, p. 107, notes the Van Rensselaer Glassworks at Albany, started 1807; Albany Glassworks; Allenville, N. Y., glassworks, about 1847; Lancaster, N. Y., glassworks, about 1840.

Figs. 8 and 9 — Henry Clay

Fig. 13 — George Washington

Figs. 10 and 11 — Henry Clay

GLASS CUP-PLATES

circle an inch and an eighth wide. A star is impressed directly below the bust. A variant shows scallops of different sizes on the rim. An extremely interesting variant of this, and the handsomest of the series, exhibits a rim of large and small scallops; the cornucopias and umbrellas, or double shields, appearing twice, only, in the border and supported by flowing acanthus scrolls. The inner rim is decorated with a somewhat snaky design, within whose convolutions two stars appear. The "N" in Henry is turned about, thus, "И." Yet another variation has a border of regularly recurring scallops. The next commonest has the name omitted and no star. Otherwise the plate is standard. Another, which is rare, has an alternately rounded and pointed edge, a slightly different inner rim — flowing lines rather than any direct pattern — and five stars.* A very interesting comparison of this cup-plate border can be made with the one on the Victoria cup-plate, which is, of course, an English piece. It closely resembles the Clay, the only difference being the heads. The time of Clay's great popularity was, I believe, in 1844, when he was the Whig nominee and ran for the Presidency against Polk. This was some seven years later than Victoria's coronation, but an English plate would naturally have an earlier pattern. English workmen, as we know, were brought over to Sandwich by Deming Jarves; they may have carried with them the design, or it might have been copied from imported glass.

THE LARGE HEAD OF HENRY CLAY (*Fig. 12*) — One of the rarest and most desirable of glass cup-plates, ranking second only to the octagonal Washington. It is three and three-eighths inches in diameter, and the head itself is five-eighths of an inch high and half an inch wide. It has a stippled border with conventionalized fleur-de-lis. The inner circle has Henry Clay printed at the top; underneath sprays of laurel at the right, oak and acorns at the left, tied with a bowknot.† The head is really lifelike; evidently an attempted portrait with ambrosial locks, stock and cravat of the period. The coat sleeves, even, show the gathered-in effect of the early forties. Apart from any rarity and historical interest it is a beautiful piece of glass.

THE OCTAGONAL WASHINGTON (*Fig. 13*) — The desired cup-plate of all collectors. It is the same size as the Fulton steamboat and the frigate *Constitution;* the edge is scalloped, and the head is really magnificent, profiled as it is against a sunburst set in a stippled circle. Next there is an encircling wreath of laurel leaves, and a conventionalized scroll and flower border just inside the scalloped edge. The rarest of all historical cup-plates, probably,

Fig. 12 — Pseudo Henry Clay

because in the particular time that it was made, the sweeping popularity of Washington had lessened, perhaps since no direct political significance then attached to him. Beautiful as the design is it can never have been much in demand, or the plates would not now be so rare.

RINGOLD—PALO ALTO (*Fig. 14*) — The third rarest of the heads. A crude plate three and three-eighths inches across, with an edge of large and small scallops; of clear glass and with no stippling at all.‡ The head, however, is a very finely modeled bust nearly an inch and three-quarters in height, and so carefully depicted that the hair, stock, military collar and epaulets are plainly discernible. On the left side of the bust is the word Ringold; on the right, Palo Alto. This is a commemorative cup-plate made in 1846, the date of Major Samuel Ringold's death on the field of Palo Alto. This battle was the opening wedge in the Mexican War, and, for a brief time, Ringold was a national hero. He soon dropped out of remembrance, however, which, perhaps, accounts for the rarity of the plate.

This piece has none of the Sandwich characteristics, and, in view of the fact that Ringold was a Marylander, I have no doubt that the cup-plates *may* have been stamped at the Baltimore Glass Works, though there is also a chance that the Dyottville Glass Works of Kensington, Philadelphia, may have pressed the Ringold plate, for this firm is known to have made the Taylor and Ringold bottles. I have seen but four of these plates, and all were picked up in Philadelphia, which scores another point for Dyottville.

HARRISON (*Figs. 15 and 16*) — Moderately rare; three and a half inches in diameter, and with an edge composed of small scallops. The draped border resembles the one used on one of the Bunker Hill cup-plates. At the top, set in a dotted space, is the word Harrison, with a star on either side and a star as a period; below is the date of his presidency, 1841. The inner circle shows a rim of stars with the bust in the center and the words Maj. Gen. W. H. Harrison above, born Feb. 9, 1773, below. It is interesting to compare this cup-plate with the political medal of the same date, for both, of course, mark the spirited and picturesque Log Cabin Campaign. Allowing for the natural differences of material and size, the copper and glass heads are almost precisely similar. The coin may easily have been used as a model. A rarer variant of this plate has the word President and the date 1841 omitted, undoubtedly the fault of some mould; unless the unmarked example was sold during the campaign preceding the election.

LOG CABIN WITH CIDER BARREL, FLAG AND TREE (*Figs. 17 and 18*) — One of the smaller cup-plates, three and a quarter inches in diameter. It has a small scalloped edge, a border of sprays and flowers, and a central design of a Log Cabin with a Flag, a Tree and a Cider Barrel; symbols, of course, of the Hard Cider Campaign of Tippecanoe, and resembling very closely the design on the reverse side of the Harrison medal. A variant, very rare in-

---

*Not illustrated.

†This plate must be wrongly labeled. The old warrior represented has not the faintest resemblance to Clay. The suggestion is that of Zachary Taylor. Examples of mislabeling are common in blue Staffordshire; why not in glass? This plate is reproduced in larger scale to facilitate comparison of the portrait. May it not be of English manufacture?

‡Variant edge has scallops and points.

Fig. 14 — General Ringold

Figs. 15 and 16 — General Harrison

Figs. 17 and 18 — Log Cabin—Tree and Barrel

Fig. 19 — Fort Meigs Cabin

Fig. 20 — Cabin with Flag

Fig. 21 — Chimney Cabin

GLASS CUP-PLATES

deed, has an acorn border, which may prove that this Log Cabin was made at Sandwich, for there is an interestingly traditional little story of Deming Jarves's controversy with the captain of the vessel who carried his wares to Boston; of his threatening to build a ship of his own, and of the captain's retort, "The acorn isn't yet planted which will grow the oak that is to build your ship." And of Deming Jarves's answer to the taunt in the naming of the ship, which he immediately built, *The Acorn*. This idea, naturally, would apply to all acorn designs, and is pure conjecture.

FORT MEIGS LOG CABIN (*Fig. 19*) — About as rare as the first Log Cabin. It is larger, a trifle over three and a half inches. The edge is scalloped, the border a wreathing of acorns, and the central design a log cabin, heavier and lower in construction than the one on the Cider Barrel and Flag Cabin. On the border, at the top, is the word "Tippecanoe" (Harrison was so called from his victory over Tecumseh), below "Wm. H. Harrison"; while just above the log cabin are the words "Fort Meigs," in memory of the first skirmish of the War of 1812.

LOG CABIN WITH FLAG (*Fig. 20*) — Very rare, and one of the smallest of all cup-plates, measuring just a fraction over three inches. The edge is a plain, small scallop, the border has two encircling lines, and the ground on which the Log Cabin stands is indicated very much as the waves in the ship cup-plates are.

LOG CABIN WITH CIDER BARREL AND OUTER CHIMNEY (*Fig. 21*) — Three and a quarter inches, very heavy and crude, with a rare twisted scalloped edge, and a large, heavy log cabin occupying the center of the plate. This design more resembles the Fort Meigs than the two others, but it is bigger, shows a wide front view, a side displaying a wide, substantial chimney, and an ample cider barrel rolled under the window. It is by far the rarest of all the Log Cabins.

THE BEE HIVE (*Figs. 22 and 23*) — One of the smaller three-inch cup-plates, and decidedly one of the prettiest of all the historical ones. It has a plain scalloped edge, a graceful border of laurel leaves and a lacy stippled inner circle adorned with a bee hive outlined with nine bees. There is a variant, a heavier plate,

Figs. 22 and 23 — Bee Hive

crude and smaller, with a border that shows a shell pattern. I have heard that there are other types, too, and since the Bee Hive is a typical Harrison symbol, fashioned into appropriate and useful ink bottles by the firm of Whitney Brothers of Glassboro, and woven into 1841 table linen, I have no doubt of this statement, although I have never seen them.

THE 1831 EAGLE (*Fig. 24*) — Three and a half inches in diameter, with a scalloped edge, a charming stippled border, ornamented with flower sprays and fleur-de-lis, and, at the bottom, what may be interpreted as four pine trees. In a way, these trees may be symbolic of the event the plate commemorates, the settlement of the boundary line between the United States and Canada. The inner circle is stippled and decorated with arabesques and four stars. This encloses the eagle with head to the right and shield on breast. Below the eagle the date, 1831, is marked. Fairly common.

PLAIN EDGED EAGLE (*Fig. 25*) — Size three and three-eighths inches. A stippled edge decorated with arabesques and a large eagle, head turned to right, is set in a stippled center. There is no shield on the breast, but the eagle appropriately grasps arrows and an olive branch. Probably dedicated — as most of these eagles were — to the jingoistic "spread-eagleism" of the time. About as rare as the Dated Eagle.

SMALL EAGLE WITH DOTTED EDGE (*Fig. 26*) — The width is three inches, perhaps a shade more. The edge is scalloped, with dots in each scallop. The glass is plain, and the central eagle, facing the right, has a shield on breast and holds arrows and the olive branch. Also, scattered around, are thirteen stars, symbolizing, of course, the Thirteen States. A very rare plate.

THE GRAPEVINE EAGLE (*Fig. 27*) — One of the prettiest of the eagle plates, and rare. The edge is alternate points and rounds; stars, scrolls, and a fleur-de-lis-like motif — all in clear glass — adorn the stippled border. The central eagle (still with olive branch and arrows) is very tiny, three-quarters of an inch perhaps. It is set in a small dotted circle, and the outer rim is quite charmingly decorated with a grapevine.

THE FLEUR-DE-LIS EAGLE (*Fig. 28*) — An equally desirable

Fig. 24 — Eagle, 1831

Fig. 25 — Plain Edged Eagle

Fig. 26 — Eagle with Dotted Border

Fig. 27 — Grapevine Eagle

Fig. 28 — Fleur-de-Lis Eagle

Fig. 29 — Eagle with Thirteen Stars

Figs. 30 and 31 — Eagle with Thirteen Stars in Sun-burst

GLASS CUP-PLATES

plate, measuring three and three-eighths inches. The edge is plain scalloped, the border stippled and adorned with leaves and formal flowers of bright (clear) glass. The eagle is a trifle larger than the Grapevine Eagle, and this time the enclosing ring is stippled glass. The eagle has a shield, arrows and olive branch, and the outer rim (which gives the plate its name) is composed of fleur-de-lis and little starlike flowers.

EAGLE WITH THIRTEEN STARS (*Fig. 29*) — A rare cup-plate, which measures three and a quarter inches. The edge is scalloped; the border is made up of a conventional design made of pineapples, acroteria and rosettes, the latter resembling daisies. The eagle is large; head turned to right; shield, arrows, and olive branch. In a semi-circle above the eagle are stamped thirteen stars.

EAGLE WITH THIRTEEN STARS IN SUN-BURST (*Figs. 30 and 31*) — This cup-plate measures three and three-eighths inches, and the edge is scalloped with alternate points and rounds, and the rounds are dotted. The border is stippled and embellished with "fine fingering"; the eagle is a little smaller than the one just described, but shows the conventional shield, arrows and olive branch; and thirteen large stars set in a stippled border form a circle around it. A crude variant shows crowded borders and a close-clipped scalloped edge. At the Essex Institute in Salem there is another interesting variant of this plate, in which, the edge is plain, the scallops being omitted. A rare type.

THE FORT PITT EAGLE (*Figs. 32 and 33*) — The most beautiful of all the eagles and the second rarest. It is large, measuring three and three-quarters inches; the edge is scalloped, and the border that beautiful peacock design found on English plates. The eagle is medium-sized, but very finely done; there is more of an attempt at plumage than in the others. There are twenty-four stars,— a fact which dates the plate subsequent to the admission to statehood of Missouri, in 1821, and previous to that of Arkansas, in 1836; for Missouri was the twenty-fourth state. I date it Pittsburgh, 1835. It looks like a memorial to commercial progress, of whose further exemplification a collecting friend of mine has a steamboat cup-plate marked Pittsburgh Glassworks, 1836. It is more than probable, since this eagle plate represents Fort Pitt — the first name of Pittsburgh — that it should have been stamped in that city and at those works. The details are

very fine; the shield, arrows, and olive branch very clearly impressed, the sparkle of the glass, white and radiant. The words Fort Pitt are printed on a scroll that the eagle carries in his beak. A variant of this plate, the plain-edged type, is sometimes found, but it seems hardly so fine.

THE HOP-VINE (BLACKBERRY-VINE) EAGLE (*Fig. 34*) — In my experience, rarer than any other eagle. It is three and one-quarter inches in diameter, as heavy as the Ringold and very nearly as crude in texture. The edge is plain, the border an interesting and very graceful vine. The very small eagle is encircled by a dotted ring; the rest of the center by concentric circles. The glass is very full of bubbles showing improper "cooking," and the plate bears none of the Sandwich aspect. I am inclined to attribute it to some New York State glassworks.

BUNKER HILL (*Figs. 35, 36, 37 and 38*)—There are four Bunker Hill variants, all very well known. All have scalloped edges; two have braided, two draped borders. The largest is three and five-eighths inches. This is the Bunker Hill with the Braided Border, indicating the stonework of the monument. There are stars at the crossings of the braids and thirteen stars around the monument in the center. In the outer circle is printed, "Bunker Hill Battle Fought June 17th, 1775."

The second Braided Border is a little smaller, three and a half inches; the monument shows no stones, only twelve stars are displayed, and the plate is rather crude. There are two circles of printing, "Bunker Hill Battle Fought June 17, 1775," and "From the Fair to the Brave." The more usual Draped Border has an outside rim of printing, "Cornerstone Laid by Lafayette June 17, 1825. Finished by the Ladies"; otherwise the printing is the same as on the second Braided Border plate. This monument has stones, but lacks the stars. The second Draped Border is precisely the same except that it has twelve stars impressed around the monument. I think that there is no doubt whatever that these Bunker Hill plates were made at Sandwich. They are a distinctly Massachusetts design, of course. "From the Fair to the Brave" and "Finished by the Ladies" mean that the money for completing the monument was given by Massachusetts women, and a quaint little legend, handed down to me by an old lady of seventy, who in her turn had heard it from a woman forty years older, says that one way the women raised their necessary funds was

Figs. 32 and 33 — Fort Pitt Eagle, Scalloped and Plain   *Fig. 34* — Hop-Vine Eagle

Figs. 35 and 36 — Bunker Hill—Braided Border   *Figs. 37 and 38* — Bunker Hill—Draped Border

GLASS CUP-PLATES

by selling these cup-plates. I merely give this for what it is worth.

*   *   *

And so ends my tale of historical glass cup-plates. May I add a few "Don'ts"?

Don't call all pressed glass Sandwich. That's as bad as all eighteenth-century glass being labeled *Stiegel* and all eighteenth-century furniture *Chippendale*. Deming Jarves happened to be the first in the field, and you must remember that all successful enterprises have their imitators.

Don't confuse cup-plates with butter plates. Butter plates have no flattened surface on which to rest the cup.

Don't let dealers sell you the *Cadmus*, and insist it is the *Mayflower*.

Don't forget to look carefully at the borders and edges, for that is where the difference in variants is most likely to occur.

Don't — having bought cup-plates — pile them one on top of the other, for that way is sure to nick the edges. Better to follow my plan and put them in a cabinet drawer against black velvet. This keeps them safe, and accentuates their lustre.

Don't forget that cup-plates are still to be found on distant farmhouse shelves, perhaps up in the attic at your grandmother's.

Last of all, don't forget that cup-plates offer one of the most beguiling of all possible quests for the collector.

"WESTERN VIEW OF SANDWICH (Central Part)" in 1839

This woodcut, reproduced from John Warner Barber's *Historical Collections,* " shows two Congregational churches, town house, and in the distance some of the buildings connected with the glassworks." It will be observed that the artist makes up for the diminishment of the factories, due to the requirements of perspective, by depicting smoke emerging from their chimneys in volume sufficient to cover the upper heavens,— sure indication of successful activity.

Notes on Historical Glass Cup-Plates

By Alice Van Leer Carrick *&* The Editor

[*Illustrations from the collections of Mrs. R. C. Taylor, Mrs. C. S. Bull, Mr. A. H. Scott, Mrs. L. G. Verrill, Mrs. A. E. Folsom, Mrs. M. B. Cookerow, Mrs. C. A. Brouwer, the Peabody Museum, the George Shepley library, and the Essex Insitute. The generous co-operation of these interested owners is appreciatively acknowledged* — Ed.]

IT is now nearly a year since my original study of historical cup-plates was published in Antiques. The purpose of this study was to offer a check list of known plates. It carried with it the obligation of endeavoring to identify the various designs shown and, where possible, to explain their significance.

As the check list was printed, it inevitably contained some errors. There were also, of course, many omissions, for hardly a day passes without the discovery of a new design. In several instances, further, the identifications and attributions have aroused differences of opinion. Out of these various circumstances and the forces which they set in motion has emerged a considerable amount of new material, very uneven in both quality and quantity; but, in general, of sufficient interest and value to be worth placing before readers of Antiques as informal notes, which, in turn, may well serve as a body of reference in case the check list is eventually published in concise and reasonably well balanced book form, in which chief emphasis would be placed on conclusions rather on the reasons back of them.

These notes concern two topics: 1, new light on the already well known plates; 2, newly encountered plates. They can not well be separated. I shall take up the well-known plates which call for discussion in the same order as that in which they appear in Antiques for February, 1922 (Volume I, p. 61), shall give them the same numbering, and, where it seems advisable, shall repeat the old illustrations.

The Cadmus

In case of newly encountered plates I shall either apply new numbers to new examples or shall use an old class number with a letter to indicate a sub-class.

I. Cadmus vs. Constitution

Cadmus, No. 1. Constitution, No. 5
(Both described in Antiques, February, 1922)

Some question has arisen as to whether the *Cadmus* and the *Constitution* plates were really intended to represent different ships or should properly be designated merely as the *large* Constitution and the *small* one. Some persons, it is understood, now use that designation.

The evidence is as follows: A water-color drawing by Anton Roux (*1765–1835*), in the Peabody Museum at Salem shows us the *Cadmus*. No frigate in the American navy ever bore this name. In the present instance the high bulwark, the painted port holes and the general shape of the vessel indicate that she was a merchantman. The *Cadmus*, by the way, was built in 1816 by Thatcher Magoun at Medford, Mass.

Likewise in the Peabody Museum occurs a five-foot model of the *Constitution*, which, in 1813, was given to the Salem East India Marine Society, by Captain Isaac Hull. It is the only accurate contemporary model known and was followed by the United States naval authorities when the *Constitution* was restored in 1907. The actual frigate was built in Boston in 1797.

The ordinary landlubber might well be forgiven if he should fail to perceive any very clear marks of difference between the two ships depicted, the one in water color, the

The Constitution

The Ship Cadmus
From a water color by Anton Roux in the Peabody Museum, Salem.

The Frigate Constitution
From a model in the Peabody Museum, Salem.

other in the rounded wood. When two such similar forms are reduced to the dimensions and material of cup-plate decoration, it
seems absurd to try to distinguish between them on the basis of
appearance.

At this point tradition appears to offer the safest guide. Tradition calls the small vessel the *Cadmus*, the large one the *Constitution*. It finds verification in the case of the second vessel in such
marks as the angle of the bowsprit, the shape of the stern, and
the placing of the row of portholes.

Granting, then, that the large plate represents the *Constitution*,
probability would yet favor a plate depicting the *Cadmus*. Lafayette's visit to America bulked very large in the events of the
day and was signalized by the newly established Sandwich
works.* To represent the *Chancellor Livingston*, and to omit
representation of the ship which bore the hero himself to this
friendly shore would have been an oversight of which Deming
Jarves would hardly have been guilty.

What may be the *Cadmus* appears likewise on a crude early
salt here pictured. The color of the glass and the general aspect
of the dish seem to imply early manufacture at Sandwich.

The following quotation from a contemporary newspaper will
serve to show how important was Lafayette's visit:

"General La Fayette, accompanied by his son, George Washington La Fayette, Mr. Auguste La Vasseur, a companion, and
one servant, arrived here yesterday morning in the Ship *Cadmus*,
captain Allyn, after a pleasant passage of thirty-one days from
Havre. The fact of his arrival was made known by the Telegraph
at an early hour, and it spread through the city with electrical
rapidity. Broadway was soon thronged, and the Battery crowded
with people." . . . He landed at Staten Island. . . . "The news of
the General's arrival had spread through the surrounding country with the rapidity of lightening; and from the dawn of day
until noon, the roads and ferry boats were thronged with people
who were hastening to the city to participate in the fete."

The Committee of Welcome chartered the steamship, *Robert
Fulton*, and the steamboats, *Chancellor Livingston*, *Oliver Ellsworth*, *Henry Eckford*, *Connecticut*, *Olive Branch*, and *Nautilus*,
which were used as an escort. They were ranged as an aquatic
guard between the south part of the Battery and Governor's
Island, and thence proceeded in order to Governor's Island. The
West Point Band played during the ceremony *See, the Conquer-
ing Hero Comes*, *Hail Columbia*, and the *Marsellaise*.

---

*See the B & S salt illustrated in ANTIQUES for April, 1922.

STEAM SHIP BENJAMIN FRANKLIN.

CAPT. R. S. BUNKER, will leave Providence
on FRIDAY next, 12 o'clock, M. Passengers by leaving their names at the Marlboro' Hotel,
or at A. J. ALLEN'S, No. 72, State-street, will be
provided with Coaches.　　　　March 11

COPY OF THE BENJAMIN FRANKLIN ADVERTISEMENT
　For some reason the masts and rigging are omitted. But otherwise note close
　similarity to cup-plate.

EARLY SANDWICH SALT
Shows alternate ship and eagle medallions.

II. BENJAMIN FRANKLIN, *No. 4*.

The study of this plate has been complicated by the appearance of an imitation, which is illustrated and discussed in
ANTIQUES for December, 1922 (Volume II, p. 252). There seems
good reason for believing that this plate was pressed at Sandwich; for the steamship *Franklin* occasioned great excitement in
and around Boston. The *Columbian Centinel* of September 10,
1828, quotes at length from the *Commercial Advertiser* a description of this new vessel:

"She has been several times put upon trial, and answered the
most sanguine expectations of owners, is now ready for service,
and, we understand, will depart hence tomorrow afternoon for
Providence, and thence on an excursion of pleasure for Boston.
She has been built according to the plans, and under the superin-
tendence of the veteran Captain E. S. Bunker by whom she is to
be commanded. In addition to her two engines of great strength
and power, she is ship-rigged, having three masts;† the length is
144 feet; breadth of beam 32 feet; breadth of guards 21 feet; making her extreme breadth 53 feet. Depth of hold ten feet. Her model
is of a graceful cast. The stern combines neatness, taste, and
beauty. In the centre is an excellent bust of the great philosopher
whose name she bears, on the left of which is the figure of Fame,
with her trumpet in her left hand, and, in her right, an olive
branch with which she is in the act of crowning the patriotic
sage. On the right is the Muse of History with her scroll to record
the deeds and the lessons of wisdom which fall from his lips. And
there are other emblems carved in relief upon the stern: such as,
books, a globe, mathematical instruments, and implements of
husbandry, with leaves of oak gilded, etc. She sits upon the water
like a swan, and is indeed a noble and stately ship.

"The interior of the ship has been finished with an eye solely
to neatness, plainness, comfort, and convenience. The ship was
built by Brown and Bell under the direction of Captain Bunker
himself. The engines were constructed by Ezra R. Dod of the
Sterling Works. The joinery, which is
finished in the very best manner, by
J. Wells and S. B. Macy.

"The design of the interior of the
ship, which is in all arrangements
most complete, has been taken without essential change or alteration
from those of Captain Bunker, upon
which the old *Experience* packets

The Benjamin Franklin

†Omitted, perhaps for reasons of space, in
the advertising column.

LANDING OF
LAFAYETTE
Cover of snuff box

The Robert Fulton

which formerly plied between Hudson and New York, were constructed in 1807, nearly twenty-two years ago. The *Experiment* was the first vessel built in the United States with the express design of conveying passengers only, and we think it no mean compliment to Captain Bunker that for twenty-two years, while so many able and accomplished artists have been engaged in constructing steam and other packets of every size and variety of form and beauty, for convenience of arrangement, beauty of design, and comfort of construction, the last was built upon the model of the first, as the *ne plus ultra* of this department of marine architecture.

"But enough for one day. The *Benjamin Franklin* will be put upon service tomorrow, and if she proves, as we believe she will, the *crack boat* of the Sound, we may write a letter to ourselves upon the subject from Boston." (Taken from the pages of the *Commercial Advertiser* "on Monday last.")

Here is part of a description of an excursion to Salem that took place September 17, 1828. It is the immense excitement in Massachusetts about the boat that makes its cup-plate seem to me a Sandwich piece. "This excellent steamer made an excursion to Salem on Saturday, and took from thence even 600 passengers and after skirting the shores of Marblehead, Nahant, and Lynn, passed over to Cape Ann shore, and returned after a long run to Salem." The tickets seem to have been fifty cents for the round trip.

Probably the first advertisement of regular passage was October 4, 1828. It is reproduced on page 21.

III. THE ROBERT FULTON, *No. 6.*

Here is the story of the *Fulton*'s part in the welcoming of Lafayette:

"The appearance of the *Robert Fulton* as she came down the East River from the Navy Yard, escorted by the *Connecticut* and *Oliver Ellsworth*, all superbly decorated, was rich beyond description. The yards were manned to the round tops with about two hundred seamen from the *Constitution*, who made an elegant appearance. Directly in the rear of the *Chancellor* was the *Robert Fulton*, whose lofty masts and widespread arms, which literally swarmed with men, towered proudly above her less pretending, but not less gay and beautiful consorts.

"It was the *Chancellor Livingston*, however, which was honored by the presence of the Committee, and Lafayette went on board of her under a triumphal arch, and over richly carpeted steps.

"The Battery was crowded with respectable people of both sexes, Castle Garden was filled; every boat that arrived to take its station was completely crowded with elegantly dressed ladies and gentlemen."—From the New York *Spectator*, Aug. 20, 1824.

A contemporary engraving presents this scene. It was used by Clews for a blue china pattern, and appears likewise on a snuff box belonging to Mrs. L. G. Verrill of Rochester, N. H. The latter is here reproduced. Mrs. Hudson Moore, in the *Old China Book*, affirms the inaccuracy of this picture, since, as she states, the *Robert Fulton* had but one mast instead of three. This is, in turn, at variance with the implications of the description of the Lafayette reception. But the existence of three masts, or of one, might appear to vitiate my earlier identification of this cup-plate as the *Robert Fulton*, for the glass representation displays no mast whatsoever. Yet this is not necessarily the case. The cup-plate in question has the appearance of Sandwich glass, its border is very similar in pattern to that of the *Chancellor Livingston*, which facts imply a relationship between the plates. That its shape is octagonal like that of the *Constitution* cup-plate, may here also imply some relationship, for on the gala day the *Fulton* was manned in part by seamen from the *Constitution*. There is no certainty in all of this. Each student of the subject will draw such conclusions as he sees fit. But if he is unduly troubled by the absence of masts on the cup-plate, he is referred to the advertisement of the *Benjamin Franklin*, which represents that vessel as innocent of masts as a diving bell.

Pittsburgh Steamboat

There remains the possibility that this nondescript craft to which so much attention is here devoted is, in reality, nothing better nor worse than a river steamer such as that pictured on the razor illustrated in ANTIQUES for December (Vol. II, p. 267). Yet it seems to me rather a possibility than a probability. I am inclined to view the 1836 Pittsburgh cup-plate, noted below, as a conscious reversion to the earlier Sandwich type exemplified in the *Robert Fulton*.

IV. THE PITTSBURGH STEAMBOAT, *No. 7a.*

"Union Glass Works, Pittsburgh, 1836." This is the legend on this plate. It is three and one-half inches in diameter, octagonal, and rather crude in effect. The border is scalloped and patterned with little ovals; at each octagonal point is a larger figure; around the inner border are conventional figures, two small eagles, and the numbers from one to eight. The central design (enclosed by the words quoted above) is a small side-paddle steamboat an inch and one-half long, flying the Stars and Stripes, and with a very realistic curl of smoke, the kind that children draw. The boat I have not been able to identify; I searched through the lists published in Hall's *The West*, in vain. Out of the hundred and seventy-three steamboats built at Pittsburgh none was dated 1836.

Nor are contemporary pictures helpful; the closest resemblance I found in the steamboat printed on a *Reward of Merit* card which admonished the receiver to remember his Creator in the days of his glad, glad youth. Such illustrations, I believe, were intended to give children a knowledge of mechanical contrivances, and of the busy world outside. Still, Ohio River commerce was so justly important in the early nineteenth century that the cup-plate really needs no explanation. An Ohio River steamboat was an object of great consequence. To quote from an enthusiast of those beginning days, "It was all that the Western country needed; and the name of Fulton should be cherished with that of Washington; if the one conducted us to liberty, the other has given us prosperity—the one broke the chain which bound us to a foreign country; the other has extended the channels of intercourse, and multiplied the ties which bind us to each other."

Henry Clay, *8 and 9*

George Washington

Henry Clay, *10 and 11*

V. HENRY CLAY and PSEUDO HENRY CLAY or HENRY CLAY turned to right.

Henry Clay has suffered at the hands of the imitator, but it is the *Henry Clay*, Nos. 8, 9, 10, 11, that has, or have, a grievance on this score. Concerning the extremely rare *Henry Clay* turned to the right, it was suggested in AN-TIQUES for February, 1922, that the head shown on that plate was more likely to be that of General Zachary Taylor, mistakenly used and hence wrongly labeled. Curious confirmation of this theory has recently come to light. One of Mrs. Verrill's snuff boxes depicts the rough and ready general. Forehead, nose, mouth, and chin are quite those of the individual of the cup-plate. With due allowances for translation into glass this would seem to be the man. The sharp-featured, straight-haired Clay bears no resemblance whatever to the plate.

If further confirmation were needed it might come from the study of a large lithograph, belonging to Dr. J. Milton Coburn of South Norwalk, Conn. In its delineation of the general this lithograph is almost identical with the engraving on the snuff box. It bears, however, this legend, "Entered according to the act of Congress in the year 1847 by Edw. Clay and F. Mitchelin." Is it not reasonable to suppose that Edward Clay, the publisher, was hastily accepted as the subject of a lithograph used as a basis for a cup-plate designed in honor of Henry Clay, the statesman, and that the error was not discovered until some few plates had been made and marketed? The extreme scarcity of the plate would thus be accounted for.

VI. OCTAGONAL WASHINGTON, *No. 13*.

The enormous adoration of Washington had perceptibly lessened two decades after his death, but the feeling was once more at high tide with the second visit of Lafayette. The blue Staffordshire china bearing the likenesses of both Washington and Lafayette, Lafayette at Washington's Tomb,

WASHINGTON SEAL
Illustration from Cloquet's Recollections of Lafayette

etc., are evidences of this. I am inclined to place the Washington cup-plate as one more Lafayette link. In a book, published in France the year after Lafayette's death, 1835, *The Recollections of the Private Life of General Lafayette*, by M. Jules Cloquet, M.D., it is stated that, in the library of Lagrange Lafayette, is "a seal habitually used by him, and given to him by Mr. Barnet, consul for the United States in Paris. It represents the head of Washington surrounded with rays." This is an interesting coincidence even if it is nothing more.

VII. MAJOR RINGOLD, *No. 14*.

Ringold appears to be somewhat more common than was indicated in my previous discussion of this plate. There is a variant of the plate as shown. It displays scallops and points.

VIII. GENERAL HARRISON, *Nos. 15 and 16*.

In previous discussions of this plate I spoke of the political medal of the time as being closely like it. A reproduction of this medal, taken from one in my possession, is illustrated on page 24.

IX. LOG CABINS, *Nos. 17 and 18*.

The close relation between campaign medal designs and cup-plates finds further exemplification in the resemblance between the small metal and enamel Harrison Campaign medal and the log cabin, tree, and barrel cup-plate illustrated.

X. LOG CABIN WITH LIBERTY CAP, *No. 21a*.

To the log cabin series must now be added the *Log Cabin with Liberty Cap* which, as probably the rarest of log cabins, deprives No. 21 of that emi-

Major Ringold

ZACHARY TAYLOR
Cover of snuff box.

Pseudo Henry Clay

HENRY CLAY
From an old lithograph.

Log Cabin with Liberty Cap

Log Cabin—Tree and Barrel.

The Plow.

General Harrison

nence. It is three and three-quarter inches in diameter; and of rough glass somewhat similar in touch to *No. 20*. The edge consists of large and small scallops. The plate displays cider barrel, bench, and tree, and, in addition, a flag pole surmounted by a liberty cap.

While Harrison emblems are under discussion, it is worth while to point to an interesting log cabin tea plate in which the Harrisonian log cabin is further embellished with an equally Harrisonian plow—likewise, no doubt, generally indicative of agriculture, just as the ship is indicative of commerce. Manufacture is probably symbolized in the glass factory.

What this factory represents is left to the judgment of the student. It has been called the Dyott works, but comparison with an old print belonging to Mr. Arthur H. Scott of Media, Pa., does not entirely support the attribution. In a case of this kind, so small a matter as the presence or absence of chimney caps may be of vital importance in the process of identification. The crude wood block of Sandwich published in ANTIQUES for February, 1922, shows the glass works pouring forth smoke from two capped chimneys. The careful capping of the stacks on this tea-plate is, therefore, not to be ignored.

Strict adherence to the lit-

Log Cabin Tea Plate
Bears emblems of agriculture, commerce and manufacture. The last is signalized by a glass factory.

eral presentation of various apparently minor details, and indifference to what an artist would consider basic exactitudes, is characteristic of the untrained or partially trained delineator. This is a fact not to be overlooked in studying resemblances in the field of the minor arts.

The care with which the makers of moulds for souvenir pressed glass followed copy will be shown by a comparison of the *Chancellor Livingston* cup-plate with the contemporary lithograph, from which it may, quite possibly, have been derived.*

XI. THE PLOW, *No. 22b*.

Probably dedicated to rural thrift and agricultural activity and hence produced in honor of Harrison, occurs this very attractive cup-plate. It is so rare as to be, perhaps, unique.

Within the year a number of hitherto unpublished eagles have come to light. These will presently be shown and discussed in ANTIQUES. Meanwhile additional material on the subject of cup-plates—whether in the form of substantiation, well-founded doubt or new discovery—will be very welcome.

*See frontispiece.

DYOTT GLASS WORKS
From a lithograph.

HARRISON CAMPAIGN MEDAL AND TOKEN
Note the similarity of the head to that on the cup-plate.

CUP PLATES OF THE PHILADELPHIA AREA

By HELEN McKEARIN and JAMES H. ROSE

FOR SOME TIME a few students have believed that cup plates were produced in the Philadelphia area. The theory advanced in *American Glass* (pp. 350, 352) that the Ringgolds, running-vine cabins, and other cup plates with identical serration patterns (*Fig. 2*) were made in the Philadelphia area was based on circumstantial evidence. In our experience a good seventy-five per cent of the known specimens of these plates have turned up in the region around Philadelphia, and the character and treatment of their designs differ in many respects from both New England and Midwestern practice. Besides, in the case of the Ringgolds it seemed a reasonable point of origin since Major Ringgold was more a local than a national hero, with his greatest popularity in the Philadelphia-Baltimore area. And if we attribute the Ringgold plates to that locality, we may also attribute the related items.

To the layman the number of varieties in each series might seem to indicate production in several factories, and for his benefit we explain briefly that all of these particular plates were pressed in molds having the serration pattern on the surface die and the design on the plunger. Since the measurements correspond, it is evident that the design could be varied at will simply by changing the part of the die attached to the plunger, while a change in the serration pattern meant nothing more difficult than changing the surface die. Thus with one die for each design (the two varieties of Ringgolds, the log cabin, and each of the three conventionals) plus four surface dies each with a different serration pattern, a factory could make twenty-four varieties of cup plates. Such a method was, of course, very economical, especially for a firm which bought its molds from an independent moldmaker. Not only could any number of made-to-order design parts be purchased separately, but also relatively few of the less expensive surface dies, which could be, and were, used over long periods of time, would be needed. It is interesting to note that twenty of these twenty-four possible varieties have been numbered by Albert C. Marble, and a twenty-first, a cabin with even serrations, is in the collection of Mrs. Palmer Graham. We are confident that the other three will turn up, for instance, a variant of 826-661 with even scallops as on 412.

The most likely date of the Ringgolds is 1846, the year of the major's death. But we do not believe that all the plates shown in Figure 2 are as late as that. The running-vine cabins, for example, are surely mementoes of the Harrison campaign and so date from 1839, or, at the latest, 1840. The three conventional groups cannot be precisely dated but might be said to record three steps in the decadence of design. The 826-661 series which is at the peak of the lacy type probably dates from about 1835. While the 81-80 series may be considered a more effective and consistent design than that of the 84-85 series, both are on the downgrade to Victorian coarseness. So it seems likely that they were pressed in the 1840's, the 81-80 series slightly antedating the 84-85. Thus these plates in Figure 2 represent a recognizable output over a period of about ten years (roughly from 1835 to the fall of 1846).

While all this evidence seemed conclusive we realized the danger of creating a new ghost like that of the Stoddard-three-mold fiasco,

a ghost that might prove ubiquitous and hard to lay if new facts turned up to discredit our assumption. Yet we felt very strongly that collectors should be turned from their far too facile faith that all pressed glass of the lacy period originated either in Massachusetts or the Pittsburgh-Monongahela district. And so we were much gratified by the receipt of an important piece of further evidence in its support from Mrs. Claude N. Campbell, great-great-granddaughter of Charles B. Austin, one-time proprietor of the Union Glass Works, Kensington, Philadelphia. In Mrs. Campbell's family there are four Ringgold cup plates like 634, with a strong family tradition of their having been made at this Union Glass Works. According to Mrs. Campbell, these Ringgolds came to her mother from a cousin who had been employed at the Excelsior Glass Works at Kaighn's Point, in New Jersey. Mrs. Campbell's mother also received from the same cousin a conventional cup plate like 421.

The history of the Union Glass Works is still somewhat obscure, though there is nothing in what we now know to indicate that glass was not pressed there; on the contrary, there is some evidence that it was. Jarves in his *Reminiscences* says that in 1820 a group of workmen left the New England Glass Company "to embark on their own account their savings of many years in the doubtful enterprise of establishing flint glass works in Kensington, Philadelphia under the title of the Union Flint Glass Company." An uncharitable undertone of "I told you so," if not of scorn for mere workmen attempting to turn entrepreneur, seeps through his brief account of their tragic failure. "The works passed into other hands," whose or when he does not say. The year in which the remnants of these New England glassworkers lost their financial interest was probably 1826. Thomas Porter, writing in the 1831 edition of Mease's *Picture of Philadelphia,* under the heading *Union Glass Works,* states that the Union Cut and Flint Glass Works was established in 1826 "by a company formed for the purpose." The company was probably that of Charles B. Austin and Company, a firm which met with considerable success under the guidance of its founder, Charles Baldrey Austin.

Until recently we have had only a few additional facts regarding the Union Glass Works and Charles B. Austin & Company. Briefly they are: specimens of their cut glass were shown in the exhibitions of the Franklin Institute in 1827 and 1831; various wares were exhibited in 1841 and 1842, in the latter year the colored glass receiving special mention; the company maintained warehouses at 10 Minor Street and 23 Dock Street in Philadelphia; Charles Austin was the agent; and by 1848 the works were operated by the firm of Lancaster & Hartwell. The picture has been filled in a little more by information from Mrs. Campbell and by evidence from directories.

Charles Austin, who was born in England September 9, 1787, was probably connected with the glass industry and was one of the many skilled artisans who escaped the hard times resulting from the Napoleonic wars by coming to the United States. He and his family sailed November 2, 1818, and landed in New York City, January 13, 1819. Since a Charles Austin was listed as a glasscutter at 7 Park in the New York City directories from 1821 through 1824,

FIG. 1 — "A VIEW OF PART OF THE UNION GLASS COMPANY'S WORKS KENSINGTON NEAR PHILAD^a."

Fig. 2 — Cup Plates of the Late Period (c.1835-1846). Attributed to the Philadelphia area. Numbers 81, 80, 826, 421, 336, and 661 occur in dirty apple-green as well as in clear glass. It seems likely that a Ringgold or log cabin in green may turn up. *Cup plate numbers used in text and illustrations are those of Marble's check list.*

and no other glasscutting firm is listed at that address, it is likely that he established his own shop there.

Just when he left for Philadelphia or who was associated with him in forming Charles B. Austin & Company we do not know. But by 1837 William Bennett and John Capewell, family connections and both capable glass men, were associated with the works. When Austin died in October 1840, William Bennett assumed management of the works. That within a short time the affairs of the company became involved is indicated by a lawsuit of "Ann Austin Administratrix of Charles B. Austin deceased Vs. William Bennett, Maria Capewell Bennett, Joseph Capewell, and Sarah Synar." In 1844 the firm was dissolved and it would seem that the works were idle until 1847. In October of that year the Union Glass Works exhibited at the Franklin Institute. Hartwell & Lancaster, who are listed in 1848 as the proprietors, probably took over in 1847.

In the meantime John Capewell, possibly during the period of the lawsuit, left the works and in 1842 with his brother James established the Excelsior Glass Works across the river at Kaighn's Point, South Camden, New Jersey. Here they made a high grade of glassware, specializing in cut and engraved. Undoubtedly they did pressing too. It is possible that the Capewells may have taken with them some of the molds from the Union Glass Works, including the surface dies for cup plates. These they might have used in conjunction with new design dies which they would have had made for the Ringgolds and perhaps also for the late conventionals of the 81-80 series. Thus there would be a continuity from the Union Glass Works, and the theory of origin for the entire series in the Philadelphia area would still hold.

Even if the Union Glass Works did not make the Ringgolds and the late conventionals, we still feel that they produced the earlier cup plates in the group, for the company was in operation during the period of early pressed and lacy glass manufacture. By 1826, the year the works began to prosper, at least two firms, the Bakewells of Pittsburgh and the New England Glass Company of Cambridge, Massachusetts, had been experimenting in the new art of mechanical pressing and had obtained patents in 1825 and 1826. In the following year the Jersey Glass Company secured a patent on an advanced method. Since this new money- and labor-saving method of production was adopted by virtually all manufacturers of tableware in the country it would be almost a miracle if the Union Glass Company failed to follow suit. In fact, it is not at all unlikely that the John McGann of Kensington who in November 1830 took out a patent on a pressing process far more complicated and advanced than any other on record at the time was associated with the company. (The only other glass factory in Kensington at that time of which we have record was the Philadelphia and Kensington Glass Works of Doctor Dyott, in 1833 christened the Dyottville Factory, which was a bottle and vial factory and did not make tableware until the 1840's when it changed ownership.) Moreover, the very intricacy of the McGann patent indicates that simpler pressing had been previously practiced at Kensington.

We have belabored the idea of the relative earliness of pressing at the Union Glass Works because we are convinced that many less subtle patterns preceded even the comparatively early 826-661 group. If this be true then there should be in existence cup plates which are peculiar to the Philadelphia area and of a cruder, hence earlier, type than those shown in Figure 2. Such plates, to fit ideally into our theory, should show characteristics in design and technique exclusive to the region, although traces of New England practice might be expected since it is likely that pressed ware of the New England Glass Company and the Boston and Sandwich Glass Company was popular in Philadelphia before the Union Glass Company began pressing. In the cup plates of Figure 3 these conditions are nicely realized.

We believe the plates in this group antedate 1830, excepting possibly 76 which is very Victorian in design. At first glance one might be tempted to assign 785 to the New England district. The large scallops of its rim are traditionally associated with New England and even, perhaps erroneously, with the New England Glass Company, as is also the sheaf-of-wheat pattern of its shoulder. A basket of flowers appears on the earliest salts of New England origin as well as on lacy salts and the so-called Providence sugar bowl. These New England manifestations of the motif are not, however, nearly so well conceived or modeled as that in 785. To the best of our knowledge but two examples of 785 are known to collectors and both of these turned up in the Philadelphia area.

Again in 462 (*Fig. 3*) we find the large New England scallop and the sheaf of wheat, both by the way indicative of early manufacture, but combined with a center pattern that from the New England point of view is unorthodox. Note the six-pointed star that reappears in the much later 81-80 series, and especially the acorn which gradually became one of the outstanding motifs of the

Philadelphia district. Although we know of three specimens of 462, we have been able to trace but two of them and these came from dealers in eastern Pennsylvania.

Still with the big New England scallops but lacking any other recognizable Massachusetts characteristic, we find 76 (*Fig. 3*), whose incidence in the Philadelphia region is truly remarkable. Although it is a very rare plate, we have owned fully a dozen examples that have been traced to eastern Pennsylvania. Moreover, we have seen a few toddy plates identical in pattern, all found in the area. Finally, 76 has a frosty upper surface like that found on 785 and 462. In fact, the incidence of a frosty or "sick" upper surface in these three plates is extraordinarily high. While we do not consider this conclusive evidence of a common origin it is so unusual to find "sick" cup plates that it is not unimportant.

Another early plate, possibly the earliest of all those we are considering, is 153 (*Fig. 3*). This shows no direct stylistic affiliations with any particular section but does demonstrate the widespread early habit of basing patterns on cut-glass designs. All, or virtually all, the specimens of both this plate and its variant, 759, of which we know have turned up around Philadelphia.

The last of these very early plates is 767 (*Fig. 3*). Besides a typical New England scallop it has the shoulder heart and the heavy stippled band in the center that are ordinarily associated with early Sandwich and New England Glass Company design, but the spacing and its center cross are completely unlike anything encountered from these factories. The distribution of this plate is confusing, to say the least. All the specimens known to us have been found either in western Pennsylvania or Ohio but it differs so radically in design and technique from accepted Midwestern practice that it seems incredible that it was made there. So, *tentatively*, we lean toward a Kensington attribution.

Thus far in this group we have been considering plates that we think antedate 1830. We believe this is unquestionably true in the case of 785 and 153, and probably true in the case of 462 and 767, but 76 is a stumbling block. It has the early type of scallop, it is often rather thick and heavy, and it frequently shows the sickness of 785 and 462; but the design shows a Victorian fussiness. It may or may not have been made before 1830. It should be noted, however, that the plates in Figure 3 were made without benefit of the cap ring, a gadget that, on the basis of its history in the Patent Office, we believe was in rather common use by that time.

Next in chronological order we come to the plates shown in Figure 4, which we place about 1830. 291 has one New England feature in the concentric bands, including the strawberry diamond, in its center, and perhaps another, much modified, in the alternating simple motifs on its shoulder. This plate and its variant, 816, which are scarce but not rare, are found much more often in eastern Pennsylvania than elsewhere. In the metal (we were about to say in the flesh), 296 seems at first glance to be an earlier plate than 291. It is heavier and cruder but its design is more mature and disciplined. Possibly more conclusive, it was made with a cap ring while 291 was not. The chances are that 296 postdates 1830, but by very little. So far as we know it is seldom found outside the Philadelphia area.

All the plates in Figure 5 we believe were made after 1830. While one of them is an eagle and the others conventional they are related through a running-vine motif which they have in common, an approach to naturalism characteristic of the period. All of these plates but 386 turn up largely if not always in the Philadelphia

FIG. 3 — CUP PLATES OF THE EARLIEST PERIOD (*before 1830*). Clear glass.

district. The latter is quite common and is often found as far afield as Ohio although even there its highest incidence is along the old National Road (now U. S. Route 40), in the early days the best road from the East. The unusual and artistically absurd practice of having a pattern on the top as well as the bottom of the plate as in 19 and 386 may derive from the very rare eagle of New England provenance, 504. Note the reappearance of the acorn motif in 141, 386, and 552, as well as the vague resemblance to the jewel-like drops of 76 in the beads pendent below the bellflowers of these three plates.

In conclusion we call attention to the astonishingly high incidence of a peculiar green, somewhat like a slightly dirty apple-green, in these plates as noted in the captions. The occurrence of this same color in plates which we have good reason to believe were made at different times would seem to indicate the use of a particular recipe over a long period of time, especially since the shade is a very unattractive one and seldom met with in other areas. Note, too, that 552 has been found in a very beautiful shade of amethyst. 386,296, and 421 are encountered quite commonly in faint but still definite tints of green and amethyst, as though the melting pot had been used just previously for a mix either of green or amethyst and had not been thoroughly cleaned. While these tints could have been caused by too much or too little black oxide of manganese, we feel they have significance considered with the other evidence. In fact, we feel strongly that our theory as to the origin of all these plates is much enhanced by the evidence of color.

Not wanting to spoil collectors' fun in further speculation on the other possible patterns from the Philadelphia area (and they undoubtedly were many), we will content ourselves with pointing to a certain similarity between 76 and 151-346 and add that the apparent connection is enhanced by the occasional occurrence of lavender specimens of 151. For the collector of larger pieces of lacy glass who is usually far more firmly wedded to Sandwich attributions, we call attention to Lee's *Sandwich Glass,* Plate 101, lower left, which matches our 153, as well as to the already noted toddy plates matching 76. We have little doubt that many large pieces of hollowware stem from this area, but we leave further speculation to specialists in that field. Further research and comparative study, we feel sure, will vastly increase the meager number of patterns here attributed to the Philadelphia area and probably made at the Union Glass Works.

EDITOR'S NOTE: In the past ANTIQUES has published several articles on the general subject of cup plates. We are listing these below for the benefit of our readers.

Historical Glass Cup Plates, by Alice Van Leer Carrick, February 1922 (pp. 61-66).

Notes on Historical Glass Cup Plates, by Alice Van Leer Carrick and Homer Eaton Keyes, January 1923 (pp. 22-26).

A Check List of Colored Cup Plates, by James H. Rose, August 1933 (pp. 63-64).

Early Glass Pressing at Cambridge and Sandwich, by Lura Woodside Watkins. Part 1, October 1935 (pp. 151-152). Part II, December 1935 (pp. 242-243).

Rims and Reasons, by James H. Rose, August 1936 (pp. 68-69).

Pressed Glass a Debtor to Staffordshire? Editorial Note, August 1937 (p. 78).

Fresh Reflections on American Glass, Editorial Note, February 1938 (pp. 82-83).

Cup-Plate Fragments Excavated at Sandwich, by Lura Woodside Watkins, September 1938 (pp. 132-133).

A Question in Cup Plates, by Mildred K. Pike, January 1939 (pp. 16-18).

The Fort Pitt Glass Works, by John Ramsay, April 1940 (pp. 190-191).

FIG. 4 — CUP PLATES OF THE EARLY-MIDDLE OR TRANSITION PERIOD *(c.1830).* 291, faint green tint. 296, faint green tint and faint amethyst tint.

FIG. 5 *(above, left)* — CUP PLATES OF THE MIDDLE PERIOD *(c.1830-1835).* 19 occurs in green, also in faint green tint and faint amethyst tint. 386, faint green tint and faint amethyst tint. 141, green. 552, green, also amethyst.

FIG. 6 *(above, right)* — CUP PLATE *(c.1835).* A plate not discussed in the text since its design shows no stylistic affinities to other plates of the area as they are now known. It is found nowhere, however, but in the Phila-delphia region, and the authors are convinced that it was made there.

FIG. 7 *(below)* — NEW ENGLAND CUP PLATES. Compare with plates here attributed to Philadelphia area. 468 and 180 exemplify the running vine. 176, early New England type of scallop; compare also shoulder heart with 767. 101, scallop and stippled band. 124, big scallop and strawberry diamond; compare with Figures 3 and 5.

MIDWESTERN CUP-PLATE DESIGNS

By JAMES H. ROSE

FOR NEARLY twenty years the glass specialists and the better informed collectors have quite generally agreed that a not inconsiderable fraction of our collectible early glass had its origin in obscure factories west of the mountains. As they became more familiar with types and techniques they discovered that they could distinguish between examples made on the seaboard and those hailing from the hinterland, and gradually specific characteristics became recognized clues to regional origins.

Thus, in the cup-plate field, there is a tacit and virtually unanimous consent that six peculiarities in design are, beyond any reasonable doubt, indications of midwestern manufacture. If, however, the expert is goaded by the skeptic into extending his critical faculties beyond these too few basic symbols, he inevitably falls back upon the old cliché about "feel." Actually, there is no such thing. "Feel" is only the piling up in the subconscious of many bits of evidence, and it remains intangible, a mysterious sixth sense, only until someone takes the trouble to analyze, arrange, and catalogue these bits of evidence.

So if we can segregate certain hitherto unidentified mannerisms of design that appear very frequently in conjunction with the six universally accepted midwestern motifs, we shall have measurably increased the tangible evidence and, let us hope, limited the use of the vague generalities in which we are now forced to take refuge. Moreover, we shall have substantially bolstered the force of our six axioms.

For the benefit of the beginner as well as for convenience and clarity in our future argument, let us first consider the six fundamental traits of midwestern design. They are, in what would seem to be the probable order of their introduction (numbers given refer to Marble's classification of cup plates):

(A) The use of a large, plain (in the sense of having no stippling or other pattern) type of serration. It should be noted that while these serrations are deeply indented, there is still a considerable margin between the deepest indentation and the beginning of the shoulder pattern. Since plates having this feature are always fairly crude and are rare, they seem to represent very early midwestern practice, at least the earliest we can at the moment rec-

ognize. This serration is shown in plates 658, 456, 451, 351, etc.
(B) The use of a peculiar cloth-like stippling. Here again we seem to be dealing with a very early technique. Note that it appears in the plates mentioned above and also that it seems to have persisted into somewhat later manifestations as, for instance, in 299, 416, and 279.
(C) The use of an exaggeratedly high foot or table-rest — in fact the use of a foot at all — as shown in its extreme form on such plates as 451 (coupled with A type serrations and cloth-like stippling), in 658 and 351 (again with our A and B motifs), in 299 and 416 with B, and so on.
(D) The use of a type of scallop-and-point serration which is related to our A type but which appears to be slightly later in origin and almost certainly was simply a further development, a refinement, of the A type. Here again, it should be noted that it is the relative plainness, not the form, that indicates midwestern manufacture. The scallop and point were used in both east and west, but only in the west do we find this wide gap between the rim of the plate and the beginning of the shoulder pattern. See 429, 503, 410, and especially 713. In this last plate we again encounter our C device, the table-rest.
(E) The use of the bull's-eye and bull's-eye-and-point type of serrations. (It is true that Sandwich, or some eastern factory, used a variation of this but only, so far as I know, on one piece — a large plate; see Lee, Sandwich Glass, Plate 122, top. But this in no way resembles the midwestern type of bull's-eye which is best exemplified by 284 and 487.) No eastern cup plate known to us today has anything remotely resembling a bull's-eye border. For typical midwestern uses of these two motifs see 416, 55, 249, 73, and so on; note that many of these show other midwestern characteristics already discussed.
(F) And, finally, the use west of the mountains of a coarser stippling than is generally encountered on eastern plates. Here we are on rather dangerous ground for, while this is the midwestern characteristic most often cited, it is not always true and must be considerably modified lest it become a dangerous tool in the hands of the amateur. Look, for example, at those indubitably eastern

222

Fig. I. Motif used on cup plates 562, 456, 416, 658, 567.

Fig. II. Motif on 284, 279, 416, 713, 487, 567, 562.

Fig. III. Motif on 658, 451, 567, 456, 284, 487.

Fig. V. Motif on plate 449.

Fig. IV. Motif on 469, 23.

Fig. VI. Motif on 269, 445.

Fig. VII. Motif on plate 56.

plates, 105, 132, 295, etc., where the stippling is even coarser than we commonly find on midwestern plates. Our proposition should be stated conversely, *i.e.*, that no truly fine stippling (as fine, let us say, as that on 1) is found on midwestern plates. Thus, coarse stippling means nothing unless coupled with other known midwestern motifs, but *really fine stippling always indicates eastern origin.*

These six characteristics are quite generally accepted as typically midwestern. We can even go so far as to say that no one of them appears on any known eastern plate. Let us now go still further and see whether we can discover additional motifs occurring commonly in conjunction with these first six and, of course, never appearing on known eastern plates.

(I) The earliest of these new motifs to appear seems to be the peculiar form of lunette or C-scroll found in 658, in combination, with A, B, and C characteristics; in 456 again with A, B, and C; in 416 with B, C, and E; in 575 with C and E; in 567 with C; in 562 where the C-motifs form a four-sided figure; and so on.

(II) Further examination of typical plates shows us a peculiar leaf form that occurs in a truly astonishing number of plates. In cup plates this motif assumes two guises: trefoil as, for example, in 284, and cinquefoil as in 279. Tying it in with our midwestern axiomatic techniques we find it in trefoil form in 284 along with a bull's-eye serration pattern, while in 487 it is coupled with the bull's-eye and point type. Its incidence in that extremely interesting series, 456, 465, 299, 546, and 416, permits us to hazard a guess that, relatively speaking, it is a device that did not come into use in the earliest period. It is missing in 456, where we find the most primitive type of serration in conjunction with very crude cloth-type stippling, and in 465, again with this same stippling. With the further development of this series and the further refinement of its stippling, the trefoil comes into its own. Plate 279, in which the motif assumes its cinquefoil shape, has been authenticated as a Pittsburgh product (see ANTIQUES, August 1937, pp. 90, 92). This leaf form was very popular in the midwest, and we will not belabor the point beyond directing attention to such plates as 562, 73, 673, and 713.

(III) Still further inspection reveals the frequent occurrence of what, for want of a better term, we may call the porthole device. In its most archaic form this is merely a series of plain circular or semicircular reserves in a stippled band on the shoulder of a plate, as in 451, 658, 456. Gradually, it was modified into such forms as we find on 284, 567. Of course, the east as well as the west understood the dramatic value of relatively large plain surfaces framed in stippling, but the practice in the east seems to have been to tie these plain surfaces into the pattern. This was difficult if not impossible on a small surface and the device was used on no eastern cup plate, but is rather commonly encountered there in larger pieces. This, of course, ties in with the rather broad generality that the east was committed to the use of a more delicate scale than the west. Finally, it should be emphasized that our consideration of this particular motif is limited strictly to its appearance on the curve of the shoulder.

(IV) We now come to the widespread use in the midwest of a sort of rayed or sunburst effect on the shoulders of cup plates, as in the eagles, 22 and 23, and the conventionals, 423, 469, 352, etc. It is true that this motif was used at a considerably later date on plates that are very probably of eastern and perhaps Sandwich origin, such as plates 187, 218, 220, etc. So far, however, as its early use is concerned, it was confined to the west. It would be unwise to assume that the east pirated this motif from the west, since it seems more than probable that both sections stole it from the French where it was extremely popular in all branches of design.

(V) Another shoulder pattern frequently used in the west was a leaf form or palmette enclosed in a crude gothic arch. See 449 (note the feet or table-rests in an undeveloped form), 359.

(VI) Another palmette device that appears on midwestern plates is the anthemion with streamers or scrolls, as in the eagle, 269, and in the conventional, 445. This same motif occurs also on larger plates (see Lee, Plates 156, 157).

(VII) Finally, we come to the use of a conventionalized leaf motif, pointed at both ends, as a shoulder decoration. This is another characteristic midwestern device, appearing on such typically western cup plates as 56.

The motifs here enumerated and illustrated are specific and may be readily identified. Thus, by careful examination of a cup plate and analysis of its design, we may go far toward crystallizing the definite components of "feel." We may, too, distinguish readily and accurately between many of the cup plates produced in the east and those of the midwestern glassmaking area.

LACY GLASS WINDOW PANES

Their Use, Process, and Origin

By JAMES H. ROSE

THE LITERATURE ON LACY GLASS WINDOW PANES that I have been able to discover is limited to brief discussions in ANTIQUES for February and December 1938. It may be summarized as follows: A Bakewell, Page and Bakewell advertisement of 1836 mentioning "Pressed panes for steamboats," quoted by Rhea M. Knittle in *Early American Glass* (New York, 1927), was the basis for attribution of the few panes then known to that famous Pittsburgh glassworks. A certain waviness of surface readily observable on the blank sides of these panes led to the theory, first, that they were not pressed in the ordinary fashion but on the contrary were rolled, and, later, that they were simple castings.

When these articles were written, the mechanics of early pressing was imperfectly understood. It was then reported that two patterns of lacy panes had been discovered, though it now appears that the examples found were all of the same pattern. In the intervening eight years at least three new patterns have turned up and a thorough investigation has been made of early pressing techniques so that a reexamination of the pioneer conclusions is advisable. Such an inquiry should cover three specific problems: 1. *Use*. Were these panes intended for use exclusively on steamboats? 2. *Process*. Were they cast, rolled, or pressed in the normal fashion? 3. *Origin*. Who made them?

Use. The pane in Figure 1 came from the door of a corner cupboard found near Lisbon, Ohio. Like all the others it measures, roughly, 5 by 6⅞ inches and is about ¼ inch thick. Since most cupboard doors of the period had much larger panes this is most likely a very rare or perhaps even a unique use. It can even be argued that the cabinetmaker built his cupboard, so to speak, around some available panes. Judged by design this pane was made between 1835 and 1840.

Panes of the pattern shown in Figure 2 are from the sidelights of the doorway of a house built about 1850 in Franklin County, Indiana. Half the panes were clear glass and half were amethyst and these were set alternately. The design here seems to be the earliest of all the four known patterns, dating probably about 1835.

A correction can now be made of the note in ANTIQUES for December 1938 which told of panes from a house built in Oxford, Ohio, in 1851, and described them as of a design "different in detail" from those of the Indiana house recorded in the February 1938 issue. Actually all the panes are of the same pattern and came from the Indiana house. Though the house was not built until about fifteen years after the date ascribed to the panes on the basis of their design, information provided by Mrs. G. V. Chapin of Oxford, Ohio, tends to substantiate this dating. The original owner of the house was Doctor William Ashton, who settled in Franklin County in 1834 and first lived in a loghouse, building his brick house about 1850. According to his grandson, the panes were stored in a box in the original dwelling and later placed around the doorway of the new home.

The panes of the type shown in Figure 3 came from door panels, not sidelights, in the old Schenley residence in Pittsburgh. In feeling their design is very close to that of the Lisbon cupboard pane and this suggests a date of 1835 or 1840. According to data furnished by George Wisecarver and George E. Born, the so-called Schenley mansion was built in two sections. Dates for the first structure are given

FIG. 1 *(above, left)*—LACY GLASS PANE from the door of a corner cupboard found near Lisbon, Ohio. 5 by 6⅞ inches. This pane is unique. *Collection of George C. Cannon.*

FIG. 2 *(above, right)* — LACY GLASS PANE in amethyst from Franklin County, Indiana. 5 by 6⅞ inches. Clear and amethyst examples of the pattern are owned by Doctor Parke G. Smith (see ANTIQUES, February 1938, p. 81). *Collection of Doctor Grace O. Doane.*

FIG. 3 *(right)* — LACY GLASS PANE from the old Schenley mansion, Pittsburgh, Pennsylvania. 5 by 6⅞ inches. *Collection of George E. Born.*

FIG. 4 *(far right)* — LACY GLASS PANE marked with maker's name. 5 by 6⅞ inches. Said to have come from a hall lantern in Wheeling, West Virginia. This pane is unique. *Collection of George C. Cannon.*

variously as 1825 or "the 1830's," while the addition is said to have been built in 1840 or 1845.

The pane in Figure 4 came from southeastern Ohio with a history of having been used in a hall lantern in Wheeling. The design is of extraordinary importance and interest for several reasons. It bears the imprint of Curlings and Robertson, proprietors of the Fort Pitt Glass Works, and is a pirating of the well-known Eastern (Sandwich?) tray. According to the McKearins, Morgan Robertson entered the Curling firm in 1834, but this pane was made much later, probably after 1840. Its stippling is of the irregular variety characteristic of the '40's and '50's.

Thus of the four known patterns of panes not one is directly traceable to steamboat use but this by no means proves the panes were not so used. River boats of so early a date have long since been dismantled and it is improbable, to say the least, that any direct proof of this use of such panes will now be found. Indeed, is any needed? The Bakewell advertisement seems sufficient. The available evidence does prove, however, that cabinetmakers, manufacturers of lighting devices, and especially builders and glaziers found them convenient and used them wherever their size was suitable.

Process. Glass *can* be cast, it is true, but not into intricate or delicate patterns because of its great surface tension. Considerable pressure would be necessary to force it into the tiny depressions constituting the designs found here. Those who wish to explore this casting process further should consult C. J. Phillips' excellent book, *Glass, The Miracle Maker* (New York, 1941, p. 173 ff.).

Theoretically it would have been possible to cut any of these patterns into a metal roller which would then have been rolled across a gather of glass that had been dropped into a dam-type mold, but the difficulties of such a procedure are tremendous. Consider the problem of centering the design on a 5 by 6⅞-inch blank. Made in this fashion easily ninety per cent of the output would have been imperfect.

Both the "cast" and "rolled" theories seem to be based on misconceptions about the causes of the uneven surfaces found on early pressed glass. A gather of glass begins to cool, particularly on its surface, the minute it is removed from the pot. It is carried to the pressing machine and held over the mold while a workman shears off the amount of glass he considers correct to produce the article to be pressed. Now this sheared gather drops into the mold in a shape resembling a tadpole which drops *tail first,* not, as is commonly pictured, head first. This thin string or tail of glass — remember it is preceding the body of the gather into the mold — has cooled to a temperature dangerously near the setting point before it even touches the mold. Perhaps depending upon the steadiness of hand of the workman, such a string normally takes one of two forms in the mold: a "coiled snake" effect that on pressing produces more or less faint circular or spiral waves; or, more rarely, an accordion pattern that shows up after pressing as lateral waves.

At this point it becomes evident that the advocates of the "cast" and "rolled" theories picture these panes as having been made with their plain surfaces up. On the contrary practically all flat pieces were pressed plain side down or, in other words, with their designs on the plunger. This is a dogmatic statement and space does not permit its full discussion but a study of Figures 5 and 6 should convince the skeptical. Figure 5 represents a cross section of one of these panes with dotted lines indicating vestigial fins. Such fins appear where the parts of a mold join and there is no denying their evidence. Figure 6 shows a schematic cross section of a mold made by extending these fins and joining the extensions. The plunger, *P,* comes down, forces the gather of glass out along the base mold, *BM,* to the walls of the cap ring, *CR,* and impresses the design on

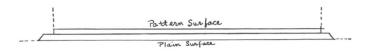

FIG. 5 — CROSS SECTION of typical pane with draw angles exaggerated. The dotted lines are extensions of fins or mold marks.

FIG. 6 — SCHEMATIC CROSS SECTION of mold based on the fin locations shown in Figure 5. A gather of glass is dropped into the receptacle formed by the base mold (BM) and cap ring (CR) and the plunger (P) is brought down forcing the glass into the *shape* formed by the base mold and cap ring and into the *pattern* cut on the face of the plunger.

the surface. The glass sets almost at once and the plunger is withdrawn. The cap ring, *CR,* is then lifted (note that its draw-angle must permit this); the mold is inverted and the finished pane falls out and is taken to the annealing furnace.

Origin. All of the known panes are of the same size, 5 by 6⅞ inches, which may indicate that but one base die and one cap ring were used with interchangeable design plungers. The fact that one design die carries the Curlings and Robertson imprint could lead to the conclusion that this firm made all of the four known patterns. There is some supporting evidence for this theory. According to Mr. Born, the Schenley residence was built by James O'Hara for his daughter, Mary, who married William Croghan. Mary Croghan, their daughter, married Major Schenley. Now James O'Hara with his partner, Isaac Craig, started the Pittsburgh Glass Works in 1797. In 1800 the superintendent of this glass works was William Price, the same Price who in 1827 with Robert Curling started the Fort Pitt Glass Works, predecessor of Curlings and Robertson. It is possible that O'Hara kept in touch with his former workman and, needing panes for the new house, secured them from this firm.

This hypothesis, however, seems too flimsy to warrant so positive an attribution. Probably 5 by 6⅞ was a standard structural size of the period and so Bakewell as well as the Fort Pitt Works would have pressed the same size. Both firms advertised such panes; both firms must have made them. It is also not unlikely that similar panes were pressed by other factories in the Pittsburgh-Wheeling glassfield but, since there is no recorded instance of lacy panes turning up east of the mountains, they are probably a purely Midwestern product.

So far, with but four finds, such panes may be classed among the great rarities in early pressed glass. The chances are that part of this seeming rarity is due to pickers' not understanding their importance if, indeed, they recognize them at all. As more people become familiar with them it can be safely predicted that additional patterns will be found.

Wheeling lacy glass

BY JAMES H. ROSE

STEAMBOAT PANE; 5-1/6 inches by 7. This is the first marked piece of Wheeling lacy glass to be recorded. A similar pane in the Grossman collection measures 5 by 7. It may, or may not, be significant that both panes are one-eighth inch longer than any of the other known (i.e., Pittsburgh) lacy panes. Each element in its design should be compared with analogous motifs in the other illustrations. *The Corning Museum of Glass.*

WE HAVE KNOWN FOR YEARS that glass was pressed in Wheeling as early as 1829, but although pressed glass of that period had to be lacy and good lacy at that, the few pieces we have attributed to Wheeling have been relatively coarse and comparatively late. All attractive midwestern lacy has been called "Pittsburgh"—too hastily, it turns out, if the lacy pane shown here is a fair example of Wheeling work. Without its inscription it would be assigned with no hesitation to Pittsburgh. It has everything—the shell, the rose, the sidewheel river boat—formerly considered evidence of Pittsburgh origin.

But J. & C. Ritchie (I follow here the account given by Josephine Jefferson in *Wheeling Glass*) were Wheeling glassmakers. The factory was founded in 1829 by John Ritchie and Jesse Wheat and did business under the name of Ritchie & Wheat until 1831, when Wheat left to start Wheat, Price & Company. John Ritchie tried it alone for a while and then, in 1833, sold a half-interest to his brother, Craig Ritchie, and the firm's name became J. & C. Ritchie. It was in this year that they made the lacy pane, as George Wilson bought into the company in 1834 and its name then became Ritchie & Wilson.

The pane's discovery calls for a re-examination of the two plates related to it stylistically, the rose and the steamboat shown here, and also of a larger group of plates allied to these two by cap-ring analogy that includes the *Constitution*, the eagle, the basket of flowers, a unique strawberry diamond, a late sunburst and, most important, the acorn, illustrated here in compote form.

These acorn compotes were purchased by Mrs. John J. Grossman many years ago in a Pittsburgh second-hand store. With them came a history that they were the first pieces pressed in a glass factory that had just moved to Pittsburgh's South Side and that, no doubt because of the coincidence, they had been presented to a Rev. H. Reck who had just started a new church, also on the South Side. Through a nice piece of research John Grossman has established the date of Bakewell's move to the South Side as 1853; he has also discovered that the Rev. H. Reck founded the Grace English Evangelical Church on the South Side in 1852, and that the "present" (as of 1889) church was built in 1853. Since the dates of the founding of both church and glasshouse are the same, the Bakewell origin of the compotes is confirmed—and so too, by extension, is that of the whole series of related plates.

But how are we to explain the resemblance of a Wheeling pane to a group of Pittsburgh plates? The range of possibilities is large but four solutions seem more plausi-

ROSE PLATE; about 6½ inches in diameter. This rose design occurs in circular as well as octagonal form and in several sizes, including cup plates. Its shoulder shells, or anthemia, have streamers but are otherwise remarkably like that on the pane. Its rose is not as well modeled.

Collection of Mrs. John J. Grossman.

STEAMBOAT PLATE; about 6½ inches in diameter. Recorded only in octagonal form and in this size. Again the shoulder anthemia resemble the shell on the pane as does, superficially, the sidewheel river boat. Cup plates with similar steamboats but with a varying shoulder pattern exist.

Collection of Mrs. Grossman.

ble than the others. First, there is the possibility that all these dies are the work of one free-lance moldmaker. Inasmuch as Pittsburgh was the larger town and probably had more artisans, this talented man's habitat is more likely to have been there than in Wheeling. On the other hand, he could have started in Wheeling and been lured away by the fleshpots of Pittsburgh. Either way, he did better work for Ritchie than he did for Bakewell; but this might be explained by the Ritchies' telling him to spare no efforts on their advertising pane while Bakewell's instructions to him were to keep costs down.

Or the problem may be one of simple piracy, the deliberate copying of one factory's wares by another. If such was the case, there is no clue as to which of our glassmakers was the pirate.

Third, it is not impossible that Bakewell bought Ritchie's molds when the latter failed about 1840. If the date of that failure had coincided with the Pittsburgh fire of 1845, in which it seems likely that Bakewell's molds suffered some damage, this would be an attractive theory. The five-year gap in dates is not fatal, however, since Bakewell could have bought the molds on the earlier date. In that case, both factories made these plates, Ritchie before Bakewell.

Finally, the resemblance of pane to plates may be pure coincidence, no more than might be expected from two moldmakers working in the idiom of their region and their period.

In spite of the fact that the pane's discovery has not so far led to the recognition of other pieces of Wheeling lacy, we may be sure that no small amount of it was made there and that, in all probability, it looks much like that which was made contemporaneously in Pittsburgh. Until we have further evidence, it is safer to call unmarked pieces from the area "Midwestern" than to label them "Pittsburgh."

ACORN COMPOTE; 7¼ inches by 4. This compote, one of a pair, has a history of having been pressed at Bakewell's South Side factory in Pittsburgh in either 1852 or 1853, an astonishingly late use of an earlier mold. Found more commonly in plate form, it is related by base mold (cap-ring and surface die) analogy to a long series of Midwestern plates, including the rose and steamboat plates shown here.

Collection of Mrs. Grossman.

Mr. Rose, a frequent contributor to ANTIQUES, is an authority on American glass. He organized the Corning Museum's 1954 exhibition *American Pressed Glass of the Lacy Period* and wrote its catalogue; and he is co-author, with Ruth Webb Lee, of *American Glass Cup Plates*.

Unrecorded rarities in lacy glass

BY JAMES H. ROSE

Variant chain-border tray. 11 9/16 x 8⅛ x 1¾. *Collection of William J. Elsholz*. The tray shown here has a star at each side between the chain border and the leaf scrolls. These stars are lacking on the recorded variety which, however, shows a curious and perhaps significant change in stippling at this spot as if something (the stars?) had been erased and the background restippled. More important, on this unlisted tray the border links are stippled on both top and bottom, while the standard type has stippling on the backs of the links only. Even in the known type a few examples have turned up with incompletely filled links or handles due to failure of the glass to flow. The roughness of stippled surfaces would obviously impede easy flow and, since fins show that these trays were pressed upside down, the obvious correction would be to buff the stippling off the tops of the links (the bottom in pressing) to facilitate flow. This would seem to indicate that the variant tray shown is the earlier, experimental version. On the other hand there

seems to be some evidence that in these chain-border trays we are dealing with the output of more than just two molds. The garden variety of tray in Mr. Elsholz's collection measures 11¾ x 8¼ x 1½. The McKearins in *American Glass* give the size as 11¾ x 8½, while Mrs. Lee in *Sandwich Glass* records 11½ x 8. While in pieces as large as these we can expect some diversity of size due to warping, annealing sag, or some similar factor, the disparity recorded seems excessive. Jarves mentions brass as well as iron molds, but a brass mold with its melting point lower than the working temperature of glass would have had a very short life. The assumption has been that it was used only for special-order work or for a very elaborate or intricate mold where the relative softness and workability of brass would ease the moldmaker's labors and reduce costs. Since no mold was more difficult to cut than that of the chain-border tray, it is not impossible that the diversity of size noted above is due to the use of several short-lived brass molds.

Tray. 7 13/16 x 5⅝. *Collection of George C. Cannon.* This is a midwestern pressing related through the lancet leaves of its cavetto to the well-known series of round and octagonal "acorn" plates. Oddly enough, the familiar Sandwich casket exactly fits this piece, suggesting that some similar piece of hollow ware may have originally accompanied this tray. Only two of these trays are known, the other in the collection of Mrs. John J. Grossman. This great rarity may be due to the irregularity of outline. A mold of such shape would be particularly liable to damage, as would be the trays made from it.

In recent years the intense interest in lacy glass has brought out of hiding many hitherto unknown pieces, many more than can be shown here. Since selection from among these riches has been arbitrary some account of the process seems necessary.

Cup plates and salts were never considered. Each is a highly specialized field with a literature and a reporting system of its own. Toddy plates and sauce dishes were also disregarded but for opposite reasons. Practically nothing is known of the range of pattern in either field so that almost any toddy or sauce is likely to be unpublished, although it by no means follows that it is rare.

This left some forty pieces for consideration. Of these a remarkable sugar bowl was excluded because neither of the two known examples has a cover. It seemed best to defer publication until a complete specimen is found. Six superb compotes were eliminated since the patterns of all their bowls are on record in either plate or dish form. Several lamps and a candlestick were discarded on similar grounds; they were unrecorded combinations of recorded parts.

The remainder was judged on the basis of earliness, design, and size. No one of these factors predominated. If an eight-inch dish had a pattern less interesting than a seven- or even a six-inch one, it was cast aside albeit with reluctance. Conversely, if two pieces had equally interesting designs, the larger was chosen. This boils down to what is called "importance." But this term is not an absolute, and in the many borderline cases other judges might have made different decisions.

Some attempt has been made in the following notes to suggest reasons for the great rarity. This is pure speculation and should be so regarded. It is arguable that rarity is due to a lack of commercial appeal so that few examples of a specific item got into circulation, or that such pieces as were sold were broken due to large size or awkward shape, or that a mold was technically unsatisfactory and was soon discarded, or—and this last is probably the most likely—that a mold cracked or was otherwise damaged before many pieces were made in it. But to assign any one of these in a specific case is very risky indeed.

Finally I must disclaim any omniscience. Beyond doubt other equally large, attractive, and early pieces exist unknown to me. I will be grateful if collectors and dealers will call them to my attention.

Oval dish. 8¼ x 5½ x 1¾. *Elsholz collection.* The strawberry diamonds in the triangles at sides and ends are generally considered proof of early work. The radial lines just inside the serrations are seldom seen but occur again in the deep bowl from the Innes collection shown on the following page and, since that bowl is unquestionably eastern and probably Sandwich, this dish is probably from the same source. The most striking feature of the design is the use of the curious and, I think, unique diagonal checkered bands. Mr. Elsholz's dish is the only known specimen and its rarity may perhaps be accounted for by the difficulty of getting glass to flow over the extraordinarily rough surface.

Oval vegetable dish. 9⅞ x 6 15/16 x 1⅜. *Collection of Lowell Innes.* A midwestern piece with regionally characteristic big bull's-eye and point serrations. But two of these magnificent dishes are known. The other is the property of the Historical Society of Western Pennsylvania. Unless it lies in the vulnerability of the serrations, no reason for this great scarcity is apparent.

Large, shallow bowl. 12 x 1¾. *Collection of Mrs. Paul Esterly.* The cross pattern is a well-known eastern device in the early days of pressing and points to an origin in that area, probably at Sandwich or the New England Glass Works. The most astonishing thing about this piece is that while Mrs. Esterly's is the only one known in this tremendous size, two others slightly smaller (11 inches) exist. One is in the Elsholz collection, the other in the collection of Mrs. Oscar R. Haase. The large size, hard to make and easy to break, may account for the rarity.

Deep bowl. 9 3/16 x 3¾. *Innes collection.* The wide band in plaid pattern and the treatment of the trefoil tulips point to an eastern and probably Sandwich origin. The radial flutes near the rim resemble those of the oval dish from the Elsholz collection illustrated on the previous page. This bowl is unique in form as well as pattern. In fact, it is not unlikely that its rarity is due to its shape, which tended to sag if taken from the mold a second too soon or if exposed to a bit too much heat during annealing. Most deep pieces from the early period, where thick, heavy metal was the rule, are straight-sided to avoid such buckling.

Large bowl. 9⅛ x 2⅜. *Elsholz collection.* This, the only known specimen, shows some stylistic affinity (the cross pattern) to Mrs. Esterly's large bowl, and to the Elsholz oval dish in its extreme use of the strawberry diamond. It seems certainly to be very early and of eastern manufacture. It has still another claim to distinction in four small ball feet, which are unique.

Covered sweetmeat. 7¼ to top of finial, 6½ across. *Elsholz collection.* The typical midwestern hairpin foot shows the origin beyond doubt. Only one other example is on record, in the Cannon collection. The mold with its turned-over rim and the die for the terraced cover (the standard was pressed separately and attached by a wafer) was a complicated one and must have been quite expensive. But this cannot account for the extreme rarity, which must be due to breakage of the finished product or, more likely, to damage to the mold before many of these pieces were made.

Covered butter dish. 4⅞ to top of finial, 4⅞ across. *Elsholz collection.* While several of these little dishes are known lidless, this seems to be the only complete one on record. The plain finial is unusual but is very like one on a sugar bowl that is generally credited to Sandwich and may be a clue to origin. There is no apparent reason for its scarcity.

Large plate. 9⅝. *Collection of Dr. Grace O. Doane.* The bull's-eye rim stamps this unique piece midwestern. The flat shoulder and the stylized shells are, in cup plates, considered to be marks of Curling's practices at his Ft. Pitt Glass Works. The rarity is probably due to the large size.

Small octagonal plate. 5⅛ side to side, 5⅝ point to point. *Esterly collection.* An unrecorded, possibly the earliest, member of the midwestern plate series which includes the *Constitution-Union,* the steamboat, the basket of flowers, the rose or chrysanthemum, and the acorn. No other example known.

A lacy glass rarity

Illustrated in James H. Rose's article, *Unrecorded rarities in lacy glass* (ANTIQUES for March 1954), was a lacy glass tray, measuring seven and thirteen-sixteenths by five and three-eighths inches, of which only two examples were then known. (Another has since been reported.) "A midwestern pressing," as Mr. Rose described it, the tray is "related through the lancet leaves of its cavetto to the well-known series of round and octagonal 'acorn' plates." He went on to point out that the tray exactly fits one of the known Sandwich caskets and suggested that "some similar piece of hollow ware" originally accompanied it.

His surmise was confirmed when the glass casket illustrated here came to light. Now part of the collection of George S. McKearin, Hoosick Falls, New York, this apparently unique specimen was on view with the matching tray described above in the recent exhibition *Pressed Glass of the Lacy Period* at the Corning Museum of Glass, Corning, New York. A midwestern product of the early period, c. 1830-1835, it is noteworthy for its elaborate design—which, as Mr. Rose suggests, may be one reason this and certain other rarities in pressed glass either were not made in quantity or have survived in few examples.

Enormous bowl: 14 by 3 inches. The design is familiar to all collectors and, in its smaller manifestations, is one of the most frequently seen of all lacy patterns; in this tremendous size, however, it is unique. Furthermore, it is the largest known piece of lacy glass. Its origin is probably New England in the 1840's. *Henry Francis du Pont Winterthur Museum.*

Unrecorded rarities in American glass

More lacy items

THE PIECES OF LACY GLASS pictured here have been chosen as worthy additions to the group shown in ANTIQUES for March 1954 (pages 224-227). None has been published; none was chosen on the basis of color; only the Winterthur bowl, the largest known piece of lacy, was selected because of size; yet each is in its own way truly exceptional. —JAMES H. ROSE

Lacy candlestick: 5¼ inches high, its base 3¾ inches square. Only one other piece, a lamp with its font in the blown-three-mold Horn of Plenty pattern, is known with this handled, lacy base. This rarity is probably due to the difficulty of getting glass worked at the low temperature characteristic of the period to flow through the handle mold: as the illustration shows, the glass forming the handle congealed before its two sections met. *Collection of Harold G. Duckworth; Lawrence photograph.*

Lamp: 12 inches high, its base 4¼ inches in diameter. While this imposing lamp has ringed knopping that resembles New England practice it rests on a Western toddy-plate base (an unrecorded, plain-rim version of No. 800-A in Lee and Rose, *American Glass Cup Plates*) and so unquestionably was made west of the mountains about 1835 or 1840. The wonder is that it has lasted as long as it has with so unstable a form. It is the only Western lamp recorded on a toddy-plate base. *Duckworth collection; photograph by Ben Lawrence.*

Opaque white lamp: 6¾ inches high, base 3½ inches in diameter. The base is pressed in a small waffle pattern and at first glance seems to be an unrecorded cup plate—but is not, since it has a domed center. As this lamp, one of a pair, appears to be the only known example of the use of this foot, it is likely that something happened to the mold before many were made. The origin is New England, probably before the year 1830. Right, lamp with lacy foot: 10½ inches high, its base 4½ inches in diameter. The lacy foot is one that is seen fairly frequently. The lamp owes its distinction to the skill of the blower. *Both lamps in the collection of William J. Elsholz; photograph by Leo Knight.*

Shallow bowl: 8¼ inches in diameter and 1¾ inches deep. Smaller pieces, mostly plates, are known with vaguely similar centers and shoulder patterns but this, in addition to being the largest of these related pieces on record, has an elaborate rose-and-thistle motif on its inner shoulder. Though the origin is unquestionably the eastern United States, it is not necessarily New England; there is some evidence, by no means conclusive, pointing to a source in the Philadelphia area. The period is apparently c. 1835 to 1840. *Duckworth collection; Lawrence photograph.*

Compote: 11 inches in diameter and 5⅝ inches high. While it is a truism that a stem and foot may be added to any bowl, such occurrences are, to say the least, infrequent. This particular bowl has not so far been published in compote form and is thus a find of major importance. The origin is New England about 1835. *Elsholz collection; Knight photograph.*

Large compote: 10½ inches in diameter, 6¼ inches high. Several bowls are known in this pattern, but the present specimen is the only one recorded in compote form. Its majestic size is not apparent in the illustration. Although its origin is almost certainly New England, c. 1835, it was found about thirty miles north of Pittsburgh—demonstrating the unreliability of attributions based on where a piece was found. *Elsholz collection; Knight photograph.*

Plate: 7�5⁄₁₆ inches in diameter. The strawberry diamonds of its cavetto are a well-known indication of early work. The curious shoulder pattern of alternating Maltese crosses and chevrons is, however, a new element in pre-lacy design, and the plate appears to be unique as of this writing. Presumably New England, early cap-ring period, c. 1830. *Collection of Preston R. Bassett.*

Shallow bowl: 6⅝ inches in diameter and 1¼ inches deep. The tulip pattern of the cavetto is, except for its eight-pointed-star center, well known to all collectors, but the continuous grapevine shoulder design is an unrecorded motif in such association. The origin is not certain but is perhaps New England somewhere close to 1840. *Elsholz collection.*

Rectangular dish: 6¾ inches long by 5¼ inches wide. This little dish with its geometric design may be unique. It was made somewhere in the Midwest, probably between 1835 and 1840. The tumbler with its Gothic arches is 2½ inches high and is an extremely rare survival, perhaps even unique. Pressed drinking glasses from the lacy period are virtually unknown. The best guess is that it was made in New England about 1830. The small handled mug is 2 inches high and seems to be the only other drinking glass on record from the lacy period. Unless Deming Jarves, who owned the patent on pressing handles in this fashion, leased his process to other factories, the mug is Sandwich, about 1835. One other heart mug is known, in the Ewing collection. *All three pieces in the collection of Louise S. Esterly; photograph by Patric P. Jacovidis.*

Compote: 4¾ inches in diameter, 2¾" high, with a foot 2¼ inches square. A few shallow bowls are known in this intricate Western version of the hairpin pattern but this is the first compote to be reported. Its importance is increased by its previously unrecorded square foot, pressed in a geometric design. The origin is probably the Midwest, c. 1835. *Duckworth collection.*

Candlestick: 14¾ inches high, its base 4 inches square. As in the case of Mr. Duckworth's tall lamp, the puzzling feature here is the maker's foolhardy disregard of stability, a factor of major importance in a lighting device where overturn could have meant disaster. The pressed base occurs in at least three slightly varying forms, two of which are Eastern and one probably Western. This prohibits any dogmatic statements concerning origin, although the annulated knopping does suggest New England chair work. *Duckworth collection; Lawrence photograph.*

American lacy and pressed glass in the Toledo Museum of Art

BY JOHN W. KEEFE, *Assistant curator for European decorative arts, Art Institute of Chicago (formerly with the Toledo Museum of Art)*

Fig. 1. Most of these early examples indicate the dependence of the American designer upon the Anglo-Irish tradition of cut glass, as witnessed by the frequent use of strawberry-diamond and fan motifs. Exceptions which mark the beginning of purely American designs and motifs are the Industry bowl in the center here, the opalescent plate (above, right), and the elaborately patterned plate below that. *Clockwise, starting at top:* Clear lead-glass bowl, c. 1825-1835; New England area, perhaps New England Glass Company; diameter 6 inches. Greenish-opalescent lead-glass plate, c. 1825-1830; probably Boston & Sandwich Glass Company; diameter 5⅞ inches. Pale-green lead-glass plate, c. 1825-1835; probably New England Glass Company, perhaps Sandwich; diameter 5⅞ inches. Clear lead-glass plate, c. 1825-1835; probably New England Glass, perhaps Sandwich; diameter 5¾ inches. Clear lead-glass plate, c. 1825-1835; New England Glass; diameter 5⅞ inches. Light-green lead-glass plate with light red streaks, c. 1825-1835; probably New England Glass, perhaps Sandwich; diameter 5⅞ inches. *Center:* So-called Industry bowl, c. 1840; perhaps Sandwich, or New England Glass Company; diameter 6¼ inches. The log cabin and barrel were Whig symbols of the 1840 Presidential campaign, and the plowman represented Harrison, "the Cincinnatus of the West." Four variants of this bowl are recorded. *Except as noted, all of the objects illustrated are the gift of Mrs. Harold G. Duckworth to the Toledo Museum of Art.*

THE RICHNESS OF the American lacy and pressed glass collection at the Toledo Museum of Art is largely due to the generosity of a private collector, Mrs. Harold G. Duckworth. She and her husband began collecting early pressed glass in the mid-1920's and the result of their collecting acuity, presented to the museum after his death in a series of gifts beginning in 1964, is one of the most representative groups of these wares ever assembled. Inevitably, in telling of a collection of this size its actual scope will be somewhat distorted, for only the rarest objects or the rarest color variants have been chosen and certain forms such as cup plates and salts have been left out simply because they form specialized collections.

Pressing of glass had been employed as early as the

151

Fig. 2. Extremely rare bowl in Princess Feather medallion pattern alternating with Cross in Diamond, c. 1830; attributed to Sandwich; diameter 10 inches.

Fig. 3. All the glass objects here are attributed to Sandwich, and except as noted, all are in the Scrolled Peacock Eye pattern. Given the tendency to pirating among all designers of the period, there may be some question as to whether Sandwich or Meissen originated the popular Peacock Eye pattern; the variant plate at the right, however, shows how quickly designs were modified. *Left to right:* Plate, c. 1830-1835; diameter 6⅛ inches. Dish in unusual light blue, c. 1830-1850; diameter 4¼ inches. Rare covered mustard cup, c. 1835; height 3¼ inches (this has a matching plate 4⅜ inches in diameter). Meissen porcelain plate, Germany, c. 1830; pink cavetto with gold border; diameter 7⅞ inches. Plate with variant Star Medallion cavetto, c. 1835-1845; diameter 5¼ inches.

closing years of the eighteenth century in England and Holland for the feet of candlesticks, bowls, and glasses, and the technique was also used to shape mushroom and rayed stoppers for decanters; but until the 1820's it was not sufficiently mechanized to be commercially feasible for the production of larger objects.

Although Americans did not originate pressing, it is certain that its perfecting was largely the result of work by American inventors. The best known of these was Deming Jarves, a founder of both the New England and the Boston and Sandwich glass companies; Jarves held a number of important pressing patents and was extremely influential in promoting pressed-glass manufacture. Perhaps it was the connection of Jarves with the Boston and Sandwich Glass Company which led to the widely held belief that all lacy glass was produced at Sandwich. This is known today to be untrue, for the technique was not limited to any single manufacturer or region, and patents, recipes, and designs were consistently pirated. That both lacy and conventionally pressed (non-lacy) glass were produced in every major glassmaking area is attested by the regional variations which appear. In lacy glass, pieces made in the Midwest tend to exhibit relatively coarse stippling, and certain Midwestern plates and dishes stand

Fig. 4. *Left to right:* Shell and Leaf pattern plate with unique center treatment, c. 1825-1850; probably Sandwich; diameter 6⅛ inches. Extremely rare window pane, c. 1835-1840; probably Midwestern; height 6¹⁵⁄₁₆ inches. Extremely rare candlestick with ribbed and beaded socket and lacy base, c. 1840; probably Sandwich; height 5½ inches. Extremely rare dish in Pipes of Pan, or Devil, pattern, c. 1835-1845; New England area; length 8⅛ inches. Amethyst compote in Princess Feather medallion pattern, c. 1835-1840; probably Sandwich; height 6⅛ inches; rare form and color. Rare creamer in Gothic Arch and Sheaves (Palm) pattern below with Peacock Eye and Chain above, c. 1830-1835; perhaps Sandwich; height 4⅛ inches.

Fig. 5. Cake tray, c. 1835; attributed to Sandwich; length 11¾ inches. Pieces like this tray —an extremely rare form—were very difficult to press evenly, which frequently caused incomplete filling of the scalloped border and the handles. This is an exceptionally fine specimen.

on small round feet which appear in the pattern as a bead motif, while Eastern examples usually rest on a flat base or a rope ring.

The method for both lacy and conventionally pressed glass consisted of cutting a gather of molten glass from the pontil rod and dropping it into a mold. A shaped plunger was then brought down into the mold, forcing the molten glass into all its indentations and impressing the design into the glass. The technique produced a more distinct pattern than the soft contours of mold-blown glass and was therefore ideally suited to imitation of cut wares.

In spite of this relatively simple means of embellishment, the problems encountered by the early makers were considerable. Prior to the invention of the cap ring (some time before 1830), pieces tended to be of uneven thick-

ness; similarly, underfilling caused handles and borders to be left incomplete (see Fig. 5). More serious was the dull, cloudy effect caused by contact of the heated metal plunger with the molten glass, which could only be corrected by reheating. Obviously, this reheating would result in a loss of sharpness in both shape and pattern. The glassmakers' solution to this was to create over-all patterns which successfully masked the clouded quality of the glass. By using the stippling characteristic of lacy glass, the designer increased the refractive qualities of the material, imparting a silvery sheen.

Given these manufacturing handicaps, it is not surprising that early lacy and conventionally pressed wares relied heavily on the Anglo-Irish tradition of cut glass, which too was thick and geometrically patterned. Pressed glass fre-

Fig. 6. Pair of candlesticks with lacy sockets, molded double melon knops, and pressed stepped bases; c. 1830-1835; probably Sandwich; height 10 1/16 inches; this is a rare form, extremely rare in pairs. Amethyst spill holder in Bull's Eye, or Lawrence, pattern; c. 1850-1870; attributed to New England Glass; height 5 9/16 inches; rare form and pattern. Lamp with blown font and pressed classical base, in opaque white glass; c. 1835; attributed to New England Glass; height 10 3/16 inches; this form also occurs in clear glass. Candlestick with opaque blue socket composed of small dolphins, mounted on a square-based clam-broth dolphin stem; c. 1840-1850; New England area; height 8 5/8 inches; considered the rarest of the dolphin candlestick forms. Extremely rare lamp in single Tulip pattern with blue font, green shaft and base; c. 1840-1850; New England area; height 12 inches.

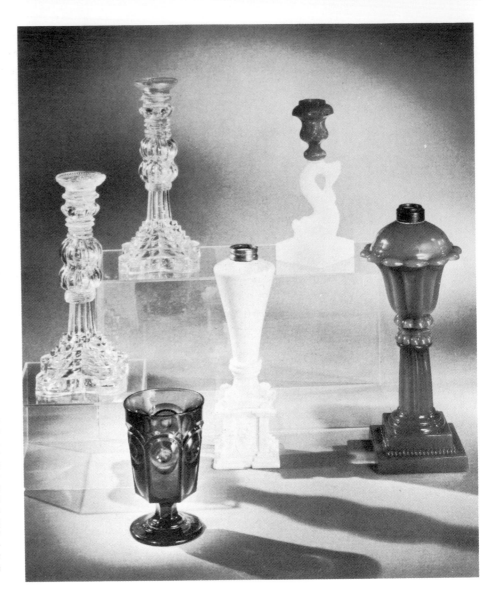

Fig. 7. Canary-yellow plate in Sandwich Plaid pattern, c. 1835-1845; Sandwich; diameter 8 1/16 inches; rare for its canary-yellow color, although the pattern is not so rare as the plain-edge Sandwich Plaid. Extremely rare opalescent glass claret goblet in Colonial pattern, c. 1840-1850; perhaps Sandwich; height 5 1/2 inches. Green plate in variant Roman Rosette pattern, c. 1835-1840; Midwestern area; diameter 5 11/16 inches; rare in any color. Light-amethyst goblet in Colonial pattern, c. 1840-1850; New England area; height 6 inches; rare in color.

Fig. 8. Fiery opalescent glass spill or spoon holder in Lyre (Harp) pattern, c. 1840-1850; McKee Brothers Glass Company, Pittsburgh, or Sandwich; height 4⅝ inches; opalescent pressed glass in any form is rare. Rare compote in Plume pattern, c. 1830-1840; Wheeling, West Virginia, area, or Sandwich; height 4½ inches, diameter 7½.

Fig. 9. Sapphire-blue bowl in Buckle pattern, c. 1860-1870; probably Gillinder and Sons, Philadelphia; diameter 9¾ inches. A rare color for this form, though patterns of this type are typical of the later Middle Period in the United States.

quently repeated its ribbing, strawberry-diamond, and fan motifs, as well as the diapered centers taken from slightly earlier English ceramics (Fig. 1). By 1830, however, these merely imitative patterns had begun to be eclipsed by designs incorporating scrolls, beaded and floral motifs, and figural designs which soon took on a distinctly national character (Fig. 2). It has been suggested that some of the American designs of this period borrowed from the Belgian and French, although the foreign prototypes show a more refined eclecticism and a stricter use of Gothic and Renaissance design elements. All glass designers consistently drew upon a variety of sources and used them in many combinations (Fig. 3). It cannot be overemphasized that this ability of the mold maker to create a greater variety than had previously been available made pressed glass the popular favorite. Until the closing years of the nineteenth century, pressed wares alone were able to keep up with the constant public demand for novelty of form and color (Figs. 4, 5).

By the mid-1840's, the buying public had begun to tire of stippled lacy types and to turn to pressed glass of a plain geometric character. This type of conventionally pressed glass took well to fire polishing, so cut glass could be more closely imitated. Popular motifs were panels, flutes, thumbprints, and diamonds (Fig. 6). By 1850,

lacy glass was out of fashion, and plain geometric patterns were the new favorites. Wares of this type were produced in an increasing variety of forms and colors to meet the demand for novelty. Today, the pressed-glass collector cherishes pieces in a rare color or shape, although these may have been design experiments which in their own day proved to be unpopular (frontispiece and Figs. 7, 8). Pressed objects of this heavier, rather monumental type were made in greater variety through the 1870's. With the invention of "lime" glass in West Virginia about 1864 these wares almost flooded the market, causing great economic problems for the manufacturers of lead glass and cut decoration.

By the late 1860's, however, there was another change in popular taste. Having moved from the intricate surfaces of the lacy variety to plain geometric patterns, the public was now receptive to more elaboration (Fig. 9). The pattern glass which resulted was made in large sets and included celeries, tumblers, plates, and covered dishes. Glass of this type had been made some fifteen years earlier, but it now reached a new level of favor. Basically, such patterns combined the plain geometric qualities of typical Middle-Period pressed glass with secondary motifs (Fig. 10).

The taste for more elaborate designs had its flowering in the exotic pressed glass which became popular from about 1870 on. From this period date such types as Three Face, Lion, and Westward-ho (originally Pioneer), the last of which boasts a crouching-Indian finial and elk and buffalo in high relief (Fig. 11). From this same period also came the late opaque-white wares known today as milk glass.

These pronounced shifts in taste were a significant comment upon the expanding American economy of the nineteenth century, which brought an unprecedented variety of goods before the buying public. Significant too was the fact that this type of glass, which had so severely threatened the market for cut and engraved wares, was in the last years of the century eclipsed by its more costly counterparts. At the Centennial Exhibition of 1876, pressed glass was less noticed by the public than the cut wares shown by the Boston and Sandwich, New England Glass, Dorflinger, and Gillinder companies.

No study of nineteenth-century American glass can be conducted without a knowledge of pressed glass. While other types existed contemporaneously, none was so popular or so well able to follow public demand. Lacy, conventionally pressed, and pattern wares did not include all of the nineteenth-century glass manufacture in America, but they constituted an important element; and not the least of their contributions was the fostering of glassmaking as an important national industry.

Fig. 10. Dark sapphire-blue cologne bottle in Bull's Eye, or Lawrence, pattern, with cut neck; c. 1850-1860; attributed to New England Glass; height 7 inches; rare in pattern, color, and form. Jade-green spill holder in Cable pattern with applied gilt decoration, c. 1860-1870; Sandwich; height 5¾ inches. Rare in any color; this particular color is extremely rare. The Cable pattern is said to commemorate the laying of the Atlantic cable in 1858. Cerulean-blue spoon holder in Ribbed Grape pattern, c. 1850 or later; probably Sandwich. Height 5¾ inches; this color may be unique in this pattern.

Fig. 11. Compote (one of a pair), celery vase, and pitcher in Westward-ho (Pioneer) pattern, c. 1870-1880; probably Gillinder; heights 11⅜ inches, 6⅝, and 7 inches. *Gift of Mr. and Mrs. Joseph S. Riegel.* Opaque white pitcher with design of swans and water plants on body, and beaded rim; c. 1880 or later; United States Glass Company, Gas City, Indiana; height 5¼ inches. *Gift of Mrs. E. M. Belknap.* All of these illustrate the very late Middle-Period taste for exotic patterns and finishes in pressed glass. In the 1890's pattern glass of this type was replaced in popular favor by brilliant-cut glass.

Lacy Hairpin in French and American glass

BY LOWELL INNES

COLLECTORS OF American lacy glass have too long looked at French lacy askance or with distaste. Nevertheless students have accepted the fact that many lacy salts and plates of identical patterns were made in France and America. The lacy Sandwich covered dish and the Meissen porcelain one which appear on Plates 151 and 152 of Ruth Webb Lee's *Sandwich Glass* (1947 ed.), as well as the lacy New England area bowl and the Meissen porcelain compote published as Numbers 239 and 242 in James H. Rose's *Story of American Pressed Glass of the Lacy Period* (catalogue of a 1954 Corning Museum exhibition), make it clear that German and American manufacturers were also using the same patterns (in these cases, variations on the Princess Feather). Recently several Meissen plates have been found in the pattern we call Roman Rosette (Fig. 1.) Since both these patterns are clearly far better suited to glass than to porcelain, it is now the consensus that the design originated here and was copied in Germany.

To find a long-accepted Midwestern lacy pattern in a French catalogue, however, is a bit unnerving. It ought to make collectors less dogmatic, more receptive, and more willing to admit that Continental lacy has merit. In 1831 a Paris firm, Barbier, Launay & Cie., was formed to distribute the products of Baccarat and St. Louis. The next year Barbier, Launay acquired the Cristallerie de St. Cloud but sold it four years later with the understanding that no more glass would be made there for fifty years. Soon after 1836 Choisy-le-Roi and the Cristallerie de Bercy came under the Launay firm, which by 1834 had

become Launay, Hautin & Cie.; it served as a distribution and advertising agent for Baccarat, St. Louis, Choisy-le-Roi, and Bercy. From time to time Launay, Hautin issued trade catalogues. Sometimes sections were reserved for each factory, sometimes different factory pieces pictured on the same page were identified by letters such as *B* for Baccarat and *S! L.* for St. Louis.

On page 30 in the second part of a Launay, Hautin & Cie. catalogue of about 1842, a saucerlike dish on a pedestal (Fig. 2) is shown. Its design was called *m: à perles* (pressed in beads) and its form, *Baguier f.̃ évasée* (flaring ring stand). In this country the pattern has long been called the Midwestern Hairpin and in fact the ring stand itself (Fig. 3) has been published as a compote, "probably Midwest" (ANTIQUES, February 1957, p. 162). Stem and base present a problem in technique as well as in design. The smooth stem, shaped in a mold, joins the saucer to a square base with small graduated diamonds on its underside. Probably stem and base were pressed in one operation. Nevertheless, the round shaft seems to have been fitted into a hole in the base just as lamp fonts were pegged. The part where the shaft emerges on the underside of the base has been polished. Clearly, the piece was pontil held for fire polishing.

The counterpart of this French ring stand, the five-inch American nappy shown in Figure 4 (right), lacks the brilliance achieved by skillful fire polishing. In the French piece the design was on the base mold; in the American, on the plunger. Another marked difference is the result of the use of the cap ring on the nappy. Such

Fig. 1. *Left:* Meissen plate in shades of pink, with gilding; c. 1850. Diameter 8½ inches. *Right:* opalescent lacy glass plate in Roman Rosette pattern; New England, c. 1845. Diameter 9¼ inches. This pattern was also produced in the Midwest. *Collection of Walter E. Simmons.*

Fig. 3. St. Louis ring stand, c. 1842. Diameter 4¾ inches, height 2¾. The square foot has graduated diamonds on the underside. This piece has been published as "probably Midwest" (ANTIQUES, February 1957, p. 162) because the pattern of the bowl is identical with the pattern known in this country as Midwestern Hairpin. *Toledo Museum of Art, Duckworth collection.*

scalloped and pointed serrations occur frequently on Midwestern pieces. Though French and other Continental manufacturers seemed to prefer having the design of the shoulder a border for the whole, as in the ring stand, they also used the cap ring when it suited their purposes. The center design of both pieces is the so-called Midwestern Hairpin: in both it has a sixteen-rayed center; sixteen bordering lancets, each edged with thirty-four stippled dots; and finally, a border of sixteen medallions with rayed centers. Except for differences in technique of manufacture the center designs are identical.

In Lee and Rose's *American Glass Cup Plates,* Number 205 seems identical, except for its scalloped rim, to the French pattern, and on page 166 the authors say: "This is the only instance known to us of this peculiar rim. So far as we know, the only set so far discovered turned

Fig. 4. *Left:* bowl of the St. Louis ring stand. *Right:* American small bowl, c. 1840. Diameter 5⅛ inches, height 1 inch. The scallop-and-point rim pattern is also found on plates and cup plates from the Pittsburgh area. *Author's collection.*

Fig. 5. Pressed covered sweetmeat on
Midwestern Hairpin base—a very rare piece; c. 1835.
Both cover and bowl of this dish carry a design similar to
that on the St. Louis ring stand.
Height over all, 7¼ inches; diameter 6½.
Collection of William J. Elsholz.

up in California, so distribution is no guide to origin." The cup plate has sixteen lancets, sixteen rays, and sixteen medallions, exactly like the St. Louis ring stand. It also has a turning pimple on the top center, which Lee and Rose "believe . . . to be a purely Midwestern trait." This need not, however, prevent us from considering the possibility that the cup plate is French.

In an article in ANTIQUES for March 1954 (p. 224) Mr. Rose shows two rarities with the lancet motif, a tray (Fig. 8a) and a covered sweetmeat (Fig. 5). The terraced cover of the sweetmeat carries practically the same Hairpin design as that on the ring stand. William J. Elsholz, who owns it, kindly let me have its statistics. The cover has eighteen center rays, eighteen lancets, and eighteen bordering medallions, where the ring stand has sixteen of each. The terraced line of the cover breaks the continuity somewhat, but a careful examination shows that the curves from the double lancets touch the medallions exactly as do those on the French piece, and the medallions include the same starlike blossoms. A marked difference, however, is the series of clear circles below the medallions. On the French piece it is a series of clear diamonds. As one looks down into the bowl of the sweetmeat he sees the cover pattern repeated.

The low, flaring Hairpin base on Mr. Elsholz' covered dish was widely used in the Midwest. It is impressive on blown sugar bowls with copper-wheel engraving (Fig. 6), and it also embellishes early blown candlesticks and lamp fonts (Figs. 7, 7a). Since it appears on late pressed compotes, too, we cannot date it with accuracy. The Hairpin base is a smaller version of the French piece and its American counterpart. Twenty rays, lancets, and medallions occur instead of sixteen. The stippling is less brilliant, and it lacks the artistic strength of larger examples of the lancet. The plain bull's eye in the medallion instead of the French design's rayed motif dulls the effect somewhat.

There has been little attempt to attribute the Midwestern Hairpin to one factory. On blown and pressed pieces like sugar bowls, candlesticks, and lamps the variety of styles forbids exact attribution. During the 1830's and 1840's at Pittsburgh, the Robinsons, the Curlings, Parke, Campbell and Hanna (Union Glass Works), and Bakewell were pressing excellent Midwestern lacy. So were the Ritchies of Wheeling. The Hairpin base could have been used by all of them on blown and pressed pieces. One pressed compote on the Hairpin base is in the Princess Feather pattern, the coarsened form that Bakewell made fairly late.

An interesting outgrowth of the Hairpin design is the

Fig. 6. Free-blown engraved sugar bowl on
pressed Midwestern Hairpin base; c. 1835. Height 7 inches.
Domed cover, galleried rim, panels at base of bowl,
and generous proportions bespeak the Pittsburgh area,
as does the leaf-and-fruit design
executed in copper-wheel technique.
Henry Ford Museum, ex coll. McKearin.

Fig. 7. Blown candlesticks
on pressed Midwestern Hairpin base; heights 8 and 8⅛ inches.
These candlesticks are attributed to the Pittsburgh area;
probably 1830's. *Corning Museum.*

Fig. 8. Pressed Midwestern casket, c. 1835. Both casket and tray (below)
utilize the lancet-and-leaf motif found on the Midwestern Hairpin base
and in the bowl of the St. Louis ring stand. Height over all, 5 inches;
dimensions at rim, 6⅜ by 3¹⁵⁄₁₆ inches. *Corning Museum.*

Fig. 8a. Tray matching Midwestern casket;
5⅜ by 7¹³⁄₁₆ inches. *Corning Museum.*

Fig. 7a. Detail of Hairpin base
of candlestick in Fig. 7.

Fig. 9. Two Midwestern lacy plates from the Pittsburgh area, c. 1840. Centers in acorn-and-oak-leaf design; on shoulders, the lancet-and-leaf motif found on the Midwestern casket; in the French piece and in the Midwestern Hairpin base none of the lancets is stippled. *Left:* round plate with bull's-eye rim (38 eyes), an indication of Pittsburgh origin; diameter 5 inches. *Right:* octagonal plate with rim of thirty-two bull's eyes separated by stippled points; diameter 8 inches. This is illustrated on Pl. 143 (No. 3) of the McKearins' *American Glass;* No. 1 on that plate has the same distinctive rim. *Author's collection.*

Fig. 10. *Top:* unrecorded Pittsburgh lacy oval tray, c. 1840. Center shows large lancet and leaves almost out of proportion to the rest of the design, and the shoulders, arches with bisecting sunbursts; scallop-and-point rim. The pattern of fleurs-de-lis between the arches is found on some Midwestern octagonal vegetable dishes. Length 7⅞ inches, width 5⅜. *Bottom:* salt dish, c. 1840; top size, 2¾ by 2⅛ inches. In the Neals' *Pressed Glass Salt Dishes* (GA 3) this model, with its similar treatment of arches and emphasis on circles, is attributed to the Pittsburgh area. *Author's collection.*

wide use of the lancet in large pieces like the Midwestern casket and its tray (Figs. 8, 8a), the J. Grossman compote on a Roman Rosette base (Rose, *op. cit.,* No. 354), and the acorn-and-oak-leaf plates in Figure 9. Note that on these plates *the lancets are alternately clear and stippled,* rather than all clear like the ones on the French ring stand. On neither the round five-inch nor the larger octagonal acorn-and-oak-leaf plates are the lancets *edged with beads.* Sometimes the center of these plates is stippled, sometimes it is not. That difference bears no relationship to the alternate stippling of lancets or the absence of beads around the lancets. The clear lancets on the Midwestern casket and its tray and on the unrecorded tray in Figure 10, however, are bordered with beads.

The scarcity of American pieces in the exact design of the St. Louis piece strongly suggests that the Midwestern lacy Hairpin base came first and American designers borrowed and adapted lancets to become integral parts of a larger design, as on acorn plates, compotes, trays, and the Midwestern casket. If we accept the theory that the larger American pieces shown were pressed in the early thirties we can sustain no claims for the French as originators—unless other catalogue material exists.

We must admit, however, that if the French copied the Hairpin base, they also refined it. Their intertwining of medallion and lancet makes for unity and grace in the design. The Launay, Hautin & Cie. catalogue of the early forties also provides clear evidence of the excellence of St. Louis workmanship. But for the present, the exact relationship between French and American design must remain an enigma.

I am indebted to the Corning Museum of Glass for use of the Launay, Hautin & Cie. catalogue and to Paul N. Perrot for guidance and help.

Rarities in Pattern Glass

By RUTH WEBB LEE

Illustrations, except as noted, from the author's collection

THE value of antiques is determined not by one but by several considerations. Beauty of design, quality of workmanship, choice of material, rarity, usefulness, historical associations, all tend to influence appraisal, though the order of their importance varies with the preferences of individual collectors. The appeal, necessarily, is always to a particular temperament. There can be no just quarrel with those who set design above rarity, or historical association above usefulness.

It must be admitted today that a greater number of American collectors are interested in pressed pattern glass than in any other type of antiques. Throughout the depression the volume of sales and the range of prices of such glass actually rose. Dealers frankly agree that the passion for pattern glass helped to keep alive the regard for antiques in general. It brought customers to the shops. The reason is self-evident. Despite hard times, the desire to own antiques persisted, and collectors gratified it by purchasing pressed glass.

Research into the origin and age of various patterns, the establishment of an accepted nomenclature, the ascertaining of exactly how many forms are obtainable by those who desire to accumulate sets, all have helped. The reiterated objections of collectors who demand extreme age for their treasures — that pattern glass is not old enough to rank, for example, with Puritan furniture or colonial silver — has not checked the movement. As a matter of fact, there are pressed patterns collectible in sets that date back to the 1840's and possess, accordingly, a very respectable antiquity. Such glass harmonizes with still older furniture and surroundings. Great-grandmother was doubtless using just such glassware on a table that she inherited from *her* great-grandmother. And, by reason of its fragility, glass that belonged to grandmother is relatively more venerable than a Windsor chair, *circa* 1800.

The element of usefulness, another value-making factor of pressed glass,

Fig. 1 — "BELLFLOWER" OCTAGONAL SUGAR BOWL
A more complicated form than that usually encountered and suggesting a date in the 1840's. *Formerly in the collection of Mrs. C. C. Viall*

cannot be overlooked. Such glass is bought for practical as well as for sentimental reasons. It is enjoyed every day. It need not be enshrined in a cabinet. As an essentially American product, it "talks American" to lovers of American antiques. I have enjoyed exceptional facilities for noting the steady increase in the number of its collectors. Men, women, and children in all sections of the United States are today acquiring pressed glass. Even in Europe the contagion is spreading. Today's mail brought me a letter from a collector in Soviet Moscow!

The acquisitive yearning which is expressed in efforts to acquire a table service of *Ashburton, bellflower, comet,* or whatever the pattern may be need not subside with the completing of the set. Though scoffers may insist that the pattern lacks the element of rarity, there is a vast satisfaction in discovering the twelfth item of a sought-for dozen. And if this emotion is less intense than that experienced in unearthing an individual piece so unusual as to be almost unique, pressed glass still affords good hunting.

In many of the early patterns occur items apparently made in such limited quantity that very few specimens are obtainable today. The demand for these particular items may have been insufficient to justify continuing their manufacture, or the entire line may have been speedily discontinued for technical or commercial reasons, such as a too complicated mold, or too high production costs, or lack of appeal to the buying public. Again, some now desirable piece may have been made by a factory that did not remain long in business. Whatever the reason, all that collectors need realize is that pressed-glass rarities exist and that they are worth searching for and acquiring.

Bellflower

The earliest mention of the *bellflower* pattern that I have found appears in a catalogue of M'Kee Brothers of Pittsburgh. This pattern goes back to the late 1850's, and is listed as *R.L.*, presumably *ribbed leaf*. That some articles in this classification were

Fig. 2 — OPAQUE RIBBED COLOGNE BOTTLES, NOT TRUE "RIBBED LEAF"; "RIBBED IVY" CELERY VASE
The bottles are not true *bellflower* and may be of foreign origin. The celery vase in the *ivy* pattern is perhaps unique.
From the collection of George S. McKearin

Fig. 3 (above and centre) — "Horn of Plenty" Oval Compote and Round Compote
Both probably made at Sandwich. The oval form is very rare

Fig. 4 — "Horn of Plenty" Claret
One of the handsomest of the pressed wine glasses

Fig. 5 — "Horn of Plenty" Covered Dish

made at a still earlier date is indisputable. The rarest *bellflower* piece I believe to be the octagonal sugar bowl, shown in Figure 1. I know of one perfect specimen, from which the photograph was taken, and one other, complete but imperfect. Both were found in Western states. We are justified in surmising that this exceptional bowl was either an experiment on the part of a short-lived factory, or that the makers, finding that the round sugar bowl of the type usually found today was more easily and cheaply produced, discarded the eight-sided mold.

To a collector of *bellflower*, the quest for an octagonal bowl will furnish a fresh aim in life. Next in order of rarity in the same early pattern are the colored specimens, such as the amber egg cup, the opal egg cup, the sapphire-blue spoon holder and syrup jar, the milk-white syrup jars, and other forms. The clear cake plate on a standard is almost unobtainable today. The cologne bottles shown in Figure 2 I have always suspected of a foreign origin. The design is not the true *ribbed leaf*, though it comes very close to that. These bottles, marked as well as unmarked, are to be found in opaque white, opaque jade green, and so on. The *ribbed ivy* celery vase, shown in the same illustration, is the only one I have seen to date.

Horn of Plenty

The *horn of plenty*, so much in demand by collectors today, is rapidly becoming one of the scarcer patterns. In this group the oval compote on a standard is probably the most elusive item. One is shown in Figure 3. It is heavy, brilliant, and rather

suggests a large pickle dish. The standard has the heavy loops at the base, usually associated by collectors with Sandwich pieces. I strongly suspect that this compote may have come from the famous factory on the Cape. It should be noted that the disc design on the bowl is carried out on the base as well. To date only two of these dishes have come to my notice.

Next in rarity in this pattern is the small oblong covered dish shown in Figure 5. I have owned one and know of two others. It is undoubtedly one of the earliest pieces of this pattern. *Horn of plenty* claret glasses are so seldom found as to challenge the persistence of any collector. Tall and slender, with a delicate, graceful bowl, they are desirable for more reasons than their extreme rarity. Another noteworthy piece is the butter dish of which the cover knob is a head of Washington, queue and all. One has been found in clear yellow. Look for its twin if you specialize in what is hard to find. The *horn of plenty* spoon holder also may be obtained in opaque white and clear yellow. Six-inch compotes on a high standard, covered or open, were usually listed in the early catalogues as "sweetmeat dishes." They are rare in any early pattern, and particularly so in *horn of plenty*. It is well to note the petal standard and the waffle design in the base.

Egg Cups

Mrs. Wallace Hood of Danvers, Massachusetts, has gathered a remarkably interesting collection of those small objects originally termed "egg glasses." After assembling such of these as may be had in patterns collectible in sets, she turned her attention to exceptional specimens that sometimes are found not only in color but

Fig. 6 — "Three-Face" Champagne
Here the stem is hollow — an unusual feature in a pressed item.
From the collection of Mrs. E. H. Bristol

Fig. 7 — SPILL HOLDERS
    Apparently of the 1840's, these were used for paper spills and for cigars. Subsequent spoon holders were deeper and mounted on taller stems.
    From the collection of Mrs. Emma Fitts Bradford

what, today, are termed "spoon holders." These articles deserve the attention of rarity seekers. The examples shown in Figure 7 are early types. Many such vessels were originally made to match, in design, the bowls of whale-oil lamps. They were called "spill holders," and were dedicated to tapers or twisted paper spills which were used in lighting lamps, candles, and the wood in the fireplace at a time when matches were either expensive or unobtainable. Spill holders are of lead flint glass, some quite brilliant and others rather dull, but all of them heavy and squat. In the 1840's many of them were made and advertised as holders for cigars. Later, when spoon holders came into gen-

covered. Two of the latter, both in opaque white, are shown in Figure 10. As an old glassworker once informed me, the covers were designed to keep the eggs warm as they were served. Covers were, however, gradually abandoned, perhaps because they broke so easily as to prove a liability instead of an asset. Thereafter egg cups came *sans* covers. A collection of these dainty cups is not only charming but well worthy of study.

Spoon Holders

    I do not know of any collector who has devoted himself, or herself, exclusively to

eral use, a gradual change in form occurred. The bowls became deeper and the stems longer. The opal or milk-white specimen in Figure 11 is a good example of this transitional type.

Three Face

    There are many rarities in the later patterns, even in those of the Centennial period. Mrs. E. H. Bristol, of Foxboro, Massachusetts, has the largest known collection in the *three-face* pattern, which is a product of the early 1870's. Among the unusual specimens that she has obtained is the hollow-stem champagne glass, shown in Figure 6, and another of the type known as a "saucer champagne," with a solid stem. Nearly all of the glasses of the early pressed period that are five or five and a half inches in height are listed in the old catalogues in my possession as "champagnes," and had solid glass stems. The pressed champagne glass with a hollow stem was apparently a later innovation. If you have any doubts about the rarity of the hollow-stem types, just try to find them today! Another rarity in the *three-face* design, in partly frosted and partly clear glass, is the tall, ribbed, covered biscuit jar illustrated in ANTIQUES for April 1933.

Lion Pattern

    Of note in the *lion* pattern of the same period are oval salts and cologne bottles. The salts, both plain and engraved, are pictured in Figure 8, with the cologne bottles. The latter are the only specimens of their kind that have been found to date,

Fig. 8 — "LION" RARITIES
    Salts of unusual form, one engraved; and perhaps unique pair of toilet bottles. Though the *lion* pattern is of the 1870's, it does not lack its rarities.
    Salts from the collection of Joseph Makanna; bottles from the collection of Donald Lannin

Fig. 9 — "Morning-Glory" Pattern (*c. 1860 or later*)
Probably New England. Goblet, "champagne," and egg cup. The term "champagne" was rather indiscriminately applied to stemware of a certain height

orative of the dense white pieces of that period is the large swan dish with uplifted wings, pictured in Figure 12.

Morning-Glory

Those who would accumulate a rare pattern obtainable in sets, and who have the necessary patience and persistence, are advised to collect the *morning-glory* pattern, illustrated in Figure 9. To all appearances it is a product of the 1860's. I have never seen any documentary evidence conclusively identifying its source, though by many it

Fig. 10 — Covered Egg Cups in Opaque Glass (*c. 1850*)
Few of these glasses survive with covers, the making of the latter having been speedily discontinued.
From the collection of Mrs. Wallace Hood

in so far as I know, though there must be others somewhere. Look for them, if you seek that which is high odds against you.

Other Exceptional Pieces

Many interesting items in milk white, both early and late, are available to collectors who spurn easy finds. A pair of opal sweetmeat dishes in the *prism* pattern, shown in Figure 11, dates back to the 1850's, and possibly to the 1840's. They were probably made by M'Kee Brothers of Pittsburgh. The Liberty Bell cup in milk white

has been attributed to a New England factory.

Limitations of space preclude the enumeration or description of all the rarities in a number of other interesting patterns. Nevertheless, I hope that I have told enough to convince collectors who complain of insufficient excitement in pressed-glass hunting that they are sadly mistaken.

Fig. 11 (above) — "Prism" Covered Sweetmeats and Opal Spoon Holder
The sweetmeats are 6 inches in diameter

Fig. 12 (right) — Unusual Milk Glass
Liberty Bell cup, pressed glass with hand-fashioned ear (*1876*); swan, an exceptionally fine piece of modeling (*c. 1880*); *bellflower* syrup jug (*c. 1850*)

with the serpent handle was produced on the grounds of the Centennial Exposition in Philadelphia in 1876, by James Gillinger and Sons, in plain sight of the visitors. One of the rarest and most dec-

The Popular Ten in Pattern Glass

By RUTH WEBB LEE

Note. We concur with Mrs. Lee in decrying attempts to prepare numerically limited lists of the *best* items in any domain of collecting. The mere naming of presumably blue-ribbon specimens may quite easily convey the erroneous impression that specimens unnamed are, in some mysterious way, of inferior merit. It should therefore be noted that in the subjoined discussion Mrs. Lee carefully avoids consideration of good, better, and best, and confines herself exclusively to classifying certain designs in pattern glass on the basis of current popularity. In suggesting this new approach to an old topic we have been hopeful of accomplishing two ends: that of helping the non-specializing dealer to determine which of innumerable patterns he could most safely acquire for stock; and that of informing the collector of pattern glass as to the particular fields in which he may expect to encounter the most active competition from other ardent hunters. It is well to remember that majority sentiment is by no means invariably sound. The most successful collector may be the one who, after observing the direction followed by the crowd, turns toward another point of the compass and blazes a trail of his own.

Fig. 1 (left) — "BELLFLOWER"
Design believed to have originated prior to 1850. Produced by sundry factories. For ready reference illustrations are alphabetically arranged. For a complete list of items in each group see the author's book, *Early American Pressed Glass*

Fig. 2 (right) — "BLACKBERRY": OPAQUE WHITE
Design patented 1870 by William Leighton, Jr., of Wheeling, West Virginia

THE search for short-cuts to expert knowledge is as old as the desire to know, something born in all men, according to Aristotle. Lists of the ten "best" novels, or twelve "greatest" paintings, or six "wisest" philosophers have no value either educational or cultural; for at most they merely record the opinion of some individual or small group. Other opinions, quite different, may be fully as reliable. And after all, what the collector should do is to form his own independent conclusions based on his own observation and judgment. I have heard many criticisms of the "best" lists dealing with prints, cup plates, and so on. It is argued, not unreasonably, that such predigested material hinders rather than helps new collectors by tending to narrow their interest prematurely, and to discourage them before they are really under way. Among the "best" cup plates, for example, are many which are virtually unobtainable. Young collectors, finding that what began as a promising avocation turns into a disappointment, give up in despair. The veteran collector may be spurred on by the scarcity; but not the beginner.

Fortunately, there are not enough patterns of pressed glass to permit anyone to attempt a list of the one hundred "best" patterns collectible in sets. Selecting the "best" would provoke more debate than encourage agreement. At the same time, it *is* possible to comply with a request for a list of the ten patterns which are in the most active demand today, or which have maintained their popularity the longest. The vogue of pattern glass is not old. It began when discriminating eyes saw merit in some of the pressed American tableware displayed in antique shops. If the glass was by no means ancient, it was none the less attractive. As the vogue spread, a greater variety of patterns was carried by the dealers. Some patterns were inferior and tended to give a bad name to all pressed glass. It always was, of course, absurd to class the fine old patterns, dating from the 1840's, with ware produced in the 1890's or even later,

Fig. 3 — "DAISY AND BUTTON"
A pattern which was at the height of its popularity during the 1880's. Produced with variations by nearly every old factory specializing in tableware. *Daisy and button* is widely collected today

Fig. 4 — "HORN OF PLENTY"
Known to have been made at Sandwich and by M'Kee and Brothers, Pittsburgh, in the 1850's–1860's. The hand-expanded mouth and the hand-shaped and applied handle are indicative of early practice

Fig. 5 — "LION"
First produced in the 1870's by Gillinder & Sons of Philadelphia. Produced by a few others during a considerable period

and, in many instances, originally given away as a premium with soaps, teas, or baking powders.

In the six years since the first edition of *Early American Pressed Glass* was published, the popularity of all pattern glass has increased phenomenally. For this several reasons may be advanced. The increased ease of doing business by mail is one. Again, throughout the depression, pressed glass enabled thousands of persons to enjoy the pleasure of collecting without incurring bankruptcy. The demand for pattern glass has now reached such proportions that dealers all over the country depend upon its handling for a steady income. No sectionalism is observable among collectors of pressed glass. Everywhere the same patterns are sought, and those which today may be viewed as the leaders are the very ones most popular fifteen years ago.

Among the first patterns to win wide favor were *Ashburton* and *bellflower*. *Ashburton* has only recently reacquired its rightful name. For some years it was classed generically with *colonial*, a denomination that for a long time included several of the early, simple designs. *Ashburton* may claim to be a genuine antique, for it was produced and sold during the 1840's, nearly a hundred years ago. To the best of my knowledge, it was never offered as a premium of any kind. It occurs in a heavy flint glass of fine quality. So popular was it from the start that it was copied by a number of factories.

Bellflower has been for years the commonly accepted name for the pattern originally listed as *R. L.* (presumably *Ribbed Leaf*), of which we have records going back to the 1850's. I think it was made even before 1850. That *bellflower* also was made almost simultaneously by a number of factories is evident from the many variants extant. No collector today need apologize for cherishing a pattern that has enjoyed popularity during so many years as *bellflower*.

Two later patterns, likewise widely collected fifteen years ago and still going strong, are *lion* and *wildflower*, both dating from the 1870's. *Lion* was made chiefly by the Gillinders of Philadelphia; and *wildflower* by Adams & Company of Pittsburgh. The long-enduring popularity of *wildflower* has been due to its decorative value, for it is obtainable in several attractive tints.

In order to determine — by investigation rather than by guesswork — the most popular pressed patterns today, I have gone to some trouble to learn from shops in all sections of the country just which ones are in such demand as to keep stocks at a low ebb. Confining my selection to those patterns which it is possible to collect in sets within a reasonable period, hence not necessarily the scarcest, I would name the following: *bellflower, horn of plenty, wildflower, thousand eye, lion, three face, westward-ho, rose in snow, milk-white blackberry,* and *daisy and button.*

It is fair to list an additional ten, which have enjoyed wide popularity but for certain reasons cannot be included in the first group. These are: *morning-glory, diamond thumbprint,* purple marble glass, *New England pineapple, tulip, star with dewdrop, thumbprint, inverted fern, Hamilton,* and *Baltimore pear.* The second choice calls for some explanation. *Morning-glory* would undoubtedly rate with the first ten in point of appearance and popularity except that examples are so seldom found that few dealers outside of New England, where the pattern originated, have ever seen a piece of it. *Diamond thumbprint* would also rank among the first ten but for the fact that the goblets are virtually unobtainable. The same holds true for the fluted goblet in marble glass, illustrated in the article *Mosaic Glass and Other Types* in ANTIQUES for February 1937. *New England pineapple* might displace some one among the first ten but, like *morning-glory,* it is too hard to find outside of New England. *Tulip* makes an attractive table setting, but has declined somewhat in popularity, perhaps because it is now rather scarce. It never was abundant.

Star with dewdrop, though undoubtedly one of the most brilliant and appealing patterns, lacks a true goblet approaching the quality of the plates. In assembling sets, collectors are compelled to substitute other goblets, usually the *popcorn. Thumbprint* is another widely known early pattern, with much to commend it. Like *tulip* it has been collected spasmodically. *Inverted fern* also is sufficiently in demand to deserve honorable mention. *Hamilton* is highly esteemed, especially among collectors who themselves bear that famous name; but its popularity does not quite entitle it to rank with the first ten. *Baltimore pear* runs even with *rose in snow.* Between these two, my own choice would be *rose in snow,* because it is the earlier and is the better in design and in quality of glass. First made during the 1870's, it has been widely known for years. *Baltimore pear* has enjoyed great popularity

Fig. 6 — "ROSE IN SNOW"
Manufactured by Bryce Brothers of Pittsburgh in the 1870's, and probably by others. Collectors should be wary of recent reproductions of this pattern

Fig. 7 — "THOUSAND EYE"
Made in the 1870's, and later. Adams & Company of Pittsburgh and Richards & Hartley of Tarentum, Pennsylvania, are known to have manufactured certain types

because, notwithstanding the poor quality of the glass, many people consider it highly decorative. This pattern made its first appearance in 1888. In writing my book, I tried to draw the line at patterns made after 1890.

There is little need to discuss in detail the reasons for choosing the first group of ten. Everyone knows the *bellflower* pattern. *Horn of plenty* is another very old favorite. *Thousand eye*, as well as *wildflower* in its various hues, has been collected from coast to coast. *Lion* and *westward-ho* have been known as far back as I can remember anything about glass. *Three face* has not been quite so well known for as long a period, but the demand for it has been steadily maintained. *Milk-white blackberry* has been sought for years. It was patented February 1, 1870, by the designer, William Leighton, Jr., and produced by Hobbs, Brockunier and Company of Wheeling,

Fig. 8 — "Three Face"
Made probably exclusively by George Duncan & Sons of Pittsburgh about 1875. The example pictured is a hollow-stem champagne, and rare

Fig. 9 — "Westward-ho"
Issued by Gillinder & Sons of Philadelphia, about 1875. The *westward-ho* pattern has likewise been imitated, in goblets and sauce dishes

West Virginia. Let collectors who like rarities in pattern glass try to find a water pitcher like the one in Figure 2! *Rose in snow* has been consistently popular with the numerous collectors who like flowers. *Daisy and button* is the one pattern in the list which will develop differences of opinion. It is included because it is known and is being collected in every state of the Union. Other patterns may possess more merit; but this is the one on which most collectors cut their eyeteeth, before they turn to others. It is not expensive. Probably it is more generally collected than any other one pattern.

Statements regarding patterns most in demand are perhaps pointers for those collectors who like to follow where others lead. Hence let me warn the blindly trusting that goblets in *westward-ho*, *wildflower*, and *rose in snow* have been recently reproduced. I advise collectors to obtain one specimen which is undoubtedly "right," and keep it for purposes of comparison. Make sure that what is offered for sale *exactly* matches the genuine piece! Study, for example, the details of the design on a genuine *westward-ho* goblet. Note that the lips of the deer are closed, whereas on the reproduction they are slightly blurred, as if the animal were preparing to masticate. The original *wildflower* goblet has a full-inch fluted band around the base of the bowl, and the design is heavily stippled. On the reproduction the band measures three quarters of an inch, and the design is thinner and a trifle smaller. The imitative *rose in snow* goblet departs from the real in the design of flower and leaves as well as in the stem and in the appearance of the glass itself.

For the benefit of collectors who may seek rarities in pattern glass, I append a list of the rare articles in each of the first-named group of ten patterns:

1. Bellflower. Cake plate on standard; handled mug; colored pieces; whiskey tumbler; octagonal sugar bowl; 6-inch covered sweetmeat dish on high standard; 3-inch honey dish; footed tumbler; decanter with original *bellflower* stopper; celery vase; berry bowl; small-size water pitcher.

2. Horn of plenty. Oblong covered dish; butter dish with Washington's head forming knob to cover; claret glass; colored pieces; handled mug; large oval vegetable dish; 6-inch covered sweetmeat dish on high standard; oval salt.

3. Wildflower. Compote with square bowl, rounded at top, on high standard; oblong cake basket with wire handle; cordial and champagne; turtle salt.

4. Thousand eye. Champagne; cordial; egg cup.

5. Lion. Oval salt; cordial; all-frosted sauce dish without standard; syrup jug; covered cheese dish; miniature set; egg cup; cologne bottle; powder jar.

6. Three face. Champagne with hollow stem (the only one made in pattern glass); champagne with saucer bowl; cordial; cracker jar, covered.

7. Westward-ho. Cordial and wine; 5-inch covered compote on low standard (only one known to date); 5-inch covered compote on high standard.

8. Rose in snow. Toddy jar with plate; covered pickle jar; extra-large oval vegetable dish.

9. Milk-white blackberry. Water pitcher; celery vase; berry bowl not on standard.

10. Daisy and button. Egg cup; hat in largest size; pieces in amethyst color as well as in ruby red.

Of considerable interest is the finding within the past year of a *ribbed ivy* and a *bellflower* hat. These were apparently made in whiskey-tumbler molds, the top of the glass being rolled over and downward, forming a recognizable hat. Only one specimen of each is known at the present time.

Fig. 10 — "Wildflower"
Made by Adams & Company of Pittsburgh in the 1870's

PRESIDENTIAL PORTRAITS
IN LATE GLASS

By HOMER EATON KEYES

Illustrations from the collection of Mrs. William Greig Walker

CUP-PLATE collectors reverently cherish those few "his-toricals" whose chief embellishment is a portrait of some well-known personage. In so far as I am aware, this category embraces only seven subjects: Washington, William Henry Harrison, Henry Clay, Major Ringgold, Queen Victoria, Victoria and Albert, the Prince and Princess of Wales. The actual number of designs is of course increased by sundry variants. Nevertheless, that so few likenesses in pressed ware were turned out between the Harrison campaign in 1840 and the marriage of Albert Edward, Prince of Wales, to Princess Alexandra of Denmark in 1863 is worth remarking. Furthermore, it may be observed that, with few exceptions, these cup-plate depictions of rulers and heroes are pretty feeble productions. In general they would be quite unrecognizable had the mold cutter failed to identify vague lineaments with easily decipherable labels.

What is true of portrait cup plates is almost equally true of the allied pictorials. At any rate, the latter exhibit no elaborate compositions, and no well-defined effects of light and shade achieved by modeling. As a matter of fact, the era of pictorial pressed glass did not really begin until the decade of the 1870's. It was to flourish during the rest of the century. Its end is not yet in sight.

This rather sudden manifestation in the domain of glassmaking must, I think, be ascribed in part to the perfecting of new methods of moldmaking. Apparently the patterns of the early molds employed for pressing, like those used for blowing articles in full size, were largely, if not entirely, hand cut. Deming Jarves is quoted to the effect that preparing the mold for the once famous Union Bowl, now lost, occupied the time of two men for six months. That certainly implies manual labor, to say nothing of high cost. This cost element was, I believe, primarily responsible for the shift from the lacy patterns of the 1830's and 1840's to the coarser forms and ornamental treatments that appeared in the 1850's. Molds for the latter could be satisfactorily produced by a process of casting. Since this involved the preliminary carving of a model in wood, it necessitated the elimination of intricately interlaced and delicate lines. (For wood models see ANTIQUES for March 1927, *p. 212*.)

The next step, taken, it would seem, shortly before 1876, permitted a return to the elaboration if not to the refinement of earlier glass. This consisted in casting the molds directly from plaster-of-Paris matrices, which had either been carved by hand, or, in their turn, cast from designs modeled in wax. Plaster of Paris is soft and easily cut in low relief. If when freshly mixed with water it is flowed over a wax sculpture and allowed to harden, it will retain the impression of every detail in the original.

The modeling in wax or plaster was of course the all-important part of this method of moldmaking. The Fostoria Glass Company tells me that it frequently engaged the talent of "well-known sculptors, as well as some who were destined to become famous."

The use of plaster-of-Paris matrices likewise permitted the accurate reproduction of glass items whose copying was considered desirable. In such instances plaster casts of the item were made in as many parts as were needed to deliver it from the mold. These sections were then sent to the foundry to be produced in iron. Thus we may perceive how readily imitations of popular pattern glass may be turned out. The only point at which the counterfeiter is likely to slip is in the final stage of his operation — that of *finishing* the cast-iron mold. This process must be accomplished by hand, and calls for the same expertness essential to die cutting and engraving. Only by observing the slight departures from verisimilitude that are almost certain to occur in hand finishing may certain current copies of older pattern glass be distinguished from the genuine.

According to the Westmoreland Glass Company, the *casting* of molds from plaster is advantageous when a complicated design is undertaken. But the iron employed is softer than that used for hand-cut molds and the results obtained are less brilliant than those accomplished by the latter type.

Concerning one phase of the process of translating a photographic or engraved likeness into a plaster model I am still in doubt. Some mechanical means must have

FIG. 1 (*above, left*) — WASHINGTON OVAL PLATE: BEAR-PAW HANDLES (*1876*)
Inscribed: on handles, *Centennial 1876;* around bust, *First in War, First in Peace, first in the hearts of his countrymen*

FIG. 2 (*above, right*) — WASHINGTON GLASS HATCHET (*1876*)
Inscription illegible; Washington profile on blade. A Centennial souvenir

FIG. 3 (*left*) — GRANT CIRCULAR PLATE: SERRATE LEAF BORDER (*1885*)
Inscribed: on border, *Let us have peace . . . U. S. Grant;* around bust, *Born April 27 1822 . . . Died July 23 1885.* A memorial piece

FIG. 4 (*right*) — GRANT RECTANGULAR PLATE WITH CHAMFERED CORNERS (*1885?*)
Circular medallion bust against faceted ground. Inscribed, around bust, *The patriot and soldier . . . Gen. Ulysses. S. Grant.* Probably a memorial piece

been relied upon, at least in many instances, to transfer the original picture to the plaster surface awaiting the carver's hand. I surmise that photography may have been requisitioned for this purpose. On the other hand, some tracing implement may have served.

So much for the outlines of a technique that opened new possibilities for the glass manufacturer and his market. Every imaginable kind of pictorial souvenir article in glass could now be turned out in quantities at prices attractive to the multitude. And turned out they were, to make thousands of homes happier and more hideous.

Manufacturers of domestic wares of many kinds have, for generations, been more concerned with technical progress than with æsthetic excellence. From the close of the Civil War until today they have been tireless in chemical research, in experimentation with mechanical improvements, and in search for skilled workmen. But only within recent years have any of them given serious thought to enlisting the aid of designers who could qualify as trained artists. Partly on this account, partly because, during the period from 1850 to 1900 or thereabouts, the best of world taste was pretty bad, the lively ingenuity devoted to creating eye-catchingly novel forms and colors in glassware, and to devising ways of turning them out in vast quantities, filled the country literally with tons of varied glassware, most of it of steadily declining æsthetic worth.

That generalization, with some exceptions, must, I fear, be accepted as the truth. But it may be countered with two questions: How would you define æsthetic worth in a domestic utensil? and, To what extent are collectors of such articles actuated in their selection by purely æsthetic considerations? I could answer neither to my own entire satisfaction or to that of anyone else. Perhaps the second question finds its own answer in the fact that within the past few years the collecting of the pictorial glasses made between 1876 and 1900 has gone forward at an ever-accelerating pace. This activity becomes somewhat more comprehensible when we realize that some of this glass is associated with specific events in United States history, and that historical objects are *ipso facto* certain to become collectibles as soon as they have accumulated a little dust.

The pictorial glasses in question may be roughly divided into three groups: I. Portraits of celebrities. II. Well-known scenes or reproductions of particular pictures — such as some of the Currier & Ives prints. III. Fanciful compositions like the *Westward-ho* pattern and its analogues. From the standpoint of the collector who has no intention of subjecting his glass to practical use on the table, the Portrait group is probably the most important. Save

perhaps for the actress items, portrait glass seldom occurs in complete sets. It is represented chiefly by individual plates and trays, some of which, however, are allied in detail to formal patterns. Portrait goblets or tumblers and portrait compotes occasionally turn up, but appear to be exceptions to the general rule. The group in question may again be divided into two sub-groups: *A.* Portraits of American presidents. *B.* Portraits of other celebrities. Of these the presidential pieces may be viewed as tops.

Under the circumstances it seems high time that all the significant items in the portrait group should be listed, so that the *omnium-gatherum* collector may have a distinct idea of the goal which he may hope to reach and the distance that he must travel in order to arrive. The purpose of these notes is to make a small beginning in that direction. I hope that interested persons throughout the country will fill inevitable gaps until a really comprehensive check list has been compiled. Hence I invite assistance in what may prove to be a large undertaking. In the present installment I shall confine myself to presidential items, leaving those representing other celebrities for subsequent consideration.

Apparently, American glassmakers of the last quarter of the 1800's did not at the outset think of issuing portrait glass in connection with campaigns for the presidency. If they had, the first candidates for such memorial treatment would doubtless have been Rutherford B. Hayes and his Democratic rival, Samuel J. Tilden, who were pitted against each other in the fall of 1876, the very year of the Philadelphia Centennial Exposition. Instead, President Washington appears to be the first first gentleman of the nation to figure in our late portrait group. His bust, quite well modeled, appears in the centre of an oval plate whose bear-paw handles are clearly marked *Centennial 1876* (*Fig. 1*). In the same year and to celebrate the same patriotic occasion the rare glass hatchet of Figure 2 was doubtless produced.

The blade of this implement carries an excellent relief of the Father of his Country. Iron hatchets of somewhat similar design were likewise made as Centennial souvenirs. The owner of one of these metal versions seriously maintains that it belonged to a restricted issue made for distinguished participants in Washington's inauguration in 1789. Such, alas, is human credulity.

Subject to welcome correction, I am inclined to believe that for some years presidential timber was not considered suitable for portrayal in glass until it had been felled by death. As I have already suggested, if Hayes was thus immortalized I am unaware of the fact. The two Ulysses S. Grant plates here pictured were — one certainly, the other probably — produced after the General's death in 1885, when his inadequacies as a president had

FIG 5 (left) — GAR-
FIELD CIRCULAR
PLATE: STAR BOR-
DER WITH SHIELD
AND FLAGS (1880–1881)
Profile head, three quar-
ters bust. Inscribed, *James
A. Garfield*. Probably a
memorial piece

FIG. 6 (right) — GAR-
FIELD CIRCULAR
PLATE: INTEGRAL
HANDLES
Border: version of egg
and dart. Profile head,
three quarters bust. No
inscription. Probably a
memorial piece

FIG. 7 — GARFIELD
MEMORIAL
PLATES
Left, serrate rim, flow-
ered drape border.
Head and bust three-
quarter view, sur-
rounded by stars. In-
scriptions: *We mourn
our nation's loss . . .
Born Nov. 19 1831
. . . Shot July 2 1881*

. . . *Died Sep 19 1881.
Right*, rim, irregular
small serrations. Bor-
der, laurel branches
against stippling. Pro-
file head, three quar-
ters bust. Inscribed,
Memorial. A somewhat
similar plate is illus-
trated by Ruth Webb
Lee, as cited in the
accompanying text

been long forgotten and only his greatness as a soldier was
remembered.

The next president after Hayes was James A. Garfield, whose
election in 1880 was followed in July of the next year by his assassination at the hands of the disgruntled office seeker Charles Jules
Guiteau. Of the five Garfield
items here illustrated three are
unquestionably memorials. I
incline to believe that the other
two belong in the same category. Yet I must admit the
possibility that they were issued
as campaign souvenirs.

The florid and amply side-
whiskered Vice President Chester
A. Arthur, who was unexpect-
edly pushed into the president's
chair by the death of his chief,
has been reported among the
glass portrayals.

The first indisputable campaign items in the group under
consideration present the countenances of James G. Blaine and
his running mate in the presidential race of 1884, John A.
Logan, better known as Black

Jack Logan. We know that the Blaine and Logan tray and plates
here illustrated are campaign pieces because the two aspirants to
office were defeated by Grover Cleveland and Thomas A. Hendricks. These two banner bearers for the Democratic party appear
on a tray whose border duplicates that of the Blaine and Logan
item (see Ruth Webb Lee's
Early American Pressed Glass,
Plate 165). A tray, or plaque,
exhibiting Benjamin Harrison
and Levi P. Morton, who defeated Cleveland and Thurman
in the election of 1888, is here
illustrated (*Fig. 11*). Four years
later Cleveland was returned to
office, thus defeating Harrison's
hope for a second term.

William McKinley, I am

FIG. 8 — GARFIELD OVAL
PLATE (1881)
Dotted serrate rim; leaf border.
Three laurel-framed medallions,
Garfield, Washington, Lincoln, in
order named; United States shield.
Inscribed below medallions, *God
reigns . . . First in peace . . .
Charity for all;* in border, *In
remembrance*

able to picture on two plates. One is either a campaign or a post-election product, since it carries the motto *Protection and plenty*. It is fair to assume that this plate was issued in 1896, since it was his position on the tariff and sound-money issues that won McKinley the election in that year. The other plate memorializes the president's assassination at the hands of Leon Czolgosz, September 6, 1901. In the campaigns of both 1896 and 1900 McKinley's opponent was William Jennings Bryan, who advocated bimetallism as a cure for all the economic ills of the masses. This accounts for the

Figure 15 are pictorial allusions to the man's exploits and personal peculiarities. The eagle, however, signifies his presidency. This plate was probably issued during or at the close of the campaign of 1904, when Roosevelt became president by popular election, and not by accident.

If it turns out that the presidential subjects in pressed glass here pictured and discussed are the only ones known, I shall be greatly surprised. I shall postpone attempting to make a check list until readers of ANTIQUES have had opportunity to inform me regarding additional subjects

FIG. 9 (*above*) — BLAINE AND LOGAN RECTANGULAR TRAY (*1884*)
Ivy-leaf border. Name of each candidate stamped on bust. A campaign item

FIG. 10 (*left and right*) — BLAINE AND LOGAN PLATES (*1884*)
Border, pointed daisy-and-button arches alternating with circular arches framing oak leaves. Finely modeled and well-placed three-quarter-view bust portraits

motto *The peoples money* above Bryan's portrayal on the bowl shown in Figure 13. Evidently it was produced at the same time and at the same place as an accompanying bowl revealing the bust of McKinley and the motto *Protection and prosperity*.

McKinley's untimely death brought Vice President Theodore Roosevelt to the White House. Roosevelt had already distinguished himself and his regiment of Rough Riders in the Spanish American War of 1898. He was known as an enthusiastic hunter of big game. As president he undertook various social and economic reforms under a "square deal" slogan. His somewhat autocratic methods of dealing with men and situations were satirically referred to as "wielding the big stick." The emblems on the rim of the Roosevelt oval plate in

FIG. 11 — HARRISON AND MORTON RECTANGULAR PLAQUE (*1888*)
Ivy-leaf border like that of Figure 9. Stiff bust portraits, each stamped with name of subject. Probably a campaign item

or to assure me that none are to be found. Whether or not a flask displaying the countenance of Franklin D. Roosevelt should be included I am not sure. It is a rather ghastly piece of work memorializing the president's first-term labors in behalf of prohibition repeal.

And that brings me to a brief consideration of the portrait items from the standpoint of quality. Here a wide diversity will be observed. Most of the models were, I think, cut in plaster instead of first modeled in wax. Their scratchy aspect suggests this opinion. In the group here pictured I consider two plates, one depicting Blaine, the other Logan, by far the best. They approach the precision of medalwork. The Bryan and McKinley covered cups or bowls win the booby prize hands down. They could hardly

FIG. 12 — McKINLEY CIRCULAR PLATE (*1896*)
Gadrooned rim, star-spangled border. Bust portrait framed by shield in circle. Inscribed, *Protection and plenty.* Probably a campaign item

FIG. 13 — BRYAN AND McKINLEY COVERED CUPS OR BOWLS (*1896*)
Left, inscribed, *The peoples money . . . W^m. J. Bryan. Right*, inscribed, *Protection and prosperity . . . Maj. Wm. McKinley*

be worse. Almost invariably the subsidiary decoration of these portrait items is either stiff and ungainly or overloaded with unrelated and coarsely executed motives. The stars surrounding one Garfield bust are, however, tastefully arranged, and those on one McKinley plate are not bad. The style of lettering employed is almost unfailingly atrocious.

Be that as it may, if I were instructing a class of highschool youngsters in United States history, I should gather all of these portrait glasses that I could find and set my pupils to work finding out the whys and wherefores of each design. Thus, I think, more than one precious jewel of learning might be borne to the head.

Note. In the preceding review I may seem to imply that the *Westward-ho* pattern was produced in cast-iron molds. James Gillinder assures me that this is not the case. On the contrary, it transpires that in the 1870's James Gillinder & Sons, Philadelphia glassmakers, had in their employ two exceptionally able die sinkers. One or both of these men cut by hand the iron molds for

the *Westward-ho* series, and for similar patterns. The labor involved must have been enormous.

I may also observe that a somewhat extended correspondence with manufacturers has revealed some differences of opinion. I have quoted two authorities who maintain that the molds for portrait glass were usually cast from plaster models. Manager K. R. Haley of the Overmyer Mould Company, Greensburg, Pennsylvania, believes that the designs were usually cut in the mold by means of chisels, hammers, and other hand-manipulated tools. Mr. Haley states that many of the old-time moldmakers could take a photograph or drawing and reproduce it accurately in iron. While casting from plaster models is widely in use, some artisans capable of cutting patterns by hand still survive. It seems reasonable to surmise that collaboration between accomplished designer and skilled craftsman might today develop unsuspected artistic capabilities in a technique hitherto dedicated primarily to commercial ends.

FIG. 14 (*left*) — McKINLEY OVAL PLATE
Laurel border. Full-length figure of the President. Inscribed, *It is Gods way . . . His will be done* [the dying man's own words]. *Born 1843 . . . Died 1901*

FIG. 15 (*right*) — THEODORE ROOSEVELT OVAL PLATE (*probably 1904*)
Rustic rim. Border of Teddy bears, military and hunting accoutrements, eagle, big sticks crossed. Inscribed, in border only, *A square deal.* Profile portrait in rustic frame

PORTRAITS IN LATE GLASS

By ELIZABETH GUNN

Except as noted, illustrations from the Walker collection

IN the latter half of the 1800's, and more particularly in the last twenty years of the century, glass manufacturers availed themselves of recently developed facilities for mass production of all manner of souvenir glassware. Of the pictorial pressed glass which they turned out in vast quantities and which was absorbed for domestic use by an enthusiastic public, the type of chief interest to present-day collectors is that decorated with portraits of notable personages. Portrait glass differs from conventional pattern glass in that it occurs mainly in plates, platters, or trays, only occasionally in tumblers, compotes, or goblets, and seldom if ever in complete sets. In ANTIQUES for November 1938 (*p. 240*), the late Homer Eaton Keyes discussed the mechanical processes by which this technically admirable — if not esthetically desirable — portrait glass was produced, and established a division of the category into two groups: portraits of American presidents, and portraits of other celebrities. His presentation of eighteen presidential items was offered as a start toward compiling a comprehensive check list. Eight additional items have now been reported, and are here reproduced. At the same time, I am illustrating thirteen portrait glasses depicting celebrities other than American presidents. For helpful information in regard to pieces in both groups I am indebted to Mrs. Lucien Nelson Lindsey and Mrs. William Greig Walker.

PORTRAITS OF PRESIDENTS

Five glass items portraying James A. Garfield have hitherto been noted, three of them unquestionably memorials issued following Garfield's assassination in 1881 by Charles Jules Guiteau. To these may now be added a platter memorializing both Garfield and Lincoln (*Fig. 1*).

The majority of the other presidential items previously shown seem to have been campaign rather than memorial items. Certainly the tray with ivy-leaf border, portraying James G. Blaine and John A. Logan, was issued at the time of their unsuccessful campaign in 1884. It is worth noting that on this tray the name *Walter* appears in fine letters, partially identifying the designer of the original model for the portraits. Yet, though several American

FIG. 3 (*above*) — CLEVELAND AND HENDRICKS PLATES (*1884*)

Border of *classic* pattern. Finely modeled portraits. *Left, from the collection of Mrs. W. R. Marsh; right, from the collection of Mrs. Lucien Nelson Lindsey*

FIG. 4 (*left*) — BLAINE AND LOGAN PLATTER (*1884*)

Simple border, daisy-and-oak-leaf handles, notched rim. Finely modeled portrait busts. A campaign item

artists and sculptors of the name are recorded, none appears to have been flourishing in 1884. A matching tray, picturing the defeated candidates' opponents, Grover Cleveland and Thomas A. Hendricks, was reported by Mr. Keyes and is now illustrated (*Fig. 2*).

A similar impartiality on the part of the glassmaker is shown by other items produced for the same campaign, which was one of the most exciting in the nation's history. Counterparts of the round Blaine and Logan plates are two plates with identical border, portraying Cleveland and Hendricks (*Fig. 3*). This border, previously described as pointed daisy-and-button arches alternating with circular arches framing oak leaves, is listed by Ruth Webb Lee as *classic* pattern. The four plates in question are of particular interest because two of them are marked with the name of the artist, who doubtless executed the complete quartet. On the shoulder of Blaine and of Hendricks tiny letters spell the name *P. J. Jacobus, Scul.* Though who Jacobus was and what works he produced are not revealed in the annals of art history, Ruth Webb Lee in

FIG. 1 (*left*) — LINCOLN AND GARFIELD PLATTER (*1881*)

Bearded faces in handles perhaps intended to portray Garfield. A memorial item. *From the collection of Mrs. Lucien Nelson Lindsey*

FIG. 2 (*right*) — CLEVELAND AND HENDRICKS TRAY (*1884*)

A campaign item, matching a Blaine and Logan tray

her *Early American Pressed Glass* says that the *westward-ho* pattern was designed by a German moldmaker named Jacobus. Quite possibly it was P. J. Jacobus who was responsible for the *westward-ho* molds and even the complete *classic* series. At all events, these portraits in glass were obviously executed by a competent sculptor; for that reason the revelation of his name alone is gratifying.

The 1884 campaign inspired the production of more portrait glass souvenirs than did any other electoral contest. Of not insignificant artistic merit are two more portraits of Blaine and Logan that appear *vis-à-vis* on an oval platter — another addition to our list (*Fig. 4*). Certain similarities in the modeling suggest the possibility that the original of these portraits might likewise have been prepared by Jacobus, though the work is not signed and nothing more than a guess may be hazarded.

A companion piece to the Harrison and Morton rectangular plaque previously illustrated depicts Grover Cleveland and Allen G. Thurman, defeated candidates in the campaign of 1888 (*Fig. 5*). Both plaques have an ivy-leaf border matching the Cleveland-Hendricks and Blaine-Logan trays of 1884. The portrait of Cleveland on the 1888 plate appears to be identical with that of the 1884 item. The thrifty glassmaker must have used the Cleveland half of the 1884 mold as model for the 1888 mold, unless perchance he actually used half of the old mold, welded to a new half portraying the new running mate.

The final Cleveland item is a round plate with a labeled portrait in the center, and the word *Reform* in the dewdrop border (*Fig. 6*). This is another campaign item, probably issued in connection with the election of 1884, though Cleveland was likewise Democratic candidate in 1888 and 1892. Throughout his political career his battle cry was reform, political and economic. In 1884, however, he was elected on a platform calling for radical reforms in the administrative departments, the civil service, the tariff, and national finances.

The only Bryan glass thus far noted is a covered cup, companion to a McKinley cup, issued in connection with the campaign of 1896. A second Bryan item, labeled with the words *Our Candidates*, portrays W. J. Bryan and J. W. Kern, an American eagle, and a crowing cock (*Fig. 7*). John Worth Kern was Democratic candidate for vice president in 1908, running with Bryan in the latter's third unsuccessful attempt to win the presidency. This plate, then, portraying both candidates, with the national bird and the Democratic rooster, is one of the latest items in the group under consideration.

PORTRAITS OF OTHER CELEBRITIES

The non-presidential celebrities include naval and military heroes, foreign rulers, religious notables, and other figures who came momentarily or repeatedly before the public eye. Just as the presidential items may be classified as memorials and campaign items, this pictorial glass may be divided into two groups: memorials, issued following the death of the subject; and souvenirs, issued at the time of some event in which the subject was primarily involved. The number of Europeans commemorated on American glass is worth remarking — for there is little doubt that all the pieces here illustrated are of American manufacture. Like the presidential glass, they date from the 1880's and 1890's, with one late item of 1908.

Three heroes of the Spanish-American War found favor with the glass manufacturers. John Coalter Bates (*1842–1919*), who had served in the United States Infantry during the Civil War, was in May 1898 appointed brigadier general of volunteers for the war with Spain. In July of the same year he was promoted to the rank of major general in recognition of his services in the Santiago campaign, and in February 1899 was made military governor of the Cuban province of Santa Clara. He later gained distinction in the Philippines, where he was stationed from 1899 to 1906. It seems likely that the two-handled glass plate on which his portrait is framed in concentric borders signalized his achievement in Cuba in 1898 (*Fig. 8*).

Another Civil War veteran was the soldier and diplomat, Fitzhugh Lee (*1835–1905*), nephew of Robert E. Lee, who served the Confederacy until the end of the war, when he retired. From 1886 to 1890 he was governor of Virginia. In 1896 he became consul general to Cuba, and in 1898, major general of United States volunteers. Like General Bates, he was appointed military governor of a Cuban province after the war. His portrait on a round glass plate against a background of stars and stripes was probably likewise issued in 1898, in recognition of a Southerner's service to the Union (*Fig. 9*).

The hero of Manila Bay deserved a handsomer tribute than he received. Admiral Dewey's countenance appears on glass only once, so far as I have been able to discover. That is on a tumbler, whose stippled surface is likewise embellished with a spread eagle, American flags, and mounds of cannon balls (*Fig. 10*). This item, too, is almost certainly of 1898, the year of Dewey's Manila Bay achievement.

A final naval souvenir is an oval platter bearing portraits of Admirals Sperry and Evans above a watery waste traversed by a procession of battleships. The words *The Pacific Fleet/Souvenir 1908* in the border identify the dish (*Fig. 11*). In 1908 President Roosevelt sent the United States battleship fleet as "heralds of peace" on a round-the-world tour. Admiral Robley Dunglison Evans (*1846–1912*), affectionately known as "fighting Bob," started the

FIG. 5 (*right*) — CLEVELAND AND THURMAN RECTANGULAR PLAQUE (*1888*)
Companion to Harrison and Morton plaque. Ivy-leaf border like that of Cleveland-Hendricks and Blaine-Logan trays. Each portrait stamped with subject's name. A campaign item. *From the collection of Mrs. Lucien Nelson Lindsey*

FIG. 6 — CLEVELAND PLATE (*1884*)
Stiff portrait bust. Dewdrop border. Probably a campaign item

FIG. 7 — BRYAN AND KERN PLATTER (*1896*)
Stars-and-stripes border. Bust portraits. American eagle and Democratic rooster. Obviously a campaign item. *From the collection of Mrs. Lucien Nelson Lindsey*

FIG. 8 (*left*) — GENERAL BATES TWO-HANDLED PLATE (*1898*)
Vine and beaded border. Bust portrait

FIG. 9 (*below, left*) — GENERAL LEE PLATE (*1898*)
Openwork border. Bust portrait against background of stars and stripes

FIG. 10 (*below, center*) — ADMIRAL DEWEY TUMBLER (*1898*)
Medallion portrait, framed in laurel wreath, surmounted by eagle; flags and cannon balls on either side. Body of tumbler stippled below rope border. No plate or platter commemorating the hero of Manila is known

FIG. 11 (*below, right*) — UNITED STATES FLEET PLATTER (*1908*)
Stippled border with laurel branches. Bust portraits of Admirals Sperry and Evans, who commanded the battleship fleet on its round-the-world good-will cruise in 1908.
From the collection of Mrs. Lucien Nelson Lindsey

voyage as commander-in-chief of the fleet. After rounding Cape Horn and reaching San Francisco, however, he was forced by ill health to relinquish his command. He was succeeded by Rear Admiral Charles Stillman Sperry (*1847–1911*), who had commanded the Second Squadron of the United States battleship fleet on the first lap of the round-the-world cruise under Evans' full command.

At least two foreign rulers were portrayed in glass, Kaiser Wilhelm I and Queen Victoria. Wilhelm, the first German emperor, was born in 1797, became seventh king of Prussia in 1861, and during the siege of Paris in 1871 was proclaimed emperor. It was doubtless following his death in 1888 that the glass memorial was issued (*Fig. 12*). Victoria, who was born in 1819 and throned in 1837, celebrated her long rule with a Golden Jubilee in 1887 and a Diamond Jubilee in 1897. The compote on which a medallion portrait of Victoria appears may have been made for either Jubilee, though probability favors the latter (*Fig. 13*). A more youthful portrait of the Queen appears on a bread plate whose border carries the arms of Great Britain, the thistle of Scotland, and the rose of England (*Fig. 14*). A variant of this plate was published in ANTIQUES for October 1928 (*p. 354*).

Religious leaders, Protestant, Catholic, and Jewish, were commemorated on glass. The Henry Ward Beecher plate was probably issued in 1887, when the beloved Congregational minister died (*Fig. 15*). Born in 1813, he was from 1847 until his death pastor of Plymouth Congregational Church in Brooklyn, New York. His fame and influence were more than nation wide. Leo XIII was born in 1810, became Pope in 1878, and died in 1903. The plate bearing his portrait with papal emblems was probably, however, not produced in one of those years but in 1893 (*Fig. 16*). In that year Monsignor Satolli was appointed first permanent apostolic delegate to the United States, sent to quell opposition within the Catholic Church which had arisen following his two previous missions to this country. Sir Moses Montefiore, whose portrait appears on a third plate of religious significance, was a well-known Jewish philanthropist,

FIG. 12 (*above*) — WILHELM I PLATE (*1888*)
Square plate with notched corners. Laurel border

FIG. 13 (*above, right*) — VICTORIA JUBILEE COMPOTE (*probably 1897*)
Medallion portrait of Queen Victoria. Floral and beaded pattern

FIG. 14 (*right*) — VICTORIA JUBILEE TWO-HANDLED PLATE (*probably 1897*)
Youthful portrait of Queen Victoria in central sunburst medallion. Emblematic border.
From the collection of Mrs. Nathan Edstein

born in Italy in 1784 of a wealthy Anglo-Italian banking family. After retiring from business in 1824, he devoted himself to the Jewish cause. He worked chiefly in Poland, Russia, Roumania, and Damascus. In 1846 he was knighted and raised to a baronetcy. Still hale and hearty after a full century, he died in 1885 at the age of one hundred and one. His memorial plate bearing his portrait and name was probably produced shortly afterward (*Fig. 17*).

The year 1892 marked the four-hundredth anniversary of the discovery of America by Christopher Columbus. Quite naturally the occasion was observed by at least two glass manufacturers (*Fig. 19*). Both Columbus portrait items are marked with the dates *1492–1892* and the name *Columbus*. One of them is the only reported portrait piece that occurs in other than clear glass. It is found in milk white as well as blue.

The celebrity series is completed, so far as present information goes, by the Nellie Bly platter (*Fig. 18*). Nellie Bly was a pseudonym given Elizabeth Cochrane (*1867–1922*) by the managing editor of the Pittsburgh *Dispatch*, where she began her sensational journalistic career about 1881. After writing *Six Months in Mexico* and a series of articles on working girls' tribulations in Pittsburgh mills, she joined the staff of the New York *World*, and in 1887 startled the country with an exposé

FIG. 15 (*left*) — HENRY WARD BEECHER PLATE (*1887*)
Serrate rim; leaf border with initials *H.W.B.* A memorial item

FIG. 16 (*center*) — LEO XIII PLATE (*probably 1893*)
Profile bust. Beaded border with religious emblems in the reserves

FIG. 17 (*right*) — MONTEFIORE PLATE (*1885*)
Serrate rim; stippled border with leaves. A memorial plate

FIG. 18 — NELLIE BLY PLATTER (*1890*)
Commemorating her globe-circling trip

FIG. 19 — TWO COLUMBUS PLATES (*1892*)
Left, wheel border; profile bust portrait. *Right*, blue glass: the only colored item here illustrated; openwork border. Bust portrait. An apparently identical example in milk-white glass has likewise been reported, in the collection of Miss Elizabeth Meating of Appleton, Wisconsin

titled *Ten Days in the Mad House*. Six doctors had declared her insane and committed her to the insane ward at Blackwell's Island. Two years later her managing editor conceived the idea of beating the "record" of Jules Verne's Phileas Fogg by sending her around the world in less than eighty days. Her account of the trip, including an interview with Jules Verne in Amiens, France, built circulation for her newspaper. She herself became for a time a symbol of feminism, and mighty debates raged over the question of career versus home for women. "Nellie Bly" married Robert L. Seaman, aged and wealthy Brooklyn manufacturer, in 1895, and when he died in 1904 she assumed management of his properties. Later impoverished by protracted litigation, she returned to newspaper work on the New York *Journal*, which she continued until her death in 1922. An inscription on the glass platter summarizes her main achievement: *AROUND THE WORLD IN 72 D'S. 6 H'S. 11 M'S. NEW YORK NOV. 14, 89. SOUTHAMPTON NOV. 22. BRINDISI NOV. 24. SUEZ NOV. 27. COLOMBO DEC. 18. HONG KONG DEC. 23. YOKOHAMA DEC. 28. SAN FRANCISCO JAN. 21, 90. CHICAGO JAN. 24. PITTSBURG JAN. 25. NEW YORK JAN. 25.* The platter was undoubtedly issued in 1890, shortly after Nellie Bly's triumphal return to New York.

Among the Latest Things in Glass

From notes and illustrations supplied by NELLE B. ROBINSON

SLAG glass — more politely known as agate glass — has been favored for some years past by certain collectors of things Victorian. Such ware appears to have been manufactured by the Sowerbys at Gateshead near Newcastle, and at the Sandwich works on Cape Cod. Likewise, no doubt, the glasshouses in the Pittsburgh district, and farther to the westward, contributed to the general production.

According to Fredrick Carder, art director of the Corning Glass Works at Corning, New York, this type of glass was made from the slag acquired from blast iron furnaces or cupolas manufacturing cast iron. "Such slag," Mr. Carder writes, "was very fusible. When to some of this material was added cryolite and a little manganese, the mixture, when remelted, afforded a variety of curious color combinations.

"Cryolite, a soft, fusible fluoride, imparts to glass that dense whiteness apparent in American so-called 'cast porcelain'; 'vitro-porcelain' it was called in England. By employing cryolite to temper the shade of a dark material — black, brown, or red — various results could be obtained. Manganese with the white of cryolite would help give chocolate and reddish-brown tones."

That a variety of slag glass emphasizing the caramel and chocolate tints noted by Mr. Carder was made between the years 1900 and 1903 in Greentown, Indiana, has recently been discovered by Mrs. Nelle B. Robinson of Indianapolis, who spent no little time and trouble in verifying her facts. The combination of materials used in obtaining these particular caramel and chocolate effects, and the method of so handling them as to secure diverse chromatic intensities, were the invention of an old-time glassworker, Jacob Rosenthal by name. Mr. Rosenthal likewise suggested ideas for the patterns employed, though the actual making of these patterns was entrusted to one "Baldy" Jackson, recently deceased in Newark, Ohio.

Jacob Rosenthal was born in Pittsburgh, May 11, 1855, and began to learn his trade in that city at the early age of eleven years, when he found work in a glass factory operated by

Fig. 1 — CHOCOLATE BUTTER DISH
This and other pieces illustrated made at Greentown, Indiana, 1901–1903

Campbell, Jones and Company. In 1874, the year of his marriage, he was occupied at Bridgeport, Ohio, whence, in 1889, he went to Anderson, Indiana, to join forces with the American Glass Company. In 1899, following a merger of several glass concerns into the National Company, he was given the management of a factory at Greentown, where he remained until 1906. Thereafter, until his death not long ago, he lived in Williamstown, West Virginia.

It was during his stay in Greentown that Mr. Rosenthal, according to his own account, developed what he called "chocolate" and "golden agate" glass, from a secret formula. For two and one half years (*1901–1903*) three fourths of the Greentown factory output was chocolate glass, which was made in table sets, water sets, berry sets, creamers and sugar bowls, and such desirable novelty forms as toothpick and match holders in the shape of a dog's head, an old woman's head, a sheaf of wheat, a dolphin, and so on. Beer mugs were also on the novelty list. Following his retirement to Williamstown, where he was associated with the Fenton Glass Company, Mr. Rosenthal permitted the use of his chocolate formula, but the accompanying production was limited. The golden agate, never in copious supply, was made during a brief period only — about six months — and solely in Greentown.

Examples of the ware are almost unmistakable. But apart from the information secured by Mrs. Robinson, their dating would

Fig. 2 — GOLDEN-AGATE PITCHER AND CHOCOLATE COMPOTE

be virtually impossible. It is difficult to associate such forms and such ornament with the dawn of the twentieth century in America. Yet it must be remembered that these designs were not created by trained artists bent on finding patterns specially suited to a peculiar material, but by the factory folk themselves — a common practice today, as well as yesterday, in many American industries. While some details of ornament, notably in the cactus tumbler, betray a search for fresh motives, the majority recall the fancies of various earlier periods. Hence the confusion that examples of the glass in question might easily engender in the mind of the student of style.

Fig. 3 — CHOCOLATE MATCH HOLDER

Fig. 4 — TUMBLERS, PITCHER, CUP, AND BERRY DISH IN CHOCOLATE AND GOLDEN AGATE

178

Fig. 1 — Pattern in Marble Glass *(decades of 1870 and 1880)*
All illustrations are from the catalogue of Challinor, Taylor & Company.
Originally known as *mosaic*. Later listed merely as *No. 13 ware*

Fig. 2 — Pattern in Marble Glass *(decades of 1870 and 1880)*
"Made in colors, crystal & mosaic," and in the dense white which was
called "opal" by the manufacturer

Mosaic Glass and Other Types

By Ruth Webb Lee

Editor's Note. Glass vessels exhibiting irregular striations of white and colored metal resembling the veinings of agate were made long prior to the Christian era. A superb Roman urn cf the type, probably dating from the first century A.D., was shown in the Metropolitan Museum special exhibition of glass held from October 13 to November 29, 1936. It is pictured as Number 5 in the catalogue of the event. Pazaurek in his *Gläser der Empire- und Biedermeierzeit* illustrates opposite 274 a vase of what he calls "lithyalinglas," which he ascribes to the 1830's. Probably a Bohemian product, the vase exhibits a blue-gray hue broken with agatelike streaks of yellow and russet whose aspect despite the vitreous material recalls the finely scroddled earthenware of Whieldon. The marble glass described by Mrs. Lee represents but a later phase of the same effort to produce a vitreous substance that would resemble a semiprecious stone.

The term "slag" by which the marbled glass material is often named is appropriate. On that topic ANTIQUES for August 1933 quoted from Frederick Carder, art director of the Corning Glass Works, to the following effect: The slag acquired from furnaces manufacturing cast iron is highly fusible. When to this slag were added cryolite and a little manganese, the mixture, when remelted, afforded a variety of curious color combinations. Cryolite imparts to glass that dense whiteness apparent in American so-called cast porcelain (the late type of

milk-white glass). Again, by employing cryolite to temper the shade of a dark material various results could be obtained.

By what technique the clearly marked stratifications of marbled glass were obtained no reference work at hand explains. The old-time agate or scroddled effects of earthenware were achieved by building up a loaf of clay layer by layer of different colors, then folding and refolding the loaf until these layers were satisfactorily intermingled. Slices were then cut from the slab and shaped according to the potter's fancy. Dribbling random portions of varicolored glass into a mold and subjecting the mass to piston pressure would obviously achieve a similar result.

For some reason, cryolite glass, either white or marbled, takes a much sharper impression from the mold than does so-called crystal of whatever quality. Of this fact American and English manufacturers of the 1870's and 1880's were well aware and, in consequence, achieved some patterns of real distinction. On the whole, it is surprising that present-day manufacturers of pressed wares have thus far failed to develop fresh possibilities in the same material.

As for the dates of the wares described by Mrs. Lee, they probably fall within the 1870's and 1880's. The registry mark on an English item of the type published in ANTIQUES for January 1934 *(p. 34)* is for the year 1877.   —H. E. K.

FOR years past, many collectors have found much to admire in what they called *End of the Day* glass. They liked the ware itself, and they liked the romantic implications of the name. *End of the Day* glass, they devoutly believed, was the workman's own product, turned out after factory hours and owing its odd mixture of hues to the custom of throwing together the varied batches of unused metal remaining in the glass pots when the shop bell sounded quitting hour and the knell of parting day. That so charming a legend should be popularly accepted is by no means strange. That it is purely a figment of the imagination untainted by even the faintest trace of fact is also by no means strange. What would a host of collectors do if they were deprived of fairytales?

Now for the prosaic truth. The glass in question was made by Challinor, Taylor & Company of Tarentum, Pennsylvania, at one of the factories in what, during the 1880's, was known as "the old Pittsburgh glass district." The firm's name for the ware was *mosaic*. In course of time, however, this original trade designation was forgotten and mosaic glass became variously known in different sections of the country as *slag, calico, end of the day,* and *marble* glass. At present it is called *marble* by virtually all collectors and dealers. Unfortunately, it was not until after publishing the first edition of my *Early American Pressed Glass* that I found an old trade catalogue of Challinor, Taylor & Company

containing illustrations of this and other popular types of the period.

From the first, mosaic glass must have been highly esteemed or the number of pieces — the "line," as the old trade lists had it — would not have included so great a variety of forms. It was a difficult glass to manufacture. An old workman of the Tarentum factory assured me that considerable difficulty was encountered in making the purple part adhere to the white. Those familiar with this ware know how very brittle it is. Many dishes have been found with bubbles, sand, and other flaws. I have been told that some of the marble-glass goblets are prone to leak, not because of breakage of the pieces but because of a lack of cohesion in the material itself.

The *end of the day* legend should die a speedy death, since it is well known that the *mosaic* of the 1880's was a carefully prepared mixture of dense purple and dense white glass, which, in the process of heating, assumed the rich shadings now so popular. If leftover metal in the pots, with all its impurities, had been used, the result would not have been a combination of purple and white.

Marble glass has become extremely popular because of its decorative value in table settings. Indeed, the supply is inadequate to meet the demand, and the highest prices ever brought by goblets in American pattern glass are now being paid for the fluted marble pattern illustrated above in Figure 1.

Fig. 3 — OPAL WARE
A dense jadelike white, impressed with an exceptionally well-designed floral pattern of oriental implications

Fig. 4 — OPAL BARNYARD FOWL
These came with or without inserted eyes of colored glass. The same designs were naturalistically colored with thinly applied enamels

Marble glass was also made in England. In addition to the large, open-edged plate made by Challinor, Taylor & Company, there is an English eight-inch size, on the reverse of which appears the peacock head, mark of Sowerby, Neville, and Sowerby, now Sowerby's Ellison Glass Works, Ltd., near Newcastle, England. The English pieces may be recognized by peculiarities difficult to describe accurately. These consist chiefly in a special manner of shading the colors, probably due to a method of manufacture, differing from that employed in America. Many odd little English pieces in various marbleized effects are also to be found.

An all-over flowered pattern was also made during the same period by Challinor, Taylor & Company. A table set is shown in Figure 2. While this is an attractive design, it has not quite the charm of the fluted pattern, though a set of it makes an unusual table display. Challinor, Taylor & Company also turned out another all-over flowered pattern in milk white, so excellent in design and quality that for years it was attributed to English makers. However, it has been definitely established as an American product. In Figure 3 is pictured a bowl familiar to many collectors. It comes in opaque white painted in natural colors, as well as in color. A large round covered jar in opaque jade-green in the same design was recently found. When tapped, the glass responds with a clear bell tone, unusual in the general run of milk-white glass.

The catalogue referred to exhibits a number of large plates with open edges (*Figs. 5* and *6*). Some of these exhibit floral designs in color. I have been asked whether such plates can have been made in this country and then sent to Bristol, England, to receive their decoration.

Fig. 5 — OPAL-WARE PLATES WITH OPEN-WORK BORDERS
Sometimes these plates were used as plaques adorned with homemade oil paintings, and made still more dreadful by a ribbon run through the open border. Hung on the parlor wall, they intensified the violence of the red or electric-blue plush furniture coverings

Fig. 6 — OPAL-WARE PLATE
Assorted decorations, either printed or printed in outline and hand colored

Since the applied patterns seem to be partly printed and partly hand-colored and of no special value from any standpoint, the possibility that they were executed outside the Tarentum factory may be dismissed without further consideration.

Gaily featured in the same catalogue is an assortment of barnyard fowl — roosters, swans, and ducks, in white as well as painted in flamboyant colors. The old turkey jar is also there, in clear glass as well as in clear glass with applied colors. Perfect reproductions of these turkey jars are in the market. I find no record that the bright-green and amber glass specimens now on sale were made in earlier days. It might be well to note here that the Challinor, Taylor & Company fowl illustrated are mostly in large sizes. The greatest number of the five-inch covered hen and rooster dishes were made by Charles West of the Westmoreland Glass Company in Grapeville, Pennsylvania. He sold them originally in carload lots, filled with prepared mustard, at ten cents apiece. One of these hen dishes bearing the label of the Westmoreland Specialty Company is in my collection.

Some of the earliest of the open-edge plates in both opaque-white and black glass were made by Challinor, Taylor & Company. Other factories also made them. At one time, they were called "stamp" plates, because the owners used to cover them with canceled postage stamps. Dealers also find them today with extraordinary decorations of flowers or animals painted in oils. A bath in a strong solution of sal soda overnight will remove the artist's efforts. Other early plates of this type during the 1870's came from the Atterbury Glass Company. These have an *A* embossed in the centre of the bottom.

GLASS AT WORLD'S FAIRS

By HELEN McKEARIN

FROM the beginning of glassblowing it has seemed little short of miraculous that from a molten mass of metal a blower's breath, nicety of judgment, manual dexterity, and feeling for form could create beautiful and useful objects. So it is scarcely remarkable that from the first World's Fair, London's *Industry of all Nations* held in 1851, to New York's 1939 *World of Tomorrow*, table and decorative wares and new, ingenious applications of glass have impressed a marveling public.

The miracle of the first World's Fair was the Crystal Palace itself. A building of glass would cause little comment today, but in 1851 it seemed a fascinating architectural innovation too fragile to be practical. "The first impression conveyed to the mind" was "a sense of insecurity arising from the apparent lightness of its supports compared with the vastness of its dimensions." Hence it was little wonder that a building whose ground floor area was 772,784 square feet and whose roof and walls were almost entirely of glass should arouse fears for its stability. But once it was realized that London Bridge was no safer, Britishers were calmly proud of their engineering achievement and visitors were conscious only of its "faerie" charm. Even more astounding to the public and glassmakers of the day was the almost unbelievable great crystal fountain manufactured by F. & C. Osler of Birmingham. *Four tons* of "pure crystal glass" were required to form its huge basin, two large dishes with their faceted canopies, and the central shaft, 27 feet in height. The annealing, transportation, and assembling of the fountain were in themselves a noteworthy accomplishment. Comments of the day indicate that this glass fountain became the symbol of the Fair of 1851 as the perisphere and trylon are of the Fair of 1939.

Literally hundreds of the 1851 exhibits included or consisted solely of glass. Almost every foreign country showed some glass, and England, where the industry was attaining new heights, had one hundred exhibits. One could see examples of nearly every type of article, method of manufacture, and decoration known at the time. Besides a "great variety of glass too tedious to insert" here, many items were shown which indicated trends modern enough to be surprising today. Among them were "patent pressed" clear and colored window glass; "patent model windows fitted with different qualities of perforated plate and sheet glass for ventilation"; a portable glass pavilion for lawns; pole fire screens; "panels for church altars, ceilings etc."; table tops; water pipes; "registered model of a percolator"; "opaque plates of glass, substitutes for marble in furniture etc."; chess tables, and Venetian blinds.

The majority of displays, however, were of table and ornamental wares in an amazing range of decorative effects, forms, and colors. One saw opal, alabaster, turquoise, amber, canary, topaz, chrysoprase, pink, blue, light and dark ruby, black, brown, green, purple, and Pomona green; crystal and ruby predominated. If one may judge from the quantity shown, glass ornamented either by cutting or engraving enjoyed the greatest popularity in 1851, and, according to English standards, was the most meritorious in design. Colorful cased (overlay) glass was a close second in favor. In this category, as might be expected, the examples of Bohemian glass from Austria were considered the most skillfully executed and spectacular. Gilded, painted, and enameled wares and frosted and Venetian glass shared about equal popularity. Two innovations attracted considerable attention. One was an exhibit by William Kidd, inventor and manufacturer, demonstrating "his new process for illuminating, embroidering and silvering flat surfaces in glass" whereby designs engraved on the underside of the glass appeared to be in high relief on the outer surface. The

other, of "glass silvered by Hale Thompson's process, a recent development in glass making" was apparently of the type of glass we call mercury. Only one firm, Rice, Harris & Son, proprietors of the Islington Glass Works of Birmingham, showed pressed glass. Besides fine glass this firm displayed pressed tumblers, goblets, wines, sugar basins, butter coolers, salt cellars, honey pots and doorknobs.

At a time when our glass industry was expanding it seems unaccountable that among the many foreign exhibits there were only three of American glass. Perhaps the explanation lies in the fact that, unlike other foreign governments, ours gave no aid to exhibitors. Regarding this policy Benjamin P. Johnson, New York State agent to the exhibition, made this comment: "It is not by any means certain but that the influence of our exhibition has been far better upon the world, has more powerfully demonstrated the peculiar advantages of the energies of the people, than could have been done if the Government had made a large appropriation for the purpose of preparing articles especially for the exhibition . . . the character of our articles was such as to show the world that we worked for the great masses, not for the luxurious and privileged few."

Be that as it may, the jury on glass awarded a prize for "cut flint glass" to the Brooklyn Flint Glass Company. The basis for awards was not competitive, but comparative with a standard approved by the jury. One English critic remarked "The Brooklyn Flint Glass Company (American) have contributed creditable specimens of cut glass but the metal itself is not so pure as ours." Another said, "The American glass . . . was pre-eminent for its brillancy." And the pride of a native son found the expression in the account of Charles T. Rodgers of Louisiana, who wrote: "None exceed in beauty the contribution of the Brooklyn Flint Glass Company . . . What particularly distinguishes this is its surpassing whiteness which with its dazzling brillancy has given it, where elaborately cut articles are sought as proofs of taste and munificence, a fame that has conferred on the company quite a monopoly on this continent."

The other two American exhibitors were Cornelius & Company of Philadelphia and John Lee Chapman, of the Maryland Glass Works, Baltimore, established in 1849 for the manufacture of window glass and bottles. Cornelius & Company exhibited two chandeliers, 24 damask solar lamps, and 7 olive solar lamps. The compiler of the official catalogue gave no hint as to the nature of Chapman's contribution, but stated in connection with that of Cornelius & Company: "These castings and glasses are the product of a branch of manufacture less than 20 years old in the United States. Up to the year 1830 the whole trade in chandeliers was in the hands of foreign importers. These lamps are an American invention adapted to the use of lard and lard oil." The two chandeliers won praise but no prize. Nevertheless, for two exhibits out of three to receive high praise speaks well for American glass manufacture.

The tremendous success of the London international exhibition so impressed some adventurous American businessmen that by 1852, in spite of vigorous opposition, preparations for an American World's Fair were going on apace. It was argued that "one of the great lessons taught on that occasion was the capacity of the masses to appreciate and enjoy the pleasures which flow from refined culture in whatever direction." But the selling factor was the great financial success of the London venture. In expectation of large dividends the group persisted in the face of many discouragements, and July 14, 1853, a Crystal Palace in New York City was formally opened. It was a pocket edition of the London Crystal Palace — and a financial failure.

The exhibits of glass, while pitifully few in number compared with the hundreds in London, were comprehensive in content. More foreign glass manufactures were represented than American: Holland sent two window-glass exhibits; Germany, four displays consisting largely of fancy articles and small objects such as buttons, beads, hairpins; England, seven, mostly of window glass and industrial wares and just a few fine objects; France, six, of which

FIG. 1 — FIVE GLASS EXHIBITS AT WORLD'S FAIRS OF YESTERDAY

Left column, three prize-winning pieces exhibited in 1851 by the Brooklyn Flint Glass Works. According to the official catalogue, this firm "contributed a well-filled stand. . . . There is enough novelty of form in these works to assure us that our transatlantic brethren are fully aware of the mercantile value of Art." *Top right*, decanter shown at the 1853 Crystal Palace in New York City by Joseph Stouvenel & Company of New York. *Center*, "chili cup" of cut glass and silver exhibited at the 1876 Philadelphia exposition by Reed & Barton of Taunton, Massachusetts. It won a prize at the Chilean Exposition; hence the name. This epergne was described in the catalogue, "light and airy . . . filled with fruit and flowers, there could hardly be a more chaste or elegant centre-piece for a table." With which sentiments we beg to differ

Chili Cup: Reed & Barton, Taunton, Mass

two were of table and ornamental wares; and Austria, seven, of which only one consisted of fine wares and the others principally of small objects such as beads, buttons, and luster pendants. The finest table and ornamental glass was represented by the "noteworthy chandeliers" of Apsley Pellatt & Company, a famous English firm; the superb cut, engraved, cased, and gilded wares contributed by J. Maes, Gallerie de Clichy, France; and the "magnificent display of frosted, cased, and gilded glass" of E. Stanier, Austria. Had it not been for these exhibits it might have seemed that foreign guests were unaware that window glass was a common article of our manufacture and that we no longer needed such knickknacks as beads to trade with the Indians.

There were few American exhibits of glass. One showing in the United States group was by Berger & Walter, apparently a French firm with a branch in New York City. Also from New York were watch crystals shown by C. M. Bodine, Manufacturer; decorated and lettered wares especially for druggists by Frederick Hale & Company and A. G. Brandon; and a ruby-glass plate, cut with designs representing the arms of the United States contributed by Philip Smith. There were five exhibits of stained and painted glass — four of them individual items. "New machine engraved and etched ornamental window glass" manufactured by Cooper & Belcher, Camptown, New Jersey, was incorporated in the window of the west gallery. "Druggist glassware of all description, preserve and pickle jars, flasks; windowglass; ink bottles; wine bottles etc." were shown by Baker & Brothers of Baltimore; a firm of jobbers who early in 1853 had become manufacturers. Extensive displays of table and ornamental wares which not only maintained but enhanced our reputation for fine glass were contributed by Messrs. Joseph Stouvenel & Company of New York, the Brooklyn Flint Glass Company of Brooklyn, and the New England Glass Company of Boston. Clear, beautiful metal and skilled workmanship characterized the "great variety of glassware both pressed and cut from the manufactory of Messrs Joseph Stouvenel & Company." One is informed by contemporary critics that "The Brooklyn Flint Glass Company and the New England Glass Company are the largest manufactures, and their display of dioptric signal lamps, and of plain, pressed, and cut and decorated glass ware, is decidedly creditable to this country. The American flint glass is distinguished by its brilliancy and the purity of its color, and that of the New England Glass Company is the best pressed glass probably ever manufactured."

Although few in number the exhibits of table and decorative wares at New York's Crystal Palace were as representative of the types of articles, methods of manufacture, and various forms of ornamentation popular here and abroad as those of London's Crystal Palace. In fact, with very few exceptions, the forms, colors, and decoration were the same as those shown in 1851. No matter where it was made, the glass was "Victorian" in design.

Our next important World's Fair was the 1876 centennial celebration in Philadelphia. In the main building were over one hundred exhibits of glass, not including glass combined with metal. The groups of various types were so large that they were divided into classes: Class 214 — Glass used in construction and for mirrors, window glass, and plate glass; Class 215 — Chemical and pharmaceutical glassware, vials, and bottles; Class 216 — Decorated glassware.

The official catalogue of the fair lists 69 exhibits from 11 foreign countries: The Argentine Republic (1), Brazil (2), Norway (2), Sweden (2), Canada (1), Great Britain (6), France (6), Belgium (24), Austria (23), Portugal and Italy, the last two apparently including glass in their collective exhibits. Assorted glassware was contributed by the Burlington Glass Company of Hamilton, Canada. The decorative glassware of Argentina, Brazil, and Norway was represented by one exhibit from each country; three from France, and two from Belgium. England's fine glass was seen in small contributions from two firms, which, considering the importance of the industry, caused bitter comment among

Americans. Austria had seventeen large exhibits of fine table and decorative glass.

A discrepancy occurs between the official catalogue list of American exhibitors and the official list of awards, the latter including some firms not mentioned in the former. There were, however, at least forty-five displays of American glass. The list of awards is annoying in its lack of detailed descriptions but, since it contains interesting information, it is given here:

Albertson, J. M. Norristown, Pa.
Award for glass shades.

Atterbury & Co. Pittsburg
Award for lime glass lamp chimneys and globes.

Boston & Sandwich Glass Co. Manufacturers of cut glass.
Award. Showed "rich cut glass ware of every description including the 'Daniel Webster punch bowl'."

Bakewell, Pears & Co. Pittsburg, Pa.
Award for moulded glass tablewares. (Also showed blown crystal and opal glass ware.)

Central Glass Co. Wheeling, W. Virginia.
Award for lime glass pressed ware.

Cohansey Glass Manufacturing Co. Bridgeton, N. J.
Award. Showed cylinder window glass, bottles, vial and demijohns.

Dobleman, J. B. Greenpoint. (Long Island)
Award for flint cut and engraved tableware.

Dorflinger Glass Co. White Mills, Wayne Co., Pa.
Award for glass tablewares

Geo. Duncan & Sons, Pittsburg
Award for limeglass tablewares.

Excelsior Flint Glass Co. Pittsburg
Award. Showed lamp chimneys, silvered glass reflectors.

Fox, H. C. & Sons, Philadelphia
Award for druggist's and perfumers' glass wares.

Gillinder & Sons, Philadelphia
Award for flint glass ware

Hobbs, J. H. Brockunier & Co., Wheeling, W. Virginia
Award for lime glass tablewares.

Keystone Flint Glass Co. Pittsburg
Award for pure lead lamp glasses. Showed silvered glassware also.

La Belle Glass Co., Bridgeport, Ohio
Award for glass tablewares moulded. Showed cut and engraved also.

Louisville Plate Glass Co. Louisville, Ky.
Award for plate glass.

Mount Washington Glass Works
Award for lime glass tablewares, chandeliers and bone glass.

C. Newman & Co. San Francisco, Cal.
Award for demijohns covered with packing.

New England Glass Co. Boston
Award for flint glass tablewares and decorative pieces.

O'Hara Glass Co. Pittsburg
Award for lime glass tablewares

Rochester Tumbler Co. Pittsburg
Award for tumblers.

Smith Bros. New Bedford, Mass.
Award for opal and bone glass lamp shades

Whitall, Tatum & Co. Millville, N. J.
Award for Chemists, Druggists and Perfumers wares of lime and green glass.

Among the American exhibits not receiving awards were two from old glasshouses — glass shades, monuments, and cylinders from the Union Glass Works, Somerville, Massachusetts, and "green and colored glass ware for druggists etc." from the factory of Whitney Brothers, Glassboro, New Jersey.

American table and ornamental glass, even though it received many awards, seems to have been far less exciting and impressive

to the historians of the Fair than the English cut and engraved crystal and the extensive Austrian exhibits. From the "elegant specimens" of cut glass of the Mount Washington Glass Works one writer did illustrate a candelabrum of a "prismatic character" showing the progress made in the "last thirty years." And several praised a glass chandelier by Mitchell Vance & Company of New York; likewise a chili cup and epergne of glass and silver and a lemonade set shown by Reed & Barton. The glass, undoubtedly of American manufacture, used in the overelaborated chili cup and epergne was deeply cut flint glass, while that of the lemonade set was of flint glass too richly ornamented with birds and flowers.

The Austrian glass commanded, as usual, the greatest attention and highest praise, but the crystal of James Green and Nephew of London and J. Millar & Company of Edinburgh made a deep and favorable impression on contemporary critics. The products of these two firms "excelled in quality of flint and skill in engraved and cut decoration." Extravagant praise was bestowed upon a chandelier and a crystal pitcher from the Green display elaborately engraved on one side with a depiction of Saint George and the Dragon and having a remarkable "filigree handle enameled and gilded." In better taste, according to present-day standards, were the crystal decanters and epergne, the latter "noteworthy for lightness and delicacy of design," from the Millar collection.

Among the Austrian exhibitors were Count Von Harrach, who exhibited, as in 1851, typical Bohemian glassware, and Heinrich Ullrich of Vienna, who showed "glass articles especially adapted for the United States of America." In the opinion of contemporary critics the outstanding glass not only of the Austrian groups but of the entire exhibition was that shown by J. & L. Lobmeyr of Vienna. Besides characteristic Bohemian styles of cased glass enhanced with gilding, this firm presented glass in the Venetian tradition and crystal, particularly engraved tableware which was considered unusually fine. The most incredible piece in their display was an elaborate vase and pedestal of chaste classical form, ruined, esthetically, by extravagant ornamentation — "richness of color, gilding, high relief and delicate tracery of intricate design."

A comparison of the glass of 1876 with that of 1851 and 1853 reveals a number of interesting and of deplorable developments. Production of industrial and commercial ware had increased by leaps and bounds, while that of fine wares suffered. In America there was great emphasis upon pressed glass and lime glass for tablewares, although flint was still considered the *fine* glass. In fact, in table and decorative wares one finds that the same colors and types — cut and engraved crystal and cased glass with rich ornamentation — enjoyed approximately the same proportional popularity as in 1851. But a taste for novelty had developed side by side with a trend toward the classical in shapes, and toward

FIG. 2 — WINE OF LEAD GLASS
Engraved "New Engl^d/Glass. C^o./Boston," and on reverse side "Mass. Cent^l./Head Q^{rs}." Displayed at the 1876 Philadelphia Centennial Exhibition. *Height*, 4 ½ inches, *top diameter*, 2 ⅛ inches

FIG. 3 — "LIBBEY GLASS CO.'S FACTORY, MIDWAY PLAISANCE"
At the 1893 World's Columbian Exposition, Chicago, "spinning wheels six feet in diameter . . . draw from glass rods melted before a blow-pipe the finest threads, which are put into a loom and woven into glass fabric," from which were made "dresses, napkins, bonnets, and the most beautiful lamp shades . . ." Visitors at the 1939 New York World's Fair are still fascinated by a demonstration of glass weaving at the Glass Center

a lamentable extravagance in decoration bordering often on the bizarre. Though an occasional piece appeared which might almost be termed a work of art, or a design in tableware which would be "good" in any period, the keynote of the time, for all countries, seems to have been extravagance in form and decoration, a nearly complete subordination of the beautiful metal itself to novelty and ornamentation.

In seventeen years between the Centennial Exhibition and Chicago's World's Columbian Exposition of 1893 science and ingenuity had contributed many new types of glass and found new uses for the metal. The general expansion is indicated by the number and contents of the classes devised for the exhibits: Class 589 — Plate glass; Class 590 — Blown glass, ordinary window glass, bottles, tubes, pipes, etc.; Class 591 — Pressed glass and glassware generally for the table and various purposes; skylights, insulators, etc.; Class 592 — Cut glassware for the table and various purposes, engraved and etched glass; Class 593 — Fancy glassware, plain iridescent, opalescent, colored, enameled, painted, beaded, gilded, etc., millefiori and aventurine glass; Class 594 — Crackled glass in layers, onyx glass, sculptured glass, and reproductions of ancient glassware; Class 595 — Glass mosaics, beads, *spun glass and glass fabrics.*

Eleven foreign countries sent exhibits. From Switzerland came *glass bricks for building purposes;* from Great Britain, two exhibits in Classes 590 and 591. Cut glassware, engraved and etched tableware were shown in two exhibits from Japan and one from the Diamond Glass Company of New Glasgow, Canada. Fancy scent bottles were sent from Siam. Cut, engraved, and etched glass and various of the fancy glasswares were in displays from Sweden, Germany, Belgium and Denmark. One of the exhibits from Denmark included a glass ceiling. Austria was again the largest exhibitor, with eighteen displays contributed by "all the famous factories of Bohemia" and "illustrative of the collective results of centuries of individual endeavor." Among the exhibitors were Count Harrach, Heinrich Ullrich, and J. & L. Lobmeyr who, as in 1876, had outstanding displays. Italy made a remarkable contribution in the miniature "palace of glass and mosaic" work erected by the Venice and Murano Company to house its display of *old* and *new* glass.

The American exhibits were few and, with two exceptions, not impressive in Classes 593 through 595. The list given in one official catalogue was as follows:

Geo. Macbeth & Co. optical and lamp glasses

Prugh, Conroy & Co. Mirrors

Wire Glass Co., Philadelphia. Wire glass

Diamond Plate Glass Co., Kokomo, Indiana. Plate glass

United States Glass Co., Pittsburg Misc. glass ware

F. M. Hicks & Co., Chicago. Ornamental flooring and skylights

Suess Co., Chicago. Beveled glass and enameled glass

Geo. E. Androvette & L. Strauss & Sons. Cut glass for table and ornaments

The Tiffany Glass & Decoration Co. Onyx glass, glass mosaics, incised and engraved glass, stained glass chapel including altar, reredos etc. designed by Louis Tiffany.

Libbey Glass Co., Toledo. Cut glass ware and glass fabrics.

J. Hoare & Co. Examples of engraving and rock crystal cutting.

The American exhibits which excited both public and critics were those of the Tiffany Glass & Decoration Company and the Libbey Glass Company. In the field of ornamental wares stress was laid on pieces demonstrating Tiffany's "new process in which glass of various colors is blown into a framework of silver and silver gilt, producing the effect of jewels, crystal and precious stones." The Libbey Company had its own building which was to the 1893 Fair what the Glass Center is to 1939. Besides its display of a great variety of cut-glass objects it had a glass factory in operation. Artisans demonstrated the art of engraving, etching, and cutting glass. But in the entire Fair the most amazing thing in the field of glass manufacture was the *spinning of fibers from glass rods and weaving of fabric.* However, even though various articles made from glass fabric were exhibited — a dress, "curtain portiers, decorations for ceiling and walls, lamp shades and other fancy articles beautifully painted" — the whole thing was considered by the public to be of little practical value.

The comments of contemporary writers indicate that little change had taken place since 1876 in designs of table and decorative ware. Except for the glass exhibited by J. & L. Lobmeyr, which was deemed superior in engraving and sculpturing, according to general opinion there was "much inferior work and but little calculated to interest the artist or art lover." Only the cut glass of the Libbey Glass Company seems to have merited any sort of praise, and that for the remarkable "accuracy and depth of cutting" which rendered the results "masterpieces of mechanical skill." In fact, with taste in decoration still at neap tide, progress in making decorated glassware seems to have been on the side of technical execution and mechanical perfection.

DORFLINGER GLASS

By JANET FOSTER NEWTON

ALTHOUGH WAYNE COUNTY, PENNSYLVANIA, during the nineteenth century was noted for its many glass-cutting establishments, there were only four factories which made the glass itself. Of these, the most successful was the Dorflinger Glass Works at White Mills. The other county plants flourished briefly, but Dorflinger glass, famous internationally for the excellent quality of its metal, continued to be produced and to maintain its high standards until 1921.

Christian Dorflinger (not Doerflinger, as often appears) was born March 16, 1828, in Rosteig, Canton Bitsch, Alsace, France. In 1837 he left his parents, Francis and Charlotte Clemens Dorflinger, to learn glassmaking with an uncle in St. Louis, Lorraine. There he mastered the fundamentals, but was especially interested in the methods of ornamenting glass — etching, engraving, enameling, and gold decorating. In 1845 his father died, and Christian in 1846 brought his mother, brothers, and sisters to America. The rest of the family went on to Indiana, but he stayed in Philadelphia working as a journeyman glassblower for a firm which manufactured druggist's bottles.

On one of his trips to New York, he became acquainted with his future wife, Elizabeth Hagen, who lived in Brooklyn. And on his visits to her, he used to stop at the Pacific Hotel in New York, kept by Captain Aaron Flower, a former seafaring captain. About 1850, when kerosene oil was giving a boom to the lamp business, Captain Flower and a group of men were discussing the idea of forming a company to make glass lamp chimneys. Flower remembered the young Alsatian, and sent for Christian Dorflinger to take charge of the business. The men put up the money, and in 1852 Christian began his first factory, the Long Island Flint Glass Works, Concord Street, Brooklyn. It began in a small way, with only one five-pot furnace. At that time Christian paid off the men who had financed the scheme and bought the business for himself. In 1858 he built a new factory at Plymouth and in 1860 he branched out again with a flint-glass factory, the Green Point Glass Works in Brooklyn, where he began the manufacture of the fine glassware he loved. In a short time the two plants were doing a business of about $300,000 a year.

In 1863, Christian, who had been living, eating, and breathing glass, became ill and his doctor told him to get out of Brooklyn and forget it. So he dutifully sold the Long Island Glass Works, leased the Green Point factory to E. P. Gleason, and retired to enjoy himself. Captain Flower sent him up to his farm in Wayne County for the summer, a spot on the east side of the Lackawaxen River near White Mills, through which the Delaware and Hudson Canal ran. Christian liked the place so well that in 1865 he bought the 300-acre farm. By this time, however, he was bored with retirement, and began plans to combine his doctor's orders with his own inclination by building a glassworks at White Mills. He first built a little plant in Indian Orchard, a farming center near-by, and later in the year built his glassworks at White Mills.

The White Mills plant started with a 5-pot furnace.

FIG. 1 — WAYNE COUNTY GLASS WORKS (1865-1921). Also called Dorflinger Glass Works, and, after 1881, C. Dorflinger & Sons. Located at White Mills, Pennsylvania. Goodrich's *History of Wayne County* (1886) says, "The glass produced there combines every degree of excellence and ornamentation. Specimens of the perfection of work were exhibited at the Centennial Exposition in Philadelphia in 1876, and were not excelled by the best work made at Pittsburg or elsewhere." The plant shown here burned in 1892, and was immediately replaced by a larger one. The Canal, going from Honesdale to Roundabout (Kingston) on the Hudson River, ran south of the picture in the present village of White Mills, where the Canal officials put in a special basin to take care of the Dorflinger boats. The building in the left foreground was the office. In addition to the numerous buildings erected for the business, Christian Dorflinger the first year built seven houses for his workmen, erected a large hotel in 1867, and a mansion in 1870. Eventually there were 75 homes for the workers built around the plant, of which Dorflinger owned 50, and for all of which he had put up the money. In 1886 about 300 people were employed, and the payroll amounted to $10,000 a month. At its peak the factory employed about 650. The row of houses along the back was called "Murderers' Row," because the Irish workmen who lived there usually had a big fight each Saturday night after pay day. *This and Figures 3 and 4 from prints in Matthew's "History of Wayne, Pike and Monroe Counties, Pennsylvania"* (1886).

FIG. 2 — PART OF A SET OF DORFLINGER GLASS DESIGNED FOR PRESIDENT LINCOLN. Fruit cup, finger bowl and saucer, and handled punch (height, 4 inches). Unlike most cut glass, which is heavy, this set is exceptionally thin, fine, and delicate. The Dorflingers made sets of tableware for all the Presidents from Lincoln to Wilson. The set for President Theodore Roosevelt included the first highball glasses ordered. All these pieces, of course, were engraved with the United States coat of arms, but each set had its distinctive pattern. *Figures 2, 5, 6, 7 from the collection of Miss Katherine Dorflinger.*

By the second year there were approximately a hundred men and boys at work. Most of them were local farm lads, trained by Christian, though he also had skilled workers from Brooklyn who had been trained in Europe. In 1867 the famous glasscutting department was introduced. At that time the buildings comprised a glasshouse, and a "cutting" shop two stories high, later used as the packing department. A three-story wing was added a few years later, and also a building in which the great clay crucibles or pots were made.

Dorflinger spent as much time on the construction of these clay pots as on the actual glassmaking itself. They were made in a long, low room which was kept at a steady temperature so that the crucibles could become thoroughly and evenly seasoned. Most of the clay for the pots came from Germany, though clay from Missouri was sometimes used.

Later Dorflinger made further improvements in his plant. A new glasshouse was built, with a large basement of iron and stone extending under the whole building. It contained one eight-pot furnace and three annealing ovens. A three-story gray stone building for the increased cutting business was also built. On the second floor was a seventy-five horse-power engine to turn the hundred wheels in the cutting room below.

One of the most skilled glasscutters of the time was employed here. He was John S. O'Connor, born in Londonderry, Ireland, June 6, 1831. Before the Civil War he had worked for Turner & Lane and E. V. Houghwought & Co., both of New York City. After the War, in which he served, he returned to be superintendent of the Houghwought plant. The firm went out of business just as Christian Dorflinger was getting his glasscutting department started, and O'Connor was hired by him as foreman of the White Mills cutting shop, starting glasscutting with one frame. While there he invented many machines for glasscutting that completely changed the cut-glass industry. One of them cut glass in circular lines instead of straight. One of his patented designs was the *Parisian*, which was copied by many other glasscutters. While O'Connor was with him, Dorflinger also brought out two other popular designs which were widely imitated, *Lorraine* and *Russian*, the latter used especially for stemware. In 1892 he left Dorflinger and started his own factory in Hawley, Pennsylvania.

Christian insisted that all processes necessary for a finished product be done at his plant, with the exception of the gold decorating. For this he sent the glass away, usually to an Austrian decorator in New York who did fine work. The volume of this business, however, increased so much that he needed a manager, and he got in touch with Carl F. Prosch from Vienna, an expert designer in etching and gold decoration, who had studied at Melk on the Danube in the school conducted there by the Benedictines. Prosch was in New York as the representative of an Austrian wholesale glass agency, Bawo and Dotter, whose factories were in Bohemia and whose main offices were in Kotzschenbroda bei Dresden. In 1900 Christian Dorflinger made an arrangement whereby Prosch was to do his type of decorating on Dorflinger glass exclusively, and the two men founded the Honesdale Decorating Company, with a factory located at Seelyville, a suburb of Honesdale. In 1915 Prosch bought out the Dorflinger interest and continued the business until 1932 under the old name.

Though Dorflingers furnished the blanks for twenty-two cutting shops in Wayne County, most of the glass made at their plant was shipped to their New York store at 915 Broadway, from which the goods were sold to Ovington, Tiffany, Gorham, and other New York retail stores, and also to shops in Washington, Chicago, Philadelphia, Boston, and San Francisco. Their New York office was located at 36 Murray Street. The variety of glass patterns and forms was wide. There were fancy dishes and bonbons in the *hobnail* cut with double star; punch bowls in *brilliante* cut with glass-handled ladles to match; table bells in various colors; lamps with dome shades; flower vases, decanters, cologne bottles, crystal and dark-green water bottles,

FIG. 4 *(below)* — UPPER FLOOR OF GLASSCUTTING DEPARTMENT, DORFLINGER GLASS WORKS. The machinery used here was originally planned by John S. O'Conner, and worked out by F. W. Farnham, who patented the brushes. The funnels held the water used both in cutting and polishing. In this room the three steps in the work were done. First was the "roughing" on an iron wheel, which the men at right are doing — the deep cutting of the pattern marked on the glass with red lead. The second process, smoothing, was done with fine stone wheels. Then came the polishing, done by the men at left, with wheel brushes and wooden wheels kept constantly smeared with "putty"—the plant name for a finely-ground oxide of zinc and lead.

FIG. 3 *(above)* — GLASSBLOWING DEPARTMENT AT THE DORFLINGER PLANT. The large square furnace is where the metal was made; each square opening had a pot for the melting. The smaller furnace at the right, called the glory hole, was used by the gaffer for finishing the glass after it was taken off the blowing iron. The gentleman in the foreground leaning on a cane is a slightly fictionalized portrait of Christian. There is a better portrait of him at the Wayne County Historical Society in Honesdale, and another owned by his daughter, Miss Katherine Dorflinger. The high quality of Dorflinger glass depended on the exceptional quality of the basic ingredients used. Christian at first insisted that the sand used be from Fontainebleau, France, and he had it brought here as ballast in sailing ships. The native product he favored was ground rock from the Berkshire Glass Sand Co., Cheshire, Massachusetts, and from the Pennsylvania Glass Sand Co., McVeigh, Pennsylvania. His special laboratory analyzed each new batch of sand to find the correct proportion of other ingredients to be mixed with it. For a batch of 600 pounds of sand, usually 400 pounds of oxide of lead were added, and 200 pounds of pearl ash. Into this went very small proportions of salt petre, arsenic, and manganese.

FIG. 5 — VARIETY IN DORFLINGER GLASS (1860's). *Left to right:* dark emerald-green wineglass, probably made at Green Point; canary-yellow sherry, cut in points, also probably from Green Point; clear crystal sherry, cut in a "thumbprint"; brandy snifter, the body cut with tiny stars, and the rim engraved with a grape pattern.

trade. There do exist many such items, made by the Dorflinger workmen in their spare time and for their own pleasure, but they were not put out with the line of Dorflinger products. For some reason, also, many people erroneously list chandeliers among Dorflinger products. At one time their New York store had two for decoration, but they were brought from France, and the Dorflingers never manufactured things of this kind.

Like the other big glassmakers of the period, the Dorflingers also made pressed glass, in such objects as knobs, lamp bases, stoppers, and silencers for chair legs. But this glass was inferior in quality to that made for the cut glass, and used lime instead of lead in the metal.

In 1881 Christian's sons, William, Louis J., and Charles, went into partnership with their father, and the firm became C. Dorflinger & Sons. Christian died in 1915. The plant continued operating until 1921, when it had to close for lack of the German potash used in their product, and also because the vogue for cut glass was on the wane.

and jugs (especially in *tusk* and *Flemish* patterns) ; trays, some with beautiful straight lines, with much the same style and simplicity of decoration as the most modern 1944 glassware; candlesticks, ice-cream sets, candy jars (one of which is now in the Cleveland Museum) , and huge druggist-window bottles, a specialty of the Dorflinger firm.

The designers of these wares, with the exception of John O'Connor, are anonymous, and no record tells who should be credited with the work. The patterns were all given names when they first appeared on the market, though no list of them exists, for, unfortunately, most of the records of the plant were destroyed by fire. There is, however a pamphlet of the early 1900's, *Table Service, C. Dorflinger & Sons, New York City,* which illustrates various sets and gives the wholesale prices of the different pieces. Also there are a few people who know the glass well enough to have this information at hand. Dwight C. Dorflinger of Honesdale, Pennsylvania, a grandson of Christian and superintendent of the glassblowing department at White Mills for twenty-five years, is at work on a biography of his grandfather and a history of Dorflinger glass. He is thoroughly acquainted with all phases of his subject, and when the book is completed it should be a valuable contribution in the field of nineteenth-century American glass and its makers.

Contrary to a current popular belief, paper weights and glass canes were not part of the Dorflinger stock in

FIG. 6 — DORFLINGER STEMWARE FROM THE PRESIDENT HARRISON SET. President Wilson's order was a repeat of this service which originally consisted of 520 pieces, costing $6,000. Special-order work was a large part of the Dorflinger business. A set of fluted glassware was made by the Dorflingers for the use of the Prince of Wales when he toured Canada and the United States in 1919. Another set of interest was made for Henry Clay Pierce's fabulous, ocean-going yacht, *Yacona.*

FIG. 7 — CONTAINERS OF DORFLINGER GLASS (1860's). *Left to right:* celery glass, cut in fine restrained lines, with a narrow rim of deep rose color around top; milk pitcher, cut in what might be called a thumbprint pattern; sherry decanter, cut around top and bottom in tiny diamonds, and engraved with an *S;* covered candy jar, about 12 inches high, one from a set containing two jars and two decanters. The greater part of the Dorflinger glass was uncolored. Some of it was colored, however, green, yellow, or a beautiful shade of red.

Dorflinger glass   Part I

BY KATHRYN HAIT DORFLINGER MANCHEE

This is the first of three articles on Christian Dorflinger and his glass. In it Mrs. Manchee tells of the founding and development of the Dorflinger glassworks in Brooklyn, New York, and White Mills, Pennsylvania, and shows some of their early products. Parts II and III will appear in coming months.

IN HER PIONEERING *Cut and Engraved Glass 1771-1905* (New York, 1950) Dorothy Daniel said of Christian Dorflinger that he was "one of the truly great glassmakers of America," and I am sure no serious student of nineteenth-century American glass would disagree with this judgment. Dorflinger's influence on the industry was profound, and his reputation was international. In the sixty-nine years (1852-1921) during which his Brooklyn, New York, and White Mills, Pennsylvania, factories were in operation they may well have turned out more glass of superlative quality than all other American factories combined. The range of his products was extensive: they came in hundreds of forms, patterns, cuttings, and engravings, and they won national and international awards. Yet the very name Dorflinger is known to few except students, museum curators, and knowledgeable collectors and dealers. Even ANTIQUES has published only one article about the glass (January 1944, p. 27), and a comprehensive book on the subject has yet to be written.

A number of factors have contributed to this surprising obscurity. To begin with, Dorflinger was a modest man who shunned publicity and concentrated on one thing: the making of fine glassware. With negligible exceptions his glass was marked with only a small paper label, and inevitably very few pieces have retained these. The White Mills glassworks became one of the largest in the United States and perhaps in the world, but it was buried in the Pennsylvania mountains and the inaccessibility of its site has discouraged research which could more easily be done on factories near large cities or in less rugged country. Then, too, the skilled artisans Dorflinger imported from England and the Continent gave his glass an international flavor, and it can easily be mistaken for its European counterparts (an error sometimes encouraged by unscrupulous dealers who, according to Dorflinger's son William, even went so far as to ship Dorflinger glass to Europe and bring it back as an "imported" product which would bring higher prices—in those days!—than American glass). It is also true that many of those foreign craftsmen who left the White Mills works to be near big cities or to escape the harsh mountain winters made names for themselves in other factories turning out the same types of glassware they had made for Dorflinger, and this adds to the difficulty of attribution. Finally, there is a tremendous quantity of Dorflinger glass in existence that was supplied to cutters (the factory is said to have supplied nine-tenths of the cutting shops in the United States) who preferred it for its quality and blue-diamond brilliance—and who naturally signed the finished pieces with their own names.

I have had the good fortune to be closely associated with the Dorflinger family for many years, and to be acquainted with a number of the Dorflinger craftsmen as well. This account of Christian Dorflinger's career and the glass he made is based on family records and surviving factory documents, and on thoroughly authenticated examples of the glass itself.

Christian Dorflinger (1828-1915) was born in Alsace, France, in 1828. When he was ten an uncle associated with the renowned Cristalleries de Saint-Louis in Lorraine (founded in 1767) offered to teach his young nephew the art of fine glassmaking and for eight years Christian

Compote made at Christian Dorflinger's Long Island Flint Glass Works in Brooklyn, New York; c. 1856. This extremely rare piece exemplifies the simple cutting and sturdy forms of Dorflinger's earliest period. Of clear, brilliant lead glass, it is cut in flat panels alternating with sharp-diamond cutting. A sixteen-point star is cut on the foot. Height 7½ inches. *Corning Museum of Glass; gift of the author.*

was actively involved in every phase of this highly technical and delicate art, from the mixing of the raw material to the finished product. This intense training and exposure to the making of beautiful French glass gave him not only technical knowledge but an appreciation of fine glass and the discriminating taste which was to prove so valuable in his future career. At the end of these eight years his enthusiasm for his chosen work persuaded his widowed mother to bring her family to America to afford him greater opportunity.

Shortly after his arrival here, young Christian obtained employment in a glass factory in Camden, New Jersey. Because of his thorough knowledge of glassmaking he soon gained the admiration and respect of his associates. According to family memoirs and recollections, the youth was endowed with an exceptionally strong physique and endless drive and perseverance. He also manifested unusual business acumen for his age, and acquired a reputation for integrity and consideration of others which made him many devoted friends within and outside the industry.

By 1852, with his savings and the help of business friends and associates, he had established his own small glassworks on Plymouth Street in Brooklyn, New York. There he manufactured special lamp chimneys of his own design to complement the new kerosene oil burners. This business grew so rapidly that by 1853 the Long Island Flint Glass Works came into being to meet the ever-increasing demand for his products. He now broadened his line of merchandise and added a line of free-blown (the workmen call this off-hand) tablewares, plain, cut, and

Baby cup made for William Francis Dorflinger, first-born son of Christian Dorflinger; it carries his name and the date 1856. The only such cup Dorflinger ever made. Blown of heavy lead crystal, it is stone-wheel engraved and cut in a simple miter and silver-diamond design. Height 3 inches. *Except as noted, illustrations are from the author's collection.*

Compote and wineglass from the state service ordered from Dorflinger's Brooklyn glassworks and used in the White House by President and Mrs. Lincoln; 1861. Each piece is engraved with the United States coat of arms on a foliated and scrolled border. The lower portion of the bowl is cut in the Dorflinger silver-diamond design; the cut stem is tapered, enclosing a teardrop, and the base is cut in an eight-point star; the entire set is exceptionally thin and beautiful. Height of compote, 7½ inches; height of wineglass, 5 inches.

Celery glass, 1852-1861. Made at one of Dorflinger's Brooklyn factories, this shows the French influence apparent in much Dorflinger glass. Height 8¾ inches. *Newark Museum.*

Cologne bottle with paperweight stopper made by Nicholas Lutz at White Mills; 1867-1869. The stopper is cut of the most brilliant crystal, enclosing a deep blue flower. The slender bottle is blown, cut, and engraved; it has been in the possession of the Dorflinger family ever since Lutz worked in White Mills. Height 7 inches. Dorflinger brought this famous glassmaker from his native Lorraine in 1867; he had known him in the Cristalleries de Saint-Louis. After working in the White Mills factory for two years Lutz left to secure work in a less severe climate. Many of the items he made for Dorflinger he also made later at the Boston and Sandwich Glass Company.

engraved. In 1858, again needing more space, he moved to another Brooklyn site, on Concord Street; and in 1860 he built the Green Point Flint Glass Works on Commercial Street at the mouth of Newtown Creek. This gave him four times the space he had had earlier.

By 1861 Dorflinger's Brooklyn factories had gained such a reputation that he received through A. P. Zimandy and Company, his dealer in Washington, D.C., an order from President and Mrs. Lincoln for a complete service of tableware and accessories for the White House, each piece to be "rich cut & eng. with U.S. Coat of Arms." The cost was $1,500, and the order was signed by President and Mrs. Lincoln. This established Dorflinger's reputation as one of the leading makers of fine glass in America. From this time on, Dorflinger glass was used in the White House by eight Presidents, from Lincoln through Wilson.

At the age of thirty-three, nine years after the founding of his first glassworks, Dorflinger's gross annual sales amounted to over $300,000. However, this phenomenal success had taken its toll. His health was so impaired that

Porcelain plate with view of the White Mills glassworks,
painted c. 1879 by a Swiss decorator who had a shop
in White Mills for several years.
The Delaware and Hudson Canal appears in the center,
with the St. Charles Hotel at upper right. *Brooklyn Museum.*

his doctors advised a period of semi-retirement. Being a
practical young man he heeded their warnings, and in
1863 he disposed of the Long Island Flint Glass Works
and put the Green Point factory in the hands of trusted
associates. In 1862 he had approached a good friend,
Captain Aaron Flower, about purchasing the captain's
summer home, a charming old farmhouse surrounded by
three hundred acres of timberland (later expanded to
fifteen hundred) in the mountains of Pennsylvania, just
above the hamlet of White Mills. As Captain Flower
wished to lessen his own responsibilities at this time, he
consented to sell his entire holdings to his young friend.
The following summer Dorflinger moved his family into
their new home, which is still occupied by a member of
the family.

Within two years, rest and invigorating mountain air
had so restored Dorflinger's health that he became restive
and felt the need for more activity, so early in 1865 he
cleared a tract of land and built a small five-pot glass
furnace at the edge of the Lackawaxen River. The following year he brought certain of his expert craftsmen from
Brooklyn to train local farm lads in the art of glassmaking.

Again the Midas touch was evident. With a large capital and the income from his Brooklyn factory Dorflinger
had ample funds for expansion, and the sleepy little village of White Mills grew into a thriving glass community.
Dorflinger built over a hundred houses for his workers.
Others built their own with his financial help. The plant
itself grew rapidly. The Wayne County Glass Works, as it
was called, required so much attention that Dorflinger
decided to make White Mills his permanent home. So he
sold his Brooklyn home and leased the glassworks which
he later sold. The Delaware and Hudson Canal Company,
whose canal ran through White Mills to Honesdale and

Goblet made for the 1869 wedding of Clothilde King to Eugene Dorflinger. The only such goblet made, this was used only once, at the wedding. It is exceptionally thin. The engraving includes a garland of ribbon and flowers entwined at the top from which are suspended three oval disks, one enclosing Clothilde's monogram and the others, delicate bouquets. Tiny dots are engraved over the entire bowl in clusters of three, giving it a lacy appearance; and the sixteen points of the star cutting on the foot alternate with engraved leaves and flowers. Height 6 inches. *Corning Museum; gift of the author.*

Pitcher, also made for Eugene and Clothilde Dorflinger; 1870-1875. Free-blown, cut, and engraved with the initial *D.* Height 10⅛ inches. *Everhart Museum; gift of the Museum Association of Scranton, Pennsylvania.*

on to Kingston on the Hudson River, built a large ship basin near the glassworks so the tremendous volume of glass that was blown, cut, and engraved in White Mills and the blanks (plain blown flint-glass shapes) for cutters throughout the country could be shipped. Barges returned from New York to White Mills loaded with sand from France, potash from Germany, and red lead from England which had been shipped as ballast. Dorflinger used only the finest raw materials. The furnace pots were built to his specifications of fine glazed brick from England. Later, sand was brought from the Berkshires and other parts of the United States. Coal, wood, and water were abundantly available. The Erie Railroad built a special spur and station to help accommodate shipments and passengers to and from the glassworks.

Dorflinger needed a place to entertain his guests and business associates, so in 1868 he started construction of a thirty-six-room hotel, complete with a large ballroom (this was 31 feet by 60). The handsome mansard-roofed building, constructed of local gray stone, was completed in 1870 and christened the St. Charles at a spectacular inaugural ball given May 25, 1870, for local prominent

St. Charles Hotel is engraved on the domed cover of this graceful candy jar, made for the opening of the hotel built in White Mills by Dorflinger to accommodate visiting friends and business associates; 1869. Blown and cut of brilliant crystal, with the engraving left unpolished for contrast. The finial encloses a teardrop and is cut in six panels tapering to a point. Broad hollow-diamond cutting surrounds the base of the bowl, and there is a twenty-four-point star cut on the foot. Height 10½ inches. Always in the Dorflinger family. *Collection of June Dorflinger Hardy.*

Very thin and graceful goblet from a set once owned by Carlotta Dorflinger Atkinson, Christian's daughter. A wreath of leaves and flowers encircles the letter *D*. The stem is cut in panels and has a twenty-four-point star-cut base. Height 6½ inches. *Hardy collection.*

citizens and Dorflinger's friends from New York and Europe. By this time his land holdings had been increased to fifteen hundred acres. In 1872 a wing with seventeen marble fireplaces was added to the hotel, and Dorflinger moved his family from the farmhouse into it. It was occupied by members of the family until 1931. This elegant building became a well-known landmark. It stood until 1961, when the then owner of the property burned it down to clear the site for a new building. No sign of it remains today, but a beautiful iron fence and a long stone wall suggest the happy and almost feudal life lived there where so many distinguished guests had found a warm welcome when they came to visit the great glassworks or to attend balls and parties.

Dorflinger's four daughters were never allowed to step inside the factory, though it was only a few minutes away. It was not considered the thing for young ladies to do. I remember being surprised sometimes to find that they could not answer questions about the glass. They were sent to the best finishing schools and traveled extensively abroad. Their brothers went to schools and colleges in the United States and Europe.

Christian's own discriminating taste is apparent in the beauty and elegance of the glass he selected for his personal use. He was well aware of the growing demand for more elaborate cutting and engraving, but much of the Dorflinger glass remained relatively simple in form. Many of the most delicate pieces, even though produced in large services, have not survived. Owners of Dorflinger glass that is still extant may not be aware of where it was made and may attribute it to other American or to European glassworks. The glass illustrated in this article has been selected to show the quality and variety in form and design created even in the earliest days of the Dorflinger factories.

Dorflinger glass   Part II

BY KATHRYN HAIT DORFLINGER MANCHEE

In Part I of this article, which appeared in the April 1972 issue of ANTIQUES, Mrs. Manchee gave a brief biography of Christian Dorflinger and illustrated a number of pieces made in his factories' early years. Part III, which is to be published next month, will deal with identification of Dorflinger glass.

IN 1876 OUR growing country celebrated its hundredth anniversary with the Philadelphia Centennial, and exhibitors from the United States and Europe had their finest products on view there. Included in the Dorflinger exhibit was the so-called Centennial Set shown here—a large decanter and thirty-eight wineglasses representing the thirty-eight states then in the Union. Not surprisingly, this tour-de-force in cut glass attracted a great deal of attention. The quality of the metal in the glass on display, as well as the skillful cutting, made an important impact on American glassmaking. Cut glass became the fashion, and Dorflinger glass became the status symbol of the carriage trade. It graced the tables of the Vanderbilts, Goulds, Reids, and others of America's foremost families. Queen Victoria and King Edward VII had special pieces made for Buckingham Palace. President Mario Menocal of Cuba selected it for the presidential palace in Havana. It also graced the special train used by the Prince of Wales when he toured the United States and Canada. Eight Presidents of the United States ordered it.

Dorflinger salesmen traveled extensively and the products of the White Mills glassworks were sold through leading jewelers and commercial houses throughout the country: E. G. Tiffany and Company, Gorham, Ovington's, Black Starr and Frost, New York City; and J. E. Caldwell, Bailey Banks and Biddle, Philadelphia.

In 1881, when Dorflinger took his three sons into the business, the firm name was changed to C. Dorflinger and Sons. William was responsible for the New York end of the business, where two stores had been opened: a retail shop at 915 Broadway (about 23rd Street), later moved to 3-5 West 19th Street (two doors from Fifth Avenue); and one for wholesale and display purposes occupying

Decanter and two of thirty-eight wineglasses of the "Centennial Set," shown at the 1876 Centennial International Exhibition in Philadelphia and given at its conclusion to the City of Philadelphia. The oversized decanter has, in addition to spectacularly deep and intricate cutting, three engraved panels showing respectively the arms of the United States, the goddess of Liberty, and the crest of the City of Philadelphia with the name of its mayor and the year, 1876. The set was made with one wineglass for each of the thirty-eight states in the Union at that date, engraved with the state's coat of arms, the name of its governor, and the year. Over-all height of decanter, 16⅝ inches; height of wineglasses, 5 inches. *Philadelphia Museum of Art.*

Candy jar, c. 1879-1880; the only such piece known to have been made at the White Mills glassworks. The elegance and grace of this simple form is reminiscent of Georgian silver design, as is the gadroonlike cutting at the base of the cover. The pointed finial encloses a teardrop; cover, base of bowl, and stem are cut in flat panels, and there is a star cutting on the foot. Over-all height, 16¾ inches. *Cleveland Museum of Art; given by Carlotta Dorflinger Atkinson in memory of her father, Christian Dorflinger.*

Goblet in the famous Parisian pattern—the first cut design to incorporate the curved miter cut. John S. O'Connor originated this design and patented it in 1886. assigning the patent to the Dorflinger firm. This particular goblet, with its intricately cut foot, was never put on the market. Height 5½ inches. *Collection of the author, currently on loan to the Corning Museum of Glass.*

three floors at 36 Murray Street. Louis stayed at White Mills in the financial end of the business, and Charles helped in the operation of the plants.

In 1886 John S. O'Connor Sr., an exceptionally skilled and original glass cutter who worked for the Dorflingers for twenty-five years, from 1867 to 1892, patented the first cut design to have a curved line and assigned the patent to the Dorflinger company; the design was called Parisian. He left White Mills in 1892 to start his own cutting shop in Hawley, Pennsylvania.

In 1892 a disastrous fire destroyed many of the immense blowing and cutting shops and penetrated to most buildings, destroying many old records and directly or indirectly throwing almost a thousand people out of work. Undaunted, Dorflinger had one furnace operating within a month, and within a year the entire factory was rebuilt with the most modern equipment available.

For the next twenty years the company had its greatest prosperity. By 1903 there were twenty-seven factory buildings employing six hundred and fifty workers, and White Mills had grown to a community of some thirteen hundred people. It boasted three hotels, two churches, a public school, an opera house, a station on the Erie, several buildings of fraternal orders, a fire department, a baseball team, and a twenty-piece Dorflinger band, and it was a well-managed and happy place in which to live.

Dorflinger made numerous trips abroad to keep in touch with his family in Lorraine, to persuade skilled artisans in England, Ireland, and on the Continent to come to White Mills, and to keep up with the latest in European glassmaking. The craftsmen who came contributed a great deal to the factory's success: among them were Ralph Barber, who wrote me several years ago that "Mr. Dorflinger was the finest boss I ever had"; Nicholas

Two-handled vase cut in strawberry-diamond and fan pattern; c. 1886. This monumental piece (it is 12 inches in height) may also have been designed by O'Connor; it is thought to be the only one of its kind. *Ex coll.* Louis J. Dorflinger, one of Christian's sons. *Corning Museum of Glass; gift of the author.*

Pair of celery vases; 1880's. Exceptionally thin-blown and graceful, with copper-wheel-engraved fern design surrounding a heraldic device and the initial *C*. The flared bowl is edged with unusual cut notching, there is a tear drop in the baluster stem, and the foot is cut in a twenty-four-point star. Height 10¼ inches. *Author's collection.*

Spiral-cut wineglass; 1885-1890. A brilliant piece in one of the most difficult cuttings, this seems to be alive with light. A complete service, from goblets to cordials, was made in this design. The foot is cut in sixteen petals to form a flower. This spiral pattern was copied in pressed glass, but there it lacks the brilliance of the blown. Height 4½ inches. *Corning Museum; author's gift.*

Finger bowl in Russian pattern, from the 520-piece White House service made by Dorflinger for President Benjamin Harrison in 1889. In 1906 Theodore Roosevelt added 170 pieces to the set, including the first highball glasses bought for the White House, and fourteen dozen pieces were added by Woodrow Wilson; the set was in use until 1938. The Russian pattern was designed by Philip McDonald, one of the cutters working for the Hawkes firm in Corning, New York, and was used for a table service ordered by the Russian embassy in Washington—hence the name. Height 3½ inches. *Author's collection.*

Goblet from a 2300-piece set made for President Mario G. Menocal of Cuba in 1918. Cut in inverted Van Dyke pattern, the bell-shape bowl is engraved with the Cuban coat of arms. There were nineteen different sizes in the set, which cost $60,000. Louis C. Tiffany, who was responsible for the decoration of the presidential palace, gave Dorflinger the order. Height 6 inches. *Author's collection.*

Tumbler and plate from a set made for Henry Clay Pierce's yacht, *Yacona*. The sturdy, simple form was planned to withstand rough weather conditions. A rope design circles the rims, and on the tumbler crossed yachting flags are engraved above a ribbon bearing the name of the yacht. The bottom of the tumbler is decorated with a vertical "flash" miter cutting (with cuts of varying lengths), and its base is cut in a forty-eight-point flash star. *Yacona* was later sold, with all its furnishings, to the King of Portugal. *Author's collection.*

Champagnes. *Left:* Heavy flutes distinguish this hollow-stemmed glass, which is monogrammed and has a forty-eight-point star cut on the foot. Height 4¾ inches. *Right:* Hollow-stemmed saucer champagne, very thinly blown. Champagnes in this shape sometimes had engraving on the bowl. Height 5¾ inches. *Author's collection.*

Lutz, whom Dorflinger had known at the Cristalleries de Saint-Louis and who came to White Mills in 1867; O'Connor, who headed the cutting shop for many years; Carl F. Prosch, a Viennese whom Dorflinger persuaded to come to White Mills from New York; Johnny Johnson, who in 1914 left to work for Steuben; Joe Falk and his brother, who later also went to Steuben. Charles Northwood, Louis Aug, Oscar Levine, the Larsens, Hugo Liljequist, Art Firmstone (a cousin of Frederick Carder of Steuben), and scores of others were devoted and fine workers.

The factory's output included more than five hundred items, from apothecary jars, optical ware, and chemical wares to the highest grade of cut glass: "We make everything that is used in cut glass for the table—goblets, wine glasses, tumblers, finger bowls, carafes, decanters, oil and vinegar bottles, salad and punch bowls, berry dishes, bonbon and olive trays, ice cream sets, etc., etc. . . . We make also a large variety of useful ornamental pieces suitable for wedding and holiday presents such as cologne bottles, vases, flower globes, lamps, lemonade and water sets, etc., etc." Colors included canary yellow, ruby, cased ruby and crystal, shades of green, cased green and crystal, turquoise, the rare poppy color, amethyst, deep "Stiegel" blue to light blue, amber opalescent combinations, opaque white, and rose.

Paperweights and canes were not part of the Dorflinger line. They were fashioned by workmen in their time off.

The glass was cut and engraved at the factory on stone or copper wheels. Hand polishing on fine stone, brush, or felt wheels created a brilliance many glass men of the day considered impossible to achieve by the acid polishing used by other glassmakers; to my knowledge the glass made in White Mills was never polished by acid until after 1907. Etching was done on a less expensive line of tableware.

Silver was applied in filigree over the glass or as rims, tops, handles, and so forth. The name Dorflinger is found engraved on some of these silver mountings. I cannot account for the fact that some pieces were so engraved and others were not.

The glass was also decorated with gold. Especially notable is the goldwork by Prosch, one of the most skilled decorators of his time. Dorflinger helped Prosch set up a gold-decorating business, the Honesdale Decorating Company, in Seeleyville, Pennsylvania, not far from White Mills. There for many years Prosch decorated Dorflinger blanks exclusively. His work was marked on the bottom HONESDALE in gold, but many of the markings have worn off. Prosch bought out Dorflinger's interest in 1915 and continued to operate the Honesdale shop under his own name.

1010

One of the best-known cutting shops was that of C. J. Hawkes of Corning, New York. Hawkes used a large volume of Dorflinger blanks on which he cut many prize-winning designs and which he signed with his own name. Charles Dorflinger, in charge of production at White Mills, had a dispute with Hawkes about inventory which ended with Hawkes' not buying Dorflinger glass for a period. However, he soon met Dorflinger's conditions because he found that he was unable to obtain blanks of equal quality anywhere else. The Dorflinger firm did not sell much to the Hawkes cutting shop after 1900.

In 1915 Christian Dorflinger, the founder of the great glassworks, died at the age of eighty-seven. He was active almost to the end of his life. Those who knew and worked for him loved him almost to the point of worship. His kindness, generosity, and fairness were renowned. He was highly respected for his thorough knowledge of glassmaking. He scrutinized and controlled every step from raw materials to the finished products, never compromising with the highest standards. During his entire career he demanded that his glass be as flawless as it could be made. The whole town mourned his death, as did his many friends in business both here and abroad.

With a brief interlude during which the plant was rented to another firm, Dorflinger's sons carried on the business until 1921; then they were forced to close the great works forever. A number of factors contributed to its demise. Christian, the glass genius with his great resourcefulness, had died. Then, it was extremely difficult to secure the best raw materials during the war: lead, which is so necessary in the making of fine glass, was almost impossible to obtain. Prohibition came in, so there was less demand for fine stemware.

The town's existence was entirely dependent on the glassworks, and when it closed the workers scattered to various other factories throughout the country. Some (*e.g.*, Johnny Johnson and his brother Siegfried) left about the time of Dorflinger's death. Many went to Corning, New York, where they made Corning and Steuben glass. I have been told that at one time practically every "gaffer" in the Steuben glassworks was a former Dorflinger workman. It was my privilege to know many of these workers personally, and I prize some pieces made for me at the Steuben glassworks by Dorflinger workers.

Today there is almost nothing left of the great glassworks in White Mills except a plaque on Route 6 and a few large solid gray-stone buildings which look as though they will endure forever.

Goblet combining strawberry-diamond and silver-diamond cuttings; 1870's. The charming over-all pattern is adapted to each form in the service; the foot is cut in a twenty-four-point star. Height 6½ inches. *Author's collection.*

Goblet with Dorflinger paper label still attached, the only one ever engraved in this elaborate over-all floral pattern; 1880's. It is very thinly blown and the engraving is correspondingly delicate. There is a teardrop in the panel-cut stem, and the foot is cut in a forty-eight-point flash star. Height 6 inches. *Author's collection.*

Dorflinger glass   Part III

BY KATHRYN HAIT DORFLINGER MANCHEE

This is the final installment of a three-part article on the glass of Christian Dorflinger (1828-1915). Parts I and II, which appeared in ANTIQUES for April (p. 710) and June (p. 1006) of this year, gave a brief biography of Dorflinger, outlined the history of his factories, and illustrated a number of documented examples of his glass.

WHILE IT IS TRUE that the glass made at the Dorflinger factories (1852-1921) is not nearly so well known as that of other, less deserving makers, it is today gradually achieving the recognition which is its due. For instance, a magnificent piece of Dorflinger glass—a goblet blown and engraved in the factory's last years—was given to President Kennedy as a memento of the dedication of the Pinchot Institute in Pike County, Pennsylvania, in the fall of 1963. With this renewed appreciation the problem of identifying Dorflinger glass presents an increasing challenge.

In my earlier articles I showed some Dorflinger family pieces with unimpeachable records, as well as a number of other firmly documented examples—for instance, glass in the White House for which the order, signed by Mary and Abraham Lincoln, still exists. When there is such a record of the original purchase or a history of ownership by executives or workers in the Dorflinger factories and their descendants, there is of course no problem. But the Dorflinger output over the years was enormous, and authenticated pieces are relatively few.

How, then, can Dorflinger glass be identified? Marks are almost nonexistent. John Dorflinger (1880-1964), a relative, acid-etched a small DORFLINGER on some of the pieces from the factory's inventory which he sold after the factory closed, and a few pieces of bread-and-butter commercial ware have turned up with the name impressed on the base; but the fine glass itself, the bulk of the firm's output, was never marked except by a tiny paper label which was usually quickly discarded. The factory did produce some pieces with mountings of silver and on these the name DORFLINGER sometimes occurs—or even C.

DORFLINGER & SONS/NEW YORK, as in the case of the tantalus shown on page 100. These were not always so signed, however.

John Dorflinger did his best to keep alive and to further interest in Dorflinger glass at the small museum and store which he established in 1921 near the site of the old factory in White Mills, Pennsylvania, and maintained until his death in 1964. He gave lectures, answered questions, and kept on display some unusually fine and rare pieces from what had been the company's permanent exhibit. In 1950 Frederick Dorflinger Suydam, Christian's grandson, published a biography of his grandfather which contains much valuable information. Mr. Suydam spent many months in the preparation of this privately printed labor of love, but with modesty reminiscent of Christian himself he published it without a by-line, so some writers who have used his research have not credited their source. But in any event he did not include a discussion of patterns, or suggestions as to how to distinguish Dorflinger glass from other glass of the same period.

Here a consideration of just what types of glass Dorflinger produced should be helpful. In addition to the fine cut and engraved wares which were its principal output, the White Mills factory produced glass decorated in gold

Dorflinger paper label; actual size, ⅜ inch.
This was the only identification used on Dorflinger's fine wares from 1852 to 1921.
Except as noted, illustrations are from the author's collection.

One-of-a-kind goblet, blown and engraved at White Mills in 1917. Originally intended only for exhibition, this was given to President John F. Kennedy in the fall of 1963 as a memento of the dedication of the Pinchot Institute in Pike County, Pennsylvania.

C. DORFLINGER & SONS, NEW YORK.

Nappy and bowl in Mitre and Silver Diamond pattern;
diameter of nappy, 5 inches.
Miter cuts radiating from a pinpoint center, as in this pattern,
require exceptional skill in the cutting and polishing.

Nappy and butter dish in Mitre and Silver Diamond pattern;
from C. Dorflinger & Sons' Catalogue M (n.d.).

Goblet in Essex pattern; height 6⅛ inches.
This brilliant design was made
in table services which included goblets,
saucer champagnes, clarets, wines, cordials,
and finger bowls.

Stemware in Essex pattern, from a group of
undated working drawings found with Dorflinger factory records.

Three sizes of stemware in Heavy Flute pattern, 1919;
height of parfait glass (center), 6 inches.
This pattern was made for
the so-called royal train on which the then
Prince of Wales toured the United States and Canada.
Some ruby overlay was made in this pattern.

Green-and-crystal overlay two-piece footed punch bowl
in Montrose pattern, 1894; over-all height, 15 inches.
The matching silver ladle has a glass-tipped handle
and the name DORFLINGER engraved on the shaft.
A wedding gift to the mother of the owner.
*Collection of Catharine E. Lee; photograph by
courtesy of Corning Museum of Glass.*

No. 279ᴬ 519 STEMWARE
HEAVY FLUTE

Working drawing of stemware and a tumbler
in Heavy Flute pattern.

No. 798 FOOTED PUNCH BOWL
MONTROSE

Working drawing of footed punch bowl
in Montrose pattern.

by such great craftsmen as Carl Prosch. Cased glass, or overlay, in crystal and green or crystal and ruby, was a regular production item (examples can be seen in the Lincoln service in the White House and in museums and private collections). The colored glass items made were mentioned in Part II; and a less expensive line of etched tableware was also produced. Before the factory closed in 1921, reproductions of Italian glass were being made in color because of the difficulty of obtaining, during the war, the lead which is essential to the production of clear glass of high grade. At this time some fine copies of Stiegel and South Jersey types were made and sold as reproductions—to the confusion of collectors of early Americana!

Comparing a piece to patent office sketches, working drawings, or illustrations in company catalogues can of course be helpful, and the illustrations for this article have

been chosen with the last two in mind. Sometimes the patterns vary from item to item to conform to differing shapes, but the original theme of the design can usually be traced. (There are hundreds of patterns, shapes, and items in my files of family records, and someday I hope to publish a picture book of this material.) Piracy, however, has always been prevalent among glassmakers, and there is no substitute for a study of the glass itself. If a piece is in a known Dorflinger pattern it may still not be Dorflinger glass unless it meets certain very definite criteria. Lack of any one of these is more significant than slight changes of pattern, which may have been made at the request of a buyer.

Dorflinger glass is skillfully made, with forms and designs harmoniously related. The cut wares, meticulously hand polished, are extremely brilliant, with great refractive qualities and a "blue-white diamond" look. When held to the light the glass is clear, almost entirely free of imperfections such as striations (appearing as tiny glass threads running through the body of the glass), stones (flecks of white clay which may have broken from the pot during the melting process), black flecks, or bubbles (air pockets). It has a beautiful bell-like ring when lightly struck, the tone depending on thickness and shape of the individual piece.

What I have been describing is, of course, glass of superlative quality, and that is just what Dorflinger glass is. So much of the fine handmade Dorflinger glass was produced that there must be quantities throughout the United States and some in Europe, in use or stored in cellars or attics, much of it hidden behind attributions to English, Irish, or French factories. I hope that the guidelines set forth here will help to identify it to its owners and enable them to prize it as the great product of American craftsmanship it truly is.

Brandy-and-soda tumbler in an unidentified pattern of lightly cut vertical panels; height 4½ inches.

Pattern identified (in pencil) as *No 1800 Cut* in C. Dorflinger & Sons' Catalogue C (n.d.).

Jug and brandy-and-soda tumbler in Old Colony pattern, an exceptionally brilliant design made in seventeen items.

Various items in Old Colony pattern, from Catalogue M.

Two-bottle tantalus set in Marlboro pattern (this also came with three bottles); case of American oak, with bar, lock, and trimmings of bronze, nickeled and lacquered. C. DORFLINGER & SONS/NEW YORK is engraved on the side of the case, and the letters *H H* under the handle. Over-all height of case, 12 inches.

Working drawing of tantalus set in Marlboro pattern.

Libbey cut and engraved glass

BY JOHN W. KEEFE, *Assistant curator, Toledo Museum of Art*

Fig. 1. Ice-cream plate in Kimberly pattern, c. 1890-1892; diameter 8 inches. This popular and beautiful pattern was named in honor of Charles G. Kimberly, a New Haven, Connecticut, dealer in crockery and glassware. *Except as noted, illustrations are from the Toledo Museum of Art.*

Fig. 2. Shallow bowl in Wedgemere pattern, c. 1900-1905; diameter 9 inches. Wedgemere was another popular Libbey pattern. This bowl is in a late variant of a design submitted to the patent office in July 1891. *Collection of Mr. and Mrs. Milton C. Zink.*

BY 1888, THE YEAR Edward Drummond Libbey moved his glass-manufacturing firm from East Cambridge, Massachusetts, to Toledo, Ohio, the deeply cut, ornate glass we know today as brilliant cut was an important part of the production of almost every table-glass firm. When it began operations the Libbey Glass Company (as Libbey rechristened his New England Glass Company) was not financially able to undertake its manufacture, but by 1893 it had become, and it remained, a leader in the field. In the last years of the "brilliant period" glass decorated with copper-wheel engraving was another outstanding product of the company.

The dates of the brilliant period in cut-glass production are generally given as from 1880 to about 1915. Although it did not become a national phenomenon until the 1880's, the new fashion was really introduced at the Philadelphia Centennial Exposition of 1876, and it remained in vogue to some extent down to 1925, so these dates, like those given for most style periods, should be understood as approximate.

Cut glass has always been costly, because a high grade of metal must be used if the glass is to withstand the pressure of cutting and because it involves a number of time-consuming procedures. The deep-miter cutting of the brilliant period was even more expensive than the fine-line cutting that had preceded it. The glass had to be heavier to take the deeper cuts; to achieve the desired sparkle it had to be of even, perfect quality throughout; the processes involved were still more complicated than those used for the earlier type.

Increasing American prosperity was responsible to a large degree for the popularity of the new wares. The panic of 1873 was but a memory; homes were larger, furnishings more ornate. Then, too, the formal living patterns of the late nineteenth and early twentieth centuries required elaborately correlated table settings, and the massive, costly cut glass was admirably suited to fill this need. An Edwardian comment on prevailing taste was that no table could be considered correctly set unless it had "cost a million and weighed a ton."

At the opening of the brilliant period technological developments had advanced to the point where the cutting lathes were driven by electric motors rather than by water or steam power. Finishing wheels of soft steel, which replaced those of cast iron, created a sharper, more brilliant cut and made deeper incisions possible. Improvement in the quality of the metal followed the introduction of natural gas as a furnace fuel: heat could be easily regulated and kept constant, fusion of the metal was more rapid, and annealing more perfect. The result was an exceptionally clear glass of considerable weight. It may truly be said that by the end of the nineteenth century American craftsmen were producing as fine a glass as the world had ever known.

Once the glass had been produced, it went through three further stages in the production of brilliant-cut

Fig. 3. Table in Neola pattern, 1902; height 32 inches. This monumental piece was probably cut by John Rufus Denman, one of the Libbey company's most skilled craftsmen. It was made for the company's display at the St. Louis World's Fair of 1904.

Fig. 4. Plate in Sultana pattern, c. 1897; diameter 12 inches. The border of this advertising piece is cut and the center is engraved with the Libbey sword mark and an advertising phrase; the phrase did not appear on the mark in normal use.

wares—a procedure fundamentally the same in the Libbey plant and in all the other glasshouses. When the blank of fine, heavy lead glass was completed, the pattern to be cut was drawn on the surface, usually in a mixture of red lead and turpentine. The cutter then roughed out his pattern with a wheel of iron or soft steel which was convex, flat, or V shape in profile, depending upon the cut desired. In the cutting of an ornate pattern the wheels might have to be changed a number of times.

The second step, the smoothing process, involved coating the wheel with a fine wet abrasive and deepening the cuts already made; these were then smoothed by sandstone wheels wet with water. Like the wheels used in the roughing, the sandstone ones varied in size from two to about eighteen inches and were changed according to the pattern being executed.

Polishing, the final stage, followed the smoothing. Traditionally, wooden wheels and a gentle abrasive such as putty powder were used for this process. A higher luster could be achieved by the use of felt wheels dusted with a rouge or a similar polishing agent. About 1890, a chemical process involving the dipping of the cut glass in an acid bath came into use, although old-time glassworkers deplored the change. Today, most experts feel that the finish acquired by the acid method cannot match the sparkle achieved by the earlier means.

Cutting is still done at the Libbey factory today, but the blanks are automatically blown and are relatively light in weight. The contemporary process differs from that of the brilliant period in that stone wheels rather than metal are now used to rough in the pattern. Stone wheels, or sometimes more rapidly cutting wheels of diamond and carborundum composition, are used for the smoothing process. Wooden wheels for polishing have been superseded by felt wheels using pumice. However, today most polishing is done by the acid method: the uncut portions are coated with wax; the piece is then dipped in an acid bath and dried, and the wax is melted off. Acid polishing is being replaced in some instances (chiefly in Europe) by a mechanical process in which brushes revolving at high speed do the work. This is cheaper, faster, and neater, but the machines are initially expensive.

The copper-wheel engraving which was used to decorate many pieces of Victorian glass involves an equally laborious process. Designs are created by copper disks of varying sizes revolving on a lathe. The most skillful engravers execute their designs freehand, while others draw them in a mixture of the aforementioned red lead and turpentine. Copper-wheel engraving is also an expensive process, since it, too, takes many hours and requires the finest lead glass.

The Libbey company hired the most highly skilled cutters and engravers available. William C. Anderson, who designed for the company from 1887 until 1906, was the creator of the beautiful and popular Kimberly (Fig. 1) and Wedgemere (Fig. 2) patterns as well as Neola, the pattern in which a spectacular glass table (Fig. 3) was cut for the 1904 St. Louis exposition.

William Marrett, another talented Libbey designer, worked for the company from 1897 until 1903. He cre-

Fig. 5. Plate and finger bowl, in Strawberry Diamond and Fan pattern, c. 1895-1900; diameter of plate, 6¾ inches; of bowl, 4¾. This was one of the most popular of all cut-glass patterns and was used, with variations, by a number of glasshouses. Attribution to a specific maker is difficult without a trade-mark or definite history.

Fig. 6. Pitcher in Greek Key pattern, c. 1907; height 11⅜ inches. This design is typical of the less ornate but still opulent patterns favored in the late brilliant period.

ated the Chrysanthemum and Sultana (Fig. 4) patterns and designed the McKinley punch-bowl sets (see ANTIQUES, May 1968, p. 665). John Rufus Denman (1877-1956) was one of the company's most proficient cutters; he cut both of the McKinley bowls, as well as the twenty-five-inch St. Louis punch bowl now in the collection of the Toledo Museum of Art. Many other designers and cutters of skill were employed at the Ash Street plant in Toledo.

Before 1893 much fine American cut glass was presented to the public by prestige-conscious dealers as imported European ware. This, plus the enormous success of the Libbey pavilion at the 1893 Chicago Columbian Exposition, aroused the leading American glass manufacturers to undertake a massive advertising campaign. In succeeding years the advertisements of the Libbey company appeared in *Harper's, McClure's, Country Life,* and the *Ladies' Home Journal,* among other magazines. These did much to inform the public and to expand the market for the company's wares. So effective were they that fine cut glass, by Libbey and others, became the most prestigious gift of the period, and it was collected enthusiastically. However, as early as 1900 its popularity began to wane. Many designs lacked the clarity of patterns like the Kimberly or the Strawberry Diamond and Fan (Fig. 5). Some were confused and overly ornate. The best designs of the late brilliant period show deliberate restraint and patterns complement the form of the object on which they appear (Fig. 6).

Then, too, the public had simply tired of the glitter of a table set with cut glass. Costs within the factory itself had increased sharply, and designers began to look for patterns which would give the desired effect less expensively. After 1905, the so-called "buzz," or Pinwheel, pattern (Fig. 7) was produced in quantity; this created a glittering surface but was not so costly to produce.

Copper-wheel engraving, which had been eclipsed by deep-miter cutting, was reintroduced by Libbey and other firms in an attempt to revive the market for fine glass. Intaglio engraving of realistic flowers, fruit, and figures was executed from about 1900 to 1910; some fine ex-

amples were made through the 1920's (Fig. 8). However, after World War I increasing informality of living really spelled the end of popular interest in heavily ornamented glass. During the 1920's the Libbey company made simple, understated pieces (Fig. 9), frequently characterized by the use of colored glass and simple geometric patterns.

In 1931, the company hired A. Douglas Nash (1885-c. 1945) to design a new series decorated by cutting and engraving. Nash's father had been superintendent of the Tiffany Favrile Glass Works in Corona, Long Island, and he was well acquainted with fine glassmaking traditions.

Fig. 7. Footed punch bowl in Pinwheel pattern, c. 1900-1910; height 13 inches, diameter 10½. The "buzz," or Pinwheel, pattern was extensively used by the Libbey company in the late brilliant period because it produced the desired effect at some reduction in cost. *Zink collection.*

Fig. 8. Vase engraved with flowers, stylized leaves, and a peacock, on a mat surface; about 1905; height 20 inches. Copper-wheel engraving, revived in the first decade of this century, appealed to a public which had tired of the flashing, deep-miter-cut surface.

Fig. 9. Candlesticks and compote, geometric cutting and engraving; c. 1920-1925; heights 6¾ to 12¾ inches. These simple, elegant pieces were made by the Libbey Glass Company in combinations of clear, garnet, black, blue, and green glass, in some instances cased in the color and then cut or engraved through to the clear. The restraint of the decoration reflects the taste of the period.

Fig. 10. Group of goblets designed by A. Douglas Nash; cut or engraved, c. 1931-1935; heights 8 to 10 inches. The two on the left are in the Toledo pattern, that in the center is in the Oxford pattern, and the one on the far right is an experimental design not produced commercially.

The new Nash line was characterized by beautiful form and intricate surface detail. The series specialized in formal stemware and matched centerpiece arrangements of candlesticks, bowls, and vases. The handsome Toledo pattern (Fig. 10, *left* and *center left*) was reminiscent of brilliant-period cutting; the pink-cased goblet in the Victoria pattern (Fig. 11), which was cameo cut, required eighty hours of cutting and retailed for a commensurately high figure. The Depression, however, destroyed the market for such expensive items, and the Nash line was discontinued in 1935.

In 1936 the Libbey Glass Company, now a division of the Owens-Illinois Glass Company, hired Edwin W. Fuerst (1903-   ) to design a series of heavy blown and mold-blown pieces, to be called Modern American. The new ware was presented to a few favored customers in 1939 and to the public in 1940. The beauty of the line depended upon the brilliance of the metal and the form of the article rather than upon decorative surface detail (Figs. 12, 13). Some of the vases were decorated by simple flute cuts or by copper-wheel engraving. The cutting was executed by Denman and the engraving by another highly skilled Libbey craftsman, Herman F. Hocke (1871-1944). Both techniques were used sparingly, and the copper-wheel engraving tended to draw upon contemporary subjects and stylized animals rather

Fig. 11. Goblet, cameo cut in Victoria pattern; c. 1931-1935; height 9¼ inches. Nash's most elaborate design, this spectacular goblet was triple-cased in pink, opal, and clear. Each piece took eighty hours to complete. *Collection of Mr. and Mrs. Carl U. Fauster.*

Fig. 12. Vases in the Modern American series, c. 1940-1945; heights 6 to 9 inches. The flute-cut vase in the center was called "my favorite piece" by Edwin W. Fuerst, who designed the line.

than on mythological or elaborately realistic themes. The advent of World War II forced the discontinuation of this line in favor of war production. The Libbey company planned to produce Modern American after the war, but this was never done, and the line marked the end of Libbey's fine, completely handmade glass.

Since 1959 the Libbey company, as a segment of Owens-Illinois, Incorporated, has produced a line of tableware designed by Freda Diamond and called the 1818 series. All of the pieces in this line are automatically blown and then cut. This is the only Libbey glass still ornamented by cutting; copper-wheel engraving is not used at all.

Libbey trade-marks

The subject of trade-marks used by the Libbey Glass Company is a complex one. The company advertised that the Libbey signature was applied to every piece, but research has shown that this was not a consistent practice. Frequently marks of an earlier date than that of manufacture were applied. To compound the difficulty, the company often showed in its advertisements trade-marks which were not actually used.

The practice of affixing paper labels began around 1906, but for obvious reasons these rarely survive. The earliest of these Libbey labels was square in shape and bore the company name. Another was oval, with an open center and the company name printed in the perimeter. Labels of other shapes were used as well, but their dates are not known since the company did not register all its trade-marks.

Collectors and students should note that only the acid-etched mark on a piece of glass should be trusted: similarity of metal and an extensive use of nearly identical patterns often make attribution impossible without an acid mark or exact family history.

Following is a brief list of definitely established trade-marks and the approximate dates of their use by the Libbey Glass Company.

a. (1892-1896) Enameled, usually in red, and apparently stenciled.

b. (1896-1906) Here the L and the y are not connected. Note the sword under the whole.

c. (1901) Patented April 16, 1901, for use on pressed blanks sold to other companies for final cutting—which disproves the contention that Libbey never made pressed blanks.

d. (1906-c. 1913) In advertisements, the banner formed by the connection of the L and the y bore the phrase *The World's Best*. This was never included in the mark on actual pieces of glass. In the same period LIBBEY in an ovoid form was used, but here the L and y were not connected. This second mark is not common.

e. (1919-1930) Some authorities maintain that this trade-mark was first used in 1910, a contention that is open to debate.

f. (1933-1935) Paper label in blue and white. On some pieces of this period, the 1919-1930 mark is also found.

g. (1939-1945) Mark similar to the 1919-1930 version, but with a double-rimmed circle.

h. (1959-1968) Found on 1818 stemware; an adaptation of the old Libbey sword trade-mark.

Fig. 13. Covered candy jar in the Modern American series, c. 1940-1945; height 9½ inches. Such simple stylized engraved decoration is typical of the period.

Louis Vaupel, master glass engraver

BY CARL U. FAUSTER

IN 1968 THE TOLEDO MUSEUM OF ART celebrated the hundred and fiftieth anniversary of the founding of the New England Glass Company by mounting an exhibition entitled *Libbey Glass, a tradition of 150 years*. (The New England Glass Company was founded in 1818 in Cambridge, Massachusetts; Edward Drummond Libbey moved it lock, stock, and barrel to Toledo in 1888, where its name was soon changed to Libbey Glass Company; and its lineal descendant today is the Libbey Products Division of Owens-Illinois, Inc.) The catalogue of that 1968 exhibition said of the superb presentation chalice shown here as color plate A that it represents "the high point in American Middle Period engraved glass"—an encomium which surely puts the man who engraved it at the top of his exacting craft.

The name of Louis Vaupel, the master craftsman who executed the chalice and all the other pieces illustrated here, is well known, but very little has been recorded about his life. There is at the Houghton Library at Harvard a 191-page journal kept by Vaupel covering the years 1824-1899 (he called it *Kurze Biographie Meiner Selbst,* which translates *Brief Autobiography*), but this is handwritten in German script and it has not been translated. I am indebted to Vaupel's grandson, John Leyson Vaupel, for the biographical material which follows.

Born on June 17, 1824, in the little German town of Schildhorst, Vaupel was the son of Georg Andreas Vaupel, a lifelong glass craftsman. (Incidentally, he used many versions of his name. He began life as Ludwig Heinrich Friedrich Vaupel, but by the time he arrived in the United States he was calling himself Louis Friedrich Vaupel and he often signed himself Louis F. Vaupel, L. F. Vaupel, L. H. F. Vaupel, or even H. F. Louis Vaupel.) He went to school at Freden, about four miles from Schildhorst, and by the time he was twelve he was working after school in the local glass factory, where his father was employed. It was not at all unusual at that time for very young boys to assist in the glass factory, and it was here that young Ludwig had his first chance to see how glass was blown and decorated. In 1836 the family moved to Breitenstein, near Stolberg, where Ludwig's father and his stepbrother, Karl, had established a glassworks of their own. Here he began work as a glass blower, studying all phases of glassmaking and becoming especially proficient in engraving.

Fig. 1. Clear-glass cup engraved by Louis Vaupel (1824-1903) with a design of love birds billing within a floral wreath; signed on the base *Louis,* inscribed *Minette* and *So inniglich liebe ich auch Dich* (So deeply do I love thee), and dated 1850—the year Vaupel migrated from Germany, leaving his sweetheart, Minette Kaufhold, behind. Four years later she joined him in America and they were married. *Except as noted, illustrations are from the Vaupel family collection.*

Fig. 2. Vaupel and his wife posed for this portrait by a Hannover photographer c. 1875, when they revisited Schildhorst, the small German town where both were born and where Vaupel had his earliest glassmaking experience.

Fig. 3. Two views of a clear-glass flask also apparently engraved before Vaupel left Germany. One side shows a pair of stags in a decorative wreath and is inscribed *Louis Vaupel/1850;* the other shows a group of buildings identified as *Glasfabrik/Schildhorst.* A cipher of Vaupel's initials is engraved on the base, evidently for use as a seal. Illustrated in ANTIQUES for December 1945 (p. 378). *Collection of Mrs. Henry G. Smith.*

When he was twenty-six and had served his time in the army he returned briefly to Schildhorst (see Fig. 3), and from there he migrated to America by way of Bremerhaven. Around 1850 Germany was experiencing a serious depression, and ready employment in American glasshouses awaited any talented glass craftsman. Four years after his arrival in America Ludwig (now Louis) was joined by his sister Louisa and by his fiancée, Minette Kaufhold, daughter of a Schildhorst glassmaker (Figs. 1, 2). The couple were married at Burlington, Massachusetts, on September 12, 1854.

By 1853 Vaupel had become an engraver for the New England Glass Company, the firm characterized by the McKearins (*Two Hundred Years of American Blown Glass,* 1950, p. 81) as "undoubtedly the leading house in New England in the production of the highest quality of glassware." The Cambridge city directory first lists Vaupel in 1860 as living at 125 Spring Street, within a few blocks of the glassworks. Vaupel was superintendent of the engraving department, which included, during the 1860's and 1870's, such highly skilled engravers as Henry S. Fillebrown and Henry Leighton, both of whom did exquisite work.

The remainder of Vaupel's working life was spent there. He retired in 1885, a few years before Edward Drummond Libbey moved the factory from Cambridge to Toledo. He was only sixty-one at the time, and this early retirement was probably due to the lessening demand for expertly engraved glass and the fact that the factory had fallen on troubled times. After retiring Vaupel lived on the income from several houses he owned in Cambridge. For a few years he accepted commissions to engrave glass on the wheel he had set up in his home, but John Vaupel doubts that his grandfather did any such work after 1890, the year his wife died. Her protracted illness, involving frequent trips in search of medical help, had long been his major concern. Vaupel himself died in 1903 and is buried in Cambridge Cemetery on Coolidge Hill Road, where, John Vaupel says, "The family is all tucked in." The monument there was designed by Louis Vaupel.

During his long career Vaupel must have engraved hundreds of pieces of glass. His style naturally reflected the Bohemian influence which was paramount in Germany when he learned the art, and his earlier work was executed on thin, delicate glass. John Vaupel says that his grandfather used "a light, feathery cut, occasionally intaglio where that was called for, and usually in a wreath-like, flowery design with considerable detail on stem and leaf." Glass craftsmen were a sentimental lot, and following a common practice Vaupel often engraved a piece of glass for a member of the family, as a gift or to commemorate a special occasion; he even engraved some such pieces for himself (Figs. 3, 5, 6). His three children were named

A.

A. Presentation chalice, Louis Vaupel's masterpiece; c. 1875-1880. Hollow-baluster, panel-cut stem; cut, scalloped foot; and cutting at base of bowl. Height 9 inches. The engraving encircling the bowl depicts forest scenes with several hunters, hounds, and a stag at bay. The work is so minutely detailed that a squirrel on a branch and a snake wriggling through the tall grass can be clearly seen. Exhibited publicly for the first time at the Toledo Museum of Art's 1968 exhibition *Libbey Glass, a tradition of 150 years*. The catalogue of that exhibition called this chalice "the high point in American Middle Period engraved glass."

B.

C.

B. Goblet engraved with scene of wolves attacking a horse and, on the other side, lions and buffalo; c. 1875. Height 8⅛ inches. *Museum of Fine Arts, Boston; photograph by Milton C. Zink.*

C. This small beaker is one of several pieces Vaupel engraved and monogrammed *M N* for his married daughter. The beautifully executed engraving is typically Bohemian. Height 4½ inches; c. 1880-1890.

D. Flared beaker with patterned foot and cutting at base of bowl; height 4½ inches; c. 1880-1890. One of the few green pieces engraved by Vaupel: most of his cased pieces are ruby, with very few examples in green or blue.

D.

Fig. 4. Clear-glass compote engraved by Vaupel for his son, with monogram *L H W V* and design of grape clusters and floral garlands; height 9 inches. Utility pieces such as compotes, finger bowls, and decanters were engraved with names or monograms of members of the family to commemorate a birthday, anniversary, or similar event. The family collection currently includes twelve pieces so monogrammed.

Minette, Emilie, and Louis, and their initials occur on a number of the family pieces; it is sometimes difficult, however, to be sure which Minette or which Louis the initials stand for. The small red beaker (color plate C) monogrammed *M N* was certainly for his daughter: her married name was Newman.

It would of course be of great interest to know just which of the engraved pieces produced by the New England Glass Company during Vaupel's working years came from his hand. However, attributions of glass to a particular worker—or, for that matter, to a particular factory—are even trickier than attributions in other fields. For one thing, glass is rarely signed. It is possible to hazard an attribution on the ground of analogy to a documented piece, and for this purpose the objects illustrated here could hardly be improved on. Every one of them is either signed or firmly documented or both. All but four are still in the Vaupel family collection, and of those four one (Fig. 3) carries signature, date, and name of factory, and the other three (color plate B, Figs. 7, 8) were bequeathed to their present owner, the Museum of Fine Arts in Boston, by Vaupel's granddaughter.

Aside from their usefulness as a possible basis for attributions, the pieces shown here are of unusual interest to students and collectors of American engraved glass because they are, with one or two exceptions, quite unfamiliar. In his later years Vaupel refused to permit examples of his work which were still in the family to be exhibited in any museum, and he persuaded his son, L. H. W. Vaupel, to follow the same policy. I am particularly grateful, therefore, to the Vaupel family and to the Boston Museum of Fine Arts for permission to publish such an outstanding group from the work of Louis Vaupel.

Fig. 5. Goblet of clear glass, c. 1875-1880, engraved with floral motifs, heraldic device, and wreathed monogram *L V;* height 7 inches. Vaupel considered this "his" glass and it was reserved for his use. The heraldic device is a family coat of arms created by Vaupel; the original sketch is still in the family collection.

Fig. 6. Cruet engraved by Vaupel for his own use; height 7 inches; c. 1860-1870. Neck and stopper are elaborately faceted.

Fig. 7. The engraving on this small (4¾ inches high) beaker, pale ruby engraved to clear (c. 1865-1870), shows Venus and Cupid in a cartouche surrounded by flowers and foliage. Such a design is unusual in American glass of the period, but the style had long been familiar in Europe, where Vaupel learned his craft. The inscribed monogram *M V* identifies this as still another gift from Vaupel to his wife. *Museum of Fine Arts, Boston; all Vaupel pieces in the museum's collection were acquired by bequest of Dr. Minette D. Newman, Louis Vaupel's granddaughter.*

Fig. 8. Mercury, or silver-glass, goblet, engraved with flowers and foliage in a conventional repeat pattern resembling a textile or wallpaper design; signed *L V* under foot. Height 10 inches; 1860-1870. Engraving on such an exceptionally large silver-glass object is rare. *Museum of Fine Arts, Boston.*